Evaluation and Quality Development

T0316759

Reinhard Stockmann

Evaluation and Quality Development

Principles of Impact-Based Quality Management

PETER LANG

Frankfurt am Main · Berlin · Bern · Bruxelles · New York · Oxford · Wien

Bibliographic Information published by the Deutsche Nationalbibliothek
The Deutsche Nationalbibliothek lists this publication in the Deutsche Nationalbibliografie; detailed bibliographic data is available in the internet at <http://www.d-nb.de>.

ISBN 978-3-631-57693-9

© Peter Lang GmbH
Internationaler Verlag der Wissenschaften
Frankfurt am Main 2008
All rights reserved.

Printed in Germany 1 2 3 4 5   7

www.peterlang.de

Table of Contents

Preface

The starting point for this book was the observation that the topics of quality management and evaluation are scarcely linked to one another, neither in terms of their academic treatment nor in day-to-day practice. The private sector, whose primary goal is that of profit maximisation, is equipped with a range of tried and tested concepts and tools for quality assurance and improvement. The public sector, which has more of a duty to serve the common good, for a long time neglected this perspective concerning the quality of processes and products or services. Now, the instrument of evaluation is being employed increasingly in the public sector, in order to assess not only the output of programmes, measures or service offerings, but also the effects that they trigger (outcome and impact). Yet still evaluation has remained largely unconnected to quality management.

However, by contributing to the improvement of processes, e.g. in the implementation of a programme, of effectiveness and efficiency in goal attainment, of a service offering, or of the efficacy and sustainability of programmes and measures, evaluation also makes an overall contribution to quality assurance.

It therefore makes sense to bring together these two strands – evaluation and quality development – and to examine them with regards to their complementarity and divergence. In doing so, account needs to be taken of the different contextual conditions present in the private and public sectors.

With the book already available in German, Spanish, and even in Chinese, an English language version had still been lacking. I am thus grateful to Lang Verlag, which has hereby filled this gap.

Particular thanks are of course due to the translator, Daniel Durling, who took on the difficult task of producing the English language version. I also thank Julie Anne Charlton for her work in putting the finishing touches to the translation, Miriam Grapp for converting this version too into a printable manuscript, and, last but not least, Angelika Nentwig, who supported me in my search for a suitable publisher.

Bürstadt and Saarbrücken, January 2008

Reinhard Stockmann.

1 Introduction and Objectives

Quality, together with efficiency, is regarded as one of the cornerstones of an economically flourishing business. Companies are responding to the increased competitive pressure stemming from globalisation, internationalisation and liberalisation by pursuing strategies of cost reduction and quality development. The huge number of publications on the subject of quality planning, quality management, Total Quality Management etc. over the last few years declare *quality* to be the most important factor for success in the markets of the future (cf. Seghezzi & Hansen 1993: preface). The debate about *quality development*, which originated in the private sector, has long since expanded to include public administration and the great variety of charitable organisations. This sphere, known as the *non-profit sector[1]*, not only shows enormous economic potential, but also has a particular social significance. *Non-profit organisations (NPOs)* provide services for areas as diverse as culture, sport and leisure, in various kinds of advisory bodies, in the fields of welfare, interest representation, religion, and international cooperation, to name but a few.

It is not easy to establish the precise number of *people working* in the German non-profit sector or their *economic output*. Apart from the question of which definition is used, there are no uniform statistical categories covering non-profit organisations. Official German statistics for a long time gathered a large number of these organisations together under the collective heading of "organisations without a profit motive". However, this category has been abolished to conform to EU statistics, and a clear statistical record is thus no longer available (cf. Zimmer & Priller 2004: 32; Anheier et al. 2002: 20). It is apparent from the statistics for employees with compulsory social security (cf. table 1.1) that in public administration alone, with a total budget of over one trillion euros per year (cf. German Federal Statistical Office 2004: 234)[2], there are about two million employees. Apart from public administration, which some authors do not include in the non-profit sector due to its dependence on state directives (cf. Zimmer & Priller 2004: 33), there are

---

1   There is no standard definition: in general, all public and private-sector non-profit organisations can be classed as non-profit organisations. However, the term is often used to describe only organisations that are neither profit-orientated nor represent public institutions (cf. Anheier et al. 2002: 19 f.). Cf. also chapter 2.2 below.

2   Encompasses federal and state administrations, cities and local authorities, special interest associations, special state assets, social security and defence.

approximately a further five million people employed in the areas of education and teaching, health care, social welfare, and in organisations providing other public and personal services.[3] However, many employees who are not working for non-profit organisations, but for profit-orientated enterprises, are included in these statistical categories. It should also be kept in mind that, in addition to their regular employees, non-profit organisations also make use of numerous members working on a voluntary basis. The German Sports Association, for example, has over 24 million members, the Catholic and Protestant churches have about 26 million believers each, and the Federation of German Trade Unions (DGB) has about 7.7 million members.

Ascertaining the economic significance of the non-profit sector is therefore dependent on complicated calculations. The John Hopkins Comparative Nonprofit Sector Project discovered that 4.2 million people were working in the public sector and 1.4 million in the non-profit sector (using the narrower definition) in Germany in 1995. In addition, there were about 17 million people working on a voluntary basis.[4] Whilst the number of people employed in the profit-making sector decreased slightly between 1960 and 1995 (22.7 million), the number of employees in the public sector doubled over the same period, and that in the non-profit sector (excluding volunteers) quadrupled (cf. Zimmer & Priller 2004: 55; Anheier et al. 2002: 29 ff.; Badelt 2002: 659 ff.; Anheier 2000: 15 ff.).

An increased demand for certain services (such as all-day kindergartens, after-school care, retirement homes, rehabilitation and convalescent centres), as well as steps towards privatisation and the at least partial retreat of the German government from welfare state politics (cf. Anheier 2000: 18 f.), have been given as reasons for the especially strong *growth* in the non-governmental non-profit sector. Market liberalisation, in particular in the fields of health and social welfare, has allowed many private services to establish themselves in an area that was previously almost exclusively dominated by the state. The non-profit sector is therefore not only economically far more significant than generally assumed, but is also characterised by particularly high levels of economic dynamism.

In addition, non-profit organisations have an important *social function* (cf. Simsa 2002: 129 ff.). Under their narrow definition (excluding public bodies), they are described as "intermediary mediation organisations" (cf. Badelt 2002: 663) or "third sector organisations", which are distinct from the state and the market by reason of their rationale. Whilst, according to this heuristic, the state sector is run on the lines of 'hierarchy' or 'power', the

---

3   The number of foundations has increased considerably over the last few years (cf. Anheier et al. 2002: 35). The assets of the approximately 10,000 German foundations are estimated to be worth over 30 billion euros. About three billion euros are handed out every year in assistance funds.

4   The John Hopkins Project examined the following institutions, facilities and organisations (cf. Zimmer & Priller 2004: 33): societies, foundations, welfare institutions, hospitals and health trusts, charitable limited companies and similar types of company, business and professional associations, trade unions, consumer organisations, self-help groups, citizens' initiatives, environmental protection groups, and civic organisations.

economic sector functions via 'competition' or 'exchange'. In the third sector, however, the rationale is based on the one hand on 'solidarity' as an altruistic, reciprocal aid principle, and on the other hand on 'spirit' (e.g. 'community spirit'). When they take the form of religious communities, societies, associations, foundations, self-help groups or citizens' initiatives, non-profit organisations are able to mobilise alternative public forces and potential for social change, and may thus be described as the "infrastructural basis of civil society" (cf. Zimmer & Priller 2004: 15 f.).

Table 1.1: Employees with compulsory social security in Germany

Sector of economy		in thousands
Total employed		26,955
Public administration, defence, social insurance		1,741
Education and teaching		1,034
Health and veterinary services		1,973
Social services		1,110
Provision of other public and personal services		1,231
Including	*Sewage, waste collection and other disposal services*	*148*
	Special interest groups, church and religious associations	*475*
	Culture, sport and entertainment	*329*
	Provision of other services	*279*
TOTAL		7,089

Source: Statistical Yearbook 2004

It can be seen from this that non-profit organisations encompass a vast spectrum of activities and have access to considerable financial and personnel resources. They are not only an *important factor* in the areas of *employment and economic policy*, but also possess *enormous social and political potential*. Therefore, in addition to having an innovative role when it comes to modernising society and contributing to welfare creation through the provision of services, non-profit organisations are also regarded as having an important function in the integration and articulation of interests, as well as for the participation of people in society.

For a range of different reasons, the *benefits* and *quality* of services provided by state and private non-profit organisations are being scrutinised with growing frequency.

The *increase in efficiency of public administration* is considered mainly in the context of three factors: (1) Analogous to the debate about quality in the private sector, which has intensified under pressure from international competition, a long-awaited debate about the quality of public services has finally been sparked off, since successful public administration is prized as a location factor in international competition for investment. (2) The democratisation of society and the development of the welfare state have wrought massive changes in the demands made by citizens on public administration. This has then increasingly been restructured from an autonomous regulatory body into a more sophisticated services administration. There has also been organisational change. The bureaucratic organisation of the state, regarded since the time of Max Weber as a model that facilitates the rational exercising of responsibilities, has gradually come to be seen as a hindrance to their efficient execution. In order to meet new demands for the effective and efficient deployment of resources, public administration has begun to model itself on private sector principles. The ideal type from Max Weber's theory of bureaucracy has been expanded to include 'new' approaches from the fields of business management and organisational theory. This process was accelerated (3) by the financial crisis into which most European countries were plunged towards the end of the 1980s and beginning of the '90s. A shortage of resources on the one hand increased the difficulty of choosing how to allocate funds (for support, covering costs, subsidies etc.) and, on the other hand, created growing pressure to legitimise - i.e. to demonstrate the success and efficiency of - work performed. Through the liberalisation of individual, previously state-dominated, sectors, particularly in health and social services, a certain competitive pressure also emerged, leading to the professionalisation of non-profit organisations in individual fields of activity, as well as to an intensification of the *quality debate.*

This not entirely ideology-free discussion ranges from a *glorification* of non-profit organisations, especially in the area of development cooperation, where non-profit organisations are regarded as being more effective than state donors (although this has never been empirically proved)[5], to *devastating criticism.* Using case studies, Seibel (1992) was able to show that non-profit organisations are characterised by a high level of both ideology and irrationality, resulting in failures of management and a limited ability to learn. Nevertheless, these deficits have led neither to changes in the organisations being examined, nor to their collapse. Seibel interprets this as "functional amateurism", which allows non-profit organisations to 'survive' in an alternative world liberated from functional rationality. Zech (1996: 256) sees in non-profit organisations "a certain degree of compensation for the harshness of the capitalist market or the relentlessness of the principles of state regulation." Seibel's case studies only take into account organisations whose continued existence is ensured by public subsidies, however, which means that the empirical basis for gaining an impression of how efficient they are, or of the quality of their work, is entirely insufficient. Alongside highly professional service provision and convincing, high-quality provision, there are also plenty of examples of deficiencies, shortcomings, ineffi-

---

5   Evidence of this can be found in just a single case study, and thus on a far from adequate basis; cf. Stockmann et al. 2000. What is more, practical experience with non-profit organisations often points in the other direction.

cacy and inefficiency. There can no longer be any question, therefore, of the need for performance appraisal and quality development to eliminate these shortcomings.

It can be established that more and more non-profit organisations are tackling the question of *what quality means* for their type of service, and how it can be defined, measured and developed (cf. Arnold 2003: 237 & 239). Whereas in the mid '90s it was still being asserted that it was relatively easy to keep an overview of the group of health and social services organisations that had already had some experience of quality management, the number of organisations which began to deal with it from the beginning of 2000, when so-called 'internal' quality management became a legal requirement for hospitals (Weiß 2000), increased significantly (cf. Schubert & Zink 2001: V). Boeßenecker and colleagues (2003: 7 ff.) point out that 'quality' has been the most frequently discussed concept in the field of social work since the mid '90s. However, a research project with the aim of obtaining a reliable evaluation of the actual dissemination and relevance of the concept of quality development in social work, and of ascertaining how it is translated into action and the effects of this, showed evidence of "muddling through", in a manner specific to the trust or establishment concerned. Those responsible selected the particular "building blocks" which seemed in their judgement at the time to be useful and appropriate. So, in the areas of health and social services at least, which may be regarded as the spearhead of quality development in the non-profit sector, the subject might receive a great deal of attention, but its application is, on the whole, unsatisfactory.

The reasons for this can be found to a large extent in the *lack of appropriate concepts and instruments*. Therefore, procedures that were evolved for the private sector are adopted straightaway, without any proper checks as to whether they are suited to the organisational and situational conditions in the non-profit sector. This is doubtful, since – as will later be demonstrated extensively – non-profit organisations and their situation and circumstances differ enormously from business enterprises (profit-organisations) and the context in which they operate.

In the light of experiences to date with the *adoption of concepts and instruments* of the private sector for quality development, this practice is being increasingly questioned. The fact that the discussion about quality in the non-profit sector is "determined too much by reactions to impulses from the profit-oriented sector" is *coming under criticism*. Transferring the traditional instruments of control and finance, as well as 'modern' concepts of Total Quality Management, has been insufficient in order to do justice to the specific demands and management requirements of non-profit organisations. "Questions to do with measuring the success of non-profit organisations" – according to Horak (1998: 445), for example – can "at present only be dealt with in a very limited way using conventional instruments". Matul and Scharitzer (2002: 606) also find that: "There is a need for an original approach to creating autonomous quality based on the individual rationale of the non-profit organisation concerned". Therefore, it is frequently suggested that entirely new concepts and tools should be developed which go beyond adaptations from the business sector and take sufficient account of the particular characteristics of non-profit organisations (Horak 1998: 445; Badelt 2002: 662; Arnold 2003: 239; Beckmann et al. 2004: 9 f.).

13

Whilst private non-profit organisations mainly experiment with adopting models of quality management such as Total Quality Management or ISO certification, state administration is attempting instead to adapt itself within the framework of *New Public Management approaches*[6] to meet new performance and efficiency demands. Reform projects such as 'Modern State – Modern Administration'[7], for example, are intended to overcome the functional and structural deficiencies of both state and administration.

This is an attempt, on the one hand, to bring the conditions pertaining in public administration into line with those of the profit-sector, in order to be able to use the instruments of the latter. And on the other hand, traditional input-orientated management philosophy is being firmly rejected through this alignment of administrative action with output and outcome. Many state-run non-profit organisations do not operate on the open market, and their 'customers' often have little or no opportunity to switch to another supplier. In order to compensate for this imbalance, an attempt is being made to systematically incorporate a *competitive approach* in administrative activities. This is happening through the authorisation of private suppliers (e.g. private employment agencies, health and advice centres), and also by simulating competitive-type structures (e.g. via benchmarking and the invitation of tenders). It is hoped that this will trigger off professionalisation processes in both state and parastatal institutions, which have up till now provided services in a monopolistic way, as well as among the 'new' providers, leading to more effective and efficient provision and an improvement in the quality of services offered (cf. Anheier 2000: 20). The idea behind this is that when external incentives (free market elements such as competition, customer orientation etc.) are applied, administrations or non-profit organisations in general will then act like businesses, and develop a management system that functions according to principles of business management, introduce business management instruments, and focus their quality development on the requirements and needs of their customers. This involves moving away from the traditional concept of quality held by public administration, which was primarily equated with doing things in accordance with the law and the regulations, and also focusing on the needs of the customer, who should no longer be treated merely as a user or even a supplicant (cf. Schedler & Proeller 2000: 44).

Another pillar of administrative modernisation is seen in *output and outcome* (impact) *orientation*. Traditionally, public administration was managed according to input factors. The availability of funds was long regarded – and still is today, to some extent – as sufficient proof of the standard of service provision of the administration concerned, or even of political leadership. The creation of an extensive budget for the elimination of the problem of unemployment, for example, or for reducing global poverty, was in itself seen as proof of success. This principle has also been perverted by budget regulations, with the result that an office which managed to decrease its use of resources in a certain year

---

6   New Public Management (NPM) deals with the modernisation of public institutions and new ways of conducting public administration. Cf. Schedler & Proeller 2003 and Naschold & Bogumil 2000 for a good overview.

7   Cf. URL: http://www.staat-modern.de (German language website).

through efficient and effective working methods was 'punished' by receiving a proportionally smaller amount in the next financial year.[8]

In place of input orientation, New Public Management prefers the concept of *output or outcome orientation*. The quality of an administration should be measured by its actual output and the resulting outcomes. Political control should thus also be based on output and outcome guidelines. The idea behind this is that the aim of administration should not merely be to take action, but also to achieve results which relate to political guidelines, for example the reduction of unemployment or of global poverty (cf. Brinckmann 1994: 173). "Outcome-oriented administrative management" (Buschor 1993) faces several difficulties, however, as it is not always easy to identify and measure outcomes and also determine the factors responsible. It is all too easy to ascribe positive results to one's own actions and negative effects to external factors. What is more, some impacts only emerge in the long term, or, in contrast, last only a short time and thus lack permanence.

It is clear from the foregoing that *quality* has become a *central criterion*, not only in the private sector, but also for public administration, as well as for the whole of the non-profit sector. Whereas focusing on quality in the private sector is aimed primarily at contributing to protecting or improving the competitive situation, in the public sector it is intended to bring an improvement in the provision of services. Various concepts of quality management have been developed to this end in the private sector, which have increasingly been employed in non-profit organisations. Within the framework of New Public Management concepts, business and free market elements are carried over into the public sector. When the concepts and instruments of quality management are applied to non-profit organisations, however, numerous problems arise, since they have been developed for the private sector, and the non-profit sector is subject to some fundamentally different conditions. Therefore, there is a growing demand for separate concepts to be developed which take account of the structural conditions of the non-profit sector.

This book takes up the theme here: irrespective of whether the concepts used are those of quality management, of New Public Management, or of other management models, data are needed for management to be able to make decisions on a rational basis. The *concepts and instruments of evaluation,* whose main task is to establish the benefit or value of an item, are appropriate here (cf. Mertens 1998: 219). These items can be individual measures, projects, programmes, or even institutionalised services offered with an unlimited time-scale. Within the framework of evaluation, *empirical methods of information acquisition* and *systematic procedures for its analysis* using *transparent criteria* are applied, facilitating intersubjective verifiability. Analysis does not follow given standards (as with ISO) or established parameters (as in the case of Total Quality Management concepts), but rather criteria which are tailored to meet the particular conditions pertaining to

---

8 This is also the reason for the annual appearance, traditional in budgeting, of "December fever", which means spending the remaining budget funds as quickly as possible at the end of the financial year, to prevent them being lost or the budget even being cut for the coming year.

the object to be evaluated (the evaluand). As mentioned above, the non-profit sector is important not only economically and for employment and socio-political reasons, but also embraces a wide spectrum of differing organisations with very different aims. Since evaluation is a flexible concept, capable of being adapted to the specific task and situational context, and since *evaluations* primarily examine the contribution and efficacy of measures, programmes or services, they are *particularly well-suited to supporting quality development in non-profit organisations.*

The aim of this book is to develop a *theoretically-based evaluation concept* and a *methodology* that: (1) can be used to *obtain output- and impact-related data,* (2) from which *assessment criteria* can be derived that are appropriate *for evaluation,* particularly in the non-profit sector, (3) and from which a *multidimensional set of criteria for assessing quality in non-profit organisations* can be developed. Using these quality criteria, it should be possible to carry out an appraisal of the services of non-profit organisations and their impacts that is appropriate for the requirements of this sector. Accordingly, these criteria (unlike those used in business management concepts) need to be suited to the tasks and contextual conditions of non-profit organisations. In addition, it is assumed that the evaluation concept developed here can, in principle, be used *in all fields of activity* and *all phases of service provision,* from planning to execution, and even beyond any possible termination of support (e.g. in the case of special measures and programmes). It can also be used for periodic *evaluations,* just as suitably as for the setting up of *monitoring systems* for long-term observation.

In order to be able to assess the performance quality of non-profit organisations, the focus of evaluation will be on the impacts of measures, programmes or services offered, as *quality is characterised by high levels of effectiveness and efficacy.* Although the concept devised is aimed at the requirements and situational context of non-profit organisations, it can, due to its flexibility, *also be used by organisations in the profit-sector (business enterprises).*

Since evaluation is not a quality management system, it does not render such a system superfluous. If deficiencies are to be corrected and the output and effectiveness of organisations enhanced in order to improve the general quality of their activities, programmes or service provision, then evaluations must have useful consequences. There is therefore a need for a system which, based on evaluation findings and, where applicable, recommendations, will lead to management decisions that produce targeted action and activity when implemented. It is therefore *necessary to link quality management and evaluation,* two themes which have seldom been connected in the literature to date. A high level of importance is thus attached to explaining the complementary nature of these two approaches.

In detail, the *layout of the book is as follows.* Firstly, the *concept of quality* is explained in depth; then, quality management concepts used by businesses to develop and ensure quality are presented. From the many existing approaches,[9] the widely-used system of certification based on standards series (DIN, EN, ISO) is singled out here, along with models of Total Quality Management (EFQM in particular) *(chapter 2.1)*.

Based on the considerations presented earlier, the focus must now be on how *concepts of quality management* developed for private-sector, freely competing, profit-businesses may be transferred to non-profit organisations. *New Public Management approaches* represent an alternative method of quality development, but these reach their limits at the point where market- and competition-like structures can neither be introduced nor simulated *(chapter 2.2)*.

After this, *concepts of evaluation* are presented, with which data can be collected and analysed for use in management decisions, regardless of the management or quality development model employed. Evaluations can be particularly usefully integrated into those management systems that measure the quality of an organisation by whether, and to what extent, it has achieved its envisaged goals and produced intended outcomes *(chapter 2.3)*.

To conclude the chapter, concepts of quality management are compared with those of evaluation, in order to identify similarities and differences, and to elucidate their *complementary nature (chapter 2.4)*.

In *chapter 3,* firstly the central *concept of impacts* is defined, and is distinguished from other terms *(chapter 3.2)*. In order to ascertain the effects resulting from (programme) interventions, a comparison must be made between at least two situations (before and after the intervention), as changes can of course only be observed over time. As the development of programmes and services offered follows a particular procedural pattern, the concept of *life-cycle research* is used to analyse the progress of programmes *(chapter 3.3)*. Services and programmes are rendered or carried out by organisations which have multifaceted relationships with their environment. *Concepts of organisational theory* can help to analyse contexts that are internal to organisations, as well as the relationship of organisations to their environment *(chapter 3.4)*. Programme interventions are often designed to introduce reforms (innovations). What this means, under what conditions this is most likely to be successful, and how innovations spread, is the concern of *innovation and diffusion research (chapter 3.5)*. Due to the fact that many services and programme interventions of non-profit organisations are not merely directed towards achieving short-term goals, but at bringing about permanent changes, the aspect of *sustainability* must also be taken into account *(chapter 3.6)*.

No structural distinction will be made here between measures, programmes, and institutionalised services offered on a permanent basis. It will be assumed that, regardless of the form services take, they follow a certain process sequence (planning, implementation etc.), are carried out by an organisation and often entail innovations aimed at effecting

---

9 For an overview of the multitude of approaches used by non-profit organisations, cf. e.g. Boeßenecker et al. 2003; Schubert & Zink 2001; Peterander & Speck 1999; Klausegger & Scharitzer 1998.

changes that are intended to be long-lasting or permanent. An example of an institutional service is marriage guidance counselling: this has to be planned by a therapist in terms of achieving a certain objective, and carried out within the framework of several 'sessions', each building on the previous one. The service is offered by an agency (an organisation), which is active in a specific context (environment). Within therapy, 'new' models of conflict resolution (innovations) are learnt, for example, which can be applied not only in the area of marriage, but also in other contexts (e.g. work, leisure groups) (diffusion). Marriage guidance also aims to achieve more than just mediating in isolated conflicts; it is concerned with finding solutions for long-term co-existence.

Programmes are conducted along largely similar lines: a programme to reduce poverty, for example, has to be planned prior to being implemented in various stages. It is put into action by an organisation, in cooperation with other organisations or target groups (e.g. farmers or people working in the casual labour market). The aim may be to introduce 'new' methods of production (innovation), which it is hoped will be adopted by as many people as possible (diffusion), in order to achieve as high a level of effectiveness as possible. Such a programme would be oriented much more towards 'sustainability' than short-term success.

The *areas and criteria of assessment* which are to be used to constitute a set of evaluation guidelines are derived from the three aforementioned theoretical concepts (the life-cycle model, and organisational and innovation/diffusion research), as well as from a multidimensional concept of sustainability. Prior to compiling these guidelines, the criteria thus obtained will be compared with business management quality criteria, in order to demonstrate that they can be condensed into *a multidimensional set of criteria* for appraising the quality of services offered and impacts triggered by organisations *(chapter 3.7)*.

Chapter 4 deals with the *methodology of evaluation* and its *application*. The central methodological element is a *model set of evaluation guidelines*, which is based on the theoretical considerations presented in *chapter 3*, and specifies the topics and assessment dimensions. Using the model guidelines to evaluate measures, programmes and permanent services, it should be possible in principle to develop made-to-order guidelines for every field of activity or area of policy, to allow for evaluations at all stages of a programme, either formative or summative, and whether the evaluation is carried out internally or externally. The basic model remains the same; it is simply a case of supplementing, expanding, and adapting the analytical questions listed within the topic fields *(chapter 4.2)*. Of course, depending on the tasks of the evaluation, the programme phase to be evaluated, and the situational conditions of the relevant policy field, different approaches are necessary. The *application and assessment procedure* is presented in *chapter 4.3*. Whilst detailed procedural instructions and evaluation examples are given for the technical application of the guidelines, the chapter dealing with methods *(chapter 4.4)* is limited to a broad overview of the most important *test designs and data collection methods* for impact-oriented evaluations. Knowledge of the range of methods available is necessary in order to select suitable test designs and methods. A *multi-method approach* is recommended here, in order to compensate for the weaknesses of some instruments by the strengths of others. Since information on the development and concrete application of the different procedures can be found in countless reference books on evaluation methods or empirical social research, an extensive description is superfluous here.

The standards that should be adhered to when *performing evaluations,* the difficulties which may arise, and the practical demands which result from using the evaluation concept are all addressed in *chapter 4.5.* A *participatory approach* has proved best for taking account of the interests and perspectives of the various stakeholders involved in the evaluation. Various experiences have shown that such an approach not only contributes to stimulating the willingness of the stakeholders to cooperate and increasing the validity of the results, but first and foremost also enhances the usefulness of an evaluation. The greater the extent to which an evaluation is accepted, the greater the chance that any recommendations arising from it will be translated into action later on.

Chapter 4.6 deals with the different stages of evaluation. *Practical advice for the planning and execution* of an evaluation is also given, with the focus on distinctive requirements resulting from the evaluation concept developed here and from the participatory approach proposed.

Chapter 5, the final chapter, provides a summary and assessment of the approach to evaluation developed here, with regard to the objective of this book, which is to enable non-profit organisations to act more effectively and thus to contribute to their quality development. There is a review of the historical development of this approach over the last ten years or so, preliminary forms of this concept having already been applied in numerous evaluations.

This book therefore has another purpose, which is to standardise, bring together, and develop further the conceptual formulations that are scattered throughout documents in various publications and (in some cases internal) evaluation reports, in such a way that they can be used by organisations in general for *impact-based quality development.* For this reason, not only is the theoretical evaluation concept and its methodology presented in detail here, but practical advice is also given for its application.

2 Quality Management and Evaluation

2.1 Quality management

Quality improvement and assurance are central challenges facing modern businesses in their efforts to survive in the market, and they thus align their management with this maxim. The main concepts employed to achieve this are outlined below. Firstly, however, we will explore the change of meaning in the term 'quality'.

2.1.1 Quality

Although the *term "quality"* is used extremely frequently nowadays, a review of the literature reveals that a concise, universally applicable definition is still lacking. Even in the business administration field, where the term is used continually in the context of quality management concepts (cf. Widmer 2001: 11; Mayländer 2000: 9), it is impossible to find such a definition. The term remains fickle, and has the most diverse meanings and uses attributed to it. This is due not least to the fact that we can differentiate between objective and subjective properties. In industry in particular, the concept of quality was in the past defined using *technical criteria*: "High quality was equated with high technical performance, high stability and a long life-cycle, combined with efficient functioning and freedom from errors" (Seghezzi 1994: 5; 2003: 23 f.).

According to this definition, the measure of quality is adherence to technical norms and specifications. In this way, quality could *seemingly* be judged based on *objective criteria*, independent of the person carrying out the assessment. However, if the specified technical norms, e.g. a very long life-span or absolute freedom from errors, cannot be achieved, the seemingly objective criteria must also undergo a *subjective appraisal*, which will produce very different results depending on the product or service[10] in question. For example, most people would accept it if, after a few years of use, their food mixer or television set incurred a fault and needed to be repaired. In the case of a heart pacemaker, on the other

---

10 Quality can be ascertained not only for products and services, but also for processes (cf. Kreutzberg 2000: 15 f.; Eversheim 1997: 11).

hand, whose function is to safeguard survival, this level of tolerance certainly doesn't exist. Thus the specification of a margin of error, which does not automatically lead to a less positive quality appraisal, may be derived not only from the type of product in question, but also be based on subjective considerations.

In the 1960s, as the *customer perspective* started to be considered, subjective elements increasingly found their way into the quality discussion. Users were questioned on their satisfaction with the product. Their assessment of 'fitness for use' - the usefulness and usability of a product - became the focus of people's understanding of quality. The appraisal of product features thus becomes a highly subjective act, which is influenced by the personal needs of customers. So, in addition to a product's freedom from errors, usefulness and usability, dimensions such as expedience, manageability, aesthetics, and prestige associated with the product may also be applied to evaluate its quality[11].

This development was taken into consideration in the formulation of an internationally recognised concept definition:

"Quality is the totality of features and characteristics of a product or service that bear on its ability to satisfy stated or implied needs" (ISO 8402 standard).[12]

This definition still incorporates the original content on efficient functioning and freedom from errors. However, abstract norms do not constitute the measure of quality here; rather, it is determined by the *satisfaction of needs and demands specified by customers*.

Quality appraisal is consequently dependent not only on subjective utility considerations, but also on the *situational context, cultural particularities* and, ultimately, the *type of product* (e.g. food, machine, repair/consulting/teaching service). The quality of cloudy drinking water (a product) in the dry Somali desert (situational context), for instance, would be judged differently by a German (cultural background) to by a Somali. It is also significant whether the customer is served this product in a five-star hotel or in a nomad tent in Somalia. This also applies, of course, to the assessment of staff service quality, of the type of hotel etc. It is thus impossible to formulate cross-sectoral, cross-cultural, non-

---

11   On the notion of quality in general, cf. e.g. Rothlauf 2004: 67 ff.; Zollondz 2002: 5 ff., 141 ff.; Kreutzberg 2000: 13 ff.; Seghezzi 1994: 5 ff.; 2003: 9 ff.; Juran 1991: 12 f. On the notion of quality in the service sector, cf. e.g. Beckmann 2004; Möller 2003; Raidl 2001: 20 ff.; Schubert, Zink 2001: 1 f., 1997: 2 ff.; Eversheim 1997: 4 ff.; CEDEFOP 1997: 6 ff. On quality in non-profit organisations, cf. e.g. Poister 2003; Scherer 2002; Meyer 2002; Badelt 2002; Daumenlang & Palm 1997: 2 ff.; Eversheim, Jaschinski & Reddemann 1997: 34 ff., and on quality in New Public Management, cf. e.g. Bremen 2004; Rossmann 2003; Schedler & Proeller 2000: 64 f. On quality management in the service sector, cf. e.g. Hansen 2003; Igl 2002; Mayländer 2000; Peterander, Speck 1999, and in the education sector, cf. e.g. Holtappels 2003; Eder 2002; Boysen 2002; Weinert 2001.

12   The 'Deutsches Institut für Normierung' (DIN) (German Standardisation Institute) (Internet address: http://www2.din.de/en) and the International Organization for Standardization (ISO) administer and maintain standards.

situation-specific quality criteria, which implies that all this general ISO definition imparts is the wisdom that quality is what the customer considers it to be. This *conceptual haziness* deepens yet further if we consider other aspects of the quality discussion. The literature points out that products should not be viewed in isolation, and that the provision as a whole should be considered when assessing quality. This comprises not only the product itself, but also its presentation, customer instruction in its operation, and the accompanying service provision. Some argue that on-time service rendering or even price should also be incorporated into the notion of quality as further appraisal dimensions. By the same token, aspects such as the environmental compatibility of a product, its health properties, or political correctness could all also be integrated into the concept as quality criteria.

It can be stated that the *quality of a product or service cannot be defined in a universally applicable way*, but is rather measured according to the *utility appraisal of the customer*. This appraisal can be carried out based on various *criteria*, which in turn can be of vastly differing significance depending on *situational context, cultural particularities* and *product type*.

2.1.2 Quality management models

If quality is primarily characterised by the product utility generated - by customer satisfaction with the product or service - and it is assumed that this satisfaction is only possible if a product is functional, i.e. error-free, then the task of quality management (QM) is to assess, create, and continually improve the utility of a product/service, as well as to ensure extensive freedom from errors (cf. Juran 1991: 13 ff.; Seghezzi 1994: 7). Quality management comprises the executive functions concerned with planning and implementing quality policy. The activities necessary for this are usually divided up into the following areas: quality planning, quality control, quality assurance, and quality improvement (cf. Seghezzi 1994: 18; 2003: 63 ff.; Eversheim 2000: 14 f.; Kreutzberg 2000: 24; Zollondz 2002: 189 ff.).

Quality planning involves the specification of quality goals and criteria, as well as of guidelines for the implementation of quality aims. In order to be able to derive the quality requirements of products to be created or services to be rendered from the quality policy decided upon, the needs and expectations of potential customers must be ascertained. Subsequently, the method of translating these into new, improved services must be planned, as well as how to configure the necessary production processes. The task of quality planning is thus performed by various fields within a business, e.g. by the market research, product development, production planning, process development departments etc. This highlights the fact that the realisation of quality is a task for all employees in a company.

Quality control ensures that processes and operations are managed in such a way as to create products and services that are as error-free as possible, and that meet the quality requirements of potential customers. To this end, actual quality is compared with target quality within the framework of process monitoring, in order to be able to even out any deviations that emerge.

Quality assurance pursues a dual aim: its purpose is to engender trust in efforts made to ensure quality both inside and outside of the company (particularly among customers and clients).

The fourth quality management task is to achieve continual q*uality improvement* with respect to products and processes, as well as to strengthen the quality consciousness of employees so that a quality-oriented corporate culture develops.

A *quality management system (quality assurance system)* should ensure the fulfilment of quality requirements specified by managers. It encompasses the organisational structure, responsibilities, processes, and the means for realising quality management.

Even a straightforward inspection and control system is a kind of quality management system. If, however, the aim is to develop quality consciousness among all employees, so that they feel jointly responsible for the quality of a product or service, then more extensive quality management systems are required. The guiding idea of such systems is the establishment of a quality culture, that is laid down in a comprehensive body of principles and standards. In order to monitor it, adhere to it, and manage it, a control system is set up[13]. Fig. 2.1 illustrates the interrelationships between individual quality management tasks.

Various models are available for structuring quality management. They can be based either on a series of standards (ISO 9000-9004), or on the guiding principles of comprehensive quality management (Total Quality Management = TQM), which also form the basis of well-known quality accolades such as the Malcolm Baldridge Award and the European Quality Award.

All models share some common features: the systematic design of the organisational structure, the handling of processes, and the safeguarding of the quality of the product to be made or service to be rendered. Standards and norms are intended to help create a uniform information base, by which companies can be appraised and compared with each other. The critical evaluative criterion here is the quality of the product or service (cf. Raidl 2001: 53).[14]

13　Quality management systems are occasionally also compared to the nervous system of an organism (cf. Rühl 1998: 24), which is a very descriptive analogy: it establishes current situations, and forwards information on them to the appropriate organs (quality planning). Conversely, it also transports status reports from the organs (quality assurance) to the brain (quality management), which then issues appropriate commands (quality control), in order to achieve continual quality improvement. The nervous system is operating rationally, completely and in a coordinated fashion if it combines all organs, and if a uniform organising principle is present.

14　It is virtually impossible to keep an overview of the quality management literature. The following is just a selection of important contributions: Rothlauf 2004; ISO 2004; Nauen-

Figure 2.1: Quality management tasks

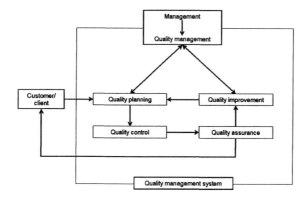

The *ISO 9000-9004 series of standards* represents a comprehensive framework for quality management[15]. The norms specify the steps a business needs to take in order to create an individual quality assurance system. There are no sector-specific specifications. On the contrary, it is assumed "that the same standards can be applied:

- to any organisation, large or small, whatever its product
- including whether its 'product' is actually a service,
- in any sector of activity and
- whether it is a business enterprise, a public administration, or a government department"
- (ISO 2005).

dorf 2004; Gucanin 2003; Oakland 2003; Brauer 2002; Seghezzi 2002; Hummel & Malorny 2002; Zollondz 2002; Töpfer & Mehdorn 2002; Pfeifer 2001; Raidl 2001; Schiersmann et al. 2001; Uehlinger 2001; Kreutzberg 2000; Cappis 1998; EFQM 1998; Malorny 1998; Masing 1998; Wilmes & Radtke 1998; Wunderer 1998; Radtke 1997; Schubert & Zink 1997; Wunderer et al. 1997; Heinrich 1996; Malorny 1996; Feuchthofen & Severing 1995; Zink 1995 & 1994; Frehr 1994; Runge 1994; Oess 1994; Saatweber 1994; Seghezzi 1994 & 1993; Witte 1993; Schildknecht 1992.

15   The basic principles and central concepts of quality management are explained within ISO 9000.. The actual requirements of the quality management system are contained within ISO 9001. ISO 9004 provides a set of principles for improving organisational performance. Its makeup is based on the content of ISO 9001, but it aims to achieve extensive quality management that goes beyond demands for standards, in a Total Quality Management sense (cf. Brauer 2002: 8). For further information, cf. URL: http://www.iso.org (last accessed on 27/7/2005).

ISO is not an instrument for defining quality level; instead, it specifies the minimum requirements of a quality management system. Its aim is to fully document workflows. It is based on the assumption that the highest quality levels are achieved if production is logically planned, standardised, and transparent for all participants. ISO standards govern all areas that need to be defined and organised within a quality management system.

The whole ISO 9000 series of standards has been reworked over the last few years, and was reintroduced in December 2000 in its revised form as ISO 9000: 2000. The modified norms are based on eight principles of quality management (cf. ISO 2005):

(1) Customer focus
Organizations depend on their customers and therefore should understand current and future customer needs, should meet customer requirements and strive to exceed customer expectations.

(2) Leadership
Leaders establish unity of purpose and direction of the organization. They should create and maintain the internal environment in which people can become fully involved in achieving the organization's objectives.

(3) Involvement of people
People at all levels are the essence of an organization and their full involvement enables their abilities to be used for the organization's benefit.

(4) Process approach
A desired result is achieved more efficiently when activities and related resources are managed as a process.

(5) System approach to management
Identifying, understanding and managing interrelated processes as a system contributes to the organization's effectiveness and efficiency in achieving its objectives.

(6) Continual improvement
Continual improvement of the organization's overall performance should be a permanent objective of the organization.

(7) Factual approach to decision making
Effective decisions are based on the analysis of data and information.

(8) Mutually beneficial supplier relationships
An organization and its suppliers are interdependent and a mutually beneficial relationship enhances the ability of both to create value.

The strong orientation of the standards (ISO 9001: 2000) towards process flows in an organisation is deemed 'new' in comparison to the previous ISO model (cf. Brauer 2002: 24). The following is understood under processes: "Processes are recognized as consisting of one or more linked activities that require resources and must be managed to achieve predetermined output. The output of one process may directly form the input to the next process and the final product is often the result of a network or system of processes" (ISO 2005). The core tasks of a company are portrayed as a control loop between incoming customer demands and targeted customer satisfaction (cf. fig. 2.2). The successful implementation of the control loop should lead to the goal of 'continual improvement' being met.

ISO 9001: 2000 differentiates between five overarching processes of a quality management system that define "what you should do consistently to provide products that meet customer and applicable statutory or regulatory requirements" (ISO 2005):

(1) Quality management system
Creating a quality management system in accordance with ISO is primarily about describing the processes in a company, as well as those between the company and cooperating firms (e.g. suppliers), and, based on this, specifying measures that ensure the quality management system is indeed created, documented, applied and monitored. A company must firstly identify and analyse the processes needed for the creation and operation of a quality management system (e.g. leadership activities, resource provision, product realisation, measurement and analysis), before they can then be managed. Of particular importance is the creation of comprehensive quality documentation. This should include the following (cf. Matul and Scharitzer 2002: 62).

- Quality manual: contains all written information on the targets, organisation, tasks, processes and structures of a company's quality assurance system.
- Quality assurance plan: governs procedures, measurement methods, and the process arrangement of activities.
- Quality assurance procedures: provide detailed regulation of quality assurance measures.
- Quality records: serve the documentation of aggregated internal and external information (e.g. on customer satisfaction), measurement results, analysis outcomes, and activities related to the quality assurance system.

(2) Management responsibility
ISO advocates a top-down approach. Management defines the goals and the quality policy that is to be implemented, and is responsible for ensuring that all employees support the quality management system, as well as for making sure that it is continually enhanced and adapted to optimally suit the company's quality policy and customer demands.

(3) Resource management
The company management is not only responsible for developing a vision and managing its implementation; it must also provide the necessary resources. On top of personnel and financial resources, this also includes the provision of an infrastructure (buildings, process equipment, auxiliary services such as transport and communication) and a working environment that is conducive to the attainment of quality goals. Through ongoing training, all employees should be given the capabilities to optimally fulfil the tasks given to them by management.

Figure 2.2: Process model of quality management from ISO 9001

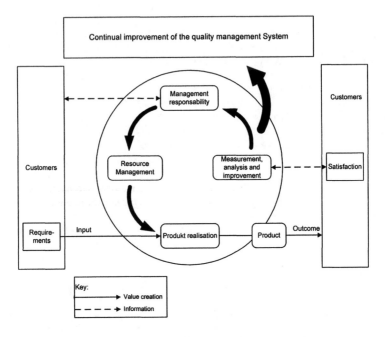

Source: based on Brauer 2002: 25

(4) Product realization
Product realisation encompasses all processes necessary for product/service provision. In the foreground is the customer, whose expectations and demands should, in accordance with the process model, form the focus of a company's activities, and who is, at the same time, the intended recipient of the product or service. In order to satisfy customers, their demands must therefore firstly be ascertained and reviewed with regard to their feasibility. Based on this, a development plan with clearly defined process phases and integrated control mechanisms is created. When procuring products, it is necessary to ensure that suppliers are capable of meeting specified demands efficiently. Product/service provision in the company is subject to detailed process control, the results of which are constantly monitored. In addition, the product's conformance to specified requirements is continually checked using surveillance and measurement equipment.

(5) Measurement, analysis and improvement
The aim of data collection and analysis is to safeguard company performance and customer satisfaction, as well as to trigger improvements. To this end, whilst customer satisfaction is being measured, attention is also given as to whether planned results are achiev-
able through the processes employed, and what sources of error and weak points need to
be overcome. Internal audits should, among other things, provide information on whether
the quality management system is fulfilling the tasks allocated to it. Unwanted developments should be identified as early as possible, ideally prior to their occurrence. The continual improvement of processes, including the quality management system itself, represents a primary corporate goal.

If a company has successfully introduced a quality management system, it can have its
fulfilment of the ISO standards certified by an officially recognised organisation (e.g.
TÜV[16] or DEKRA[17]). This should make clear that the company in question is quality-
orientated. However, ISO 9000 certification is no guarantee that all employees adhere to
the rules out of conviction, that the company operates a modern quality management system or that the processes defined also undergo optimisation (cf. Vilain 2003: 23 ff.;
Seghezzi 2003: 219 ff.; Zollondz 2002: 250 ff.; Raidl 2001: 67; Zink 2001: 94 ff.; Schubert 2001: 113 ff.; Mayländer 2000: 18 ff.; Scheiber 1999; Rühl 1998: 25 ff.; Fuhr 1998:
47 ff.; Wunder 1995: 12 ff.; Kegelmann 1995: 160 ff.).
   An equally well-known quality concept, which will here be explained in somewhat
more detail, is *Total Quality Management (TQM)*, which is extraordinarily bold in its in-
tent to make quality the most important determinant of a company's success. TQM is thus
frequently elevated to the status of a universally dominant corporate concept. The fundamental principles are very similar to those used within ISO (cf. Rothlauf 2004: 53 ff.; 83
ff.; Seghezzi 2003: 253; 1994: 57; Hummel & Malorny 2002, 1997: 44 ff.; Mayländer
2000: 17; CEDEFOP 1997: 6; Witte 1993: 90 ff.; Schildknecht 1992: 125 ff.):

(1) Customer orientation
The customer is the key to the success of every business. All processes and activities in a
company are thus aligned with the fulfilment of customer needs. In order to achieve
strong customer orientation, detailed knowledge of customer requirements, expectations
and satisfaction should be systematically acquired and applied within the company. The
goal is to create long-term customer loyalty.

(2) Process orientation
Focusing on operational processes and their continual improvement is one of the cornerstones of TQM. Processes rather than results should thus be at the forefront of firms' actions. As every activity is viewed as a process, a constant improvement potential emerges,

---

16   Technischer Überwachungsverein (German product testing agency).
17   Deutscher Kraftfahrzeug-Überwachungsverein (German vehicle inspection agency).

which makes a crucial contribution to the enhancement of quality and productivity. The aim is to minimise cost-intensive quality controls and the re-working of products. Faults should be avoided as far as possible (zero error approach). If they do occur, they should be treated as a source of learning. Implementation is carried out by management, which employs planning, organisational and control measures aimed at enhancing process quality.

(3) Continual quality improvement and assurance
All employees in a company should be involved in efforts to achieve quality. Based on the 'constant improvement' motto, organisations carry out continual quality enhancement programmes. In order to ensure the participation of employees in such programmes, they are motivated by, for example, results-oriented pay. Each person is thus responsible for the quality of their work. Internally, the customer-supplier principle is introduced, which states that "anyone who requires the output of our work as the basis for their work is our customer" (cf. Heß 1997: 87).

(4) Management
Management is the driving force which ensures that customer, employee and process orientation are introduced into the company. Managers thus have high demands placed upon them. The following functions form essential parts of leadership behaviour (cf. Rothlauf 2004: 60):
- Commitment and role model function in relation to comprehensive quality
- Appraisal of the efforts and success of individuals and project teams
- Establishment of an ongoing TQM culture
- Support for TQM through the provision of suitable resources and aids
- Commitment to customers and suppliers
- Active promotion of comprehensive quality, including outside of the company.

A cooperative leadership style is demanded of managers, embracing all executives and employees. In addition, the role of supportive manager is becoming more and more important, with the focus on the mobilisation of employees and their potential.

Many of the TQM concepts originally developed in Japan, and later on in the USA and also in Europe, are associated with quality awards. Internationally, the US American 'Malcolm Baldridge National Quality Award', which is divided into seven main categories with a total of 28 individual criteria, has attracted the most attention up to now. On the one hand, these criteria serve many companies as internal guidelines for creating their own quality management system, whilst on the other hand being applied for company appraisal in the awarding of the quality prize (cf. Eversheim, Jaschinski & Reddemann 1997: 59 f.; Zollondz 2002: 261 ff.). Organisations that receive awards are those that have been able to achieve outstanding quality and productivity improvements through the application of the TQM model.

In Europe, the *European Foundation for Quality Management (EFQM)* model and its prize, the 'European Quality Award' (EQA), have attracted the most interest.[18] Its main features do not differ significantly from those of its American archetype. The amount of attention given to security and environmental protection issues led to the inclusion of just one additional dimension: 'public interests' (cf. Seghezzi 1993: 30).

The model is configured – like ISO – in such a way that it can be applied to any organisation, regardless of sector, type, size, or socio-cultural context, at least within Europe. The fundamental outline of the EFQM model is based on the three pillars of TQM – people, processes and results – and follows the *basic principles* detailed below (cf. Rothlauf 2004: 50 ff. & 442 ff.; Seghezzi 2003: 255 ff.; EFQM 2003a: 5 ff.; 2003b: 6 ff.; 1998: 4 f.; Hummel & Malorny 2002: 11 ff.; Mayländer 2000: 23 ff.):

- *Results orientation*
  According to EFQM (2003a: 5), excellent organisations are agile, flexible and reactive in their behaviour, in order to meet the changing needs and expectations of stakeholders. They thereby act with foresight, observe the competition, and undertake careful planning based on all available information. The goal is to achieve results that "delight all the organisation's stakeholders" (ibid.).
- *Customer focus*
  As customers are seen as being the ultimate judges of product and service quality, excellent organisations know, and have a very detailed understanding of, their customers. They gear themselves towards their needs and expectations in order to create lasting customer value: "They also understand that customer loyalty, retention, and market share gain is maximised through a clear focus on the needs and expectations of both existing and potential customers" (ibid.).
- *Leadership and constancy of purpose*
  Excellent organisations have visionary, inspirational management that consistently pursues the organisation's objectives. Managers define the organisation's focus, communicate it, and have a persuasive, motivating effect. They display exemplary behaviour and performance, and in doing so "lead by example" (ibid.).
- *Management by processes and facts*
  Excellent organisations are managed "through a set of interdependent and interrelated systems, processes and facts" (ibid.). For this purpose they are equipped with a management system that is based on the needs and expectations of all stakeholders, and is oriented towards their fulfilment.
- *People development and involvement*
  Excellent organisations have competent, flexible, motivated employees, whose contribution is maximised through their continual development and involvement. Excellent organisations support the personal growth of their co-workers, in order to be able to

---

18 For further information, cf. URL: http://www.efqm.org (last accessed on 01/09/2006).

benefit from their expertise. Through appropriate protection, reward and recognition, loyalty to the organisation can be enhanced.

- *Continuous learning, innovation and improvement*
Learning is utilised to create innovation and opportunities for improvement, thus "challenging the status quo and effecting change" (ibid.). The organisation can learn from its own activities and performance, as well as from those of others. For this purpose, the expertise of all employees is drawn upon.

- *Partnership development*
Excellent organisations are characterised by their "developing and maintaining value-adding partnerships" (ibid.). They recognise that their success can depend on such partnerships. Partnerships put them in a situation to be able to achieve enhanced value creation for their stakeholders by optimising their core competencies. In order to attain common goals, partners work together and offer mutual support by sharing experiences, resources and knowledge.

- *Corporate social responsibility*
Excellent organisations exceed the relevant minimum regulatory framework, and strive to understand and respond to the expectations of their stakeholders in society. They are thus characterised by high ethical standards, which are reflected in the values of the organisation.

Figure 2.3: The EFQM European Quality Model

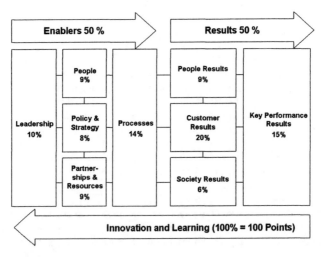

Source: http://www.efqm.org

These principles are also reflected in the agenda of the European Quality Award, which can be divided up into two main blocks – enablers and results – with a total of nine criteria and 32 sub-criteria (cf. fig. 2.3).

(1) At the heart of the EFQM model is *management behaviour*, the role of which is to ensure the long-term success of an organisation. This can only be achieved – according to the EFQM model

- "if top and middle management continually initiate improvements, and secure their implementation through personal involvement" (Radtke & Wilmes 2002: 29). Crucial to the assessment of the leadership criterion is evidence of systematic, pre-emptive behaviour, and a consistency of commitment across all fields and on all levels. This is deemed to be especially important, "as employees tend to act as exemplified by managers" (ibid.).[19] The *leadership* criterion is divided into five sub-criteria in the EFQM model:[20]
- Leaders develop the mission, vision, values and ethics and are role models of a culture of excellence.
- Leaders are personally involved in ensuring the organisation's management system is developed, implemented and continuously improved.
- Leaders interact with customers, partners and representatives of society.
- Leaders reinforce a culture of excellence with the organisation's people.
- Leaders identify and champion organisational change.

(2) According to EFQM, the *policy and strategy* of a company are based on a vision or mission. The "value system of the organisation" should find expression in formulated policy and its implementation in corporate strategy. The appraisal process should involve setting out how the various stakeholders are to be included in the formulation, implementation, review and improvement of policy and strategy. The assessment of all 'enablers' is aligned towards examining the extent to which managers and employees implement or configure resources and processes in a way commensurate with strategy. The *policy and strategy* criterion is divided up into four sub-points:[21]

- Policy and strategy are based on the present and future needs and expectations of stakeholders.
- Policy and strategy are based on information from performance measurement, research, learning and external related activities.
- Policy and strategy are developed, reviewed and updated.

---

19   For further explanation of the sub-criteria, cf. also Radtke & Wilmes 2002, as well as EFQM 2003a, 2003b, 2003c.

20   Taken directly from http://www.efqm.org/uploads/introducing_english.pdf (last accessed on 01/09/2006).

21   Ibid.

- Policy and strategy are communicated and deployed through a framework of key processes.

(3) The *people* criterion comprises all activities that a company employs to release employee potential and continually improve business activity. In order to involve employees from the whole company in continual improvement processes, holistic employee management concepts should be developed, systematised, and refined. The *people* criterion has five sub-points:[22]
- People resources are planned, managed and improved.
- People's knowledge and competencies are identified, developed and sustained.
- People are involved and empowered.
- People and the organisation have a dialogue.
- People are rewarded, recognised and cared for.

(4) Management has the task of deploying *partnerships and resources* in such a way as to ensure the implementation of company policy and strategy. The *resources (and partnerships)* criterion comprises the following aspects:[23]
- External partnerships are managed.
- Finances are managed.
- Buildings, equipment and materials are managed.
- Technology is managed.
- Information and knowledge are managed.

(5) *Processes* are at the heart of a TQM-oriented company, and should act as a catalyst between input and output. In assessing this criterion, consideration is given to the basic treatment of processes, as well as to the management of all value-adding business processes in a company. In the foreground are measures for the continual identification, management and control of customer-oriented business processes, as well as for implementing creativity and innovations. The *processes* criterion is divided up into five sub-points:[24]
- Processes are systematically designed and managed.
- Processes are improved, as needed, using innovation in order to fully satisfy and generate increasing value for customers and other stakeholders.
- Products and services are designed and developed based on customer needs and expectations.
- Products and services are produced, delivered and serviced.
- Customer relationships are managed and enhanced.

---

22 Ibid.
23 Ibid.
24 Ibid.

(6) The remaining criteria are concerned with an organisation's results. The *customer re-sults* criterion is allocated by far the biggest weighting, with 20 per cent of all available appraisal points, as it takes top priority in an excellent organisation according to EFQM. It deals with the performance of a company with regard to the satisfaction of external customer requirements. It can thus be observed how customers rate the quality of a firm's products and services. Knowledge about customer demands, expectations and desires should ensure that product and service development and production do not ignore market realities. Only detailed measurement and analysis of customer satisfaction is seen as being able to provide a basis for continual improvement: "It is necessary to get feedback from the customer on whether the products or services have generated satisfaction or even enthusiasm" (Radtke & Wilmes 2002: 83). In addition to "measurement results from the customer's perspective", "performance indicators" are also applied, such as the proportion of regular customers; customer acquisition and loss; failure, error and return rates; on-time delivery; letters of thanks and awards. The *customer results* criterion comprises:[25]

- (Customer) perception measures.
- Performance indicators.

(7) The *people results* criterion considers direct and indirect measurements in order to assess the achievements of an organisation with regard to employee satisfaction. According to EFQM, in an excellent organisation employee satisfaction is one of the most important variables. It is calculated by comparing subjectively-perceived input to a company with the working climate discerned by the employee. As employee satisfaction is deemed a prerequisite for all planning processes and strategic decisions in an organisation, it needs to be systematically measured and analysed. In addition to these "measures", key data (performance indicators) are also gathered (e.g. on levels of training, frequency of accidents at work, employee turnover etc.), in order to be able to draw conclusions as to employee satisfaction. Under the *people results* criterion, two aspects are distinguished:[26]

- (Employee) perception measures.
- Performance indicators.

(8) In contrast to Japanese and American quality awards, the EFQM model explicitly comprises the category *society results*. This criterion is used to assess to what extent an organisation is orientated towards the needs and expectations of the public with regard to social and environmental responsibility. If an organisation meets these requirements – according to the EFQM assumption – then it can be "sure of the acceptance and support of society" (Radtke & Wilmes 2002: 92). EFQM expects the effects of such a positive image to be a superior supply of labour, good relations with trade unions and professional associations, good political contacts, better cooperation with the authorities, and preferential treatment as a supplier or customer. In addition to "measurement results from soci-

---

25 Ibid.
26 Ibid.

ety's perspective", which can be obtained through, for example, surveys, sub-criteria such as engagement in society, impact on local employment levels, or environmental protection measures are used, which are gauged using "performance indicators". With regard to *society results*, EFQM again differentiates between:[27]
- (Social) perception measures.
- Performance indicators.

(9) The criterion *key performance results* refers to the operating results of an organisation, which "ultimately shed light on the quality of processes in the organisation" (Radtke & Wilmes 2002: 96). This criterion, second only to customer satisfaction in terms of importance, highlights the fact that the survival and advancement in the market of a company can only be secured through positive long-term operating results: "For organisations managed as free-market enterprises, the generation of profit is crucial to their existence" (ibid., p. 97). Company reports, consolidated with additional data, e.g. profit and loss statements, data from the balance sheet, credit rating data, share price data, as well as data on error rates, flexibility, process capabilities, market share and supplier appraisals, can all be employed in carrying out the assessment. Under *key performance results*, EFQM differentiates between:[28]
- Key performance outcomes.
- Key performance indicators.

In summary, it can be stated that the 'enabler' criteria (leadership, policy and strategy, people, resources and processes) facilitate the examination and appraisal of the behaviours, activities and processes in an organisation, as well as their degree of application. *The 'enabler' criteria deal with what an organisation does.* As the ultimate aim of all efforts to enhance quality is the improvement of operating results, the main focal points on the results side are the systematic measurement of (operating) results, the appraisal of employee and customer satisfaction, and the assessment of the appearance of the organisation from the outside (social responsibility/image). *The results criteria are concerned with the outcomes achieved by an organisation through its activities.*[29]

At what level an organisation is at the start of an EFQM process - and what progress is made - is reviewed using a self-assessment process. EFQM sees *self-assessment*[30] as being a comprehensive, regular, systematic audit of the effectiveness of processes and structures within one's own organisation. The nine main categories and 32 sub-categories presented in the model are used to carry this out. Within the framework of this self-assessment, existing organisational solutions are analysed and evaluated using a so-called

---

27   Ibid.
28   Ibid.
29   For more detail, cf. http://www.efqm.org.
30   The exact procedure to be followed in carrying out the assessment and points allocation is presented in detail in EFQM brochures, and illustrated using examples.

RADAR logic[31]. As a *result* of this process, the organisation receives, on the one hand, a points rating of between 0 and 1000 points, which describes the *level* at which the organisation finds itself, and, on the other hand, a *structured list of strengths and weaknesses,* which outlines the organisation's *improvement potential.* If a company puts itself forward for the European Quality Award (EQA), a written report must be prepared, detailing the strengths and weaknesses of the organisation in accordance with the EFQM criteria. This documentation is examined by trained, accredited EFQM assessors together with the organisation. For the awarding of quality prizes, a sector-specific applicant ranking is created. In practice, however, most organisations employ EFQM much more as an internal instrument, without applying for a quality prize (cf. Langnickel 2003: 38 ff.; Seghezzi 2003: 287 ff.; Vomberg & Wallrafen-Dreisow 2002: 257 ff.; Schüberl & Egger 2001: 133 ff.; Klausegger & Scharitzer 1998a: 384 f.).

2.1.3 Advantages and disadvantages of the ISO and EFQM models

The ISO model and TQM models such as EFQM need *not* be viewed as *contradictory* or as mutually exclusive alternatives, since the requirements of ISO certification are essentially congruent with the 'enabler' criteria of the EFQM model (cf. Pinter 1999: 26). The EFQM model can thus also be understood as a continuation of the ISO model. The two models simply identify different focal points, yet *can be used in conjunction with one another* (cf. Raidl 2001: 81; Mayländer 2000: 34 ff.; Matul & Scharitzer 2002: 61 ff.).

If we compare the two approaches (cf. fig. 2.4), it is apparent that both represent relatively complete quality management systems, with the ISO concept focusing primarily on the fulfilment of standards and the EFQM concept, on the other hand, on the customer. Whilst EFQM is above all concerned with self-monitoring, ISO is a traditional, expert-oriented system that is to be viewed largely as externally controlled due to the existence of prescribed standards. It thus carries with it the danger that a fixation on directives may, whilst improving the quality management system, lead to processes of bureaucratisation that serve merely to stifle creativity and innovation (cf. Stahl & Severing 2002: 50). Another criticism is that the ISO 9000 standards series is too statically focused on the actual situation, with criteria for corporate success not included to a sufficient degree. It is also argued that the ISO model is too industrially-oriented, meaning its application in service firms or even non-profit organisations can be problematic (cf. chapter 2.2). This criticism applies to the revised ISO model as well.

---

31 RADAR comprises the following aspects: Results, Approach, Deployment, Assessment, and Review. According to EFQM, these aspects describe "the standard to be measured in the EFQM model, against which measurements are made... On the basis of these aspects, the effectiveness of an organisation can be assessed and enhanced with regard to all 32 sub-criteria". For detail on the procedure followed here, cf. Radtke & Wilmes 2002: 24.

Moreover, the specified corset of ISO standards has little motivational effect on employees, and can therefore lead to considerable acceptance problems. EFQM, on the other hand, is much more flexible, permitting multifaceted development processes with outcomes that are not always predictable. Even though the introduction of EFQM is usually controlled by management, employees are at least actively involved in the implementation process if not in decision-making. This represents an advantage of the EFQM approach, as standards such as those in the ISO model and criteria such as those in the EFQM model can only achieve their intended effects if all managers and employees are prepared to not only passively support them, but also to actively promote their implementation and observance. It can nevertheless be viewed positively that awareness of organisational processes is raised merely by working with ISO or EFQM and their standards/parameters, with resultant beneficial effects on quality improvement (cf. Radtke & Wilmes 2002: 28 f.).

Figure 2.4: Differences between the ISO and EFQM models

ISO	EFQM
✓ Fulfilment of standards	✓ Focuses on the customer
✓ Traditional, expert-oriented system	✓ Self-directed, also possible without external assessment
✓ Remote management via specified modules	✓ Flexible model that can be adapted to the relevant sector
✓ Focuses on process orientation; attributes high importance to technical, temporal and personal optimisation	✓ Continual improvement is of central importance
	✓ Results-oriented
✓ Frequent external assessment ensures objective results from experienced auditors, but is costly	✓ Cost-effective assessment, as no external auditors required
	✓ Bias possible if only self-assessment carried out
✓ International recognition	✓ European recognition, associated with quality awards

Source: based on Raidl 2001: 81.

Whilst the ISO model envisages the provision of objective results through regular external assessment by qualified auditors, the EFQM model is based first and foremost on the process of self-assessment. If, however, the responsibility for appraisal resides with a trained, internal EFQM assessor or criteria manager, then there is a danger of receiving one-sided (professionally blinkered) judgements. If external consultants are called upon, on the other hand, costs can rapidly spiral, which is not consistent with the fundamental principles of EFQM.

Another positive aspect of EFQM is that, through the possibility of participating in a European or national quality prize competition, the concept of benchmarking[32] is given attention. This enables an organisation to determine its position relative to that of others, and to initiate targeted measures for improvement.

ISO deals primarily with the internal structures and processes of an organisation, with the aim of optimising technical, temporal and personnel processes and procedural structures. EFQM, on the other hand, incorporates the economic and social environment of an organisation to a greater extent. By attaching high importance to customer satisfaction, EFQM also focuses on the 'target group' (customers) in endeavours to achieve quality. Whilst this criterion plays a central role within the framework of the EFQM model, the current ISO 9001: 2000 standard merely certifies the area "monitoring and measurement". This only assesses, however, whether or not an organisation "monitors" customer satisfaction, ignoring whether or not it is actually achieved (cf. Voss & Stoschek 2005: 2). Moreover, ISO-based audits are still seen as concentrating too strongly on processes and their optimisation. Employee opinions and feedback are seen to be largely disregarded. In addition, criteria deemed important under EFQM, such as employee satisfaction, social results, and key performance results, are given little attention even in the revised ISO standards series (cf. ibid.).

The EFQM model is credited with the fact that its diverse criteria penetrate – according to Heller (1993: 17) – every corner of the organisation, focusing on the dimensions of the value chain that an organisation can influence directly (cf. Wunderer 1998: 75 f.). However, the associated implementation processes of self-assessment are extremely time-consuming.

EFQM is further criticised for being an extremely complex model, with its nine components and 32 sub-criteria, placing high demands on those wishing to apply it. Moreover, because it deals with abstract principles, each organisation must complete the framework individually. There are no industry- or sector-specific criteria, yet this is seen by EFQM (2003a, b, c) as being an advantage, as it affords users a high degree of flexibility. This assessment applies equally to the ISO model.

---

32 Benchmarking is a method with which, through a direct comparison with other successful businesses, differences can be identified and internal improvement potential ascertained. For this purpose, products, services, processes and methods are compared with the best-performing company. The aim is to attain this 'best' standard. (Cf. Bayer 2004: 58 f.; Mertins 2004; Grieble 2004; Jahns 2003; Leidig & Sommerfeld 2003; Deutsche Gesellschaft für Qualität (German Society for Quality) 2002; Siebert 2002; Siebert & Kempf 2002; Elsweiler 2002; Bornemeier 2002; Fahrni et al. 2002; Puschmann 2000; Jackson 2000; Horváth 1996: 396 ff.; Camp 1994 & 1995; Mertins et al. 1994; Clutterbuck 1993; Weber 1991: 295 ff.).

It must be seen as particularly problematic that the parameters specified by EFQM and standards defined by ISO are by no means theoretically derived or even substantiated. They can thus not escape the accusation that they are, to some degree, arbitrary. This applies especially to the weighting factors (points) in EFQM, which appear to be random, a criticism which pertains to the equally-weighted division into 'enabler' criteria and results as well as to the nine sub-groups.[33]

Overall, it can be observed that *the application and diffusion of ISO and TQM models* has *increased* in private organisations in recent years. According to ISO figures, around 634,000 organisations in 152 countries have introduced ISO 9000 standards, concerned with quality management, and/or ISO 14000 standards, relating to environment management. Data relating solely to ISO 9000 and to Germany are not issued (cf. ISO 2005)[34]. The European Foundation for Quality Management (EFQM), which was founded in 1988 by 14 European businesses, had a global membership of around 2,500 in 2005, 500 of those in Germany.[35] In the light of about 40,000 organisations in the industrial sector and 638,300 organisations in the service sector in Germany alone (cf. Statistisches Bundesamt, Fachserie 9)[36], this figure appears very modest. It should be noted, however, that many organisations apply the EFQM model without becoming members. Figures on this are unavailable, however. What is more, it can be observed that more and more organisations in the *non-profit sector* are taking an interest in models of quality assurance, triggered by the heightened discussion about quality and customer orientation.

As mentioned already, interest has really taken off since the mid- to late-nineties, particularly in the fields of health and social services[37] - in which legislative controls have also demanded that heightened attention be paid to the issue – as well as in the education[38] and training[39] sector. Even in the field of development cooperation[40], and within

---

33   Further critique can be found in Wunderer et al. 1997. For information on experiences of implementing TQM, cf. Michels 2004; Nüllen 2004; Egger 2002; and the summary of Guhl 1998: 133 ff.

34   http://www.iso.org

35   http://www.deutsche-efqm.de

36   German Federal Statistical Office, subject-matter series 9.

37   Beckmann et al. 2004 (social work); Arnold 2003 (social economy); Boeßenecker et al. 2003 (social work); Hansen & Kamiske 2003 (service provision); Woehrle 2003 (social economy); Boysen & Strecker 2002 (social work); Gissel-Palkovich 2002 (youth welfare service); Igl et al. 2002 (care); Matul & Scharitzer 2002 (non-profit organisations); Schuhen 2002 (welfare work); Schwan, Kohlhass et al. 2002 (counselling); Gebert & Kneubühler 2001 (care); Schubert & Zink 2001 (health and social services); Garms 2000 (social projects); Hoeth & Schwarz 2002 (service provision); Mayländer 2000 (geriatric care); Müller-Kohlenberg 2000 (humanitarian services); Straumann 2000 (counselling); Weiß 2000 (hospitals); Peterander & Speck 1999 (social facilities); Oppen 1996 (health).

38   Heinrich & Meyer 2005 (essay for ZfEV); Kempfert & Rolff 2005 (schools); Stockmann 2005 (e-learning); HRK 2005, 2004a,b, 2002 (universities/colleges); Stockmann 2004b (universities/colleges); Meister et al. 2004 (e-learning); Ehlers & Schenkel 2004 (e-

cultural institutions[41], quality management has become a central theme, and it can thus be claimed that non-profit organisations in all branches in which they are to be found deal with the issues of quality, quality development, quality assurance, and quality management. Due to a lack of concepts of their own, they frequently try to transfer models developed for the profit-sector (such as ISO or EFQM). The Frey-Akademie[42] attempts, with considerable effort, to make this transfer easier by adapting the EFQM model to the specific contextual conditions of individual sectors and company sizes. This involves modifying the nine main and 32 sub-criteria of the EFQM model. According to their own figures, around 600 organisations in the German-speaking world use this 'custom version' of EFQM.

EFQM itself, however, does not offer any 'sector-specific versions', as it is based on the assumption that the model can be applied universally in all sectors, for organisations of all kinds and sizes (EFQM 2003a: 3 ff., 2003b: 10, 2003c: 7). The "public and voluntary sector" model (EFQM 2003c: 34 f.) thus also turns out to be largely a reproduction of the basic model with no core modifications[43]. Instead, it is once again repeated in routine fashion that the open basic structure of the model ensures such room for interpretation that the requirements of public service strategies can be met.

It is still largely unclear, however, to what extent these models can be applied to non-profit organisations (cf. e.g. Klausegger & Scharitzer 1998b: 371 & 387; Langnickel 2003: 45; Beckmann et al. 2004: 9 f.). The authors of a review of the situation in the social work field, who also carried out an international comparison, come to the following sobering conclusion:

> "The expectations and hopes associated with the discussion and implementation of quality concepts and procedures, relating to quality measures making social pedagogic services more transparent, effective, easily manageable, of higher professional value, more reliable, and more closely aligned with the wants, interests and needs of recipients, have scarcely been fulfilled" (Beckmann et al. 2004: 9).

---

learning); Holtappels 2003 (schools); Haindl 2003 (schools); Deutsche Gesellschaft für Qualität (German Society for Quality) 2001; Kückmann-Metschies 2001 (universities/colleges); Olbertz & Otto 2001 (education); Arnold 1997 (adult education); Feuchthofen & Severing 1995.

39   Heinrich & Meyer 2005; Bethke 2003; Liebald 2003; Holla 2002; Deutsche Gesellschaft for Qualität (German Society for Quality) 2001; Stark 2000; Arnold 1997 (adult education); Bardeleben 1995; Feuchthofen & Severing 1995.

40   Stockmann 2002; Arnold et al. 2002; GTZ 2004, GTZ 2002.

41   Ermert 2004.

42   http://www.freyakademie.de (German language website).

43   In the EFQM brochure, examples of performance indicators, the measurement of criteria etc. detailed under the 32 sub-criteria are merely in part related to the public sector. In addition to this, in chapter 7 there are two pages describing the general characteristics of public services and voluntary institutions (EFQM 2003c: 34-35).

41

In the following section, the question will therefore be explored of the extent to which the non-profit and profit-sectors differ structurally, as a result of prevailing underlying conditions, and what significance this has for the respective understanding of quality.

2.2 Quality in profit and non-profit organisations

2.2.1 Organisational and situational differences and their implications for the understanding of quality

Profit and *non-profit organisations* exhibit a range of common organisational features. They constitute economic entities, and can choose to take various legal forms[44]. They are regarded as spatial, technical and organisational units that have been created for the purpose of producing goods and/or services. In German official statistics, every spatially-distinct establishment – including so-called 'organisations without profit motive' – is registered as a place of work. From a sociological point of view, undertakings such as non-profit organisations tend to be long-term oriented social entities with institutional regulations governing the behaviour of those involved, and with specific goals and tasks that are to be realised by members (employees) (cf. Reinhold 1992: 429).

However, profit and non-profit organisations also display a series of crucial differences, which ultimately have an effect on their respective understanding of quality and on the quality development and management strategies employed. Most conspicuously, non-profit organisations are, by definition, not profit-oriented. If they generate surpluses, these are not allowed to be registered and distributed as profits, but must be reinvested in the organisation. Non-profit organisations are characterised by a strong solidarity and public utility ethic. In addition to full-time employees, many also have a (in some cases large) number of unsalaried volunteers. Accordingly, the management and decision-making structures in such organisations are usually more participative and directly democratic (with, for example, member/delegate meetings) than in private firms. A company, business, or enterprise, on the other hand, is understood as being a legal economic entity that strives for profit maximisation, i.e. for a return on the capital necessary for operation (cf. Gabler 1994).

Four central differences between profit and non-profit organisations, which are significant in the context of quality management, will form the primary focus of discussion here. These are: (1) the lack of *profit orientation* of non-profit organisations, (2) their lack of *competitive orientation*, (3) the fact that non-profit organisations primarily render *ser-*

---

44   In the case of non-profit organisations, this can range from registered society, to private foundation, to charitable limited company or non-profit making cooperative (cf. Zimmer & Priller 2004: 32).

vices, and (4) the special relationship with their *'customers'*, which makes the use of this term in the context of non-profit organisations appear problematic.

Before looking into these differences, the non-profit sector will firstly be characterised in more detail (cf. fig. 2.5). A fundamental distinction is made between *state non-profit organisations*, or those belonging to the *collective economy*, which perform public tasks for citizens (public administration bodies, public transport services, authorities, municipalities etc.), and *private non-profit organisations* (Anheier et al. 2002: 19). The latter are in turn divided up into (cf. Eversheim et al. 1997: 8 f.):

a) Economic non-profit organisations that represent and promote the economic interests of their members (chambers of commerce, trade associations)
b) Socio-cultural non-profit organisations that promote religious, cultural and social interests (churches, culture groups, sports clubs)
c) Political non-profit organisations that represent political and ideational interests (political parties)
d) Charitable non-profit organisations that perform support services for groups of persons in need (aid organisations, Third World organisations).

Figure 2.5: Classification of non-profit organisations (NPOs)

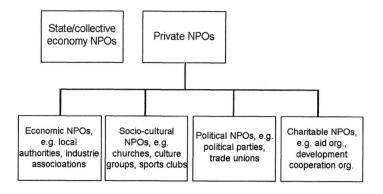

As already mentioned, by no means every author assigns all not-for-profit businesses to the non-profit sector. Rather, the non-profit sector – also referred to as the 'third sector' – is distinguished from state-run institutions. This distinction stems from Amitai Etzioni, who, at the start of the 1970s, drew attention to a "third alternative, indeed sector (…) between state and market" (Etzioni 1973: 314 ff.). In the USA, extensive *third sector* research became well established, especially in the field of business science. The emergence of a third sector was interpreted as a reaction to market and state failures (cf. Bauer 2001:

168). In Germany[45], in the course of neo-corporatist research commencing in the mid-eighties, questions of management theory accounted for most interest in the third sector. In the social sciences, the theory that non-governmental organisations are more efficient and effective than state-run organisations was given particular attention, and remains a popular idea in the field of development cooperation (cf. e.g. Glagow 1990). Today, these organisations are characterised more and more frequently as bearers of hope for effective problem-handling at all levels of politics (cf. Take 2002: 37). An international study, the Johns Hopkins Comparative Nonprofit Sector Project, in which 21 countries are participating (including Germany), is now attempting to conduct a comparative analysis of the history, structures, relationships and development processes of the third sector (cf. Zimmer & Priller 2004: 29 ff.). For this, the study employs a standard definition, according to which only those organisations that "are formally structured, organisationally independent of the state, non-profit-oriented, autonomously administered, and do not represent compulsory associations" are to be assigned to the non-profit sector (Zimmer & Priller 2004: 32).

According to this restrictive definition, non-profit organisations have autonomous administrative structures and management boards that are independent of the state. This means that so-called 'QUANGOS' (quasi non-governmental organisations), which are maintained by the state and whose business processes are not free from government influence, do not qualify as non-profit organisations. Chambers of commerce and guilds are also excluded from the categorisation, as they represent compulsory associations. Regional authorities, social insurance bodies, and state-sponsored cultural institutions are precluded as well, as they all represent public agencies.

A classification of this kind is appropriate when examining the role of the non-profit sector with regard to its socio-political significance (cf. Simsa 2002: 129 ff. & 2000; Anheier et al. 2000; Bauer 1997). Third sector organisations are understood, on the one hand, as a common feature and element of social integration and socialisation, and, on the other hand, as a mobilisable resource against state and politics, i.e. as a 'counterbalance' to state power (cf. Zimmer & Priller 2004: 21 f.). Non-profit organisations are multifunctional entities that, depending on their orientation, act as social integrators, interest representatives, and/or service providers. This multifunctionality is reflected in the large service alliances and diverse local society landscape, as well as in the array of charitable trusts.

A polymorphic symbiosis has thereby developed between state and non-profit sector. On the one hand, non-profit organisations relieve the burden on the state and on local authorities in numerous areas (e.g. in fields as diverse as social services, health, religion, international exchange and cooperation, the economy, environmental and nature protection, the representation of citizen and consumer interests, foundations and charities, as well as in the areas of culture, sport and leisure). Yet on the other hand, the state also supports non-profit organisations financially to a considerable degree. When compared inter-

---

45   For information on the historical roots and development of the German non-profit sector, cf. Anheier et al. 2002: 20 ff.

nationally, the German non-profit sector is, monetarily, "one of the most state-centred, state-dependent of its kind" (Anheiner et al. 2002: 26).

Whilst a distinction between state-run and private non-profit organisations may be appropriate from a democratic and socio-political point of view, it is not necessary to make one in the context of the success and efficiency measurement/performance assessment of non-profit organisations, as both groupings – as will be demonstrated – face very similar problems in this respect.

It can thus be stated that, with regard to quality development in organisations, the crucial difference between private enterprises and non-profit organisations lies in the presence or lack of profit orientation. *All organisations that do not exhibit profit orientation,* i.e. state-run, collective economy and private non-profit organisations, will therefore be referred to here as *non-profit organisations.*

The restricted notion of non-profit organisations employed by the Johns Hopkins Comparative Nonprofit Sector Project is equivalent to the concept of non-governmental organisations (NGOs), which Glagow (1992: 311) defines thus: "Non-governmental organisations are formalised entities separate from the market and the state that receive their resources from voluntary solidarity contributions made by society and convert them into collective goods for dealing with social problems". According to this, non-governmental organisations can here be understood as a subset of non-profit organisations.

(1) The *existence or lack of profit orientation* is not only the defining criterion for the categorisation of organisations; it is also an important influencing factor for the understanding of quality. As there is no standard criterion equivalent to profit goals for performance measurement or quality assessment in the state-run or non-governmental non-profit sectors, other dimensions must be applied (cf. Simsa 2002: 138). The success of organisations as diverse as crisis lines, sports clubs, museums, social security agencies, authorities, foundations for world peace, and development cooperation organisations cannot be ascertained on the basis of a single measure such as profit, turnover or efficiency. These examples make clear that the goals of non-profit organisations can span a multitude of issues and tasks, and that they can have manifold stakeholder groups that in turn employ mostly differing assessment criteria for judging the performance or service quality of non-profit organisations. Sponsors, donors, employees, service recipients, the media, politicians, and individual citizens, for example, will have sharply varying expectations of a service, and will accordingly judge the quality of services rendered in very different ways (cf. Simsa 2002: 138; Matul and Scharitzer 2002: 607).

It should thus be borne in mind that the organisational aims of state-run and non-governmental non-profit organisations cannot be reduced to one overarching goal, as they do not act to maximise profit. On the contrary, they are characterised by *complex goal systems*, which also serve to complicate the use of conventional management methods, most of which are oriented towards monetary aims. It is not only necessary to coordinate the various goals with each other; appropriate performance indicators also need to be defined. Monetary measures of goal attainment (profit, dividends, shareholder value), which are used as in profit-oriented businesses as gauges of success, are hardly suited to public institutions and other non-profit organisations (cf. Horak 1997: 124 f., Horak et al. 1997: 136 ff., Tweraser 1998: 437 ff.; Simsa 2002: 138; Eschenbach & Horak 2003).

(2) A further central distinction between profit and non-profit organisations is that the former operate in *markets open to competition*, and are in *rivalry* with each other, whilst a functioning market, providing the classic supply and demand framework and sanctioning any deterioration in quality, is seldom to be found for the services rendered by non-profit organisations (cf. Tweraser 1998: 438; Matul & Scharitzer 2002: 613). In the profit sector, companies whose products and services are not in demand cannot survive over the long term. For non-profit organisations, on the other hand, this consequence is not compelling due to their financing mechanisms. In contrast to profit-oriented organisations, which act for their own ends and are financed through the *payment of prices* for their products and services, which must first of all be accepted by the market if profits are to be possible at all, non-profit organisations are frequently financed by *collective fees* (taxes, contributions, donations). Many non-profit organisations thus have no compelling incentive to deploy resources efficiently, which can have a negative impact on the effectiveness and quality of service provision. The lack of a market price mechanism at the very least complicates the achievement of quantitatively and qualitatively optimal resource allocation (cf. Matul & Scharitzer 2002: 614).

Non-profit organisations are also characterised by special demand conditions known as 'asymmetric information'. Recipients of the services of non-profit organisations usually do not have the same level of information available to them as the service providers, and they frequently have no way of eliminating these information deficits. In such cases, it is often impossible for service recipients to react to deteriorations in quality (cf. Badelt 2002: 107 ff.).

In situations in which non-profit organisations occupy a monopolistic position[46], a further consideration is that they cannot (always) freely choose their service recipients, who by the same token cannot freely choose their service providers. In *free markets,* the customer makes the purchase/non-purchase decision. In doing so, he or she can examine the offers of various providers and decide upon the product that best meets his or her needs. In *non-free markets*, which are prevalent among state-run service providers and quasi-monopolists, the situation is very different. The service recipient cannot usually freely choose whether or not, or from whom, to purchase the product or service. He or she cannot change provider if dissatisfied with quality. A welfare recipient, for example, will continue to visit the local social welfare office even if he or she is treated poorly there. An unemployed person will carry on visiting a job centre support scheme even if convinced of its futility, as he or she may otherwise run the risk of losing an entitlement to assis-

---

46   E.g. the Kreditanstalt für Wiederaufbau (KfW banking group) in the allocation of credit finance for development cooperation; pensions insurance agencies; social welfare offices; the German Federal Employment Office etc.

tance. An employee cannot unsubscribe from social insurance, even if performance continually deteriorates. And a taxpayer can only escape his or her tax collector by changing his or her name or address.

For such service providers, who are not in competition with each other in free markets, who are not profit-oriented, and whose organisational existence is not in danger, a fundamental motive for ensuring quality improvement, for orienting products and services towards customer needs, and for generating as much customer satisfaction as possible is not present.

For this reason, the creation of *competition* in these sectors is being striven for more and more. German citizens, for example, are now able to change their health insurance company more easily. German students are no longer allocated to universities through the Central Office for the Allocation of Places in Higher Education[47], and public services provided by the state are also being supplemented by private contractors. Rivalry among public institutions remains very low, however, in situations where there is no free-market incentive leading to the creation of competition, which in turn allows customers to exercise choice and thereby select products and services that meet their needs and demands.

Many government departments, administrative bodies and authorities therefore employ quality management systems (if they have one at all) which deal only indirectly with the customer. They compare themselves with other public institutions (benchmarking)[48], set up quality circles[49], or give themselves citizen-friendly mission statements[50] etc. As stated earlier on, most non-governmental non-profit organisations do not have sophisticated quality management systems. Rather, it is frequently the case that individual elements or instruments from various concepts are erratically selected and employed.

(3) In contrast to profit organisations, non-profit organisations almost exclusively generate services. In the non-profit sector, no products are manufactured as a rule, and it is the non-material nature of services which dominates (cf. Matul & Scharitzer 2002: 614;

---

47   Zentrale Vergabestelle von Studienplätzen (ZVS).
48   See footnote 32, chapter 2.
49   Quality circles are workgroups that approach the process of work with an explicit reform task, and are not subject to any hierarchical classification or ties during this time. Tasks may include, for example, the improvement of workflows or communication structures, as well as, in a broad sense, the introduction of innovations (cf. Klausegger & Scharitzer 1998: 403, Bosetzky & Heinrich 1994: 170). For information on the goals of quality circles, cf. also Bungard 1991: 80. For a more general introduction to quality circles, cf. Bungard & Wiendieck 1986; Bungard 1992; Doppe 1992; Zink 1992: 219 ff.; Rischer & Titze 1998; Sommer 2001; Drescher 2003.
50   A strategic *mission statement* is a set of basic written assertions which forms the normative basis for all further strategic and operational management decisions of an organisation. In contrast to business enterprises, which often have a one-dimensional orientation towards profit maximisation, non-profit organisations pursue numerous goals, which necessitates formal prioritisation (cf. Eschenbach 1998: 15 & 437 and 2003).

Hoeth & Schwarz 2000: 12 f.). Services are not as concrete as products in their nature. A customer seeking, for example, a tax advisor, a hospital, or an employment agency, does not want to purchase a product, but rather expects an adequate solution to a problem from an expert dealing with his or her individual request. Often the customer has to participate in the rendering of the service. For example, the customer must provide the tax advisor with all relevant documents and information, the hospital patient must take the prescribed medication and attend therapy, while the unemployed person has to disclose his or her qualifications and be willing to work. Despite numerous attempts, it has not yet been possible to develop a generally accepted definition of the term *service* that also succeeds in ensuring sufficient delimitation from material products or goods (cf. Meffert & Bruhn 1995: 25, 2003: 27). If the differences listed in the literature between a service and a material product are systematised, four points of note can be identified (cf. Eversheim et al. 1997: 27 f., 2000: 6; Hoeth & Schwarz 2000: 12 f.):

The outcome of a service is intangible.

a) Persons external to the organisation providing the service are involved in service provision. A service is thus always generated through a process of interaction. As the external persons do not belong to the domain of the organisation providing the service, problems can arise in service planning and performance.

b) As the external customer participates in the rendering of services as a 'co-producer', it is difficult to standardise the production process.

c) Services are process-oriented, and therefore cannot be produced in advance and stored.

d) A number of problems as regards the determination of quality arise from these distinctive features of services relative to material products, as from a customer point of view quality assessment cannot be focused exclusively on service provision (cf. Eversheim et al. 1997: 36), an issue which will be explored in more detail later on.

In general, a *service* can be classified according to *type,* based on whether it is performed by state-run or private non-profit organisations. Public administration, the largest branch of the non-profit sector, is primarily concerned with implementing political decisions. Its precise administrative tasks stem from laws, which allow it various degrees of scope for manoeuvre in terms of its activities and formative actions. On top of protection and sovereign functions (e.g. internal and external security, law and order, environmental protection), due to the expansion of the welfare state central and local administrative bodies have taken on more and more welfare functions (social insurance, social welfare, kindergartens etc.). In addition to implementation, public administration also has an important role to play within the scope of policy preparation: political actors depend increasingly on administrative bodies for professional support in formulating decision-making bases (e.g. for the drafting of bills) (cf. e.g. Sebaldt & Straßner 2004; Sontheimer & Bleek 2000; Schmid 1998; von Beyme 1996; Ellwein 1987; Sontheimer 1977; Eschenburg 1963).

The *array of functions* of non-profit organisations ranges – as the above classification demonstrates – from parastatal tasks to the representation of the very specific interests of societies or associations. Their catalogue of services also varies greatly depending on the type of organisation in question. It may be that a non-profit organisation provides information and consultation, offers courses and proposals of various kinds, and organises and conducts programmes, events, conferences and meetings etc. Sometimes services will be provided only for members, and in other cases for a specialised, wide, or sometimes even international, public. Many of these services are akin to programmes and schemes in their nature. For example, the German Federal Employment Office carries out a programme aimed at reintegrating the long-term unemployed, the environment ministry is launching an educational campaign on climate protection, health insurance funds conduct an informational AIDS education programme, and the German Society for Technical Cooperation[51] provides advice and support for development cooperation projects.

(4) In the private sector of the economy, the customer is, alongside the company (as manufacturer or service provider), the central actor, as he or she decides on the purchase or non-purchase of products and services, therefore determining the company's development. Whilst customers participate in the market by means of payments, and have, in principle[52], full autonomy over their purchase decisions, being able to choose between alternatives, this is not always the case in the non-profit sector (cf. Boeßenecker et al. 2003: 11). Frequently in this sector, service recipients or users cannot really choose between alternative provision, and their decision-making authority is thus limited. Moreover, in many cases services are not given to those who 'pay' for them, but rather to 'eligible recipients', e.g. in the case of foundations, organisations financed through donations, social welfare offices, social insurance funds etc. It is thus questionable whether the *customer concept* can be transferred to the non-profit sector at all. The differences between the profit and non-profit sectors with regard to the *'customer relationship'* will therefore now be explored in more detail.

In the private sector, a *one-dimensional producer-customer relationship* is prevalent (cf. fig. 2.6a). Companies offer products and services on markets, and customers choose between the offers, make purchase decisions, and pay prices. In the case of non-profit or-

---

51 The German Agency for Technical Cooperation (Deutsche Gesellschaft für Technische Zusammenarbeit) is "one of the world's largest service organisations in the development cooperation field" (GTZ: 'Die GTZ stellt sich vor', n.d.). The GTZ is contracted by the German federal government, carrying out technical cooperation tasks on a non-profit-making basis. This serves to "increase the competence of people and organisations, by imparting, mobilising, or improving conditions for the application of, knowledge and skills" (ibid.). In 2004, the GTZ carried out 2,628 projects together with its partners in 131 countries. 1,030 employees who had been dispatched abroad were active, working together with just under 7,000 'national employees' from partner countries. Almost 1,000 people were employed in GTZ's head office in Eschborn. Transaction volume in the non-profit area and the "International Services" business unit amounted to 879 million euros.

52 If we disregard, for a moment, advertising, manipulative attempts at exerting influence, and limited market competition.

ganisations, however, 'customers' do not always represent a single, clearly-defined target group (cf. Daumenlang & Palm 1997: 9); the *customer concept* is much more *complex* (cf. Bumbacher 2000: 109). Martin (1993) distinguishes between "client customers"[53] and "funding source customers". In some cases, a distinction can even be drawn between the 'immediate customer', the 'client' (e.g. legislator), and the 'sponsor' (e.g. public administration). For public services in Germany (e.g. social welfare, unemployment benefits, development aid), the legislator defines the requirements, whilst the social welfare and employment agencies and the Federal Ministry for Economic Cooperation and Development[54] allocate the financial resources. The person in need - the service recipient - is the immediate user. In the case of private non-profit organisations, the donor (sponsor), the organisation that collects donations (which may also render the services), and the recipient can all be identified as 'customers' (cf. fig. 2.6b).

This example serves to illustrate that the customer concept reaches its limits at this juncture. The service recipient neither has the same options as a customer acting in open markets (freedom of choice), nor does he or she pay (at least not directly) for the acquired service. Even labelling clients or sponsors (e.g. foundations, societies, social insurance funds, authorities) as (funding source) 'customers' is problematic, as although they do indeed finance the services to be rendered, they are not service recipients. In the non-profit sector, therefore, instead of talking about 'customers', it appears more appropriate to refer, on the one hand, to *users, service recipients or, more generally, audiences or target groups,* and, on the other hand, to the client or sponsor that funds the services.

These various groups can have extremely *diverse requirements and interests,* and may therefore also judge service quality very differently. A legislator and an entity carrying out a service may primarily be interested in the range of services scheduled by the legislation being designed especially compactly, in order to save as much money as possible. The user, in contrast, is likely to be interested in an extensive design, so that he or she is able to enjoy as many benefits as possible. The person responsible for quality assurance must then decide whose interests and requirements should, within the scope for manoeuvre granted by the legislation, have priority. Whilst the customer is critical for quality assessment in the case of services rendered under market conditions, this idea cannot be applied so unequivocally for non-profit organisations. Should the legislator's demands, those of the city council, or the needs of the user be decisive for quality assessment? This conflict also arises in other cases: should donated funds, for example, be spent in accordance with the interests of donors or those of the groups in need? Should the aims of a programme's client or the requirements of its users be given stronger consideration?

---

53   The term 'client' refers here to service recipients/users, and *not,* as elsewhere in this book, to entities that commission a service.

54   Bundesministerium für wirtschaftliche Zusammenarbeit und Entwicklung (BMZ).

Figure 2.6: Producer-customer/user relationship

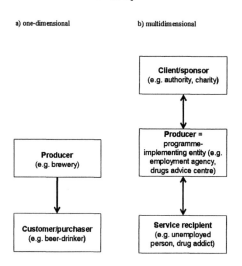

a) one-dimensional   b) multidimensional

In the field of *development cooperation*, this conflict becomes yet more complex. Thus a German implementing organisation, whether state- or non-state-run, is confronted with the problem of having to deal with at least four 'customers' (cf. fig. 2.7). These are (1) the client, e.g. the BMZ[55] or a non-governmental organisation that collects donations, (2) the government of the partner country (e.g. the health or education ministry) with which the German organisation implementing the programme collaborates, and (3) the local on-site implementing organisation that is provided with advice and support. On top of these are (4) the actual target groups (e.g. the unemployed, children, women, poor sections of the population) – the people in need whom the development programme should ultimately serve.

Which group is decisive, then, in terms of the central factor of 'customer satisfaction'? Who is crucial with regard to quality assessment? Whose needs should be satisfied primarily? Even a multifunctional customer concept – all the named actors are simultaneously 'customers' – is of no help if these 'customers' have, as is to be expected, very different ideas, demands and appraisal criteria where service quality is concerned.

These deliberations make it clear that, unlike in the private business sector, where a one-dimensional producer-customer relationship exists, in the case of many public institu-

---

55   See footnote 54.

tions and private non-profit organisations, the customer concept can only be applied to a limited extent.[56]

Figure 2.7: Multi-level relationship in development cooperation

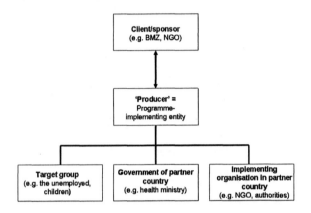

The question also arises then of whether 'customer' judgement on products and services of non-profit organisations can be applied at all as a central quality measure as in the case of profit-oriented companies. In areas where the service/product recipient does not pay directly for the service performed or product acquired, there is a danger that his or her requirements exceed the performance potential of the provider, and that quality is only assessed negatively for this reason. Whilst supply and demand regulate the price in free markets, with customers able to understand empirically what price they have to pay for what service within what scope, this regulatory mechanism is lacking outside of the private business sector. Thus welfare recipients, for example, may be tempted to continually place unaffordable financial demands on the social welfare office, in accordance with their requirements. As they do not receive the services which they desire and which might indeed be in accordance with their needs, they may be very dissatisfied with the quality of the social welfare office's service. Can, then, user assessment represent the decisive measure for the judgement of social welfare office service quality? The answer is 'hardly'.

---

56   The customer concept can not only be applied in an external sense, but also in an internal one. According to this perspective, recipients of sub-outputs within an organisation may also be classed as (internal) customers, e.g. employees of different departments (cf. Eversheim 1997: 9; 2000: 9; Daumenlang & Palm 1997: 11 f.; Juran 1988, 1999).

The situation is the same in the case of, for example, a programme aimed at the reintegration of unemployed workers. This may possibly involve severe conditions for the unemployed person, with the primary objective of relieving the burden on public finances rather than meeting his or her needs and demands. The quality assessment of the service recipient, the unemployed person, represents at best just one perspective. From the point of view of society, the programme could be very successful (with all unemployed workers placed in jobs, and public finances relieved), meaning that non-users may credit the programme with a high degree of quality, as it meets their needs and demands (the unemployment contribution falls).

Things become even more critical when considering the field of development cooperation. Here, 'customer requirements' are not only being put at the centre of political development action of late, but are also set to become the benchmark for the assessment of co-operation quality. But what would happen, to take an admittedly extreme example, if the needy target groups demanded, in accordance with their perceived requirements, weapons instead of advice, convinced that the unjust power structures can only be eradicated through force? As they would of course not receive these within the development cooperation framework, the target group would hardly be satisfied with the quality of the development service, believing that it fails to meet their requirements.

These examples highlight the fact that, where public money[57] is being used, other quality criteria must be applied on top of the satisfaction of direct 'customers'. Their satisfaction with the services offered cannot be the most important measure, simply because this *excludes all non-customers*. If university funding were to be raised massively, leading to significantly improved teaching and research conditions, this would produce extremely satisfied university 'customers' who appraise the quality of the new support programme positively as it fulfils their demands. However, the simultaneous budget cutbacks for employment creation programmes, for instance, would cause dissatisfaction among the unemployed, leading this 'customer segment' of state services to complain of deteriorating quality, i.e. weaker orientation towards their needs and demands.

It is also doubtful whether service recipients are always in a position to adequately appraise their (long-term) requirements and thus service quality. The following example from the university sector illustrates this more clearly. Nowadays, teaching appraisal is an important quality criterion at all universities. In the course of such appraisals, it can be observed that courses in which the teacher succeeds in being witty and entertaining receive particularly good marks from students. Dry, dull courses receive poor assessments. And who could blame the students? But potentially it may be the boring courses (although this needn't necessarily be the case), perhaps with high, and therefore unpopular, performance requirements, that provide the best preparation for future careers. This will only become apparent later on, though. It thus makes sense to not only have course quality appraised by students, but also by graduates who have already started their career, or by companies (which also represent stakeholders of universities).

---

57   Including donations to non-profit organisations such as churches, societies and foundations.

Accordingly it should be noted that *the customer concept appropriate in the context of competition- and profit-oriented companies cannot simply be transferred to the 'customers' of non-profit organisations.* The non-profit sector 'customer' is lacking that which characterises him or her in the profit sector: the autonomy to choose between alternative products and services, and to pay for them a price established through competition. Moreover, the one-dimensional producer-customer relationship in the private business sector does not do justice to the multidimensional network prevalent in the non-profit sector, which consists of numerous recipients on the one hand, and producers, clients and, in some cases, sponsors (donors) on the other. This has consequences for the development and safeguarding of quality. For, in contrast to profit-oriented organisations, it must first be decided whose viewpoints should be called upon for assessing the quality of the services of non-profit organisations, in order to provide a starting point for quality management.

Against the backdrop of the *differences* outlined here, it is questionable whether the application of a complex Total Quality Management concept such as EFQM, or indeed ISO-based standardisation, can satisfy the quality requirements of non-profit organisations. To conclude, a number of *fundamental discrepancies* will now be explored. In the ISO and EFQM model, the particular role of management is highlighted, which develops the mission, the vision and the values of an organisation (cf. chapter 2.1.2). This may well present problems for non-governmental non-profit organisations that have more participatory, more democratically-oriented organisational cultures. This also applies to the determination of policy and strategy, which in non-profit organisations is, by definition, not oriented towards making profits. Another fact that is disregarded is that, in a lot of non-governmental non-profit organisations at least, not only are employees active, but numerous volunteers need to be integrated into the organisation too.

With regard to the resource criterion, it can be observed that, in the case of non-profit organisations, finance provision usually occurs in a completely different way to that in business enterprises. Financing takes the form of either a state allocation or a compulsory levy, or is based on voluntary contributions, donations or allowances.

The biggest discrepancies can be identified on the results side under customer satisfaction and business results, which together make up over a third of all available EFQM appraisal points.

As has already been illustrated in detail, the customer concept has, if any, only limited applicability to non-profit organisations. This is not only due to the lack of decision-making autonomy and competition, but also to the fact that the classic market transaction of goods/services in exchange for money often does not exist, as those who finance services are not (always) the recipients thereof. Whilst profit and return on equity are defined by EFQM as central success criteria (key performance results) for companies, these cease to apply in the case of non-profit organisations.

Of course it may at this point be argued that these shortcomings could be corrected within a modified ISO or EFQM service model. However, in the "public and voluntary sector" EFQM model, which, as stated already, has only been marginally adjusted from the standard version, this claim is not supported. This also applies to the ISO 9000 model, modified in the year 2000. Within the framework of the ISO/EFQM philosophy, this is also consistent, as it is argued that ISO and EFQM can be applied to all organisations, regardless of sector, type and size (cf. ISO 2005; EFQM 2003c: 7). Adaptations would ultimately only represent cosmetic tinkering, and would not do justice to the particular organisational and situational conditions of non-profit organisations portrayed in detail here.

In summary, it can be stated that *profit and non-profit organisations differ* in respect of a range of characteristics (cf. fig. 2.8) relevant for the understanding of quality and the quality development and assurance strategies based upon it. The organisational goals of non-profit organisations are not aligned with making profits, and goal attainment can often not be ascertained using monetary measures. Frequently there is just slight competition between non-profit organisations. At most there is competition for donations, particularly in the case of charitable non-profit organisations (such as aid and Third World organisations in the fields of health care, welfare and development cooperation etc.). What would be a significant motive for quality improvement thus does not apply. People will usually not leave a culture group, sports club, political party, or religious organisation because it is badly managed. In the case of many non-profit organisations there is absolutely no, or only a very limited, possibility of exercising choice (e.g. authorities, social insurance institutions etc.). Furthermore, the customer concept does not do justice to the client-producer-recipient network: 'customers' (service recipients) alone cannot carry out the assessment of the quality of services rendered by non-profit organisations. For many non-profit organisations, the judgement of non-'customers' of the quality of their services is at least as important as that of their users.

Against this background it appears distinctly *problematic* to simply *transfer management techniques, organisational principles, organisational cultures and quality concepts* that have been developed in, and for, profit organisations to the non-profit sector. The largely "unquestioning adaptation of business management terminologies and policies" has thus come in for increasing criticism (Beckmann et al. 2004: 9 f.). Simply adopting the terminology of the profit sector does not create equivalent situational conditions for non-profit organisations. Frequently the non-profit sector is dealt with as if there were competition – even though the choice alternatives are only very limited, and principles of competition therefore do not take hold. It is often overlooked that social norms and values, as well as political convictions - and not markets - are decisive in determining the price of a service.

Additionally, corporate-style behaviour is often called for in non-profit organisations, without allowing them the kind of scope, e.g. in personnel policy or strategic decision-making, that is present in the private sector, with which they are to align themselves. But even if an attempt to create in the non-profit sector all situational conditions that exist in the profit sector were to be successful (primarily competition; customer decision-making autonomy; exchange relationships characterised by the classic market transaction of goods/services against payment), one *crucial differentiating criterion* would still remain:

profit orientation. If they were endowed with this feature as well – which would, after all, be logical and consistent – then there would no longer be a non-profit sector. Assuming this is undesirable, or even impossible, due to a range of socio-political reasons as well as market failures in certain social fields, then the organisational and situational diversity between the two sectors should also be realised.

Figure 2.8: Differences between profit- and non-profit-oriented organisations

Profit organisations (companies)	Non-profit organisations
✓ Profit motive, act for their own ends	✓ No profit motive, act for benefit of others
✓ Financing through prices attained for products and/or services	✓ Financing through collective fees (e.g. taxes, contributions, donations)
✓ Clear main objective (e.g. profit maximisation)	✓ Complex goal systems
✓ Clear measures (e.g. profit, dividends, shareholder value)	✓ Measures have to be defined (variable, multidimensional)
✓ Open competition	✓ Partly no competition at all, partly limited competition
✓ Free choice of provider	✓ Partly no choice, partly limited choice of provider
✓ Products and services	✓ Services
✓ One-dimensional producer-customer relationship	✓ Multidimensional, multi-level relationships (e.g. sponsors, clients, producers, service recipients)

Attempts to alter the situational conditions of non-profit organisations towards those in the profit sector, and to redesign organisations accordingly, have at times produced downright compulsive pressures, and sometimes even give the awkward impression of things being done merely for their own sake. A lack of free-market regulation does not automatically constitute a deficiency to be removed with all available resources. As shown by numerous examples, even markets do not represent perfect regulatory mechanisms. Moreover, there are a range of socio-political objectives that cannot be achieved by markets. State-run and non-governmental non-profit organisations are therefore necessary. They exhibit, however, different organisational structures and situational conditions to profit organisations. It is imperative that these *differences* are given *consideration* in the development of quality management concepts and quality development tools.

2.2.2 Quality development through New Public Management

As explained already, due to differing organisational and situational conditions, there is growing doubt over whether quality development and management concepts devised for private enterprises can be applied in non-profit organisations. A further management approach is thus presented here, one that is enjoying increasing popularity, primarily in the fields of state and local administration: the *New Public Management (NPM)*[58] *model*. Its aim is to improve performance and the process of service provision in public administration. In going about this, it employs various strategic principles that are intended to produce enhanced customer and competitive orientation. In addition, the concepts of New Public Management present a new element – output and outcome orientation – which goes beyond the scope of private-sector TQM and certification models.

NPM pursues the following *strategic goals*:

1. Customer orientation
As already illustrated, the customer concept common in private industry, which is central to quality assessment, cannot simply be transferred to public administration. However, customer orientation nevertheless represents a meaningful goal. According to NPM, a customer is classed as anyone who receives individual services from an administrative unit (cf. Schedler & Proeller 2000: 58, 2003: 59). Klages (1998: 125 f.) draws a distinction between customers internal and those external to the administration. He also distinguishes "citizens" in general from particular "target groups" of the administrative activity. Thirdly, Klages differentiates customers based on their relations with the administration, in order to identify spheres and possibilities of influence of various customer groups. The OECD (Shand & Arnberg 1996) divides customers up into seven different types, based on service entitlement. However the customer concept is defined for non-profit organisations, it is clear that it must have a multidimensional nature.

2. Competitive orientation
A further principle of NPM is the systematic inclusion of the notion of competition in all areas of state activity. This is based on the basic idea that the market is better placed than regulations to bring about efficient, effective service provision. As detailed earlier on, this is achieved by the creation of either market conditions (through opening up markets to other providers) or quasi-market competition (through performance agreements or competition within the public administration), or through the application of market instruments

---

58 For more detail on this topic, cf.: Pede 2000; Naschold & Bogumil 2000; Buschor 2002; Saner 2002; Reichard 2002; Mülbert 2002; Rehbinder 2002; Christensen 2002; McLaughlin 2002; Wollmann 2002 & 2003; Ritz 2003; Schedler & Proeller 2000 (2003); Nöthen 2004; Dent 2004; Koch 2004a & b; Pitschas 2004; Reichard 2004; Mastronardi 2004; Lienhard 2005; Nolte 2005.

(e.g. cost-performance analysis, performance comparisons, price competition, benchmarking) (for more detail, cf. Schedler & Proeller 2000: 158 ff., 2003: 166 ff.).

3. Output and outcome orientation
Traditionally, as is well-known, public administration is controlled via input factors. Through the allocation of various inputs (e.g. financial resources, personnel, equipment), the administration can be made active in specific, assigned areas of activity. As the usefulness of resource allocation is not necessarily examined on the basis of services rendered, results achieved, or even outcomes produced, efficient, goal- or even sustainability-oriented actions are hardly encouraged. On the contrary: traditionally in public finances, especially economical operation can even lead to resource cutbacks in the budget for the next financial year.
Another central element of NPM is therefore an orientation towards output and outcome:

> "Available resources should no longer form the topic of discussion and orientation of administrative activity, but rather the outputs (products) generated or the outcomes produced through these outputs."
> (Schedler & Proeller 2000: 60, 2003: 62 f.).

This means that political management should align itself with output and outcome requirements. The underlying logic here assumes that the objective the state wishes to achieve is the outcome, rather than merely the operation of the administration.

4. Quality orientation
The creation of extensive quality consciousness and management is considered a further aim of NPM. In conjunction with customer orientation, this means that it is not only important how a service is performed within the administration, but also what benefit customers derive from it. Building on Garvin (1984: 25 ff.), the following quality dimensions can be identified for public institutions. These will be explored further later on (cf. chapter 3.7.3):
- Product-related
- Customer-related
- Process-related
- Value-related and
- Political quality.

While private non-profit organisations are yet to employ quality improvement and assurance concepts extensively, but rather use individual tools at best, state-run non-profit organisations (public administration) are increasingly resorting to the *concepts of NPM*. The policy is aimed, on the one hand, at creating market-like conditions (competition), and, on the other hand, at adopting elements of quality management (customer orientation, quality dimensions). However, the difficulties already outlined, stemming from the particular organisational and situational conditions of non-profit organisations, can ultimately not even be overcome with the concepts of NPM. As supply and demand can usually not be regulated by markets (prices) in the case of non-profit organisations, and as the customers of these organisations constitute a complex, multidimensional network with various interests and assessment criteria, another important supplementary mechanism is necessary for quality control – *output and outcome orientation*. If NPM concepts put this aspect at the centre of their quality strategies, new possibilities for action emerge in comparison with the TQM and certification models previously presented.

While output orientation – the ascertainment of the results (products) of administrative activity – was for a long time at the forefront of the German reform discussion, more recent discussion focuses on the actual effects of administrative activity. Thus the talk is of *"outcome-oriented administrative management"* (Buschor 1993). The view that the quality of administrative activity must be measured based on outcomes caused has now become prevalent, "as the task of the state is only accomplished when the desired effect has been produced" (Brinckmann 1994: 173; Ösze 2000: 54 ff.).

A groundbreaking solution for non-profit organisations thus presents itself. The production of competition-like structures, orientation towards the needs and demands of target groups (users, target audiences) for which certain services are to be rendered, and the creation of quality consciousness all serve the *aim of getting services rendered to trigger planned impacts. Quality development* in non-profit organisations should therefore be oriented towards *increasing outcome optimisation. The more thoroughly the intended outcomes are achieved among target groups and in the policy fields where the interventions take place, and the less these outcomes are counteracted by unintended negative effects, the higher the quality of a non-profit organisation's services can be rated.*

However, the orientation of the activities of non-profit organisations towards outcomes achieved involves a range of *methodological difficulties*. The detection and measurement of outcomes, as well as the identification of their causes, can present empirical social research with major problems. What is more, immediate and long-term, intended and unintended effects must be differentiated from one another, identified, and examined for interrelationships and cause factors within complex cause-effect structures.

Yet control of public administration, or of non-profit organisations in general, based on outputs and outcomes only becomes possible if this problem can be overcome. The unanimous opinion is that this cannot be achieved with traditional controlling and finance instruments. New appraisal concepts and analytical instruments are thus required for outcome-based governance.

The concepts and instruments of *evaluation research* are suitable for this purpose, enabling not only the processes of planning and service rendering to be analysed, but also the services performed, goals attained, and impacts produced to be empirically examined and appraised. Regardless of whether TQM, ISO certification, NPM, or other management concepts are applied for governing non-profit organisations, data are in any case necessary to provide a rational decision-making basis. With the help of the theoretical and methodological concepts and tools of evaluation research, this task can be accomplished.

Evaluation lends itself particularly to use in conjunction with management concepts that are based on output- and outcome-oriented governance (e.g. NPM).

2.3 Evaluation[59]

2.3.1 Definition, aims and functions

In a similar way to the notion of 'quality', the concept of *'evaluation'* is also enjoying a surge in popularity, and is used to describe a diverse range of practices. Carol Weiss (1974: 19), in her seminal work on the topic, pointed out then that evaluation is an "ambiguous word which can refer to the most varied forms of assessment". Thirty years on, this has hardly changed. Evaluation not only describes a specific activity whose objective is to obtain and assess information; it also refers to the result of this process. *In a scientific context* – as opposed to in everyday evaluation activities – empirical information retrieval methods and systematic information assessment procedures are applied on the basis of certain criteria, which are disclosed in order to facilitate intersubjective verifiability. In contrast to subject-specific scientific research, evaluations do not represent an end in themselves. They do not serve pure cognitive interest, but should create value and contribute towards making processes more transparent, documenting impacts, and revealing relationships – ultimately in order to facilitate decision-making. Among their objectives are to configure processes more effectively, to deploy inputs more efficiently, to increase output, to enhance effectiveness, to ensure sustainability etc. Evaluations can – like quality management systems – help to enhance the quality of a measure, programme or service.

The appraisal of issues and circumstances, however, is not based on prescribed standards (as in the case of ISO) or parameters (as in the case of EFQM), but on criteria, which can be extremely diverse. These are very often oriented towards the utility of an object, situation or development process for certain people or groups. The *assessment criteria* can be defined by the client of an evaluation, by the target group, by affected interest groups ('stakeholders')[60], by evaluators themselves, or by a combination of all of these.

---

59 The following are examples of suitable introductory texts: Weiss 1974; Wittmann 1985; Scriven 1991; Chelimsky & Shadish 1997; Patton 1997; Wottawa & Thierau 1998; Owen & Rogers 1999; Vedung 1999; Rossi, Freeman & Lipsey 2004; Stockmann 2004a; Fitzpatrick, Sanders & Worthen 2004; Stockmann 2007.

60 Weiss (1998: 337) defines 'stakeholders' as: "Those people with a direct or indirect interest (stake) in a program or its evaluation." On top of sponsors and clients, the following are also stakeholders: programme managers and employees, recipients of the programme's services and their families, other organisations associated with the programme, interest groups, and the public in general, i.e. all those "who may otherwise affect or be affected by

Clearly the assessment of utility within an evaluation can turn out very differently depending on the criteria selected.

This not only depends on who generates the assessment criteria, but also on:

- For what purpose the evaluation is to be used (what function it is supposed to have)
- What tasks the evaluation is intended to fulfil (on which programme phase it concentrates, what analytical perspective it employs, what kind of cognitive interest it pursues)
- How the evaluation is carried out (what test paradigm it is based on and what methods are used)
- Who performs the evaluation (the programme-implementing organisation itself or an external entity).

This represents an outline of some central questions that every evaluation has to deal with.

General functions of evaluations

Evaluations are first and foremost conducted with the aim of acquiring information for decisions within the scope of management and control processes. Mertens (1998: 219) provides a generally accepted definition: "Evaluation is the systematic investigation of the merit or worth of an object (program) for the purpose of reducing uncertainty in decision making". Decisions based on evaluations can contribute to, among other things, the detection of implementational problems, the increasing of a programme's effectiveness, the reduction of costs, the raising of efficiency, efficacy etc. Evaluations thus support management in securing or developing the quality of programmes or measures, or, generally speaking, of services. *Evaluations* therefore represent a *constituent of quality management*. For this purpose, they can fulfil four interrelated *general functions* (cf. fig. 2.9):[61]

(a) The gaining of knowledge
(b) Exertion of control
(c) Creation of transparency and possibilities for dialogue in order to drive developments
(d) Legitimation of measures implemented

---

decisions about the program or the evaluation" (ibid.). Cf. also Fitzpatrick et al. 2004: 174 f.; Scriven 2002.

61   There have been numerous attempts to provide a typology of evaluations. Cf. e.g. Alkin 2004; Fitzpatrick et al. 2004; Rossi, Lipsey & Freeman 2004; Stufflebeam 2001; Stufflebeam et al. 2000. One proposal that has received much attention is that of Eleanor Chelimsky (1997: 100 ff.), which differentiates between three "conceptual frameworks": evaluation (1) for widening the knowledge base, (2) for purposes of control, and (3) for purposes of development. The advantage of this classification is that each concept has a specific affinity for certain approaches and design types. In this book, this classification is followed only to a limited extent.

Figure 2.9: General functions of evaluation

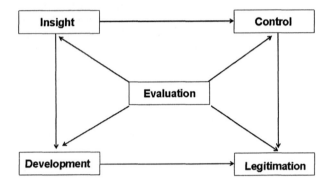

More specifically:

(a) Evaluations should provide *knowledge*, in order to give management decisions a rational basis. There may be an interest, for example, in knowing whether the implementation of a programme functions smoothly; what needs the target group has; whether measures reach the target group; what kind of acceptance the programme enjoys; whether implementing organisations are in a position to realise the programme effectively and efficiently; how the underlying conditions have changed; what effect this has had on programme implementation, goal attainment and the programme's impacts; what contributions the programme has made to solving the problem identified; or whether the changes observed can indeed be attributed to the programme or to other factors, etc. The goal of information collection is to gain insights, in order to then analyse these using the assessment criteria agreed upon, or specified within the programme, and to derive management decisions from this. The insights, and assessments thereof, presented by the evaluators need not necessarily be consistent with the assessments of the entities carrying out the programme or those of the target groups, which may also differ from each other.

Evaluations are not always commissioned by finance providers (sponsors) or implementing agencies, although this is frequently the case. Scientific evaluations are characterised primarily by cognitive interest. In such cases, the focus is not on the acquisition of information for the rationalisation of decisions, but rather on the analysis of the internal structures and processes of the political-administrative system. Such insights, gained directly in the social field under examination, have an otherwise almost unattainable degree of external validity (cf. Kromrey 2001: 114), and can of course, in the long-term, also contribute to the improvement of programme, measure and service quality.

(b) Without gaining any insights, i.e. knowledge of the evolution of structures and processes, no evaluation would be able to create benefit. However, decision-making is not always at the forefront of the application of insights, but rather *control*. Here the primary objective is to determine whether the goals specified in the planning phase have been achieved. 'Success' criteria such as effectiveness, efficiency, acceptance and sustainability can be used for this purpose. On top of legal controls (courts of law), political controls (politics), and economic controls (auditing), 'control' evaluations represent a further form of control of administrative activity (cf. Kromrey 2001: 115). Even in cases where evaluations are not primarily intended as controls, they usually reveal whether all those involved in a programme are performing their tasks, complying with duties assumed, and whether their skills and competencies suffice etc. That is to say, some form of control, direct or indirect, is associated with every evaluation.

(c) Insight – as well as control-oriented evaluations – provide findings that can be used for the *development* of a programme. The disclosure of insights facilitates a *dialogue* between various stakeholders (sponsors, implementing organisations, target groups, and other involved or affected parties). The results obtained permit the assessment, for example, collectively and transparently for all parties, of how successfully cooperation is proceeding, where the greatest successes are to be found, and where shortcomings have arisen, in order to then draw conclusions for future procedures. *Learning processes*, which should be used to further develop programmes, are at the centre of this evaluation function. As will be shown, this function plays a central role in formative (programme-shaping) evaluations.

(d) A further function of evaluation is to *legitimise* programmes or measures that have been implemented. The data set obtained through an evaluation provides the possibility of verifiably proving what output and outcomes have been achieved over time with what input. Sponsors and implementing organisations can thereby demonstrate how efficiently they have managed financial resources and what degree of impact their projects and programmes have caused. Through ex-post evaluations, the sustainability of programme outcomes can also be specified. Particularly in times of scarce financial resources, this evaluation function gains increased significance, with programmes often in competition with each other and political actors having to set priorities and make choices. Using evaluation criteria (e.g. effectiveness, efficiency, relevance, sustainability etc.), the legitimation of programmes or measures can be demonstrated and communicated. However, it is frequently the case that evaluation results are only used internally, i.e. that they are not made transparent to the public, and are not used to legitimise work performed.

Evaluations also very often have *"tactical' functions* ascribed to them. These are present if the results of evaluations are only to be used for the legitimation (sometimes even retroactively) of certain political decisions, e.g. because a programme is to be continued or, conversely, phased out. It has even become 'hip' for politicians "to use evaluations as baubles or as bolsters" (Pollitt 1998: 223), as decorative symbols of a modern policy, without wishing to seriously use the results of evaluations. This kind of 'tactical' function, however, is hardly consistent with the actual purpose of evaluation, but rather represents its dysfunctional side.

Evaluations can thus have various functions, which are, however, closely related to one another rather than being independent. Without the gaining of knowledge, none of the other functions can be performed. Conversely, it is also the case that if the focus is on other functions, these evaluations always produce knowledge as well. The commitment to a primary function governs the approach and determines the design and execution of an evaluation. Depending on whether the focus is on the acquisition of insights, control, the identification of development potential, or the legitimation of work carried out, different approaches and procedures can be employed.

Evaluation tasks
Evaluations can not only assume different orientations, but may also have varying *tasks*. Evaluations can be employed to:
- Improve the planning of a programme or measure (ex-ante evaluation) (cf. Rossi, Lipsey & Freeman 2004: 336 ff.)
- Monitor processes of implementation (ongoing evaluation)
- Ascertain the effectiveness and sustainability of interventions retrospectively (ex-post evaluation) (cf. Rossi, Lipsey & Freeman. 2004: 360 ff.).

Evaluations can thus be more *formative* in their nature, i.e. actively constructive, process-oriented, and communication-promoting, or more *summative*, i.e. concerned with summarising, producing balances, and results orientation (cf. Rossi, Lipsey & Freeman 2004: 34 ff.). In principle, both evaluation perspectives can be adopted for all *phases of a programme*. However, as there are scarcely any starting points for a summative evaluation in the planning and design stage of a programme, an evaluation can only be of a formative nature here. During the implementation phase, formative as well as summative evaluations are possible. Ex-post analyses are usually summative evaluations, as the constructive aspect is lacking. By producing appropriate informational feedback loops for follow-up projects, however, they can also take on formative significance (cf. fig. 2.10).

Aside from ex-ante evaluations, which examine the requirements of a programme or intervention measure, evaluations can perform the following *tasks* (cf. fig. 2.11).

(a) They can serve to monitor *processes*. This relates to the identification of problems in the implementation of a programme, as well as the question of whether planned time schedules are adhered to. Here it should be determined, among other things, whether measures find acceptance with the various stakeholders, what conflicts of interests arise, whether enough qualified personnel are available to implement measures, how implementing agencies undertake communication and coordination among themselves and with the programme's target groups, whether technical and financial resources are sufficient for goal attainment, and whether innovations introduced within the programme are effective.

(b) The *review of goal attainment* is normally carried out using the target values specified during planning, which is why this evaluation function is also known as a 'target/actual comparison'. It is strictly oriented towards targeted goals. However, a range of problems can arise here, and it is frequently the case that:

- Goals are formulated very ambiguously and are abstract in their nature
- Documented goals differ from those actually pursued (rhetoric of legitimation)
- Goals change over time
- Different actors involved in realising the goals pursue differing aims (cf. Stockmann 1996a: 102 ff.).

Figure 2.10: Evaluation research dimensions

Programme phases	Analytical perspective	Cognitive interest	Evaluation concepts
Programme design/planning phase	Ex-ante	"Analysis for policy" "Science for action"	Preformative/formative: actively constructive, process-oriented
Implementation phase	Ongoing	Both possible	Formative/summative: both possible
Impact phase	Ex-post	"Analysis of policy" "Science for knowledge"	Summative: summarising, balance-producing, results-oriented

(c) Evaluation is usually not just about performing a straightforward target/actual comparison, but is also concerned with recording as many impacts as possible (ideally all of them) that are triggered by a programme or intervention measure. Aside from planned outcomes, the primary objective is to also ascertain unintended effects, which may either support or run counter to goal attainment. Only by producing an *overall balance of impacts* is it possible to see if the positive or negative effects of a programme prevail.

(d) Evaluations should not only determine whether things are "on the right track" (process view), i.e. whether it is to be expected that goals can be reached to the planned extent with the material and personnel resources provided, within the specified time frame; they should also reveal whether "the right things are being done". That is to say, evaluations question the very aims of programmes and measures. It should be examined whether the programme facilitates *relevant developments or innovations* at all, or whether a different path needs to be taken altogether.

(e) Of course it is not sufficient to simply record impacts and assess their contribution to development. Rather, it is of central importance to deal with the question of whether the intended and unintended impacts observed can be attributed at all to the programme, or whether they stem from external factors. Solving the *problem of causality* is one of the most difficult tasks of evaluation. Experimental designs would represent the best option for examining causal hypotheses, as they are the most likely to accommodate the technical requirements of testing a causal structure. These are the chronological order and linking of measure and impact, and the controlling of external variables, either through randomisation and/or matching when measuring the relationship between measure and impact, or through the inclusion of all conceivable external variables (cf. Campbell 1969: 409 ff.).

Figure 2.11: Task profile of evaluations

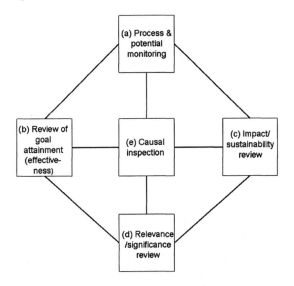

Because, for a variety of reasons, experimental designs can hardly be sensibly employed in evaluations in practice, alternatives are required. Yet these are not always sufficiently suitable for proving cause-effect relationships in a valid and reliable way (for more detail, cf. e.g. Stockmann 1996a: 107 ff.; Rossi et al. 1999: 235 ff.; Rossi, Lipsey & Freeman 2004: 233 ff.; Kromrey 2001: 116 ff.). This topic will be explored further in chapter 4.6.

2.3.2 Implementing evaluation

Evaluation paradigms

Of importance for the planning and implementation of an evaluation is what *research paradigm* it is based on. Broadly speaking, two main approaches can be distinguished.[62] One views evaluation as an empirical scientific procedure which follows critically rational research logic and, in principle, considers all common empirical research methods applicable. Evaluation is thus to be understood as applied social research, which has to consider particular research requirements, and which involves a specific interest in insight and application, at the centre of which is the usefulness of evaluation results in 'practice' (cf. Vedung 2000: 103 ff., Kromrey 2001: 113).

The second main approach associates evaluation with different aspirations, and is based on different assumptions. The existence of a 'true' reality that can be 'objectively' understood using empirical scientific procedures is disputed. Rather it is assumed that 'reality' is constructed socially from various perspectives, which may be in conflict with one another. As individual stakeholder groups take up positions of varying power, an overemphasis of certain interests can result. An evaluation is therefore not concerned with producing as 'realistic' a representation and assessment of circumstances encountered as possible, but rather with changing these circumstances in favour of disadvantaged persons. Evaluation thus becomes a transformational act. In its most radical form, evaluation turns into a constructivist combination of negotiations, organisational development, and group therapy, which in no way seeks overarching scientific explanations, but rather serves the emancipation and empowerment of deprived stakeholders (cf. Pollitt 2000: 71).

This *'cold war of the paradigms'* is by no means settled for good, but over the last few years many evaluation researchers have stressed the similarities rather than the differences. To this effect, there is a broad consensus that evaluations need to take the perspectives and needs of stakeholders into consideration, that quantitative and qualitative procedures (multi-method approaches) should be employed as far as possible, and that evaluations should be of benefit to clients and stakeholders. Only then will they be able to bring about processes of political and social change (cf. Rossi et al. 1988: 10, 2004: 16 ff., Chelimsky 1995: 6).

In the course of the professionalisation of evaluation research, in the late 1970s various organisations in the USA developed a range of criteria with which to ascertain the quality of evaluations (cf. Rossi, Lipsey & Freeman 2004: 404 ff.). The "Standards for Evaluation" originally presented by the Joint Committee on Standards for Educational Evaluation have had the widest acceptance and are those on which the *standards* formulated by the German Evaluation Society[63] are also modelled. These postulate that evaluations:

---

62   For information on their origins, cf. Campbell 1969; Cronbach et al. 1981; Cronbach 1982; and, as a summary, Mertens 2004.

63   Gesellschaft für Evaluation (DeGEval).

- Should be of use, i.e. oriented towards the informational requirements of users *(utility)*.
- Should be carried out realistically, prudently, diplomatically and cost-effectively *(feasibility)*.
- Should be conducted legally and ethically, and with due regard for the welfare of those involved in the evaluation, as well as those affected by its results *(propriety)*.
- Should reveal and convey technically adequate information about the features that determine the worth or merit of the programme being evaluated *(accuracy)*.

The understanding of evaluation that underlies this book is oriented towards the *empirical scientific model*, as the now commonly-held view is accepted here "that an analysis can simultaneously comply with strict scientific standards and be of maximum benefit for the client and other stakeholders" (Rossi et al. 1988: 10).

This does not mean that participatory procedures are ruled out, but they should focus primarily on the design and application phase. The aims of an evaluation, the assessment criteria and, to a certain extent, the course of action too, can be ascertained in a participatory way, and represent guidelines for the evaluation. However, within an empirical scientific procedure, information collection and analysis is the task of the evaluators. The assessment and interpretation of results, on the other hand, can be carried out participatively. The utilisation of findings presented by an evaluation and the conversion of (participatively) developed recommendations into measures and activities is the responsibility of clients or other stakeholders. The participatory approach will be taken up again later on (in chapter 4.8.2) (cf. Rossi, Lipsey & Freeman 2004: 48 ff.).

Internal and external evaluation
In principle, evaluations can be performed internally or externally. An evaluation is seen as *internal* if it is conducted by the same organisation that carries out the programme. If this internal evaluation is done by the department (unit) assigned with the operational implementation of the programme, this is referred to as *'self-evaluation'*. If a different department within the organisation (e.g. an evaluation or quality assurance department) performs the evaluation, this still represents an internal evaluation, but not self-evaluation.[64] Such 'in-house evaluations' offer a number of advantages: they can be carried out swiftly and at little expense, the evaluators usually possess high levels of subject knowledge, and results can be implemented directly.

The main drawbacks of internal evaluations stem from the fact that evaluators do not on the whole possess sufficient methodological competence, are lacking in independence and distance, and may be so attached to their programme that they fail to recognise more promising alternatives.

External evaluations are carried out by persons not belonging to the sponsor or the implementing organisation. External evaluators are thus usually characterised by greater independence, as well as extensive methodological competence and professional evaluation

---

64   Cf. Vedung 1999: 104 ff.; Scriven 1991: 159 f. & 197 f.; Widmer 2000: 79 f.; Caspari 2004: 32.

knowledge, and are familiar with the field in which the programme operates. In addition, external evaluations can give added legitimacy and influence to forces of reform within an organisation, which are required in order to spark processes of change (cf. Pollitt 2000: 72). On the other hand, however, external evaluations can arouse anxieties among those being evaluated, leading to defensive reactions. Problems may also arise during the later implementation of evaluation results. External evaluations of course incur additional costs. This does not mean, though, that an external evaluation is always more expensive than an internal one. If the costs incurred within the scope of an evaluation by persons inside the organisation involved in it are calculated, there will not necessarily be much difference financially between external and internal evaluations. Internal and external evaluations are often *combined*, in order to bring together different points of view, and to make use of the benefits of both methods.

2.3.3 Excursus: monitoring and controlling

Evaluations can be extended to create a system of *continual monitoring*. Monitoring can operate at the level of the system as a whole (society), a policy field, a programme, or individual intervention measures. It enables input, output and outcome data to be obtained. A well-known example of a monitoring system at the *policy field level* is environmental monitoring, which provides data on the condition of the environment. At the level of society as a whole, a system of social indicators, for example, provides information on the development of living circumstances, thus supplementing official statistics.

At the *programme level*, the function of a monitoring system is to provide management with a continual stream of data on the progress of the programme and on goal attainment. Rossi, Freeman and Lipsey (1999: 231) thus come up with the following definition: "Program monitoring is a form of evaluation designed to describe how a program is operating and assess how well it performs its intended functions" (cf. also Rossi, Lipsey & Freeman 2004: 171). In contrast to evaluations, which are carried out on a one-off basis at a certain point in time, monitoring is a continuous task, an ongoing, routine activity. Its aim is to examine whether planning guidelines are realised with maximum efficiency, in compliance with available resources, and within the scheduled time frame, and whether targeted goals are attained. Monitoring thus controls whether implementation goes according to plan. In doing so, the programme plan and development hypotheses on which it is based are not questioned. This, along with the analysis of relationships, is the task of evaluations. The causal attribution of changes observed plays a subordinate role in monitoring; it is a largely descriptive activity through which data should be collected as reliably as possible at periodic intervals, providing time series which help to identify developments (cf. Kissling-Näf & Knoepfel 1997: 147). This can be achieved only with great difficulty, if at all, within the scope of individual evaluations.

The functions of monitoring share many *similarities* with those of *controlling*[65], meaning the concept of the latter also warrants inspection. Like the concepts of Total Quality Management (TQM), controlling is a business management approach. While TQM was developed primarily in the marketing field, though, controlling has its roots in accountancy.

Controlling can be understood – from a functional viewpoint – as the subsystem of organisational management that "coordinates planning and control, as well as information provision, in a results-oriented, system-shaping and system-linking way, thus supporting the adaptation and coordination of the whole system" (Horváth 1996: 141). So, controlling helps management to adapt the system as a whole to environmental changes, based on results targets, as well as to perform tasks of coordination.

Most controlling concepts are based on system-theoretical considerations (cf. Horváth 1996: 138 ff., 2002: 98 ff.; Eschenbach 1996: 45 ff.; Habersam 1997: 113 f.; Eschenbach 1999: 8). The organisation is seen as a social system which is divided up into management and execution subsystems. As a social system, the organisation interacts with its environment. The role of management is to react appropriately to the demands of the environment, and – as far as possible – to actively shape them. Management must thus correctly assess the prevailing complexity and dynamics, and develop forward-looking strategies that ensure the existence and prosperity of the organisation. The more complex the environment, the greater the environmentally-induced controlling requirement. Since the complexity of organisational design usually increases with increasing environmental complexity, the organisationally-induced controlling requirement also grows.

As it is assumed that environmental complexity and dynamics have greatly increased over time, management must now react swiftly and flexibly to rapidly changing demands, as well as improving its innovative ability. In order to achieve this, management requires information, the provision of which is a central task of controlling:

> "In the context of the information function, controlling has the task of ascertaining informational requirements, and obtaining, storing, and editing information, as well as forwarding it on time to the right recipients" (Eschenbach 1999: 9).

Controlling should not only provide information, but also work towards ensuring that, based on this information, decisions are precipitated and measures implemented. By creating transparency, controlling produces inherent necessities, which increase the pressure

---

65 For information on the origins of controlling, see the brief, concise overview of Gerlich 1999: 3 ff. For detail on the concept and method of controlling, cf. also Ehlers & Schenkel 2004; Baum 2004; Spraul 2004; Bethke 2003; Friedl 2003; Piontec 2003; Jung 2003; Czenskowsky 2002; Bähr 2002; Baier 2002; Müller 2002. For specific information on education controlling, cf. e.g. Hummel 1999; Landsberg & Weiß 1995.

to make decisions and carry out actions.[66] Management must then ensure that the decisions it takes are implemented in the organisation.

Coordination represents the second major function of controlling, and is concerned with "bringing the complexity of organisational management under control" (Hoffmann et al. 1996: 48). Controlling should first and foremost ensure the coordination of information generation and provision with informational requirements, as well as coordinating the planning and control system with the information provision system (cf. Horváth 1996: 143).[67]

The extent to which a controlling system is institutionalised in an organisation, not only in a functional sense, but also among its employees, depends primarily on its size. In small firms, controlling is not institutionalised at all as a distinct business function, with managers performing controlling tasks themselves or turning to external service providers. The range of tasks and amount of managerial responsibility attributed to controlling are dependent not only on the type and size of the organisation, but also on leadership style, the historical development of controlling within the organisation, and numerous other factors. In practice, employees responsible for controlling range from those without any managerial competence (who carry out solely service functions) to those who take informal responsibility for crucial management tasks:

> "In practice, people with the title controller have functions that are, at one extreme little more than bookkeeping, at the other extreme, de facto general management" (Anthony 1988: 28).

The support function of controlling can, depending on requirements, be limited to information provision and coordination, or can mean – as advocated in most American concepts – making genuine contributions to decision-making. An examination of German controlling concepts shows that most incorporate the informational aim, necessitating "that controlling secures the provision of management with planning and control information, as well as with methods and models" (Eschenbach and Niedermayr 1996: 55). Controlling aims such as the safeguarding of responsiveness, anticipatory ability and adaptability are also mentioned, meaning, in this context, that controlling should provide information on expected environmental changes and those that have already occurred, and their effect on goal attainment, as well as supplying internal planning and control information.

---

66   The discussion on the demarcation between management and controlling will not be explored here. For information on this topic, cf. Eschenbach 1999: 10; Horváth 1996: 141; Eschenbach and Niedermayr 1996: 71.

67   Eschenbach and Niedermayr (1996: 70) see the coordination tasks of controlling primarily in the creation and maintenance of business management frameworks and instruments (system-shaping coordination), as well as in the system-linking coordination of the management system. The latter function is rejected by Horváth (1996: 143) and Schneider (1994: 330) as too far-reaching.

The coordination function is also highlighted by most German controlling concepts, but the decision-making function receives scant attention (cf. ibid.). There is thus broad consensus that controlling should serve to support managers in taking planning and control decisions, meaning it has a kind of service function. Controlling is therefore often compared to a 'piloting service' (Gerlich 1999: 8; Eschenbach and Niedermayr 1996: 51; Horváth 1996: 141; Deyhle 1995: 6).

In concrete terms, controlling assists management in strategy planning and development, strategic control and early warning, operational planning and budgeting, and calculating operational forecasts (cf. Eschenbach 1999: 28). Various tools are employed for these purposes. Operational controlling is primarily oriented towards internal aspects of an organisation, and deals with developments that manifest themselves in the present through expenditure and earnings. There is thus a focus on the use of decision-oriented cost and revenue calculation. For this, operational controlling typically employs, above all, internal accounting tools - key figures, transfer prices and budgets, as well as those tools used in forecasting (for purposes of target/actual comparison).

Strategic controlling, on the other hand, is future-oriented, and enjoys greater importance the more strategically aligned an organisation. Strategic controlling is intended to enhance the adaptability and innovativeness of the organisation, by identifying exogenous and endogenous environmental changes and inducing management to take action in good time (cf. Habersam 1997: 97). A number of tools are used to achieve this, including strengths/weaknesses analysis, industry/competition analysis, potential and portfolio analysis, cost structure analysis, and implementation and results controls.

With regard to the prevalence of tools employed in German organisations, empirical investigations show that, in the main, classic controlling instruments such as budget control, variance analysis, reporting, costing etc. are used. Strategic instruments are used to a far lesser extent (cf. Niedermayr 1996: 144 ff.). One criticism is that strategic controlling instruments largely represent merely an adaptation of operational tools, with a lack of theoretical orientation and practical testing (Habersam 1997: 83; Weber 1995: 141; Langguth 1994: 1; Küpper, Weber and Zünd 1990: 288). Furthermore, the controlling approach is criticised for being based on a one-sided conception of people "which views the employee as a squanderer of resources and thus as necessitating control". Controlling is also accused of being scientifically hazy and being based on a belief in the effectiveness of planning: it is viewed as a technocratic approach that serves the subtle controllability of the organisation and its employees (cf. Habersam 1997: 75 f., 134).

An examination of the dispersal of controlling by economic sector shows that it is frequently employed in manufacturing and in service industries (particularly financial services). In non-profit organisations and public administration, on the other hand, only a low awareness of controlling is to be found (cf. Eschenbach 1999: 4), even though it is assumed that controlling can be applied in all organisations and social systems. Controlling is a management tool or leadership component that is not in principle tied to any specific aims (e.g. making profits), particular business activities (e.g. the production of goods or rendering of services), or to organisations of certain sizes (cf. Küpper, Weber and Zünd 1990: 282; Habersam 1997: 96).

The *'balanced scorecard'* arose from criticism of the purely financial nature of figures used in organisational management (cf. Greiling 2001: 9; Koch 2003: 15 ff.), and can be understood as an extension of strategic controlling.[68] The balanced scorecard is a tool for implementing and enforcing corporate strategy. David Kaplan and Nolan Norton (1997), who developed this concept, assume that the implementation of a formulated, internally-communicative strategy is a pre-requisite for organisational success. 'Classical' financial data ultimately serve as the decisive criteria for measuring an organisation's success. However, the implementation of strategy is based on key figures which, in addition to the financial side, also shed light on customer, business process, and learning and development perspectives. There is still little known about the degree of use of the balanced scorecard in Europe (cf. Weber & Schäffer 2000: 1; Horváth & Gaiser 2000: 18; PwC 2001: 4 ff.)[69], but it seems to have been enjoying increased popularity over the last few years.[70]

In summary, it can be stated that controlling is a management subsystem that provides information and relevant data about environmental changes that have already occurred, as well as about possible future ones, in order to create a base for implementing adaptive actions and measures that shape the environment. Controlling also supplies internal data to continually inform decision-makers about the relationship between planned and actual developments (target/actual comparison), in order to facilitate purposeful adjustments (management decisions). In addition, controlling performs coordination functions for management, by creating the conditions necessary for harmonisation of the activities of separate management subsystems, or, generally speaking, of the organisation. To these ends, planning, control and information systems, among others, are established.

If we *compare* the functions of *controlling* with those of *monitoring*, there are a number of commonalities, but also fundamental differences. Monitoring is, like controlling – and also TQM, but unlike evaluation – a continuous activity, whose objective is to inform management continually about the relationship between planned and actual developments (target/actual comparison) using data internal and external to the organisation, so that it can carry out goal-oriented adjustments. Common to both procedures is that they provide information for decisions, and thus make a contribution to decision-making, yet are not a

---

68 For information on the balanced scorecard, cf. e.g. Jossé 2005; Friedag & Schmidt 2004; Horváth & Partners 2004; Wunder 2004; Ahn 2003; Preißner 2003; Uebel & Helmke 2003; Morganski 2003; Niven 2003; Schlemmer 2002; Steinacher 2002; Tonnesen 2002; Wüst 2001; Fratschner 1999; Friedag 1998.

69 For a summary critique of the balanced scorecard, cf. Diensberg 2001: 21 ff.

70 For information on the use of the balanced scorecard in non-profit organisations, cf., in particular, Niven 2003; Stoll 2003; Langthaler 2002; Greulich 2002; Scherer 2002; Krönes 2001; Schön 2001.

part of the process itself. This is carried out by the management and not by controllers or evaluation experts.

There are, however, a number of *differences* between the two procedures. An important one is that monitoring is only assigned an information provision function, whereas controlling also performs a coordination function. Another difference is that the reporting scope of monitoring is far wider. While controlling systems in practice continue to concentrate primarily on cost aspects, this area is often neglected by monitoring systems. Instead, monitoring systems also provide data on intended and unintended impacts. While controlling is heavily focused on structural factors, monitoring also gives consideration to process- and system-related issues. This prevents monitoring from being reduced to a technical planning aid. The very reason that monitoring is necessary is that the planning and implementation of measures are understood as an ongoing, continuous process that has to react to changing environmental conditions. Because stakeholders are also frequently incorporated in monitoring systems, which is rarely true in the case of controlling, the criticism of controlling that it is a subtle way of manipulating employees does not apply to monitoring. In contrast, while 'stakeholders' may be actively involved in defining assessment criteria, indicators and measures in monitoring systems, controlling is governed by set 'controls'. Controlling follows a 'top-down' approach, while monitoring is administered as a 'bottom-up' system.

Because monitoring represents a specific form of continuous evaluation, the scientific/theoretical principles of evaluation also apply, and all known evaluation methods can be employed. These are far more extensive than the procedures used in controlling, which are strongly focused on costing. One consequence of this is that qualitative as well as quantitative data are used within monitoring processes, whereas almost exclusively monetary or quantitative measures are used in controlling. While controlling is a very rigid procedure, monitoring is much more flexible - what is to be measured, and how it is to be done, can be determined in an interactive process.

As controlling is derived from the businesses management and monitoring from the social science field, the procedures stem from different traditions and are usually applied in different areas (business enterprises vs. non-profit organisations/programmes). There has thus been little effort made up to now to combine the two instruments. This seems a genuine possibility, though. Monitoring approaches could help to enrich controlling in terms of content and method, to 'democratise' it, and to open it up to 'subjective' reality (to the various perspectives of stakeholders). Conversely, monitoring could be enhanced by controlling through adopting aspects and methods of costing.[71]

---

71 Habersam (1997: 186 ff.) performs a comparison of the fundamental points in the controlling and evaluation discussion. However, he concentrates the comparison solely on the emancipatory constructivist approach of the '4th generation of evaluation'. In doing so he fails to acknowledge that this approach is by no means the only one represented and accepted in the field of evaluation research. In this respect, the comparison he carries out

It is also worth noting that, despite their identical scientific (business management) roots, even *TQM and controlling* share scarcely any common ground. Indeed, the two concepts differ fundamentally. In TQM the view is prevalent "that quality cannot be enforced through controlling, but rather is generated in the workplace, that quality assurance is not the task of one department, but rather concerns everyone" (Daumenlang and Palm 1997: 7). TQM is thus oriented towards individual employees. Yet it is out of the question that every company and organisation should have to solve the problems of external and internal information provision, as well as of the coordination of the management system. These should rather be the main functions of any controlling system. However, in practice controlling concepts have so far played hardly any role in quality management (cf. Müller and Zenz 1996: 42). An investigation in the course of the joint "process-oriented quality controlling"[72] project, sponsored by the German research ministry, showed that controlling tends to deal with technical parameters and is deemed to be primarily reactive (cf. Müller and Zenz 1996: 42). This may be especially due to the fact that controlling continues to be too heavily oriented towards costs and not enough towards aspects of quality (cf. Kreutzberg 2000: 23).

2.3.4 Summary

In summary, it can be said that the tool of evaluation can fulfil various *functions* and diverse *tasks*. The most important activity in the case of ongoing and completed measures is the review of *goal attainment* and *effectiveness* (or sustainability). Common to all evaluations is the task of collecting, analysing and assessing information (data) based on selected criteria. How this is done depends on the choice of underlying *research paradigm*. Evaluations should comply with prescribed *standards*, regardless of whether they are carried out internally or externally.

Monitoring may be described as a special form of evaluation with limited functional scope. It is usually administered internally (i.e. performed by the organisation that offers a particular service or implements certain intervention measures) and, in contrast to evaluations, which are usually done sporadically, represents a continuous activity whose goal is to collect data on scheduled progress, i.e. processes of development. In doing so, the goals of the product/service, programme or measure themselves are not questioned - this is the task of an evaluation.

Monitoring has been shown to exhibit many parallels with *controlling*. However, its scope is wider than that of controlling, which continues to be characterised strongly by the investigation of cost aspects, an area often ignored by monitoring.

---

gives a somewhat skewed picture. A further comparison of evaluation and controlling can be found in Gerlich (1999: 15).
72   "Prozess-orientiertes Qualitätscontrolling".

In the next section, the quality management concepts discussed earlier in the book (in particular TQM) will be compared with those of evaluation. The *aim of this comparison* is to examine whether these different concepts portray mutually-exclusive, competing, or complementary concepts for quality development in non-profit organisations. A comparison of the two concepts shows a range of similarities, but even more differences (cf. fig. 2.12).

2.4 Comparison of quality management and evaluation concepts[73]

2.4.1 Similarities

Common aim and origins
A central similarity between TQM and evaluation concepts is that both are oriented towards contributing to the *quality improvement* of a product or service, which can include the implementation of programmes or intervention measures. Pollitt (2000: 62) alludes to the fact that both endeavours to improve quality and evaluation procedures are of American descent. Mertens (2000: 42) identifies the *origins* of evaluation as being in the USA in the early 19th century, when the government commissioned independent inspectors to evaluate prisons, schools, hospitals, and orphanages. The first 'professional' evaluations were carried out in the 1960s within the scope of the Great Society laws.

Modern quality management often refers to Deming and Juran[74] as its founding fathers in the 1950s. After that, quality management procedures were most notably developed in Japan (cf. e.g. Ishikawa 1980), and it wasn't until later on, in the 1980s, that they started to gain significance again in the USA. Pollitt's (2000: 62) assumption that evaluation and quality management exhibit traits characteristic of their US cultural roots, which are based on the belief "that improvements result from the application of rational-technical expertise" and effectively get adopted automatically if they demonstrate their superiority, surely underestimates the contribution made by Japan to the concepts' development. Evaluation and quality management are shaped to a far lesser extent by "traits of American optimism" (ibid.) than by characteristics of the modern age that are based on criteria of rationality.

Both procedures can thus be seen as *important instruments of modern societies*, and are – at least to a certain extent – based on a belief in the ability to plan and control political and social processes. Quality management and evaluation, as has been shown here, aim to create rational decision-making bases for management – even if they approach this in different ways. Employees and citizens also expect decisions to be comprehensibly legiti-

---

73   Monitoring is understood here as a specific form of evaluation, and is therefore not mentioned separately.
74   Cf. e.g. Deming 1952, 1982; Juran 1951, 1991, 1993.

mised. Evaluation and quality management have developed into *symbols of modernisation*, which at times serve a decorative purpose rather than the will to convert recommendations into actions. It has become 'fashionable' "to use evaluations as baubles or as bolsters" (Pollitt 1998: 223). Both procedures are in danger of degenerating into expensive rituals if they are employed more for tactical than for implementational purposes (cf. Stockmann 2000a: 15).

Figure 2.12: Similarities and differences between EFQM and evaluation

SIMILIARITIES
✓ Aim of quality improvement
✓ US-American roots
✓ Instruments of modern, rational organisational management/politics
✓ Acceptance problems

DIFFERENCES	
EFQM	**Evaluation**
✓ Origin: private sector, particularly manufacturing	✓ Origin: public sector, non-profit organisations, programme management
✓ Business administration	✓ Social science
✓ Field of application: profit-oriented private enterprises, competition	✓ Field of application: no profit orientation, little competition
✓ Customer-oriented, clearly defined target groups	✓ Target group-oriented, complex stakeholder network
✓ Centralised orientation: top-down	✓ Participatory procedure (bottom-up), but also top-down
✓ Assessment criteria given	✓ Assessment criteria variable
✓ Obligation to 'shareholder value' creation	✓ Obligation to 'stakeholder value' creation
✓ All employees involved in implementation	✓ Employees partially excluded from implementation
✓ Continuous activity	✓ Periodic activity
✓ Internal (self-assessment process)	✓ Internal and/or external
✓ Narrow, customer-oriented field of enquiry	✓ Broad field of enquiry, intended and unintended impacts, causal analysis

Acceptance and implementation problems
It can also be stated that *implementational difficulties* provide both procedures with similar problems. Especially in the case of external evaluations, for example, it is by no means rare for findings to be obtained, at times at great expense, and the resulting recommendations not implemented. This is not only due to a lack of political will, but also to the fact that organisations and bureaucracies have great powers of persistence that cannot be overcome through the presentation of evaluation findings and resulting recommendations alone. In addition, there are of course evaluation results that are politically unwelcome, which those responsible prefer to hush up rather than making them public and using them for reform.

In the case of quality management, the procedures particularly at risk of finding little *acceptance* are those that are not interactive, focus on pleas to follow rules, produce complex handbooks, necessitate costly processes, and at times create new bureaucratic structures (cf. Zbaracki 1998: 602 ff.). Related to the at times low motivation of affected parties to implement evaluation results is the fact that quality managers and evaluators are not always gleefully-received experts. Because they reveal, examine, and (even if this is not the main motive) 'control' shortcomings, it is not uncommon for them to come into conflict with clients and evaluees. Moreover, affected parties may feel restricted in their professional autonomy. In this regard too, external approaches that fail to incorporate relevant persons in the evaluation or quality management system are likely to create the greatest problems with acceptance and, later on, implementation.

2.4.2 Differences

Different fields of origin and application
The essential differences between quality management concepts and evaluation can primarily be attributed to their different origins. Quality management emerged in the *private sector*, and has come to be an integral component of every profit business. Evaluation is a product of the *public sector*, and is thus subject to different conditions. Quality management and evaluation accordingly have *differing theoretical roots*: whilst TQM concepts follow primarily business management-oriented approaches, evaluations borrow their methodology mainly from fundamental social-scientific research. This produces different priorities and perspectives. By concentrating the comparison on the TQM and evaluation concepts presented earlier, it is possible to illustrate the differences more precisely.

TQM concepts were initially developed above all for manufacturing companies, although their application has since started to be tested in the service sector as well.[75] The

---

75 Cf. the overviews of Boeßenecker 2003; Busse 2003; Haindl 2003; Igl 2002; Gaschler 2002; Gissel-Palkovich 2002; Schubert 2001; Mayländer 2000; Peterander 1999; Guhl 1998 and Huber 1998.

extent to which TQM can be applied in non-profit organisations remains controversial.[76] As discussed, non-profit organisations exhibit different characteristics to businesses enterprises, and usually operate in a differently-structured situational environment.

Profit maximisation and competition are the reasons why private-sector businesses strive, on the one hand, to improve the quality of their products and services, in order to increase sales potential, whilst on the other hand trying to make their organisational structures more efficient and to streamline their personnel structures - for the purpose of cutting costs etc. TQM contributes towards enhancing competitiveness and, ultimately, increasing profits and improving market position. However, if competition and profit maximisation do not exist as significant motives for quality improvement, the use of TQM, as well as EFQM, has proved to be problematic (cf. Selbmann 1999: 8).

Public sector organisations enjoy, as a rule, a guaranteed existence. Their 'survival' is assured even if they do not perform optimally, if customers are dissatisfied with their output, and if organisational goals (if these are indeed formulated in such a way that they can be operationalised and measured) are not achieved. It is only recently that a quality offensive has become evident in the public sector as well. The claimant, patient, or unemployed person is viewed as a 'customer' to be satisfied. Intervention schemes are no longer able to justify their success through input factors alone; rather, they must be able to provide proof of their effectiveness, or even sustainability, especially in times of scarce financial resources.

Another difference in the application context of TQM and evaluation is *customer orientation*. TQM demands central alignment with customer requirements. For this, a clear producer-customer relationship is necessary, which is present in the case of business enterprises. Companies then see confirmation of their quality if customers are satisfied with the product. However, in the case of numerous public establishments, such a one-dimensional producer-customer relationship does not exist, as has already been discussed at length. Instead, they are usually presented with a multidimensional customer network. Furthermore, in the non-profit sector the 'customer' lacks central characteristics inherent in the concept (e.g. decision-making authority, the market transaction of product/service in exchange for money). It is thus highly questionable whether the customer concept can sensibly be applied in the non-profit sector at all. Instead, it has been suggested that, in this case, they are referred to as users, audiences, or target groups.

Holistic versus specific orientation
In addition to the application context, a fundamental difference between TQM and evaluation is that a TQM concept (e.g. EFQM) represents a comprehensive, complex, co-

---

76   At the Vienna University of Economics and Business Administration, an interdisciplinary research body for 'non-profit organisations' has been created, which examines the management of such organisations and seeks to develop management aids. Cf. http://www.wu-wien.ac.at/Nonprofit-Organisation/forschung/uebersicht.htm (German language website).

ordinated system for ensuring quality. It incorporates all members of an organisation, internal structures and processes, and the organisation's immediate environment.

Evaluation, on the other hand, is *not* a quality management system! It also observes internal and external structural and general conditions – indeed much more extensively than TQM models – but *evaluation lacks the decision-making element*. Evaluations provide information, assessments and recommendations for requirements defined by decision-makers. Yet decision-making, and the implementation of measures recommended by evaluations, remains the role of management.

Centralised versus participatory orientation
A further major difference between TQM and evaluation is the situation of the client and the *relationship to other stakeholders*. In a business enterprise, the leadership/management decides on the organisation's strategies. Participants, in particular employees and customers, are allocated with tightly-defined roles. Employees are primarily seen as producers, and customers as recipients, of products and services. If external experts are incorporated in the TQM process, there is a clear prevailing functional relationship. Their job is, first and foremost, based on management guidelines, to contribute towards improving the quality of an organisation's products, by convincing employees of the TQM philosophy and motivating them to collaborate.

In addition, the *assessment criteria* in a *TQM model* are *pre-defined* (whilst ISO is even more rigid in this respect). EFQM, for example, distinguishes between nine main criteria and 32 sub-criteria, which, although they must be interpreted according to sector, are even fixed in terms of their weighting. Modifications are not intended.[77]

In *evaluations*, on the other hand, the *evaluation goals* and *assessment criteria* are *freely definable*. They can be specified by decision-makers/clients (directive), evaluators (science-/experience-based), target groups and stakeholders (emancipative), or by all of them together (participatory). Participants (stakeholders) frequently play an important role in the goal formulation and application phases, at least.

They are not simply employees or customers whose satisfaction or needs are measured; they can play an active part in shaping the evaluation process. If an evaluation is based on the emancipatory paradigm, employees of the organisation being evaluated, as well as the various stakeholder groups, also collaborate in performing the evaluation. Yet even if the empirical scientific paradigm of evaluation, on which this comparison is based, is employed, stakeholders can exert far greater influence on an evaluation than is the case under TQM. Thus, in evaluations, multiple 'client' perspectives arise, with multiple objectives, and diverse interests and measures of value. *Evaluations* should first and foremost contribute towards improving the situation of stakeholders.

---

77 Of course no company can be prevented from modifying the EFQM model and omitting, replacing, or altering criteria. But in such cases, the model no longer complies with EFQM, but is rather an internal creation. Applying for the European Quality Award would then also of course be out of the question.

In TQM, the focus is on customers, yet only in the sense that they are to be satisfied, so that they will demand the product or service and thus increase the company's profits, improve its market position etc. That is to say, the customer only takes centre stage on a superficial level; the primary goal is to increase 'shareholder' value. As this is only possible, according to the TQM philosophy, if the customer is satisfied, his or her needs and quality demands are accommodated. In short, this means that while TQM has an obligation to *'shareholder value'*, evaluation serves *'stakeholder value'*.

Different levels of employee participation
A further difference between TQM and evaluation is the *involvement of employees* of the company or of the organisation being evaluated. Although evaluations offer stakeholders greater potential for participation in the design, assessment and application phases, in the data collection and analysis phases they are primarily of importance as information carriers. Under the emancipatory paradigm the situation is different, with employees and stakeholders actively contributing to shaping the evaluation as a whole.

In the case of TQM this is different, in the sense that management prescribes the *TQM* strategy and its implementation from above (*top-down approach*), yet actively incorporates all employees of a company in the execution process. Only if employees can be motivated and convinced of the virtues of TQM, so that they internalise its principles and employ them consistently in their daily work, does TQM have a chance of succeeding. While empirical scientific evaluations involve the employees of organisations being evaluated, as well as other stakeholders, primarily in the design phase, offering them the possibility of making a contribution towards planning (goal definition, assessment criteria selection), under TQM there is hardly any scope for negotiation here. Goals and means are largely determined using standards (ISO) or parameters (EFQM). *Evaluation* can thus be developed as a *participatory bottom-up process*, which is hardly true of TQM. On the other hand, employees are involved in implementation under TQM, which is not true in the case of (empirical scientific) evaluation.

Continuous versus periodic activity
TQM is, in principle, a *continually* running programme that covers the whole organisation. *Evaluation* is a *periodic activity* for which there is often a particular cause, and for which the terms of reference are redefined in each case. However, evaluation can also be extended into a continuous activity, particularly in the form of a systematic *monitoring* system. As explained earlier on, this can be applied at different levels, and at the programme level serves to monitor planning guidelines and goal attainment. Within the scope of a monitoring system, data are continuously collected and analysed. While monitoring has the task of observing scheduled implementation, the function of periodically-performed evaluations is to scrutinize the goals themselves, the programme plan, and the development hypotheses on which it is based.

Monitoring is an internal process whose objective is to provide management with information relevant to decision-making. Evaluations, on the other hand, are often also carried out externally. Evaluations often use the data collected in the course of monitoring, as they cannot be obtained to a comparable extent in the course of a relatively short evaluation. However, it is often the case that the monitoring systems used do not have sufficient output- and outcome-related data available, but are rather focused on documenting input-related factors.

Generally, it is feasible to carry out a combination of monitoring (as a routine, continuous task) and periodically-performed evaluation, in order to deal with the issue of scheduled progress ("are we still on course?") as well as that of direction ("is the course taken even the right one?"). Such outcome-based monitoring and evaluations systems have been applied only infrequently up to now (cf. Pollitt 2000: 72).

Internal versus external activity
TQM is primarily a *self-assessment process*. It can either follow set standards (ISO) or be carried out as an interactive process (EFQM). While an EFQM system is possible even without any external appraisal or participation, ISO is, as explained earlier, a largely externally-managed process. In the case of certification (ISO), or within the framework of an appraisal to attain a "European Quality Award", assessment is carried out externally by organisations such as TÜV or DEKRA[78], or by certified EFQM assessors.

Evaluation too can be performed as an *internal* as well as an *external activity*. Particularly within a monitoring system, evaluation is organised as an internal, continuous process for supervising programme development. As a periodical activity with a specific remit, it can be carried out either internally or externally. The advantages and disadvantages of internal versus external evaluations have already been detailed.

In spite of some similarities in principle, however, it should be stated that TQM normally represents an internal activity, whereas evaluation is mostly external, and it thus appears justified to attach more weight to the differences than the similarities (a view also subscribed to by Pollitt 2000: 66).[79]

Scope and depth of the area of analysis
In terms of the depth and width of the areas of analysis of evaluation and TQM, the two methods differ fundamentally. This becomes especially clear if we take another look at the parameters used under EFQM. The two most important results parameters concentrate on the satisfaction of customers and the securing of long-term business success ("key performance results"). Employee satisfaction and social responsibility are indeed measured too, yet they account for only 150 out of 500 results points. The remaining 350 assessment points are for customer satisfaction (200) and operating results (150). What is more, employee satisfaction at least could just as well be counted amongst the 'enabler' criteria,

---

78   Cf. footnotes 16 and 17.
79   For information on self-evaluation, cf. above all the contributions compiled by Maja Heiner (1996).

as satisfied employees are an absolute necessity for a well-functioning TQM system. So, TQM is primarily concerned with improving quality via 'enabler' criteria, in order to satisfy customers and thereby ensure the long-term success of the organisation.

Evaluations, on the other hand, are employed to acquire and assess information, in order to create transparency for decision-makers. They do this by supplying relevant data for the planning and implementation of measures, as well as for the assessment of their outcomes. The *scope and functional range of evaluations* is significantly *wider* than that of TQM. Within evaluations, on top of cost-benefit aspects and programmes' efficiency and effectiveness, dimensions largely disregarded in TQM concepts are also measured, namely the relevance, efficacy, or even sustainability of a programme, service or product.

A profit-oriented company need not be interested in whether the good produced or service offered is socially necessary. It is only concerned about whether there is a market for it; that is to say, whether purchasers can be found for the product/service that are prepared to pay an appropriate price for it (i.e. one that secures long-term profitability). Whether a Tamagotchi is socially necessary, or whether it simply represents a waste of valuable resources, is an irrelevant question for business enterprises. The crucial question is whether there are customers who are prepared to purchase this product for the price demanded.

The effectiveness of their strategies thus only usually interests *business enterprises*, as will be explained, in respect of whether a demand exists, whether it is met by the product manufactured, and whether customers are satisfied with this. The measurement of intended outcomes thus focuses on a *narrow range of interests*. This is very different within an evaluation. Here, it is not only a case of carrying out a straightforward target/actual comparison to compare goals attained with those aimed for; not only are the intended outcomes among target groups examined; rather, the scope of outcome monitoring is far wider. Internal impacts (within the organisation being evaluated) and external impacts (in the organisation's environment) in all conceivable fields are examined. Furthermore, unintended impacts are measured as well. So, an impact analysis within the scope of an *evaluation* attempts to ascertain as many outcomes as it can, in order to produce as *intricate an impact balance* as possible.

TQM is not concerned with this. The issue of whether beer and cigarette sales promote alcoholism or increase the numer of cancer deaths is an unintended outcome that might be of interest to society, but not necessarily to the relevant company, as long as drinking and smoking customers are satisfied, sales are assured, and the target profit margin is thus reached. The social impact of this firm, which may well enjoy particular success directly due to the deployment of TQM, need barely concern it. The (hopefully) unintended consequences such as addiction and illness must be borne by society.

Furthermore, evaluations are not usually interested in the measuring of impacts alone, but also in the *attribution of causes*, i.e. in the discovery of cause-effect relationships. In this respect too, we can proceed on the assumption that evaluations are more extensive in their conception than TQM models. TQM is only concerned with company-specific cause-effect relationships. More comprehensive, broader analyses can thus be neglected if the company does not appear to be affected. Evaluations, in contrast, endeavour to undertake a causal analysis that incorporates the whole social context.

2.4.3 Summary

Although TQM and evaluation ultimately both pursue the goal of contributing to the quality improvement of products and services (including programme provision), and although both procedures are instruments of modern societies that function according to criteria of rationality, as well as having to deal with similar problems of acceptance, *the differences outweigh the similarities*. TQM and evaluation not only have different theoretical roots, but also different backgrounds and application contexts.

Another fundamental difference between TQM and evaluation is that, while TQM represents an all-encompassing (holistic), coordinated quality assurance system (covering everything from information provision and appraisal to decision-making and implementation), evaluation has primarily an information acquisition and assessment function. Evaluations are used to collect and appraise data, as well as to derive recommendations for action, in a target-oriented fashion. But decisions on action and the implementation of those decisions do not form part of the evaluation procedure. TQM is therefore also a component of performance management, but evaluation is not (cf. Pollitt 2000: 67).

Moreover, although TQM is a concept that can be designed either in accordance with standards or more interactively, overall it is less participatory than evaluation. TQM is a top-down approach that in principle involves less open actions than evaluation. Yet TQM is unconditionally dependent on the acceptance of employees; without this the model cannot work. Evaluation, on the other hand, can be carried out even without the consent of the employees being evaluated. This is inadvisable, however, as their non-acceptance impairs not only information collection, but above all the preparedness to implement evaluation recommendations.

The two procedures also differ in terms of customer orientation. TQM focuses on the customer, and evaluation on stakeholders. Under TQM, the satisfaction of the needs of the customer (i.e. the buyer of the good produced or service offered) is the main concern. Evaluations, on the other hand, are more complex, encompassing target and non-target groups, intended and unintended effects, and the social context. Evaluations are interested in shedding light on causal relationships, and do not limit themselves to variables relevant for the development of sales-driving strategies. The social consequences, relevance, effectiveness and sustainability of service provision or intervention measures are also examined.

TQM is ultimately only interested in customers, making them the benchmark of its activities, because the prosperity of the company is dependent upon it. The actual goal of a market-oriented company is to increase profit, market value, and *shareholder value*. Evaluation, on the other hand, has an obligation to serve *stakeholder value*. Target groups should derive optimal utility from a service or programme to as great a degree as possible, without others being disadvantaged or even harmed. Therefore, customer satisfaction cannot be the all-determining criterion for quality assessment, but instead the whole context (unintended effects, implications for other stakeholders not belonging to the target group etc.) must be illuminated and subjected to assessment.

Based on the clear differences, it is not surprising that TQM and evaluation are rarely employed in unison (cf. Pollitt 2000: 70, Davies 1999: 153). However, they constitute *complementary rather than mutually exclusive concepts, with differing potentials.* Even though the conditions under which evaluation and TQM might complement each other have barely been explored thus far (cf. Pollitt 2000: 76), it is not difficult to envisage possibilities for combined application. First and foremost, users of the different approaches could *learn from each other*:

One lesson to be learnt from the quality management discussion is that evaluation should not remain a periodical activity, but should rather serve the *continual provision of information.* By taking the form of a systematic monitoring system, evaluation can be extended into this kind of continuous activity, and be combined with periodical individual evaluations. Know-how from the field of controlling can also be used in the process. The interaction of monitoring and evaluation allows the advantages of internal and external evaluation described in this chapter to be combined. As has been explained, the implementation of evaluation results often represents a problem, as the process is normally not closely enough associated with the quality management system. Here, the view must be promoted that *quality improvement is the task of every employee* – as occurs in companies that practise TQM. This also applies to the improvement of the quality of public services and programmes. The implementation of evaluation results is not only the task of management, but of all employees.

So, what appears generally necessary, above all in the public sector and non-profit organisations, is *increasing the acceptance of quality assurance measures.* The employment of monitoring and evaluation should not just be seen as an expense factor, but rather as an instrument that leads to the efficient and effective use of funds. Evaluations produce transparency, and through their insights create decision-making bases that can contribute towards preventing undesirable developments and lowering costs.

Quality development measures have been appreciated for some time in organisations, yet *TQM is too one-dimensionsal* in its orientation. It neglects questions of relevance as well as intended and, above all, unintended impacts that are not just limited to customers (target groups). Especially for organisations with a demand profile of a highly social nature, impact and sustainability evaluations could contribute towards:

- Tapping new sources of information
- Carrying out broader analyses and assessments that encompass social factors
- Giving greater analytical weight to the problem of cause-effect identification[80]
- Assessing additional factors such as social relevance and sustainability

---

80   Davies (1999: 156) believes that the primary way in which evaluations could enrich quality management would be by providing the know-how for designing causal analyses.

- Revealing and highlighting value conflicts arising from the use of different measures of value and assessment criteria within an organisation
- Revealing and highlighting goal conflicts arising from diverse interests.

In both application contexts, evaluation could be used to firstly *reveal* the *shortcomings* of the *quality information systems* present in organisations, and to support, and give additional legitimacy to, quality offensives.

Due to the organisational and situational differences between profit and non-profit organisations detailed here, it is to be assumed that *adopting complex TQM concepts such as EFQM, or even ISO-based standardisation, is not sufficient for the quality development of non-profit organisations.* They require the *concepts and tools of evaluation,* in order to provide management with comprehensive information about the context in which non-profit organisations operate, and about central success variables such as goal attainment, effectiveness, sustainability, social relevance etc., as well as to carry out systematic causal analyses. This information is indispensible, at least for the governance of non-profit organisations.

Furthermore, evaluation concepts offer *greater chances of participation* than TQM or ISO models. Through the participatory determination of evaluation aims and assessment criteria, it is possible to accommodate the multidimensional 'customer network' characteristic of non-profit organisations. By considering the needs and demands of individual stakeholders in the selection and weighting of assessment criteria, a *multidimensional appraisal system* is created, which forms the basis of quality assessment and improvement. A participatory approach is also to be recommended because it can serve to remove fears and reservations about the evaluation, and induce concerned parties to actively cooperate. Transparency of results and an open discussion of the resulting recommendations also increase the chances of them being implemented by participants.

In order that decisions are ultimately made, however, and their implementation coordinated and monitored, *a functioning quality management system is required.* Because evaluation does not incorporate any decision-making or management elements, a link between evaluation and a management system is absolutely necessary. Data obtained through evaluations, assessments carried out based on pre-agreed criteria, and the resulting recommendations, constitute essential, but often insufficient, conditions for quality development.

Various quality management systems are appropriate for use *in conjunction with evaluation.* Least suitable for this purpose would be especially rigid systems, such as ISO, which present a fixed framework of standards. Evaluation is likely to generate the greatest benefit within management systems that are designed more openly and flexibly. In the context of non-profit organisations, the *concepts of NPM* provide a starting point here. Although the competitive orientation which it propagates, as shown in this chapter, cannot be applied in all non-profit organisations, while the customer concept often appears extremely problematic in this context, the development of comprehensive quality consciousness and management is indispensable for quality development in non-profit organisations. Its primary advantage over other quality management concepts is the strategic goal of output and outcome orientation. The orientation of quality development towards *improved service provision* and *higher levels of effectiveness* is a *guiding example* for non-profit organisations. Evaluation is vital for output- and outcome-based management, as it is through this process that the necessary data on output, goal attainment, and intended and unintended impacts are obtained.

While NPM models can barely be applied without the support of evaluation, as it makes output- and outcome-oriented management possible, evaluation can also be combined with other quality management concepts. As explained earlier on (cf. chapter 2.1.2), even a simple decision-making and control system constitutes a quality management system. The *aim of this book*, however, is not to develop a quality management system that is as suitable as possible for non-profit organisations, i.e. one that corresponds as far as possible to their particular quality requirements. Rather, it is to develop a theoretical conception of, and methodology for, an impact-based monitoring and evaluation system, from which, on the one hand, evaluation criteria and quality dimensions can be derived that are suitable for assessing the output and impacts of organisations, especially non-profit organisations, and that, on the other hand, provides an empirical data collection framework with which the need for management-relevant information can be covered.

3 Theoretical Conception of Evaluation

3.1 Overview

As discussed earlier on, non-profit organisations render a diverse array of services. In addition to security and sovereign functions, state-run non-profit organisations have primarily welfare state duties to fulfil. Private non-profit organisations, on the other hand, are characterised by a broad spectrum of different *services*. On top of continuous tasks (e.g. nursing, social and youth welfare, citizen services, debt advice etc.), both state and private services also encompass individual intervention measures (e.g. the restoration of a cultural monument, reconstruction aid following a flood disaster etc.), as well as the implementation of projects and programmes (e.g. for improving environmental communication, developing deprived regions, integrating the unemployed, rehabilitating drug addicts etc.).

Programmes, projects and other political intervention measures are usually based on a 'policy'. A *'policy'* can be defined as a self-contained strategy for action relating to a specific subject or problem area (cf. Bank & Lames 2000: 6).[81] *Programmes* and *projects* form the central elements of such strategies, and are concerned with achieving goals that are deemed to be desirable (cf. Bussmann et al. 1997: 66 f. & 83). A programme involves a bundle of interrelated measures. Very broadly defined, the term programme refers to: "The general effort that marshals staff and projects toward some (often poorly) defined and funded goals" (Scriven 2002: 285). Royse et al. (2001: 5) define a programme as "an

---

81 In accordance with the Anglo-Saxon use of the concept of policy, a distinction is usually made between three dimensions: (1) policy, (2) politics, and (3) polity. (1) *Policy* refers to the content dimension of the concept. The main focus is on all state-society interactions, e.g. how problems are identified and dealt with by the political-administrative system, and what goal- or purpose-oriented activities the state uses to attempt to implement solutions. Such questions are examined by policy studies. (2) The term *politics* refers to the process aspect of policy. Politics research is concerned with the issue of what rules are employed to solve conflicts, what role institutions play, how interests become established etc. (3) *Polity* covers the formal aspect of policy, and is concerned with the structure it takes (cf. Druwe 1987: 393 ff.). An excellent introductory article to (German) policy studies is that of Jann (1994: 308 ff.). Cf. also e.g. Dye 1978; Windhoff-Héritier 1983 & 1993; Hartwich 1985; Feick & Jann 1988; Schmidt 1988; Derlien 1991; Schubert 1991 and 2003; Dunn 2004.

organized collection of activities designed to reach certain objectives". Projects are characterised as "the primary means through which governments (...) attempt to translate their plans and policies into programs of action" (Rondinelli 1983: 3). Regardless of how extensive or detailed development plans and strategies for action are, "they are of little value unless they can be translated into projects or programs that can be carried out" (ibid.).

In an *instrumental* sense, programmes and projects are bundles of measures designed to achieve specified targets, which are intended to help initiate innovations within social systems. In an *organisational* sense, they represent entities that are equipped with material and personnel resources, and are embedded in an organisation (executing agency), which in turn is part of a larger system context. Programme/project interventions can produce impacts both within the executing agency and in its environment (e.g. among target groups, service recipients, claimants).

According to Royse et al. (2001: 5 ff.), *good programmes* exhibit the following *features*:
- Qualified personnel
- Their own budget
- A stable allocation of funds
- Their own identity
- An empirically-based appraisal of requirements
- A 'programme theory' on the causal effectiveness of the programme
- A service philosophy
- An empirically-based evaluation system for reviewing programme results.

Programmes differ from institutional support in that they are temporary and pursue specified goals (cf. Kuhlmann & Holland 1995: 14). Although programmes are at the centre of theoretical considerations in this book, and for the sake of linguistic simplicity are referred to in the majority of cases, the concept to be developed is also applicable for the evaluation of institutionalised, open-ended, continuous tasks, as well as of individual, temporary intervention measures.

In order to achieve intended goals – within service provision or programmes – personnel and material inputs are employed. Goal attainment can relate to the production of certain services (outputs) and/or the triggering of certain impacts (outcomes). Because the notion of *impacts*, as the dependent variable in a development process, plays a central role in the monitoring and evaluation system to be conceived here, it will be discussed in more detail below *(chapter 3.2)*. I will then present the individual theoretical approaches which are to form the fundamental basis of the impact-oriented concept for the evaluation of service provision, measures and programmes developed here. In the course of this, the following assumptions are made.

In order to be able to establish impacts, at least two states of affairs must be compared with each other at different points in time. Impacts manifest themselves in changes over time, which means any impact analysis must take a process perspective. It stands to reason, then, that the theoretical approach of *'life-cycle research'* be applied. Although this model was developed for the analysis of human life-cycles, it has come to be employed in many other fields as well. In this case it is to be used for the analysis of programme processes. Chronologically, programmes follow a typical development pattern, just as the life-cycle of an individual does. In the same way as the life-cycle of a person is made up of a series of decisions between institutionally-defined alternatives (cf. Meulemann 1990: 89), 'life-cycles' of programmes (and the evolution of service provision) result from a sequence of decisions on the realisation of a programme concept, and on various planning and implementation steps up to the completion of the programme. The *life-cycle perspective* can thus also be used as a heuristic model for the evaluation of programmes. This concept should help in examining and assessing the development of measures and programmes *(chapter 3.3)*.

For the planning and implementation of programmes, organisations are required - referred to here as 'executing agencies'. The development and progress of programmes is dependent on structures within the organisation, and, conversely, exerts influence on these structures, as well as interacting with conditions external to the organisation. Thus, the use of *concepts of organisational theory* is appropriate, in order to analyse relationships internal to the organisation as well as those between the organisation and its environment *(chapter 3.4)*.

Internal structures and organisation-environment relationships also play a crucial role in the case of service provision. As discussed in chapter 2.2.1, external persons or organisations, i.e. those outside of the organisation providing the service, are involved in service rendering. Due to the fact that services are therefore always created through a process of interaction, the organisation-environment relationship is of particular significance in this context too.

The parameters obtained from concepts of organisational theory are to be used to determine the competence of organisations that carry out programmes or render services. Because programme interventions trigger effects on the implementing organisation (e.g. in order to improve its effectiveness), the parameters also serve the identification of internal (executing agency-related) changes.

Programme interventions as a rule have the goal of improving conditions identified as being deficient. To bring about positive outcomes, 'innovations' are introduced. It should thus be clarified what is to be understood by this. If the utility created by innovations is to benefit as many people as possible rather than just a small, isolated target group, the conditions under which as wide a dispersal of innovations as possible occurs should be examined. Concepts of *innovation and diffusion research* prove to be suitable theoretical starting points for this purpose *(chapter 3.5)*.

The objective is thus not simply to check whether the intended *goals and target groups* have been successfully *reached* with the help of the programme intervention or service, or to determine whether the target groups (customers) experience a benefit and are therefore *satisfied* with the changes (innovations) implemented; it should also be examined whether, and to what extent, diffusion of the innovations occurs. That is to say, the observation of impacts goes beyond the determination of direct effects on target groups to also detect the *scope of impact* or *diffusion*.

Sustainability, in the sense in which it is applied here, refers to a particular type of impacts, ones that can only be measured when support has been terminated and a programme or measure completed. It can therefore only be established using ex-post evaluation. As sustainability has become a much-used, and sometimes abused, term, the concept of sustainability used here will be presented in detail *(chapter 3.6)*.

On the basis of these three theoretical concepts (life-cycle, organisational and innovation/diffusion research), as well as the multidimensional sustainability model, the assessment criteria used (in chapter 4) to constitute a set of evaluation guidelines will be derived. Prior to this, *evaluation assessment criteria* will be compared with those of business management concepts of quality development/quality management. Here it becomes apparent that the evaluation criteria can also be used to measure the quality of organisations' outputs and outcomes, as well as the quality of the processes of service provision. The evaluation concept developed here thus facilitates not only the theoretically-based derivation of assessment criteria that can be used to form a set of evaluation guidelines, but also the establishment of *quality crtieria* which, due to their orientation towards output and outcome, are particularly suitable for appraising the activities of non-profit organisations *(chapter 3.7)*.

3.2 Impacts

In order to manufacture products or render services, companies and non-profit organisations employ *human and material inputs*, e.g. in the form of qualified labour with specific knowledge and skills, as well as in the form of machines, equipment and tools. This can be illustrated with the help of a few examples. Human and material resources (inputs) are employed, for instance, to create kindergarten places, to teach schoolchildren, to drill wells, and to build streets. The *'output'* can accordingly be specified numerically as the number of children looked after, schoolchildren taught, wells drilled, or metres of new road built. Yet this tells us nothing about the *impacts* (or 'outcomes') produced, e.g. about which children are cared for and taught, and whether they are learning anything. The number of wells drilled reveals nothing about whether water is actually accessed, drinkable, and whether it benefits the intended target groups, e.g. the poor. The construction of a road can, as is well-known, lead to a range of positive as well as negative impacts on the surrounding environment.

Outputs and impacts are frequently confused with each other. At times this confusion exists to such an extent that impacts (or outcomes) are referred to as "the products of a 'non-profit organisation', which it produces for the purpose of its non-commercial or charitable aims" (Gohl 2000: 35). Yet the products of an organisation do not consist of impacts. Impacts are rather the results of outputs, i.e. of services provided or goods produced. Nobody would suggest characterising drunks as the products of a brewery; rather, drunkenness is at best an impact of these products.

Owen and Rogers (1999: 264) thus come up witht the following definition: "Outputs are products of the program's activities, such as the number of meals provided, classes taught, participants served or materials distributed." Rossi, Freeman and Lipsey (1999: 201) phrase their definition similarly: "Program outputs are the products or services delivered to program participants or other such activities viewed as part of the program's contribution to society."

So, to be able to make statements on the *quality of programmes* or individual measures, it is not sufficient to simply measure output, as the crucial determinant of quality is whether a programme or service achieves its intended impacts (cf. Rossi, Freeman and Lipsey 1999: 275). As argued in the previous chapter, it is also not sufficient to deal only with impacts produced among 'customers' (which is the primary focus of the quality management models discussed). Rather, a broad scope of impact should be investigated, incorporating not only unintended outcomes but also socio-political and other external effects.

Based on these considerations, it can be stated that *'impacts' should on no account be confused with the 'outputs' of a programme*. While 'outputs' represent services or products of programme activities – such as the number of sick persons cared for, the number of disabled persons newly employed, or the number of environment consultations carried out – 'impacts' (or outcomes) represent changes resulting from these services, e.g. an improvement in people's state of health, changed attitudes to disabled persons, or an improved ecological situation.

If a balance of programme impacts is produced, *unintended consequences* should not be neglected, as a programme's quality cannot be viewed in isolation, but rather only in its full complexity, of which unexpected or undesired effects also form a part. Impacts can thus be differentiated according to whether they are *intended (planned)*, and consistent with the goals of the programme or service, or *unintended (unplanned)*. Intended impacts are usually appraised positively with regard to goal attainment, while unintended impacts can turn out to be either positive – i.e. supportive of goal attainment – or negative, i.e. running counter to goal attainment. Negative intended impacts are of course possible too, e.g. if certain disadvantages associated with a programme are consciously tolerated. Whether an impact is judged to be intended or unintended, positive or negative, is of course dependent on the goals of the programme or service, and not least on the perspective of the observer.

Positive intended impacts would be present if, for example, a funding increase in schools had not only led to more teachers being employed, but also to classes becoming smaller and pupils learning more. A negative unintended effect may turn out to be that teachers have been siphoned from other regions through the measure, and are now in short supply there, meaning standards worsen. Another undesired effect could be that less-qualified teachers are taken on because not enough qualified ones are available, meaning that education quality in the affected schools drops rather than improving as intended.

Positive intended effects of a road construction project could be that traffic between a town and nearby countryside is relieved, meaning farmers can enjoy better market access and sell more products, with the region's affluence therefore increasing. An unintended positive effect would have arisen – depending on the measure's aims – if lots of small transport and bus companies are then founded, creating further jobs and thus income. At the same time, the increased volume of traffic may also produce negative effects, such as pollution and traffic accidents.

Impacts can alter *structures, processes,* and/or *individual behaviour.* A structural change would have taken place if, for example, school laws or curricula had been altered to increase the practical component of lessons. Process impacts would have been achieved if, for instance, the subject matter were taught more interactively and less frontally. For this to happen, the behaviour of individual teachers would have to change; they would have to teach according to the new curricula and adjust the style of their lessons.

According to this perception, impacts can be defined analytically along three dimensions (cf. fig. 3.1).

1st dimension: structure-process-behaviour
Impacts can relate to structures (e.g. of organisations or social subsystems), processes, and/or individual behaviour.

2nd dimension: planned – unplanned
Impacts can be planned (intended) or unplanned (unintended).

3rd dimension: positive – negative
The planned or unplanned impacts can support (+) or run counter to (-) the goals of the programme or service.

Figure 3.1: Impact dimensions

Impact dimension	Planned	Unplanned
Structure	+ -	+ -
Process	+ -	+ -
Behaviour	+ -	+ -

Further differentiating factors are also significant. Impacts can, for example, be differentiated according to their type, e.g. based on whether they are of an economic, social, ecological, cultural, or political nature. Furthermore, they can be classified according to their duration, e.g. whether they appear in the short, medium or long term. And finally, they can be differentiated based on the level of their occurrence, i.e. whether they are identified on a society-wide basis (within social subsystems), that is to say at the macro level, in organisations or groups (meso level), or among individuals (attitudes and behaviour = individual level).

It should also be noted that impacts can occur directly or indirectly. An example of a direct effect would be if schoolchildren learn more because they receive more tuition.

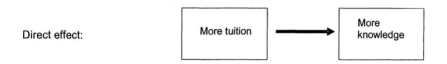

An indirect effect would be present if an increase in knowledge among the schoolchildren were to be the result of teachers being given new didactic methods which they then apply in their lessons.

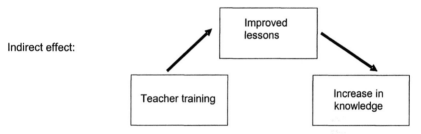

An *impact-based evaluation*[82] endeavours ideally to register all outcomes that occur. However, in practise this will never be possible. In most cases the data required for this are lacking, or existing information is not relayed (for a variety of reasons). Moreover, due to financial and time considerations, a client will hardly be willing to fund such an evaluation. Yet the most profound reason is that an evaluation measuring all impacts that occur could only ever be successful in a laboratory experiment, within which all influencing factors (independent variables) can be accurately controlled and all impacts (dependent variables) precisely measured. However, such a research design can hardly be applied in practice within the framework of evaluation research (cf. chapter 4.6). Experimental designs would also be ideal for solving the second main problem of evaluation – the identification of causal relationships between programme or service interventions (independ-

---

82 It is important to note that impact-based evaluations are not compelled to follow a summative approach; formative evaluations can also be oriented towards impacts.

ent variables) and recorded impacts (dependent variables); i.e. the issue of how cause factors of impacts can be determined as clearly as possible, and competing explanations eliminated (cf. e.g. Hellstern & Wollmann 1984: 25; OECD 1986: 34; White 1986: 4; Staudt et al. 1988: 32; Weiss 1998: 180 ff.; Rossi, Freeman & Lipsey 1999: 235 ff.; Owen & Rogers 1999: 263 ff.; Ross, Lipsey & Freeman 2004: 233 ff.).

As the *aim of impact evaluations* is to establish as reliably as possible whether an intervention causes its intended impacts, the influence of other factors that may also be responsible for the identified changes is to be excluded. That is to say, sophisticated causal attribution needs to be carried out within the mesh of observed outcomes. This task represents one of the greatest challenges of an evaluation. This is primarily due to the fact that the social world exhibits a high degree of complexity, with most social phenomena based on multiple causes. What is more, interventions only usually have a narrow scope of influence, and low potential to elicit change. Programme or service impacts are often only faintly detectable, and there is a danger of them not even being recognised at all in amongst the general 'noise'. Social science does possess numerous explanatory models for social phenomena, as well as refined methods for measuring them. However, within the scope of evaluations they are often insufficiently applicable, an issue which will be discussed further later on.

These problems complicate the identification of impacts and their causal attribution. *'Net effects'*, which are purely a result of the intervention, are to be distinguished from the *'gross outcome'*, which encompasses all impacts:

> "Net effects are the changes on outcome measures that can be reasonably attributed to the intervention, free and clear of the influence of any other causal factors that may also influence outcomes" (Rossi, Freeman and Lipsey 1999: 240 f.).

Alongside these are *effects* caused *by other factors* ('extraneous confounding factors'). This refers to all impacts that additionally arise independent of the intervention. There are also *design effects*, i.e. measurement errors and artefacts that can be attributed to the research process itself. This situation can be illustrated as follows (cf. fig. 3.2):

Figure 3.2: Effect equation

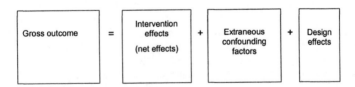

Here, the aim of an evaluation is to adjust the gross outcome for these extraneous confounding factors and design effects, in order to isolate the net effects and their causes. In this way, competing explanations for the observed impacts can be eliminated.

These impacts may also be the result of endogenous and/or exogenous change, or the occurrence of 'historic events'. There is reason for an *endogenous* explanation if a critical situation, which is to be remedied with certain intervention measures, corrects itself of its own accord. Many people recover from serious illness, for instance, without receiving any treatment from a doctor. In medicine, this endogenous transition is referred to as 'spontaneous remission'. Therefore, when new medicines are tested in pharmacological experiments, the body's self-healing powers are considered as belonging to the 'gross outcome'.

Taking the example of road construction used here, the intended goal may be to improve the affluence of farmers by giving them easier access to the town through building the road, with the market then growing and prosperity increasing. However, a process of endogenous change may also be responsible for the observed increase in affluence, with farmers growing more profitable or marketable fruits, or having tapped new markets or found new distribution channels themselves.

Furthermore, the increase in affluence among farming families could be a consequence of *exogenous* change. General structural trends such as a macroeconomic boom may have created greater demand for agricultural products, and could thus be responsible for the increased prosperity of farmers. Or perhaps an extended period of favourable climatic conditions has pushed up crop yields.

Finally, a *sudden event* can amplify or dilute the effects of an intervention. The construction of a further road, for example, could ease access to the town, and therefore the market, for another region as well, leading to excess supply and thus falling prices. Or the road may be destroyed by a storm so that it can no longer be used. A positive scenario is also conceivable, e.g. if, following a change of government, the farmers in the region affected are granted a privilege, due to political, relational or ethnic affiliation, leading to their earnings potential increasing.

The *measurement and assessment of impacts* and their *causal attribution* are the *central tasks of evaluation*. In order to fulfil these tasks, a theoretical framework is required that governs the search for intended and potential unintended impacts and eases the identification of causes. Various theoretical approaches are utilised to this end, and are presented below.

3.3 Life-cycle theories

The term *'life-cycle research'* refers to an interdisciplinary theory and research agenda that has emerged over the last twenty years, whose goal is "the depiction and explanation of individual life situations and life events, as well as of overall social processes, within a standardised, formal, categorical, empirical frame of reference" (cf. Mayer 1990b: 9).

Life-cycle research[83] refers to the examination of social processes that span the whole life-cycle, or significant parts thereof, and which are viewed in the context of institutional change and special historical conditions. *Life-cycles* are the result of a whole range of influences. Mayer (2001: 446 ff.) identifies the following influencing factors: economic and politically-determined opportunity structures, culturally-shaped beliefs, legal age standards, institutionalised position sequences and crossovers, individual decisions, processes of socialisation, and selection mechanisms. Under this perspective, the individual life-cycle, as a succession of activities and occurrences in various spheres of life and institutionalised areas of activity, becomes an object of analysis (cf. Mayer 2001: 446).

The life-cycle represents a series of conditions or features of a person, that remain for a certain length of time, and which alter over time (cf. Blossfeld & Huinink 2001: 6). Based on a logic of individual action, it is assumed that the life-cycle of a person is the result of their efforts, given the relevant underlying situational conditions, to realise an optimal life structure according to their subjective measures. They go about achieving this by using the resources available to them, and are guided by individual goals and preferences.

According to Huinink (1995), the structural characteristics and conditions of life planning and organisation can be described more precisely in three points:

(a) The life-cycle of an individual is understood as a *self-referential process*. It is defined as a "continuous series of phases delimited by events" (cf. Friedrichs & Kamp 1978: 16), between which an *endogenous causal relationship* exists:
> "Later conditions, as well as goals and expectations, are primarily to be understood and explained based on conditions, decisions, resources and experiences in earlier personal history" (Mayer 1987: 60).
Phases and sections of the life-cycle are thus viewed in a common context.

(b) The life-cycle of a person is also a *multidimensional process* that develops from numerous interrelated spheres of life. Each sphere can be understood as a sub-process of the life-cycle. So, for example, educational career, family life, the buying process, and history of illness can be viewed as such sub-processes. The various spheres of life of a person are usually not independent, but rather are linked in a reciprocal relationship with each other.

---

83 For information on the basic heuristic assumptions, cf. Mayer 1990b: 10 ff. Good overviews can be found in, for example, Voges 1983a & b, 1987a & b; Sørensen et al. 1986; Mayer 1987, 1990a & b; Binstock & George 1990; Blossfeld & Huinink 2001: 5 ff. For information on its application, cf. e.g. Blossdfeld 1989 & 1990c; Mayer & Müller 1989; Brüderl 1991; Diekmann & Weick 1993; Lauterbach 1994; Allmendinger 1995; Heinz 1995; Huinink 1995; Diewald et al. 1996; Mayer 1997; Wagner 1997; Brückner & Meyer 1998; Hullen 1998; Konietzka 1999; Kohli & Kühnemund 2000; Blossfeld & Drobnic 2001; Hillmert 2001; Sackmann 2001.

Individual life-cycle dimensions can have differing priorities for life organisation in different life situations and depending on age.

(c) The life-cycle of a person is embedded in highly complex *multi-level* social *processes*. It takes place, for example, under the formative influence of:

- Other people (parents, partners, children, friends etc.) with which the person has interactive relations, to whatever extent
- Corporate institutions and social organisations (intermediate entities, administrative bodies, companies etc.)
- Living conditions in the social and regional contexts in which a person lives or between which her or she changes
- Developed, changing social structures and historic events, which constitute socio-structural, political, legal, cultural and economic conditions underlying life organisation (cf. e.g. Preisendörfer & Burgess 1988; Huinink & Wagner 1989; Strohmeier 1989; Mayer & Huinink 1990; Brüderl 1991; Huinink 1995: 154 f.; Nauck 1997; Blossfeld & Drobnic 2001; Mayer 2001: 447).

Conversely, the individual life structure of a person affects the life organisation of other people, as well as existing structures and processes, and contributes towards social transition in a community. Individuals in principle also have the option of choosing other social and spatial living contexts, or of altering them.

The life-cycles of people are complex, highly non-linear processes. Blossfeld and Huinink (2001: 8) identify the following sources of this non-linearity: "Self-reference, temporally local interdependency of spheres of life, and vertical interdependency between different social process levels." Time is the medium that links the individual levels together. Thus in life-cycle research, changes over time in the conditions of individual actors are at the forefront of considerations.

Life-cycle research has made significant contributions to the examination of social change, especially in the areas of education, labour participation and the job market, partnerships, marriage and families, later phases of life, and age.[84] In addition, the life-cycle

---

84 Cf. e.g. Kohli 1978a & b, 1985; Müller 1978 & 1980; Baltes et al. 1986; Sørensen et al. 1986; Voges 1987; Barnett 1988; Elder & Caspi 1990; Hagestad 1990; Fuchs-Heinritz 1990; Meulemann 1990; Blossfeld 1989, 1990 a, b, c, 1993; Carroll et al. 1990; Brüderl 1991; Diekmann & Weick 1993; Blossfeld & Shavit 1993; Lauterbach 1994; Heinz 1995; Mayer 1990 a & b, 1997, 2001; Brückner & Mayer 1998; Hullen 1998; Blossfeld & Stockmann 1998/99; Konietzka 1999; Kohli & Künemund 2000; Sackmann & Wingens 2001; Hillmert 2001. For a selection of research work and additional literature, cf. the summary essay of Blossfeld and Huinink 2001.

model has been applied fruitfully in psychology[85], business administration, and organisational theory. In economics, for example, the sequence of market development stages (cf. Heuß 1965) and product cycles is examined, and ecological life-cycle balances are created to facilitate the evaluation and comparison of the lifelong effects of different product versions (cf. Schmidheiny 1992: 27). In organisational research, the life-cycle model is used within the scope of evolution and population ecology approaches.[86]

The conceptual assumptions of life-cycle research can also be utilised for programme development. *Programmes* follow, like the life-cycles of individuals, a self-referential process. Programmes progress from the initial idea, via conceptual planning and individual implementation steps, to the point in time at which their support is terminated. The time axis connects the individual phases, during each of which the implementation of specific planning and action steps ensures the successive accumulation of resources.

Programme development also represents a multidimensional process. It is made up of various programme areas (e.g. programme strategy development, organisational development, funding etc.), which are interdependent and subject to influence from each other. As in the case of individuals' life-cycles, separate 'spheres' have differing significance in different 'life situations' and depending on age.

The development of a programme is also embedded in complex, multi-level social processes. A programme is not developed independently of other existing or planned programmes. Different actors often pursue diverse aims through a programme, and programmes are developed subject to underlying social, institutional and organisational conditions. Social and regional contexts must be taken into consideration, and programmes have to adapt to economic, social, political, legal and cultural changes.

Programmes can of course also have a formative influence on structures and processes. Conversely, because they are exposed to external influences, the development of programmes is not always predictable. They are nevertheless *planned*, which is a way of trying to ensure that programme goals are attained, if possible, within specified time limits. In this respect, programme development differs from life-cycles, as it is often planned rationally from the start with reference to each individual implementation step – sometimes remotely in a planning institution, sometimes participatively in conjunction with stakeholders.

Once the programme concept has been developed and financing provided, *implementation* can commence. Those responsible for the programme endeavour – like an individual

---

85   Cf. Brandtstädter (1990) for information on the approaches and problems of "life-span development psychology", as well as Heckhausen 1990 and Baltes & Baltes 1986; Diewald et al. 1996.

86   Cf. e.g. Freeman & Hannan 1975; Hannan & Freeman 1977, 1988a & b, 1989; Aldrich 1979; Kimberley; Miles et al. 1980; Freeman 1982; McKelvey & Aldrich 1983; Kasarda & Bidwell 1984; Carroll 1984 & 1988; Astley 1985; Kieser 1985, 1988, 1989, 1992, 1993g: 243 ff.; Barnett 1988. For summaries, cf. Bea & Göbel 2002: 148 ff.; Kieser 1999: 253 ff.; Kieser 2002.

in his or her personal life-cycle – to realise as optimal a 'life' (in this case programme) structure as possible. Monitoring and evaluation tools are employed to this end, in order to collect data for the 'replanning', rerouting, and control of the programme. Programmes do not always follow a linear course. Far from it; sudden occurrences and changed underlying conditions demand not only course changes, but sometimes necessitate questioning of the intended programme goals themselves.

As age increases, i.e. as a programme's duration lengthens, the outcomes desired for goal attainment should increasingly materialise, so that the programme – if it is of a temporary nature – can come to a *close*. Even after the cessation of support, it is to be expected that a programme will continue to have effects. Very often, support programmes are carried out with the very aim of permanently transforming structures, or of bringing about changes in behaviour among certain target groups. An energy saving programme, for example, should induce people to be frugal with energy even after the support has ended, whilst a programme aimed at integrating the disabled into the process of work should give companies the chance of gaining positive experiences with disabled people so that they change their attitudes over the long term. By the same token, a programme aimed at improving the efficiency of tax administration should change the existing administrative structures and processes so that the goal is achieved even after the programme's completion.

Figure 3.3: Life-cycle model

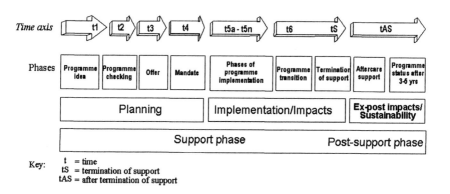

In summary, the *life-cycle* of a programme can be roughly split up into *three main phases* (cf. fig. 3.3): (1) *planning* and (2) *implementation phases* during the course of the programme, and (3) the time following the termination of programme support (*ex-post impact phase*). The start of a programme's life-cycle can be identified as the point at which the programme idea is formulated (t1). The various 'life' phases of a programme – such as programme checking, the drafting of concepts, if necessary the formulation of an offer and the assignment of an order to carry out the programme, the individual phases of implementation (t2-tn), the preparation for the termination of support (tS), as well as the period subsequent to programme support (tAS) – to name but a few – are each characterised by typical problems. They can be delimited, and may well be analysed using a range of process-produced data, which are available, for example, in proposals, quotes, programme descriptions, operational plans, progress reports, monitoring documents, evaluation reports, and closing reports.

The *heuristic advantage of the life-cycle perspective* consists primarily of two aspects:
(1) The life-cycle hypothesis offers the opportunity of recognising the *post-support phase* - during which the sustainability of a programme becomes evident - as an *integral component* of the programme's *life-cycle*. Like the sequences in the life-cycle of an individual, the separate programme phases build on each other, and are arranged over time to successively implement the goals of the programme.
(2) The life-cycle perspective also emphasises the *causal linkage of the individual phases*. It thus becomes clear that the *sustainability* of a programme is influenced *by programme selection*, and that the *material and immaterial structures created* during the *duration of support* form the basis for long-term programme impacts.

3.4 Theoretical conception of organisations

3.4.1 The underlying impact model

Institutionalised services and programmes are generated or carried out by organisations, which are therefore also referred to here as implementing organisations or executing agencies. Existing or specially-formed organisational entities are commissioned with implementation, with the objective of attaining specific goals. Frequently, attempts are made to introduce or bring about innovations (cf. chapter 3.5). These can aim to elicit, on the one hand, *internal changes* in an implementing organisation (e.g. state institution, association, foundation, or other non-governmental organisation), or, on the other hand, changes in *external social systems* (e.g. organisations or subsystems of society). That is to say, implementing organisations (programme-executing agencies) can be objects of change, as well as serving as transmitters for the diffusion of change processes.

This perspective can be illustrated using a concrete example. The chambers of industry, commerce and trade (executing agencies), for instance, decide to carry out an environmental advice programme. The objective of the programme is, on the one hand, the lasting establishment of consultation structures in the chambers, and, on the other hand, the provision of effective advice for companies on environmental issues so that they adapt their procedures and structures.

Special organisational units (environmental advisory bodies of the chambers) are formed to implement the programme, which then carry out consultations with firms. In this way, innovations (e.g. energy-saving production methods, the use of environmentally-friendly materials etc.) should be triggered among the companies receiving advice. The more companies that introduce these innovations, the greater the diffusion effects. Additional diffusion effects (multiplier effects) would arise if firms that were not advised on the issue were to adopt these innovations too (e.g. because they prove to be profitable or more cost-effective).

As *organisations* carry out programmes or offer services - which are intended to produce impacts - they and their relationships with other organisations and social subsystems are of particular significance for impact evaluations. According to this perspective, programmes trigger effects within and through organisations, and are, conversely, exposed via their executing agencies to external influences (e.g. demands) from surrounding social systems. These systems may be other organisations (e.g. those receiving advice, such as small and medium-sized businesses, skilled crafts enterprises), or political, economic, social, cultural, ecological, regional, international (etc.) frameworks. Programme interventions, the executing agency, and external influencing factors thus represent the independent variables and underlying conditions of the intended and unintended results achieved (outcomes, impacts).

This interdependency is illustrated in figure 3.4. At the centre of the 'model' is the programme, which is embedded – possibly as a sub-unit – in an executing agency. Within the framework of programme goals, the objective is to trigger innovations inside and outside of the executing agency using coordinated packages of measures. In doing do, the programme's potential impacts are influenced, on the one hand, by the executing agency – the internal environment – and, on the other hand, by the systems which surround the executing agency and thus the programme – the external environment. External environmental fields can either have a supportive effect on goals, or serve to impede or prevent goal attainment, acting as 'counteractive forces'.

In order to be able to analyse this situation, and to identify and explain relationships, *organisational theory approaches* are most appropriate. A closer look at at these approaches shows that organisations can, depending on cognitive interest, be analysed from entirely different angles.

The theoretical bureaucratic approach is primarily interested in organisations as systems of authority; theoretical structural (Tayloristic) approaches concentrate on the task fulfilment aspect of organisations; the human relations approach fosuses on the coexistence of people in organisations; the situational approach views organisations as open systems that act under certain contextual conditions; and the theoretical evolutionary approach extends this perspective with ecological development models. The decision theory approach is above all concerned with how individuals with diverse interests make rational decisions; the property rights approach is interested in the rights of disposal in organisations; the transaction costs approach views organisations as an alternative institutional arrangement to the market; agency theory deals primarily with the the institution of contract; whilst the interpretive approach centres on the everyday analysis of organisational members.[87]

Figure 3.4: Impact model[88]

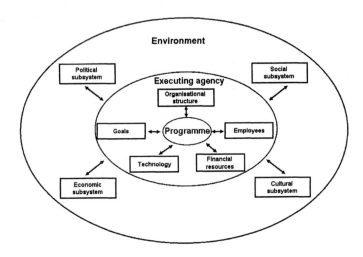

3.4.2 Organisational elements

If social change is understood as a transfer process that occurs essentially via organisations (cf. Stockmann 1987), which can be initiated or amplified by programmes and projects within organisations, then the concepts of organisational theory most suitable for explaining programme impacts are those that conceive of organisations as *open social systems* that are intended to be *rationally structured* in order to achieve specific goals (cf. Thompson 1967: 66 ff.; Scott 2003: 33 ff.; 82 ff., 141 ff.; Kieser & Kubicek 1992: 4 ff.;

---

87   Cf. the very clear synoptic description in Bea & Göbel (2002: 201 ff.). Good overviews are also those of Kieser 2002, and the compilation of chief organisational theory works of Türk 2000. Cf. also Frese 1992; Walter-Busch 1996 and Schreyögg 1999.

88   The subsystems depicted here represent merely a selection. Which subsystems are of importance to an organisational model depends on the type of programme being carried out.

Kieser 2002: 169 ff.; 1993f: 161 ff.; Kieser & Walgenbach 2003: 6 ff.; Müller-Jentsch 2003: 20 ff.). They have a *formal structure* and employ a certain *technology* in order to align the activities of their *members* with the *goals* pursued.[89] The *financial resources* available to an organisation are not an issue addressed by prevalent sociological organisational concepts. However, as this dimension is of central significance in terms of the task fulfilment and survival of organisations, it is included in the analysis carried out here. The elements that constitute an organisation can thus be derived:

- Goals
- Members (participants)
- Formal (organisational) structure
- Technology
- Financial resources.[90]

Since organisations are dealt with as 'open systems' in this book, the *'environment'*, as an external feature, represents a further indispensable component of this conception.[91] In the following section, these *organisational elements* will be briefly outlined.

Goals and strategies

Almost all definitions of organisations identify *goal* or *purpose orientation* as a defining feature.[92] The pursuit of goals is seen as the principle reason for forming organisations (cf. Barnard 1938: 37). Objectives create a common point of reference among participants (cf. Blau & Scott 1963: 2 f., Mayntz 1977: 43 & 58 ff., Scott 2003: 293), and provide the uppermost maxim of behaviour. The organisational structure is a means of controlling the behaviour of members with respect to goals (cf. Kieser & Walgenbach 2003: 7 ff.; Bea & Göbel 2002: 210).

---

89 Cf. e.g. Barnard 1938: 4; March & Simon 1958: 4; Blau & Scott 1963: 5; Etzioni 1964: 3; Hage & Aiken 1969: 366 ff.; Mayntz & Ziegler 1976: 11; Mayntz 1977: 36 & 40; Scott 2003: 19 ff.; Kieser & Kubicek 1992: 4; Bea & Göbel 2002: 2; Abraham & Büschges 2004: 109 ff.

90 In organisational research, each of these elements has been emphasised by individual authors as the most important feature, at the cost of neglecting the other elements (cf. Scott 2003: 24).

91 Cf. e.g. Udy 1959; Woodward 1965; Thompson 1967; Perrow 1967; Pugh et al. 1969; Blau 1970; Hickson et al. 1971; Gabraith 1973; March & Olson 1976; Meyer & Rowan 1977; Pfeffer & Salancik 1978; Mayntz 1977; Scott 2003; Kieser & Kubicek 1992; Kieser 1993f & 1999; Bea & Göbel 2002.

92 For information on the various concepts and problems associated with the notion of goals, cf. above all Mayntz & Ziegler 1976: 36 ff.; Mayntz 1977: 58 ff.; Hauschildt & Hamel 1978: 237 ff.; Hauschildt 1980: 2419 ff.; Kubicek 1981: 458 ff.; Scott 2003: 292 ff.; Berger & Bernhard-Mehlich 1993: 141 ff.; Aldrich 1999; Bea & Göbel 2002: 14 ff. & 210; Endruweit 2004: 100 ff.; Abraham & Büschges 2004: 109 ff.

Goals perform *numerous functions* in organisations. They can:

- Provide criteria for the development of, and decisions between, alternative strategies for action (cognitive function)
- Have the function of a source of identification and motivation for participants
- Offer current justification for past actions
- Supply criteria for the assessment of job performance, members, and action programmes
- Constitute ideological guidelines with which participants align their work.

Members

Common to members of organisations is that their activities are pooled by means of the organisational structure to achieve goals. The *formal form of social integration* into an organisation is based on contractual relationships, e.g. on an employment contract or contract for work and labour, which grant the organisation or its representatives the right to continue to specify demands and guidelines, including organisational regulations, for the member (cf. Kieser & Walgenbach 2003: 12 ff.). Membership does not relate to the personality as a whole, however, but rather only to certain actions and activities of the member. According to a somewhat broad definition, all people who make a contribution to goal attainment, in accordance with an organisation's rules, can be classed as members of the organisation (cf. Etzioni 1961, Steinmann & Gerum 1978: 5 ff., Simon 1981, Scott 2003: 21; Müller-Jentsch 2003: 26 f.; Abraham & Büschges 2004: 197 ff.).

Formal (organisational) structure

The organisational structure (or formal structure of an organisation) refers to the "patterned or regularized aspects of the relationship existing among participants in an organization" (Scott 2003: 18). The organisational structure relates, on the one hand, to the relatively stable network of social relationships that assigns individual members a certain position and status, and, on the other hand, to the system of common values and orientations that acts as a standard for the behaviour of organisational members (cf. Blau & Scott 1963: 5).[93] *Formal structures* consist of relatively constant patterns that are established by set regulations to bring about certain modes of behaviour. In order to achieve this as rationally as possible, social relations between members are consciously arranged and institutionalised. In addition to this, a *structural pattern of informal relations* also exists.

As organisations produce their goods and services based on the *division of labour*, it is necessary to officially allocate the activities required for goal attainment among individual members, as well as to *coordinate* these activities. On top of procedural guidelines,

---

93 Davis (1949: 52 ff.) makes a distinction between the normative structure, which comprises the values, norms and role expectations, and the behavioural structure, which relates to actual conduct. He refers to the two components together as the social structure of an organisation. Scott (2003: 18 ff.) also uses this terminology. Here, the common notion of organisational structure is used instead.

the hierarchy is also a central instrument of coordination. Entities endowed with decision-making and directive authority form the *leadership system*, also known as configuration. The allocation of decision-making power - the distribution of authority in an organisation - is observed along the decision delegation dimension. The *decision delegation* is greater, the more decision-making authority is officially granted to the lower levels of the hierarchy on the basis of general regulations. The use of written organisational rules in the form of organisation diagrams, handbooks, guidelines, and job descriptions etc. determines the degree of *formalisation* of an organisation. So, the formal organisational structure can be analysed using the following five *structural parameters* (for more detail, cf. Lawrence & Lorsch 1967a and 1969, Hill et al. 1974, Grochla 1978: 30 ff., Türk 1978: 101 ff., Bea & Göbel 2002: 210 ff.; Kieser and Walgenbach 2003: 16 ff. & 71 ff.; Müller-Jentsch 2003: 39 ff.; Abraham & Büschges 2004: 130 ff.):[94]

- Division of labour (specialisation, internal differentiation)
- Coordination
- Leadership system (configuration)
- Division of competence (decision delegation)
- Formalisation.

Formal organisational structures not only arise by decree from holders of certain positions with the relevant authorisation, but also through members of the organisation explicitly agreeing among themselves on specific procedures. Rules can be the result of largely unconscious collective learning processes, with members over time developing routine programmes for certain recurrent tasks, repeating patterns of action that have proved appropriate in the past. Such patterns of action are often couched in tradition, and are passed on through socialisation processes during training and work (cf. Kieser & Walgenbach 2003: 21).

Technology

Every organisation is a social entity in which a certain kind of work is performed. Scott (2003: 22) thus characterises organisations as a place where work is carried out for the purpose of transforming material energy, and as a mechanism that converts inputs into outputs. This process necessitates *technical equipment* and an *agenda* for managing production and service provision. Every organisation that performs work thus has a *technology*[95] for carrying out this work (cf. Brinkerhoff & Goldsmith 1992: 372). While some organisations use material inputs to produce tools, machines, or other hardware, others

---

94   This conception of organisational structure ties in with the bureaucracy model of Max Weber (1976), as well as with organisation theory.

95   This enhanced conceptual understanding of technology was proposed by Perrow (1965), as well as by Thompson and Bates (1957/58: 325 ff.), and adopted by Scott (2003). Under the term technology, Perrow subsumes all techniques through which objects (symbols, people, or physical objects) are altered (with or without technical equipment).

perform socialisation work: "Their products consist of better informed individuals" (ibid.). Among this latter form of organisation are, for instance, schools, universities, and training institutes. Technologies encompass the procedures applied in an organisation, as well as the technical equipment employed (cf. Steffens 1980: 2236 f.; Müller-Jentsch 2003: 23). The technology of vocational training institutes and technical colleges, for example, comprises knowledge about procedures for communicating information and skills (as are contained in e.g. teaching programmes, curricula, training systems etc.), as well as knowledge about the techniques to be employed and the technical equipment used for this (e.g. machines, tools, apparatus etc.).

Financial resources

In sociological theories of organisations, financial resources, which an organisation requires for maintaining its functional capability, are undervalued. Without financial support or self-financing, no organisation can secure its survival in the long term. While business enterprises use the sale of their products to obtain the means with which they cover their day-to-day personnel and material costs and undertake new investments, non-profit organisations are reliant on state maintenance, on the charging of fees and membership contributions, or on the receipt of donations.

Environment

No organisation is *an autarchic entity*, but is rather located within a specific physical, technical, cultural and social environment to which it must attune itself (cf. Scott 2003: 23 & 228 ff., Mayntz 1977: 45, Mayntz & Ziegler 1977: 84 ff.). The *environment*[96] has an influence on organisations in many ways (cf. Endruweit 2004: 216 ff.; Abraham & Büschges 2004: 241 ff.). Members recruited by an organisation are not socialised in the organisation itself: "Employees come to the organization with heavy cultural and social baggage obtained from interactions in other social contexts" (Scott 2003: 23). Moreover, participants are often members of numerous organisations simultaneously. Conflicts of interest are therefore possible, which may weaken the commitment to a certain organisation.

In addition, not all organisations create their own technologies: "rather, they import them from the environment in the form of mechanical equipment, packaged programs and sets of instructions, and trained workers" (Scott 2003: 23). Even the goals of an organisation are influenced by other social systems. Finally, environmental traits are reflected in the organisational structure: "Structural forms, no less than technologies, are usually borrowed from the environment" (Scott 2003: 24). Other organisations are also part of this

---

96   Contingency theory, also referred to as the situational approach, has become a particularly influential 'school'. Good outlines are provided by Kieser 2002; Kieser & Kubicek 1992: 33 ff. Cf. also Stockmann 1987a: 30 ff.

environment, and are either in competition with each other, or combine to form a network[97] for achieving goals collectively.

3.4.3 Organisational effectiveness

For programmes or services to produce the desired (goal-compliant) outcomes, they must be implemented by capable organisations (under the given environmental conditions) as effectively as possible.

The issue of how well an organisation functions, measured against a certain standard, is examined within the framework of *effectiveness analyses* (cf. Scott 2003: 350 ff.).[98] A whole variety of criteria has been used for this purpose.[99] The continuing lack of consensus as to how a meaningful, valid instrument for measuring effectiveness should look is, according to Scott (2003: 355), primarily due to the various researchers developing quite different conceptions of organisations, with each conception implying a somewhat different set of criteria for evaluating organisational effectiveness. Bea and Göbel (2002: 17) deem the application of effectiveness criteria for appraising organisational models difficult, as the demands of the criteria contradict each other in part, and precise cause-effect relationships are unknown. That is to say, there is little foundation for assigning impacts to individual organisational characteristics with regard to the organisation's goal attainment. Moreover, the significance of individual criteria varies according to the situational context of the organisation.

Within the framework of the organisational concepts employed here, according to which organisations are viewed as instruments for achieving goals, the *'quantity and*

---

97 The meaning of networks will not be examined in more detail here. They are often understood as an additional level of activity coordination, 'above', 'alongside', and also 'within' organisations (cf. Rölle & Blättel-Mink 1998: 84). Inside of organisations, networks are normally simply informal groups (cf. Endruweit 2004: 26). For information on the network approach, cf. e.g. Jansen 2002: 88 ff.; Meyer 2002; Schmidt 1998: 55 ff.; Benz 1995: 194 f.; Pappi, König & Knoke 1990). For an overview of network analysis, cf. e.g. Carrington et al. 2005; Cross, Parker & Cross 2004; Diany & MacAdam 2004; Jansen 2002a, b, & 2002. For an introduction to organisational networks, cf. Müller-Jentsch 2003: 113 ff.

98 Efficiency tests go beyond this, measuring not only whether a targeted effect is actually achieved, but also whether it was done with a minimum of input (cf. Scott 2003). Efficiency is determined by the relationship between output and input (costs) (cf. Pfeiffer 1976: 42; Staehle & Grabatin 1979: 89 ff.; Welge & Fessmann 1980: 578 ff.; Endruweit 2004: 201).

99 Cf. Yuchtman & Seashore 1967: 891 ff.; Price 1968; Child 1972: 1 ff.; Steers 1975 & 1977; Spray 1976; Budäus & Dobler 1977: 61 ff.; Campbell 1977; Mayntz 1977; Scott 1977a; Cameron 1978: 604 & 1986: 87 ff.; Scott et al. 1978; Connolly et al. 1980: 211 ff.; Cameron & Whetten 1983; Zammuto 1984: 606 ff.; Lewin & Minton 1986: 514 ff.; Scott 2003; Scholz 1992: 539 ff.; Bünting 1995; Bea & Göbel 2002: 15 ff.).

quality of products' is a central criterion. This necessitates *qualified and motivated employees*, who *accept and actively support the organisation's goals*. As organisations are in an interdependent relationship with their environment, the *acquisition and processing of information* represents a crucial activity of all organisations. In addition, an *efficient use of resources* is necessary. As long-term success depends on their ability to recognise and react to changes in their task environment, *'innovation and learning capacity'*, *'adaptability'*, and *'flexibility'* are, among others, particularly fruitful criteria for effectiveness (cf. Bea & Göbel 2002: 16 f.; Scott 2003: 352, Yuchtman & Seashore 1967: 898, Weick 1977: 193 f.), and are to be used here for its measurement.

To be able to assess the ability of an organisation to develop and maintain structures that are effective over the long term, in interdependence with its environment, the *effectiveness of individual organisational elements* as well as of the *organisation as a whole* is to be evaluated. The capability to perform effectively is appraised using *structural indicators*:[100] "Included within this category are all measures based on organizational features or participant characteristics presumed to have an impact on organisational effectiveness." (Scott 2003: 367). Industrial enterprises, for example, may thus be assessed based on the value and age of their machines, hospitals on the adequacy of their facilities, and schools on the qualification of their teachers.

However, these indicators do not measure actual task performance, but rather merely the *potential capacity of structures*. As structural indicators are thus only of limited use as effectiveness benchmarks, they are supplemented with indicators with which process measurements can be carried out. These focus on the quantity and quality of activities performed in an organisation. *Process measurements* are thus concerned with the effort of achieving an effect, and not towards the effect itself. They evaluate primarily the endeavour, not the work performed. While *structural indicators* measure *what can potentially be done*, *process indicators* measure *what has been done*. Consider the following example: with the help of structural indicators, the competence of a training supervisor can be ascertained (potential ability). Using process indicators, the activities the training supervisor has actually carried out (performance) can then be measured. The personnel component of the organisation would then only be declared effective if staff are not only qualified but also act accordingly. The performance of skilled training in a vocational training institute thus requires not only the presence of qualified personnel, but also that these training supervisors actually teach and do not, for example, pursue other activities.

For the *assessment of organisational achievement potential* using structural and process-based indicators, the features defined here as *constitutive elements of an organisation* are used. That means that organisational capability is rated more highly, the greater the extent to which:

- A goal system has been sucessfully established, which is accepted and supported by the organisation's members

---

100 For information on the concept of indicators, cf. chapter 4.3.3.

- The organisation's members are qualified and motivated, and such members can be recruited and retained
- The organisation's structure and mode of operation facilitate an effective transformation of resources into output
- Technical equipment and programme concept correspond to service/production demands
- The organisation's costs can be covered
- All elements of an organisation are sufficiently adaptable and flexible to allow for innovations that become necessary due to changing environmental conditions to be introduced without affecting performance.[101]

The issue of the *achievement potential* of an organisation is connected *to* the *life-cycle perspective* applied here, as effectiveness can change considerably over time (cf. Mayntz 1977: 137). This is especially true in the case of programmes in which the improvement of the achievement potential of implementing organisations is an explicit aim. To establish whether an organisation is capable, i.e. whether it performs its tasks effectively, and how this has changed over time, the individual elements of an orgaisation are examined with regard to their *achievement potential at different time-points*. Performance appraisals can, for example, be carried out and compared with each other when the support/programme begins (baseline), at the end of the support/programme, and subsequent to the end of the support (programme). It should also be resolved whether changes in the effectiveness of individual criteria are attributable to programme interventions or other (environmental) factors.

The impact model developed earlier on allows for *different causal approaches*. Two analytical perspectives can be taken up successively (cf. figure 3.5): firstly, the programme interventions are viewed as independent variables (IV), and the organisational elements as dependent variables (DV), in order to examine whether the interventions (inputs) – given certain underlying conditions – have effected changes in the various dimensions of the implementing organisation. The creation of acceptance of programme goals in the organisation, the training of personnel to achieve these goals, the improvement of communication structures, the optimisation of coordination or labour division (organisational structure), the provision of technical tools, and the securing of financial resources can all constitute necessary prerequisites for the attainment of programme aims.

If the individual organisational elements have been successfully shaped by the programme interventions, this result represents an internal programme output, i.e. one that relates to the implementing organisation.

---

101 Similar criteria for measuring the "performance effectiveness of an organisation" are identified by Mayntz 1977: 137 f. Cf. also Pfeiffer 1976: 42 ff.; Türk 1978: 120 ff.; Grochla 1978: 23 f.; Scott 2003: 18 ff.; Kieser & Kubicek 1992: 57 ff.; Kieser 1999: 176; Bea & Göbel 2002: 15 ff.

Figure 3.5: Causal model

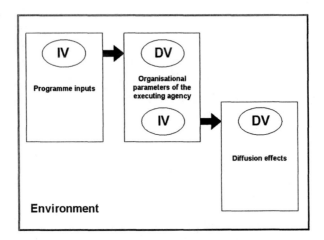

Under the subsequent analytical perspective, internal programme outputs (the organisational dimensions changed by programme inputs) become independent variables, with which changes should be brought about in areas outside of the implementing organisation. These external fields (e.g. the employment or education system, the ecosystem, the legal system) now assume the role of dependent variables. The diffusion effects of the implementing organisation in these (external) fields, which must firstly be specified, can be measured using indicators, and become the benchmark for the effectiveness of the implementing organisation. A training institution, for example, would be classed as effective if, within the framework of a qualification programme, it succeeds in providing the employment system with skilled personnel.

3.5 Theoretical conception of innovation and diffusion

3.5.1 Innovation

According to the conception of organisational theory developed here, programmes propagate *innovations* within and through organisations. *Diffusion research* is interested in the question of under what conditions processes of dispersal take place. After an explanation of the term "innovation", a model of diffusion is then introduced.

Traditionally, *innovation* is equated with verifiable technological progress. However, the concept of innovation is more complex than this, and incorporates not only scientific/technical, but also economic and social developments. 'Innovation' is thus used as a synonym for 'novelty'. According to Schumpeter's (1947: 151) much-cited, concise definition, innovations are "the doing of new things or the doing of things that are already being done in a new way". Hence, innovations are simply changes: something is, or is done, "different(ly) to in the past" (Bechmann & Grunwald 1998: 5). Viewed in this way, rediscoveries and reinventions also constitute innovations: tried and tested techniques, organisational principles, or procedures can become innovations by being transferred into 'new' spatial and/or (other) sociocultural contexts (e.g. developing countries). 'Newness' is indeed a necessary requirement of an innovation, yet it may just be a matter of 'relative' newness. What is regarded as an innovation is "ultimately determined by the point of reference used" (Ewers & Brenck 1992: 311), and this has a strongly subjective element, which in turn is subject to change over time. The question of how long something remains 'new' and innovative does not have a universally valid answer, but rather depends on the context, the points of reference applied, and not least on subjective assessments (cf. Deitmer 2004: 32; Koschatzky & Zenker 1999; Ewers & Brenck 1992: 311.).

Since Schumpeter (1911, 1939) developed a theory of innovation to explain economic cycles, political and scientific interest has concentrated on technical innovations. A distinction was drawn between *technical and social innovations* as early as Ogburn (1923, 1957), who described social change as "cultural lag". A fundamental 'genetic' difference between the two forms of innovation is that technical innovations consist of matter, i.e. are objective, and social innovations are non-objective or abstract (cf. Zapf 1989: 170 ff.). Analogous to this, Henderson (1988) drew a distinction between cultural 'hardware' and 'software'. Common to both forms of innovation is that they are core components of cultural evolution, and are the result of the human desire to design. Whilst the arisal, workings, and diffusion of technical innovations have been widely researched, there are hardly any works dealing directly with social innovations (cf. Gillwald 2000: 1).

Social innovations play a central role primarily in the context of modernisation theories, which are seen as applied versions of theories of social change. They are the most important general cause of social transition. Social innovations can thus be employed as a suitable means of mastering societal challenges (cf. Zapf 1997: 39):

> "Social innovations are new ways of achieving objectives, in particular new organisational forms, new regulations, new lifeytyles, that alter the direction of social change, solve problems better than earlier practices, and are therefore worth being emulated and institutionalised" (Zapf 1989: 17).

Social innovations advance the processes of social change/modernisation. Those that emanate from the political-administrative system are also termed 'reforms'. Reforms usually target changes within existing systems, without dislodging the cornerstones of those systems. Instead, adjustments are made to certain sections of the system with a view to achieving the desired improvements in efficiency (cf. Altmann & Hösch 1994: 9).

An important tool for stimulating such reforms is *programmes*, meaning these can be referred to as *goal-oriented social innovations*, carried out to effect changes in organisations or systems. As the implementation of programmes requires an organisational structure, innovations are conveyed via organisations. So, organisations are transmitters of social change brought about by social innovations, as well as being – in accordance with the organisational model developed here – objects of change. Social innovations can also relate to changes within organisations (e.g. changes in production structures, the use of new procedures, the redesign of organisational structures, the training of personnel). Zapf (1989: 179) thus characterises 'innovative ability' not only as an individual attribute, but also as a feature of organisations.

A list of the various *types of innovation* (cf. Mohr 1977: 24 f.) makes clear that structural elements of organisations are invariably affected (cf. fig. 3.6).

Figure 3.6: Types of innovation and organisational elements

Type of innovation	Definition	Organisational element	Example from field of training
Product or service innovation	Introduction of new products or services	Technology	Training design, curricula, careers
Procedural innovation	Use of new procedures that facilitate a more technologically advanced production structure	Technology, financial resources	Learning, teaching and training methods, production methods, funding methods
Organisational structure innovations	Redesign of the formal decision, information and communication structures, as well as a change in interaction and authority relations	Organisational structure, formal structure	Division of labour, coordination, leadership system, authority distribution, formalisation
Personnel innovation	Hiring and/or firing, as well as training, of labour	Members, participants	Personnel recruitment, employee turnover, training

Organisational or social change occurs, from a chronological point of view, in *phases*. At the beginning is an *invention*, which may be the result of research and development, or of a chance discovery. From the time of market entry or their introduction, the creations are classed as *innovations*. During this phase, the new product, procedure or behaviour is tested in practice. The conceptual differentiation between invention and innovation is attributed to Schumpeter (1947: 152), who made a distinction between the "inventor", who produces ideas, and the "entrepreneur", who implements them ("gets things done"). Rogers (1995: 11), in contrast, includes new ideas in his definition of innovation: "An innovation is an idea, practice, or object that is perceived as new (...)", i.e. inventions and innovations are considered one and the same thing (cf. also Barnett 1953: 7).

Much more important than this distinction is the delimitation of the next phase, which is characterised by the dispersal of innovations, i.e. *diffusion*. Only if changes in behaviour, for example, spread, and come to be adopted by the majority, can lasting impacts materialise and the direction of social change be influenced (cf. Mohr 1977: 28 f.; Bollmann 1990: 8 f.). During the diffusion of an innovation, processes of adjustment may occur - immanent in the innovation (as amendments), or external to the innovation (in order to bridge "cultural lags") (Ogburn 1950: 30). The latter become necessary because sociocultural structures and processes are characterised by multifaceted complexities, meaning changes in their environment cause 'coordination gaps' (maladjustments), and result in corresponding adjustments.

In contrast to technical innovations, in the case of social innovations it is pointed out that these are often "self-made social inventions" (Zapf 1989), that have not been developed in research laboratories, and also that there is no market, in the classical sense, for social inventions. Gillwald (2000: 32), however, suggests that they must be introduced into day-to-day behavioural contexts, which is roughly equivalent to market entry. Otherwise they remain, just like technical inventions that are left to gather dust, merely ideas. The diffusion of social innovations follows the same pattern as that of technical innovations (cf. fig. 3.7).[102]

Figure 3.7: Phase model of innovation and diffusion research

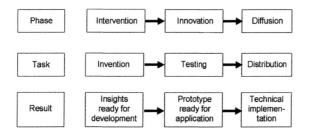

Source: based on Mohr 1977: 26

---

102 For perspectives on social scientific innovation research, cf. e.g. Tews 2004; Van den Bulte & Lilien 1999; Sauer & Lang 1999; Tushmann 1997; Nowotny 1996; Grupp & Schmoch 1995.

3.5.2 Diffusion

Diffusion research[103] is concerned with the conditions under which innovations become disseminated. According to Rogers (1995: 5), diffusion is "the process by which an innovation is communicated through certain channels over time among the members of a social system". Diffusion is thus about a specific kind of communication, "in that the messages are concerned with new ideas" (ibid.). The *diffusion process* spans from the spread of an innovation from the source of its invention to its application by users. Through this process, changes arise: "Diffusion is a kind of social change, defined as the process by which alteration occurs in the structure and function of a social system" (Rogers 1995: 6).[104]

Mohr (1977) developed a seminal model dealing with the factors that can positively or negatively influence the process of diffusion. He distinguishes between four groups of variables: (1) the first group relates to the specific characteristics of the innovation itself; (2) the second is made up of environmental variables; (3) the third set of variables relates to the people who take up an innovation idea, determine its introduction and, as the case my be, carry out its realisation; (4) elements of the formal structure of the organisation which implements the innovation form the fourth group of variables (cf. Mohr 1977: 19 ff.).

In accordance with the conception of organisations employed in this book, people who take up an innovation, get it established, and work on its realisation are treated as members of organisations. Therefore here – building on Mohr (1977: 43) – only *three groups of variables* are distinguished (cf. fig. 3.8).[105]

(1) Specific characteristics of the innovation

It has now been demonstrated in numerous studies that an innovation is more likely to be adopted "the more relatively beneficial, the more compatible with existing production conditions, the less complex, and the more testable and observable the innovation (appears) to the user" (Mohr 1977: 60).[106] These points are explained in more detail below.

The *relative benefit* of an innovation lies in its constitution of a 'better' problem solution than the existing one. This benefit can, for example, be of an econonic nature, in that the 'new' alternative is more cost-effective; it can relate to qualitative aspects (a better

---

103 For detail on the various approaches to diffusion research, cf. e.g. Tews 2004; Rogers 1995: 38 ff.; Kortmann 1995: 33 ff.; Mohr 1977: 33 ff. For information on the diffusion of innovations in non-profit organisations, cf. e.g. Rogers & Kim 1985.

104 This is very similar to the definition provided by Katz, Levin and Hamilton 1963: 240.

105 For information on the development of the diffusion process over time, and on the various adopter types, cf. Rogers 1995: 11 and 20 ff.

106 Rogers (1995: 15 f.) refers to the criteria that explain the varying innovation adoption rate as: relative advantage, compatibility, complexity, trialability, and observability.

product); or it can arise from time-saving considerations. Here, it does not matter too much whether the benefits can actually be measured objectively:

> "What does matter is whether an individual perceives the innovation as advantageous. The greater the perceived relative advantage of an innovation, the more rapid its rate of adoption will be" (Rogers 1995: 15).

A further important condition for the spread of an innovation is the extent "to which an innovation is perceived as being consistent with the existing values, past experiences, and needs of potential adopters" (ibid.).

The *complexity* of an innovation refers to the degree to which the application of a new technology appears to potential users to be relatively difficult to understand and hard to manage.

Figure 3.8: Diffusion model

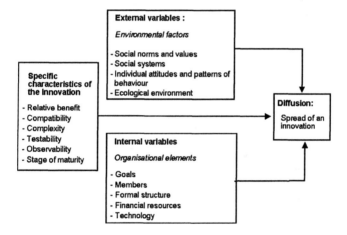

Source: based on Mohr 1977: 43

Two further factors that have considerable influence on the diffusion of an innovation are *testability* and *observability*. Only if the benefit and compatibility of an innovation can be tested and the results observed, can – in the case of a positive outcome – diffusion be expected to occur. Important here is that potential users of an innovation learn of these results via appropriate channels of communication (cf. Mohr 1977: 75; Neun 1985: 113, Rogers 1995: 16). The extent to which this occurs successfully depends on, among other things, the stage of maturity of an innovation.

(2) Variables external to the organisation

In diffusion research too, organisations are viewed as complex dynamic structures that are in a symbiotic relationship with their environment (cf. Mohr 1977: 64), which in turn consists of other organisations, networks, and social structures and systems. Thus, *variables external to the organisation* have particular significance with regard to the diffusion of innovations. It seems to be the case that items adopted are diffused most easily in a receiving society that "has already developed requirements that are practically identical to the prerequisites for development of the features conveyed" (Rüschemeyer 1971: 383).[107]

In the case of the adoption of technical innovations, analysis has focused primarily on the influence of the following factors: market size; market, demand and supply structure; chances of cooperation; external information possibilities; the presence of sufficient capital; the quantity and quality of available labour; and legislation. In the case of social innovations, on the other hand, cultural values and norms, the structure of social systems, and individual attitudes and patterns of behaviour are most significant. Which external variables come into play depends largely on the innovation in question, and can thus not be stated universally. This will be illustrated with an example later on.

(3) Variables internal to the organisation

The influence of characteristics internal to an organisation (including those of members) on the introduction of an innovation and its prospects of diffusion has already been discussed within the development of the theoretical conception of organisations, meaning further explanations can be foregone here.

Nevertheless, an important parallel between this approach and diffusion research should be noted. The long-term achievement potential of an organisation, including the ability to adapt flexibly to changed environmental conditions, is given particular significance in terms of an innovation's chances of dispersal in diffusion research, too:

> "The user of innovations must be in a position not only to apply the innovation mechanistically (technically competently), but also to adapt and modify the innovation flexibly and in a way that is congruous to problem solving progress" (Simson & Schönherr 1985: 79).

If recipients (individuals or oganisations) do not possess the ability to "creatively apply the innovation" (ibid.), the probability of *innovation inertia* or *pseudo-innovation* increases. This means that an innovation remains fixed in the state it reaches during the implementation phase, i.e. the copy of an archetype as true to the original as possible is conserved and not developed further.[108] This fixation effect should not be confused with the sustainability of a project or programme, a point which is discussed in more detail later

---

107 Mohr (1977: 37) criticises pedagogic diffusion studies, claiming "that although the potential adopters are mostly bureaucratically structured organisations, they disregard all questions of organisational structure".

108 Simson and Schönherr (1985) provide a number of striking examples of innovation inertia.

on. It should be emphasised that the diffusion of an innovation is to a large extent dependent on its internal and external acceptance. Internal acceptance is important because members of an organisation will only support the introduction and distribution of an innovation if they themselves are committed to it. External acceptance refers to the fact that actors outside of the programme-implementing organisation will likewise only adopt the innovation if they see it as being of benefit to them.

Using an *example* from the field of vocational training, the *development process of an innovation* will now be illustrated, from the point of its invention up to its widespread adoption among users. The example chosen is concerned with using a support programme to reform a country's education system, so that graduates receive those qualifications that are in demand on the job market.

The innovations developed for this purpose relate, among other things, to (cf. fig. 3.6, above):

- The development of a new education concept (e.g. dual vs. hitherto fully academic education) (product innovation)
- The development of new vocational profiles and curricula (product innovation)
- The introduction of new learning, teaching and training methods (procedural innovation)
- The reorganisation of training centres in accordance with efficiency criteria (organisational innovation)
- The qualification of personnel in order to meet the new requirements (personnel innovation).

In order to observe the factors that influence the diffusion process, only the innovation 'introduction of dual training' is to be considered further. In accordance with the first set of variables, the 'specific characteristics of the innovation', stakeholders must be able to recognise that the new form of education is actually beneficial, e.g. because:

- It is considerably more cost-efficient for the state
- It gives companies a say on the matter of educational content
- It enhances practical training
- It allows trainees to be integrated into the production process at an early stage
- Financial benefits in turn arise for companies (which offset, or even outweigh, the costs of training)
- It contributes towards improving the quality of products
- It provides trainees with better job prospects etc.

The improvements induced by dual training will only spread, however, if they can be reconciled with the production conditions, cultural norms and values, legal regulations etc. prevalent in the country. This will be explored in the context of external variables, in particular.

Furthermore, the innovation must not be so complex that it cannot be fathomed by users. If the dual training concept goes beyond the receipt of training in two locations (school and company) to encompass an extensive system of duties and rights of partici-pants (businesses, the state, trainees), the system may rapidly fall victim to its bureau-cratic rules. The complexity of the system may lead to companies refusing to accept im-portant rules (e.g. articles of apprenticeship, trainee pay, release to attend school, compli-ance with a training schedule, participation in the self-administration of the system), the state not wanting to see its educational sovereignty (e.g. to specify learning content on its own) touched, and trainees preferring to spend three years at university rather than com-pleting vocational training because they don't know of what benefit it will be to them later on.

The undertaking of pilot schemes within the scope of the support programme facilitates the testing of the new educational concept in selected training centres and companies. This also allows proof to be furnished that the promised benefits of the innovation do in-deed materialise and can be observed.

Over time, the innovation may also be improved further, thereby reaching a new stage of maturity, which would in turn have a positive effect on the degree of diffusion, meas-ured according to the number of training institutions and companies in the country that offer this new form of training, the occupations in which dual training takes place, the dual-trained graduates themselves etc.

In order for the training model introduced to be able to spread, however, a range of ex-ternal conditions must also be present. In the case of innovations in the school and train-ing field, it is particularly essential that they are consistent with the *cultural traditions, norms, and values* of a society. Not every conceivable form of training or method of learning and teaching can simply be transferred into a foreign social context. Studies by Margaret Mead (1955: 357 ff.), for instance, showed that innovations are more likely to be adopted the closer they are to being in harmony with the cultural values of relevant potential users.

The *job market* of course creates especially significant underlying conditions for train-ing institutions. It governs the supply and demand of labour in the various occupations, sectors, and salary brackets, as well as determining the price of work. Not only quantita-tive, but also qualitative aspects play a role here. The type of qualitifications demanded of labour for a certain job can vary greatly. While in some cases only basic qualifications are asked for, in other cases a skilled worker or technician with many years' training may be sought. This depends to a large extent on the labour organisation of companies, on inter-nal qualification mechanisms, and on the hitherto predominant training system.

It has been demonstrated in numerous studies that the degree to which purveyors of new technologies orient themselves towards the demands and need structures of recipients is of crucial importance for the success and diffusion of innovations (cf. Mohr 1977: 71). This should also be true where new training programmes are offered. What is more, the demand pull for new technologies has proved to be more important than the supply push emanating from the new technologies themselves (cf. Geschka 1974: 70).

For the introduction and dispersal of innovations in the *education and training system*, this system itself presents particularly important conditions and possibilities for action.

Across the general education system, specific knowledge standards are produced at different educational levels, which serve as prerequisites for further schooling. Thus the creation of curricula for secondary schools, or of training regulations for vocational institutions, must be based on these. Traditional forms of training, the role of companies in training, and the established mode of education constitute, alongside other factors, important underlying conditions for innovations in this field.

Legal issues can also play a decisive role. If the dual training concept were to run contrary to existing laws, regulations, or statutes, these would first of all have to be altered before a nationwide dissemination could become possible. This can necessitate very proctracted, complex processes of persuasion and change. Of particular importance is the political system, which defines political education and training targets, shapes the environment through legislation, provides financial resources, and even exerts influence on the occupancy of important posts.

For diffusion of the dual form of training to occur, effective providers are required, i.e. organisations that possess the ability and capacity to perform and market the offer efficiently. This would include, for example, an effective state-run school set-up that is in a position to meet the academic training requirements. For this, the academic training institutions would have to have qualified personnel, who are also committed to the dual training idea (and do not, for instance, wish to retain the fully academic system practised thus far which guarantees them benefices). They would also need a functioning organisational structure and sufficient technical and financial resources, in order to be able to provide teaching in accordance with the training concept. In the case of dual training, companies willing and able to train would also be required.

This example makes clear that *diffusion* of an innovation *only* occurs *if*:

- The innovation provides a benefit that is also discernable by participants
- The innovation does not run contrary to external conditions
- The innovation can be provided and disseminated by competent organisations.

It should be remembered that *innovations represent reforms,* which establish themselves, i.e. become initiated and institutionalised, if they solve problems better than earlier practices (cf. Zapf 1989: 177), and thereby create an observable *benefit*. Innovations cause structures, institutional regulations, and individual patterns of behaviour to change (cf. Deutsch 1985: 19 f.). This can lead to not only positive social change processes being triggered, but also to *conflicts* and negative effects:

"An innovation does not become an innovation until there is a social impact and this may involve both positive and negative effects" (Salen 1984: vi).

Innovations not only solve problems; they can also potentially create new ones at the same time. If traditional behavioural customs and sequences of actions are replaced with new ones, old structures reformed, and new rules institutionalised, then conflicts and tensions are to be expected. The introduction of innovations necessitates relearning. The more an innovation is diffused, the more people are affected by it. This entails a certain expenditure of time, thought, and mental capacity for all those concerned. Moreover, knowledge and skills acquired in the past are simultaneously devalued. It can be assumed that innovation pioneers have to shoulder a particularly high level of transition expenditure. Schumpeter (1911: 125) symbolises this by pointing out that building a path is different to following one.[109]

Innovations are expected to produce particular *groups of winners and losers*, an issue to which Deutsch (1985: 22) draws attention: "There are costs and benefits involved, but these costs and benefits are not equally distributed." This means that programme interventions that initiate innovations in order to attain specified goals trigger a highly complex mix of intended and unintended, positive and negative effects.

It should also be taken into consideration that not all organisations are equally prepared to learn. On the contrary, inactivity, or even resistance, can often be detected vis-à-vis changes, with innovations only standing a chance of becoming established and diffused if they meet with sufficient acceptance within an organistion.[110]

3.6 Multidimensional sustainability concept

Impacts also possess a temporal dimension (cf. chapter 3.2). According to the life-cycle model applied here (chapter 3.3), programmes (or services) pass through various phases, from planning, via implementation, up to the termination of support and beyond. This phase after the support or programme has ended forms the focus of sustainability concepts. They deal, on the one hand, with the future viability of problem solutions, and, on the other hand, with the question of whether changes to structures, processes, and patterns of behaviour brought about by the intervention measures are permanent, and whether they will become diffused and further developed. Before these considerations are used to develop a concept of sustainability encompassing multiple dimensions, the confusing diversity of the various uses of the term sustainability is explored, as well as definitions theroef.

Since the latter part of the 1980s, *'sustainability'* has become a central notion in sociopolitical discussions. The term has now come to permeate almost all spheres of life, and can be found as an adjective in myriad combinations of words (e.g. sustainable development, sustainable management, sustainable consumption, sustainable policies in whatever field, etc.). Because of its growing use, it threatens to degenerate into a meaningless buzzword. In order for this not to happen, it must be given a clear meaning, one that can be operationalised.

---

109 Cf. also Rogers (1995: 11), who distinguishes between "earlier adopters" and "later adopters".

110 For information on organisational learning, cf. e.g. Kieser & Walgenbach 2003: 425 ff.; Bea & Göbel 2002: 387 ff.; Argyris & Schön 1999; Hennemann 1997.

Here it is useful to uncover its *origin* (cf. Caspari 2004: 45; Meyer 2005). The concept was first introduced into broad public debate in 1987 by the 'World Commission for Environment and Development' deployed by the United Nations, which is also referred to as the 'Brundtland Commission' because of its Chair. But only through the UN conference for 'Environment and Development' in 1992 in Rio de Janeiro did it obtain global significance, and, in the course of 'Agenda 21', which was passed by 178 states, it triggered a wave of activities. After a string of follow-up conferences and resolutions, however, marked disillusionment already began to emerge at the 'Rio +10' conference with regard to the progress achieved (cf. e.g. Hens and Nath 2003).

So, the term *'sustainable development'* emerged in the context of discussions among the international community of states. Its origins are in the association of environmental considerations with the development-political approach of 'catching-up development'[111], made as early as at the first international environment conference in Stockholm in 1973. According to this approach, through the sustainable economic growth of "underdeveloped" southern hemisphere countries, global wealth inequalities should be evened out. The term 'sustainable development' arose in this context, and is by no means derived from the forestry-related concept of 'sustainable yield forestry'.[112]

With the adoption of the *'sustainable development'* approach, the growth model dominant in global politics in the 1960s was finally replaced with the idea that the improvement of ecological and social living conditions can only be achieved in the long term through the simultaneous safeguarding of natural resources (cf. Stockmann 1993a: 207). The careless use of raw materials, and the associated pollution of air, water and earth, had revealed the "limits to growth" (cf. Meadows et al. 1972) as early as the 1970s, and triggered a lively discussion on the possibilities for stable economic growth. Ecology and economy appeared to be in an irreconcilable conflict, which also threatened to lead to the long-term failure of the solution of the most pressing social problems (above all "Third World" poverty). The advance in knowledge associated with the new approach of sustainable development relates primarily to the realisation that *economic, social,* and *ecological* development processes (the "three pillars of sustainability") are inseparably related to each other, and must therefore be brought into equilibrium. However, this quite abstract vision of the future represents the end of global consensus on the matter.

The question of *how* to harmonise these *three dimensions*, and what strategies and tools to use to realise sustainable development, is just as controversial as the definition of the guiding principle itself. On reviewing the literature, Kastenholz and colleagues (1996: 1) identified more than 60 different definitions of sustainability. Different aspects are given more weight depending on the scientific discipline of the authors, the research tradition and interests to which they are bound, their understanding of nature, and their overriding

---

111 Translated from the German term 'nachholende Entwicklung'.
112 According to the German member of the Brundtland Commission, Volker Hauff, the Commission was at the time completely unaware of the forestry-related term ('sustainable yield forestry') (cf. Tremmel 2003: 89 ff.).

perceptions of value. This conceptual fuzziness has given rise to a situation in which everyone can appear to be under the 'sustainable development' umbrella, even though they are guided by highly diverse ideas (cf. Meyer 2000, 2002a & b; Meyer et al. 2003). It would seem that the *haziness of this concept* is the very thing that makes it appealing. Everyone can be in favour of it and feel part of a global, reassuring consensus movement. Yet because of this, there is a danger of the concept of sustainable development becoming an 'empty phrase', a 'catchword', a 'political buzzword', or, even worse, of this nebulous principle being abused to conceal divergent interests and impending conflicts.

Upon close inspection of the concept of sustainable development, another layer becomes apparent. In order for a plan for the future of a society, of whatever nature, to be realised, it requires political strategies and programmes. This is expressed by the motto of the global conference held in Rio in 1992 - 'think globally, act locally' - which implies *vertical* coordination of action for managing 'sustainable development' that spans the various levels of the political system (local, regional, national and global politics). Furthermore, as early as during the Rio conference – and to an even greater extent during the follow-up conference ten years later in Johannesburg – a *horizontal* coordination of action between state, economy, and civil society was proclaimed, and stipulated as a necessary condition for the implementation of the overall concept. These requirements of the 'sustainable development' principle suggest, on the one hand, that comprehensive institutional reform of global social governance is necessary, an issue which has since been discussed in the context of *'global governance'* debates (cf. e.g. Commission on Global Governance 1995, Rittberger 2002). And, on the other hand, measures for improving managerial competence at a local level are also deemed essential, and these have found their way into more recent development-political strategies through the slogans *'capacity building'* and *'empowerment'*.

Demands for a fundamental change in the design principles used hitherto ultimately cast the spotlight on questions relating to the *impacts of political strategies and programmes*. To what extent is it even possible to contribute towards the implementation of sustainable development through human intervention, and how sustainable are the effects triggered by programme interventions? So, in addition to the sustainability model relating to the macro level of society, whose aim is the optimal balancing of ecological, economic and social developments, there is also a *micro-level concept* that deals with the effectiveness of human interventions with regard to these processes (cf. Stockmann 1993a: 208).

A variety of definitions are to be found at this programme level too (cf. the contributions made in Stockmann 1993a, Stockmann 1996a: 15 ff., Stockmann and Caspari 2001, Caspari 2004: 45 ff.). This conceptual fuzziness produces processes similar to those at the macro level: all participants can be in favour of sustainability, yet their understanding of it differs greatly, and may even be contradictory.

A *sustainability concept for the micro level* will therefore be developed here, containing operational parameters, which will enable a clear appraisal of the sustainability of project and programme impacts, as well as comparative and summary assessments. For this purpose, it is necessary to switch from a normative to an *analytical understanding* of sustainability.

If the various definitions of sustainability at the programme level are gathered together, it becomes apparent that primarily the field of *development cooperation (DC)* has been concerned with this concept. This should be taken into consideration in the course of the analysis, as development cooperation measures and programmes have a specific character. They are usually oriented towards sustainability. Through project and programme interventions, solutions are sought for situations identified as being deficient, which put partners (target groups and so-called executing agencies) in a position to solve these problems on a long-term basis. In accordance with the perspective depicted in the life-cycle model, such measures and programmes go through individual phases. After various planning and implementation phases, each programme reaches the *end of its support*, with transfer payments from an external donor ceasing. This does not automatically signal the end of the programme, as the partner may then continue to manage it alone. If the partner also withdraws his or her financial support, then the *programme end* has been reached. Yet even when a programme has ended, effects are still to be expected, especially if the programme in question is a sustainable one.

This can be illustrated with an *example from development cooperation*. Let's assume that the aim of a health programme is to establish basic health centres in a particular region, and to encourage the population to seek out these centres in order to be informed about hygiene standards and prophylaxis measures, to take advantage of the medical provision offered etc., so that health levels in the region improve, infant and child mortality decrease etc.

Sustainable impacts subsequent to the termination of support by the external donor would then be identifiable if the programme – the creation of health centres – continued to receive support from the government of the partner country and to be in demand among the population. Even if the programme were to be completely ended, e.g. because the whole region had been provided with health centres, effects would still be apparent should the programme be sustainable, i.e. if the population were to continue to use the health centres rather than resorting back to relying on the services of shamans.

In the case of programmes not in the DC field, the principle remains the same. Every project or programme is of a temporary nature, i.e. sooner or later support is discontinued. Sustainable programmes are distinguished by the fact that their impacts do not cease when the programme ends. A programme aimed at reintegrating disabled people would be considered sustainable if employers continue to take on disabled workers even if they no longer receive any financial incentives from the support programme to do so, e.g. because they have seen these people to be potentially just as competent as others.

A programme for promoting the provision of environmental advice to businesses would be sustainable if the consultation centres set up using the support funds were to remain intact and continue to be used by companies after the programme had ended. Adaptations to the programme may be necessary for this, e.g. the replacement of the support funds that existed for consultation with private contributions from companies. Or the consultation offer may need to be modified to meet the needs and requirements of companies, so that they continue to demand the service and are prepared to pay a fee for it.

These examples make clear that sustainability not only refers to 'long-term effectiveness', but also incorporates other dimensions. This becomes especially apparent if the various *definitions of sustainability at the project and programme level* are inspected. Very often the terms 'sustainability' and 'long-term impacts' are used as synonyms in international dialogue. The DAC Expert Group on Aid Evaluation, for example, deems a development programme sustainable "when it is able to deliver an appropriate level of benefits for an extended period of time after major financial, managerial, and technical assistance from an external donor is terminated" (OECD 1989). Similarly, the American development organisation USAID defines sustainability as "the extent to which a program continues to deliver benefits after development assistance ends" (USAID, 1999: 13). The 'Evaluation Guidelines' of the Danish organisation Danida describe sustainability as "an indication whether the positive impacts are likely to continue after external assistance has come to an end" (DANIDA, 1999: 60).

The UNDP Handbook for Programme Managers also defines sustainability as "the durability of positive programme or project results after the termination of the technical co-operation channelled through that programme or project" (UNDP, 2000a: 12). However, its glossary lists a number of distinctions, notably between '*static sustainability* and *dynamic sustainability*'. 'Static sustainability' is defined as "the continuous flow of the same benefits, set in motion by the completed programme or project", while 'dynamic sustainability' is seen as "the use or adaption of programme or project results to a different context or changing environment by the original target groups and/or other groups" (UNDP, 2000a: 34).

A further defining feature of the concept of sustainability employed by international donor organisations, which is also used by the UNDP, relates to the fact that projects, as targeted interventions, should contribute to the changing of social systems: "The purpose of the technical co-operation was supposed to change the nature and performance of one or more or all components of the system. As such it is the evolution of the system, into which the technical co-operation has been introduced, that should be the focus of the concern with sustainability" (UNDP 1988a: 15).

Four dimensions of sustainability can be derived from these differing definitions of the sustainability of project and programme impacts.

The *first dimension* contains the element common to all definitions of sustainability – *durability*. This exists if the target group and/or executing agency *continue* the innovations achieved within the project/programme over the *long term* without external support. This would be the case – referring back to the previously cited examples – if:

- The operator of the health centres (e.g. a health authority) continues to run them after the support programme has ended, and the target groups (e.g. women) utilise the offer
- Employers continue to take on disabled people following the cessation of the integration programme

- The executing agencies (e.g. chambers of commerce, industry and trade) retain the consultation centres created through the environment programme after it has ended, and target groups (e.g. construction companies) demand their services.

This dimension of sustainability is closely bound to the project/programme, describing the long-term effects which occur subsequent to the support/programme end, and can thus be referred to as *project-/programme-oriented sustainability*.

Figure 3.9: Programme-level sustainability dimensions

Dimension	Type	Characteristics
I	Project-/programme-oriented	The target group and/or executing agency continues the innovations to serve their own interests and for their own benefit.
II	Output-oriented	Other groups/organisations have adopted the innovations long-term to serve their own interests and for their own benefit.
III	System-oriented	The innovations lead, via processes of diffusion, to an increase in the performance of the system as a whole (e.g. the health or education system).
IV	Innovation-oriented	The target group/executing agency has a potential for innovation that enables it to react flexibly and appropriately to changed environmental conditions.

Source: Stockmann 1996a: 75; Caspari 2004: 67.

The *second dimension* considers the *scope* of the impacts or benefits of a project or programme. *Output*, i.e. the number of users (service recipients) and also the nature of the user group, is used as an indicator of this. The crucial question is whether people outside of the original target group have adopted the innovations introduced through the programme on a long-term basis, out of self-interest and for their own benefit. This can come about if the executing agency is able to secure benefits for others (those external to the target group) as well, or if other organisations have adopted the innovations and thus additional social groups are being reached. The 'project environment' element of the AwZ definition of sustainability[113] is relevant here, as well as "the use of program results by other groups" from the UNDP definition of "dynamic sustainability".

---

113 AwZ refers to the German 'Ausschuss für wirtschaftliche Zusammenarbeit' (Committee on Economic Cooperation and Development), which includes in its definition of sustainability the continuing effect of development cooperation measures within the project environment (cf. Deutscher Bundestag 13/10857).

Considering the examples again, dimension II of sustainability could mean that:

- The executing agency responsible for the health centres is in a position to extend its provision beyond the original target group (e.g. women) to now also reach other users (e.g. children and men), with these new 'groups' taking advantage of this provision
- Employers not only take on disabled people, but are also prepared to give other fringe groups a chance
- The executing agencies of the environmental consultancy centres expand the provision and, in addition to businesses, now also provide advice to towns, local authorities, and private households.

A distinct diffusion of output would arise if other organisations (besides the executing agency supported) had also adopted the innovations and were now employing them for the benefit of their users.

This dimension of sustainability goes beyond the target group actually supported by the programme. The executing agency or agencies in receipt of support prove themselves to be competent in also ensuring long-term benefits for those outside of the immediate target group; or other organisations (distinct from the one supported) also adopt the innovations for the benefit of their users. The number of service providers/users thus increases, and is measured as output. This dimension is thus referred to as *output-oriented sustainability*.

The *third dimension* is concerned with the changing of the system in which the innovation was introduced (e.g. in organisations of the health, education or economic system). The central aspect of this dimension is therefore not (only) the expansion of the user group, but rather the *evolution of the system as a whole*. This refers not only to regional diffusion being brought about, and not only to once-supported executing agencies as well as other organisations using the innovation, but rather to the complete system to which the target groups and executing agencies belong being affected, i.e. to the triggering of a reform of, for example, the health, education or economic system.

In relation to the three examples, this would mean that:

- The health centre model implemented is so successful that it is introduced in the health system on a nationwide basis
- The integration of disabled people and fringe groups becomes the norm throughout the whole economic system
- The environmental consultation model established through a number of selected and once-supported executing agencies is so successful that environmental consultation becomes a major factor in the conservation of the ecological system.

An increase in the performance of the whole system in question is brought about via diffusion of the programme innovations introduced. This could happen in the following ways:

- Through the adoption of the health centre model by the health system, cases of illness decrease, child mortality falls, public health improves etc.
- Through the integration of disabled people and other fringe groups, unemployment falls, social welfare expenditure decreases, valuable new labour is gained etc.

- Through the introduction of nationwide consultation systems, the overall ecological situation improves etc.

'*System-oriented sustainability*' is thus referred to if innovations introduced through a programme lead, via processes of diffusion, to an increase in performance of a system as a whole.

The *fourth dimension* of sustainability takes into account the fact that services are not simply reproduced in the same way, but rather a target group, an executing agency, or even a system can *flexibly and appropriately adapt* in accordance with changing environmental conditions. Sustainability does not reside in the perpetuation of that which has been created or introduced once, but rather in the ability to further develop innovations. That is to say, the executing agency or target group must have an innovation potential in order to be able to consciously bring about adaptations and modifications. If services are reproduced in the same way again and again, even though environmental conditions have changed, they will soon cease to meet the requirements of target groups. If services or products are no longer in demand, however, then sustainability is jeopardised. This element, "the adaption to a changing environment", which goes hand-in-hand with innovative changes in behaviour, is contained within numerous definitions of sustainability, notably that of the UNDP.

With regard to the three examples chosen, this may mean that:
- Demand for the services of the health centres declines because they do not offer any help for current health problems (e.g. AIDS), the technical apparatus with which they are equipped is obsolete, or the personnel does not undertake further training
- The integration of disabled people comes to a halt because they have hitherto been employed in primarily low-skill jobs, the number of which then decreases, meaning disabled people now need to be better trained
- The environmental consultation centres do not recognise new trends, thus failing to alter their consultancy offer. The need for advice on ecological construction, for example, may have been fully satisfied, but questions about alternative energy production are not yet covered sufficiently (e.g. because of a lack of know-how or suitable consultants).

Sustainability profiles
An assessment of the sustainability of a programme can be carried out using the four dimensions developed here. A programme may, for example, be judged to be programme- and innovation-oriented, but not display any degree of diffusion. The sustainability *profile* would then look as follows:

Dim. I	Dim. II	Dim. III	Dim. IV
+	-	-	+

If a programme is, on the other hand, programme-, output- and system-oriented, but does not have any inherent innovation potential, then it has the following sustainability *profile*:

Dim. I	Dim. II	Dim. III	Dim. IV
+	+	+	-

In total, 16 different sustainability profiles are theoretically possible (cf. fig. 3.10), yet six of these (4, 5, 9, 10, 11, 15) are not to be expected in practice (for the reasons behind this, cf. Caspari 2004: 72).

Figure 3.10: Possible sustainability profiles

Sustainability profile	Dimension
1. `- - - -`	none
2. `+ - - -`	
3. `- + - -`	
4. `- - + -`	III
5. `- - - +`	IV
6. `+ + - -`	
7. `+ - + -`	I III
8. `+ - - +`	IV
9. `- + + -`	II III
10. `- + - +`	II IV
11. `- - + +`	III IV
12. `+ + + -`	I II III
13. `+ + - +`	IV
14. `+ - + +`	IV
15. `- + + +`	IV
16. `+ + + +`	I II III IV

Source: Caspari 2004: 72

The *multidimensional sustainability concept* developed here has a number of *advantages*:
1. *All aspects* of existing sustainability definitions are covered, with no information lost.
2. It is *not necessary* to set a *normative 'sustainability threshold'* that, depending on the definition chosen, has to be exceeded for sustainability to be established.

3. The dimensions exhibit *clear criteria* that can be *operationalised*, and they can thus be measured empirically.
4. Using *sustainability profiles,* evaluation results can be represented completely and clearly, meaning that *comparisons* over time and between programmes are perfectly *possible.*

In addition, Caspari (2004: 74 f.) has shown that the information contained within the profiles can be used for the creation of an *additive sustainability index*, without any siginificant loss of information. For this, the number of dimensions judged empirically as positive is added up. Such an index allows a summary statement to be made as to the sustainability of measures, projects, or programmes, on the basis of five levels. The greater the number of positive judgements, the more sustainable a programme is rated (cf. fig. 3.11). The benefits of such an index primarily become apparent if various programmes are to be compared with each other within a cross-sectional study. Because of its metric measurement scale, simple methods of statistical analysis can also be applied, which are particularly important when carrying out cause-effect analyses.

The *sustainability profiles* developed with the help of the multidimensional sustainability concept facilitate not only a *compression of information* through an *additive index*, but also a *comparison* of the actual level of sustainability achieved with that intended (cf. Caspari 2004: 77 ff.). Because the evaluation of sustainability deals with programmes and measures that have long been completed, and which were possibly planned and implemented a number of years previously, there is a danger of judging the sustainability of these programmes against current standards. It thus appears sensible to consider the *sustainability intended at the beginning of the programme*, i.e. to judge it in its historical form with regard to expectations at the time of its conception. This makes sense not only because assessment standards change over time, but also because reasons of content necessitate consideration of the original intentions of the programme. A project that plans to build one or more health centres, for example, may not necessarily have intended to trigger effects in the whole of the health sector. So, intended sustainability was focused on dimensions I or II, but not III. Or the integration programme for disabled people may have concentrated explicitly just on this target group, thus only aiming for sustainability along dimension I. In the case of the environmental consultancy centres too, it is clear that intended sustainability could have been specified in various ways with regard to the degree of diffusion (target group, target group-spanning, system-related).

The situation is different, however, in the case of dimension IV. Every executing agency that wishes to achieve *sustainability* with a programme along one of the three other dimensions *must*, in the long term, prove its *innovative ability*. Without the capacity to further develop innovations that have been introduced, in order to flexibly adapt them to changed environmental conditions or target group needs, in the long run neither a high level of diffusion will be possible (dimensions II and III), nor can benefit be lastingly secured for the actual target group (dimension I).

If 'intended' sustainability is to be compared with that actually achieved, then in the course of an evaluation, not only the current sustainability - that achieved upto the point of the investigation - needs to be measured, but also, retrospectively, that intended during the planning phase. This allows programmes to be measured by that which they were actually supposed to achieve, i.e. against their original aims. A *target/actual comparison of sustainability* is then possible, which facilitates an interpretation that is appropriate given the programmes' historical situation and intentions.

Figure 3.11: Additive sustainability index

Level	Description
0	No sustainability
+	Very low sustainability
++	Relatively low sustainability
+++	Relatively high sustainability
++++	Very high sustainability

Source: based on Caspari 2004: 75

3.7 Multidimensional assessment and quality model

The three theoretical approaches, along with the multidimensional sustainability concept, are now to be used to derive *impact hypotheses* and *identify areas/criteria for assessment*, in order to then develop a set of evaluation guidelines. Prior to this, the evaluation criteria obtained on the basis of the theoretical deliberations presented here will be compared with the assessment criteria used in programme evaluations, as well as with those used in the context of quality management concepts. The *aim is,* firstly, to obtain *criteria for evaluation* that are as *theoretically-based* as possible. And secondly, these criteria should not only serve to *structure* the *set of evaluation guidelines*, but should also be used for the *determination of the quality* of, specifically, programmes, and, more generally, service provision.

3.7.1 Interdependencies

If we summarise the discussions presented thus far on the theoretical conception of evaluation, it becomes clear that this encompasses various *analytical perspectives*, integrating *three theoretical approaches* that each deal with different aspects of a programme. The starting point is (1) a *life-cycle model* that focuses on the temporal perspective and processual nature of a programme. According to this model, programmes and projects consist of a series of consecutive, definable phases, in each of which successive goal attainment should be ensured through the implementation of specific planning and execution steps. The time axis joins together the individual phases, creating a causal relationship between them.

Life-cycle research implies that life-cycles are the result of a multitude of influences. Particularly if the progress and impacts of programmes are to be examined, not only should individual decisions and macro-structural conditions be considered, but also the role of organisations. Programmes that are developed as an instrumental set of measures in order to achieve defined targets, and to contribute towards triggering innovations within social systems, usually require an executing agency, i.e. an organisation to carry it out. Often organisational units are formed especially for this purpose; alternatively, existing ones are assigned with the task of implementation.

In order to examine the interdependencies between programmes, implementing organisations, and social subsystems, a (2) *theoretical conception of organisations* has been drawn upon here, according to which organisations are open social systems that are intended to be rationally designed to achieve specific goals. Constituent features of an organisation are its *aims*, *members* (participants), *formal* (organisational) *structure*, *technology*, and *financial resources*, as well as its *environment*. Based on these elements, it is possible to ascertain the *performance potential of an organisation* (its effectiveness) over time.

The programme-organisation relationship and the organisation-environment relationship are elucidated through an *impact model*. For their implementation, programmes require organisational subsystems, which are embedded in an existing or newly-formed organisational framework of the programme-executing agency (implementing organisation), which is in turn part of a larger system context. Programmes can thus produce effects within and through these organisations, whilst conversely being subject to influence by surrounding systems via the executing agency.

Programme inputs are conceived of as social, economic or technical interventions that trigger impacts - viewed as continuous processes - in other systems. These impacts are measured both within the executing agency and in external environmental fields. In accordance with the idea of causality applied here, *programme inputs (IV)* trigger changes in *dimensions of the implementing organisation (DV)* - characterised as internal impacts. Under the approach that leads on from this, the previously dependent dimensions of the implementing organisation become independent variables. The issue is then whether, and to what extent, the *executing agency (IV)*, which has been altered by programme interventions, is in a lasting position to produce impacts in *external environmental fields (DV)*.

As an important function of programmes is the introduction of innovations, (3) *innovation and diffusion research* has been employed in order to clarify the function and significance of innovations, and to present the conditions necessary for their diffusion. For this purpose, a distinction is made between *three groups of variables*: specific characteristics of the innovation itself, external (environmental) variables, and internal variables - referred to here as organisational elements.

The *three theoretical approaches* exhibit numerous similarities, and complement one another outstandingly well. The *life-cycle model* focuses on the process dimension of developments, linking individual phases together in a causal manner. *Diffusion research* is also based on a causal phase model. The two approaches are combined through a *theoretical model of organisations*. Combining the three theoretical approaches facilitates an understanding of processes, casts light on the programme-organisation-environment relationship, and allows the specification of conditions under which the diffusion of innovations introduced occurs.

According to these conditions, it is to be expected that *programmes* are *more likely to achieve* their *planned aims* (intended impacts), *the greater the extent to which the innovations introduced through programme interventions benefit stakeholders*. For this it is necessary that stakeholders identify and experience the benefit, which means that a new solution to a problem (innovation) should not be too complex and unfathomable. The innovation must be testable and lead to positive (advantageous) results (impacts) that are identified and accepted by stakeholders as being so. There is then an increased chance of it being adopted, and taken on by others, and thus of undergoing dispersal.[114]

Programme interventions are *more likely* to achieve *intended outcomes, the greater the extent* to which *innovations* introduced are *compatible* with present solutions and are not in conflict with existing values, traditions, customs, or even just past experiences. This presents a *problem*, however: on the one hand, products and services should be improved, inefficient solutions replaced, and deficient structures altered with the help of appropriate innovations; but on the other hand, the change should not be so drastic that users do not accept it. External conditions thus deserve a great deal of attention when carrying out an evaluation, as the maintenance of existing structures and introduction of innovations is a *balancing act*. Inherent in too many innovations is the danger of being rejected and thus stabilising the status quo. If, on the other hand, innovations turn out to be too small in their magnitude, old structures may likewise be reinforced.

For programmes to produce impacts, competent organisations are required with which they can be planned and implemented. *The greater the effectiveness of an organisation,*

---

114 Expressed in the language of quality management, this means that programme interventions must meet the requirements of customers (target groups, stakeholders). Whether or not this is the case could be found out on the basis of customer satisfaction.

the higher is the chance that the intended aims of a programme are achieved. Organisational effectiveness is, in turn, higher, the greater the extent to which:

- Members of the organisation accept and actively promote the programme's aims
- Personnel are qualified to lead and administer the organisation, and to fulfil central tasks (including those of the programme)
- A well-functioning organisational structure is present
- Necessary financial resources are available
- The technical equipment ('hardware') and ...
- Programme concept ('software') of an organisation (which together constitute technology) are aligned with task fulfilment.

These factors combine to facilitate the overall satisfaction of the needs of target audiences (users, service recipients etc.).

The *multidimensional sustainability concept* developed here brings the three theoretical perspectives together: it links in with (1) the life-cycle model, referring to the temporal dimension of programmes and services on offer by making clear that the ending of the support or programme does not represent the end of impacts triggered by a programme. Especially if programmes are oriented towards achieving sustainability, lasting structural, process-related, and behavioural changes are to be expected over the long term (cf. chapter 3.3 fig. 3.3).

For sustainability to occur, it is assumed, based on (2) considerations of organisational theory, that a competent and innovative organisation is required, whose members actively support the programme concept and are able to continually adapt the innovations introduced to changing environmental conditions and requirements. Innovations will only endure and be further diffused if they continue to be perceived by their (potential) users as beneficial, and create utility.

The sustainability of measures or programmes will be higher, the greater the extent to which innovations introduced are successfully disseminated, i.e. the higher their degree of diffusion. Based on (3) theoretical diffusion considerations, it is assumed that it is more difficult to reverse innovations that have been introduced, the more they have proved their worth and shown themselves to be beneficial. That is to say, the higher their degree of diffusion, the greater the chance of them being sustainable.

The programme-level sustainability concept developed here thus encompasses not only the aspect of the duration of innovation diffusion, but also the degree of its spatial spread, as well as the potential for adapting innovations to changed environmental conditions and target group needs.

Overall, based on that which has been discussed up to now, it is to be expected that *sustainability* - provided it is a programme aim - is more likely to occur:

- The greater the extent to which target group needs and organisational and situational conditions are taken into consideration in programme planning, implementation, and aftercare support

- The greater the extent to which programme aims and innovations introduced meet with the acceptance of target groups (because they correspond to their requirements and create benefit)
- The greater the effectiveness of the executing agencies that carry out the intervention measures and adapt them to changed environmental conditions
- The more extensive the diffusion of the innovations.

3.7.2 Evaluation assessment criteria

Out of these theoretical deliberations and the interdependencies derived from them, the *areas and criteria of assessment* used to constitute the *set of evaluation guidelines* can be obtained. In the process, it becomes clear that these *criteria* have not been put together randomly or, for that matter, gleaned from plausibility considerations, but rather are *theoretically grounded*. What is more, these criteria have *proved* themselves *empirically* in numerous evaluation studies.[115]

Broadly, *five areas of assessment* can be identified:
(1) Programme and environment
(2) Planning and implementation
(3) Internal impact fields
(4) External impact fields
(5) Sustainability

(1) Programme and environment
As discussed within the theoretical conception of organisations, programmes and services are carried out or rendered by organisations (executing agencies). To perform an evaluation, it is thus necessary to have precise knowledge of the programme or service provision. Although an impact- rather than a goal-oriented evaluation perspective is taken here, which is explained more closely in chapter 4.3, evaluations cannot reasonably be carried out without any knowledge of the programme or service goals. The derivation of the *programme concept* and its *goals,* of the *implicit programme theory,* and of the *relationships* that can be assumed on the basis of the theoretical deliberations presented here, is therefore of central importance. This can also be said of the *innovation concept,* i.e. the type of innovations that are to be introduced through a programme or improved through a service being offered. As the implementation of measures necessitates resources (personnel, fund-

---

115 Cf. e.g. Heinrich & Meyer 2005; Stockmann 2005b, 2004a & c, 2002b, 2001a & b, 2000a, b, c & 1996; Caspari 2004; Stockmann, Krapp & Baltes 2004; Baltes, Krapp & Stockmann 2004; Meyer et al. 2003; Ludwig & Koglin 2003; Stockmann et al. 2001 & 2000; Stockmann, Meyer, Kohlmann, Gaus & Urbahn 2001; Stockmann, Caspari, Kevenhörster 2000; Stockmann, Meyer, Krapp & Köhne 2000; Caspari et al. 2000.

ing, technical resources etc.), it should be documented what *resources* are needed and which are present.

The aim of programme interventions and services is to create benefit. *Target groups (audiences)* are usually defined for this purpose. A description of the target groups, as well as of the social groups or persons excluded from a programme (or service provision), is required for the understanding of a programme and its effects. Of equal importance is the description of the area in which a programme is to produce impacts. This area can incorporate various fields, such as the health or education system of a country; consultancy in the youth welfare service or environmental sector; support for the homeless or students; the placement of unemployed or disabled people in work; the promotion of art, culture, sport or overseas students; cooperation with developing or transition countries etc.

These areas, which sometimes represent *social subsystems*, can in general be referred to as *fields of policy or practice*, in which the programme interventions are intended to bring about impacts. The contextual conditions under which a programme is implemented or a range of services (e.g. consultation, support etc.) offered should be analysed. In doing so, changes that occur over time, which can influence the effectiveness of a programme, are to be given particular attention.

The relationships between a programme (or service on offer) and the implementing (or service-providing) organisation are dealt with in a separate chapter.

(2) Programme planning and implementation

It can be inferred from the *life-cycle model* that, on top of the type of service to be rendered or programme to be carried out, the process of planning and implementation should be analysed in its various phases, since the individual phases build on each other. In doing so, the following *hypothesis* is assumed: *programmes* that are *planned and implemented* (or services that are offered) carefully, and in accordance with target group needs and demands, are more likely to achieve specified goals and intended effects than those that neglect planning or only have limited management potential, meaning that problems that arise during implementation cannot be adequately dealt with.

In the case of support programmes with a time limit, it is especially important that systematic preparations are made for the *support end*, so that the discontinuation of funding can be compensated for. Many programmes therefore do not finish abruptly, but rather their end is announced and the available funds are gradually reduced so that recipients of the support can prepare for it. As several studies have shown (cf. Stockmann 1992a, 1996a, 2000c, 2001a), this 'transition phase' is of particular importance for the sustainability of programmes. In the case of some programmes, provisions are also made for the possibility of '*aftercare support*'. Here, personnel and material resources may continue to be transferred to a lesser extent following the conclusion of a support programme.

'Good' planning and implementation means, according to Wholey (1979), the negotiation of goals, detailed knowledge of the technical, personnel and financial resources necessary for sound programme implementation, and knowledge about the forces that stand in the way of achieving optimal implementation (cf. Cook and Matt 1990: 25). This brief characterisation still applies today, and is endorsed by the causal relationships presented.

The *quality of the programme process* can thus be determined through the assessment of:
- The preparation/planning of a programme
  This is to be rated positively if the most important stakeholders were involved in the planning phase, and if planning is based on studies (e.g. requirement and feasibility studies) and concepts that provide an appropriate assessment of the problem situation, the needs of the programme's target groups, the necessary means (interventions), the competence of the organisation given the task of implementation, and the contextual conditions.
- Programme management during implementation
  This is to be assessed positively if planning errors and implementation problems have been identified early, and appropriate managerial interventions were carried out so that the programme design was able to be adapted to changed contextual conditions.
- Preparation for the termination of support
  This phase is to be rated positively if the ending of support, i.e. the cessation of financial backing for a programme, has been initiated in a timely manner through suitable steps (e.g. the gradual reduction of funds, the development of transition plans).
- Aftercare support
  This phase does not always exist. It can be appraised positively if the intended effects of the programme are sustainably supported by targeted intervention measures.

(3) Internal impact fields

As has been discussed, in order to render a service or carry out a programme, an organisation is usually required. It is assumed that the effectiveness of the organisation has a decisive influence on service provision or programme implementation, and thus on the impacts produced. Based on *theoretical considerations of organisations*, the following *central organisational parameters* have been identified:
- Goals and their acceptance
  Whilst programme goals have already been dealt with within the scope of the analysis of the programme concept, here the focus is primarily on the acceptance of these goals and the associated intervention measures by the implementing organisation.
- Personnel
  The crucial issue is whether personnel are sufficiently qualified to be able to implement the planned intervention measures.
- Organisational structure
  This criterion relates to the extent to which the organisational subsystems (e.g. administration, procurement, production) of the executing agency work effectively, and whether the division of labour, coordination, decision structures, communication etc. are functionally managed.
- Financial resources

Of critical importance here is whether the financial resources of an executing agency are sufficient to secure its functional capability and the scheduled implementation of the programme.

- Technology (technical infrastructure)
Here the crucial issue is whether the technical infrastructure of an executing agency is suitable for fulfilling its (service) mandate and enabling the scheduled implementation of the programme.
- Technology (organisational agenda/concept)
For products or services to be produced, knowledge not only about the application of technical instruments is required, but also about a concept or strategy for product or service provision.

Programme interventions may aim to effect changes in these parameters, inducing *(internal) impacts*. Interventions may thus be oriented towards:

- Establishing new goals or reformulating old ones (e.g. by opening up a training scheme that had previously only been available to domestic residents to foreign persons as well)
- Personnel becoming qualified in new technologies (e.g. by offering courses in new computer programmes)
- Improving organisational processes (e.g. by reducing the number of levels in the hierarchy)
- Increasing revenue (e.g. by putting up the fees for certain services)
- Improving equipment (e.g. by purchasing new machines)
- Altering the organisational concept (e.g. by developing new training curricula).

As set out in detail earlier on, impacts can be analysed along three dimensions: they can relate to structures, processes and/or individual modes of behaviour; they can be planned or unplanned; and they can support or run contrary to programme or service goals (cf. chapter 3.2, fig. 3.1). In order to be able to ascertain, assess and evaluate the whole range of impacts that arise, not only intended, but also unintended, impacts must be considered, along with their 'direction'.

Hence, for the production of an *'impact balance'*, all changes (also referred to in chapter 3.2 as the 'gross outcome') should be recorded for subsequent differentiation based on:

- Whether they are net (programme) impacts that can be attributed to the programme interventions
- Whether they are the result of extraneous confounding factors, or
- Whether they are actually the result of design effects, i.e. impacts that have been 'artificially' created through the measuring process.

Only then is it possible to assess the extent to which the goals of a programme have been achieved (effectiveness).

Measures aimed at enhancing the performance of an organisation are not, however, merely concerned with fulfilling this goal, but rather are usually oriented towards further-reaching aims, such as improving service provision, increasing efficiency, and spreading services and their associated impacts. In order to clarify under what conditions this occurs, *diffusion theory approaches* have been employed.

(4) External impact fields

In order to ascertain the type of changes (impacts) and their magnitude (scope, degree of diffusion) in the impact fields referred to here as external (from the point of view of the implementing organisation), the *impacts on the target audiences*, towards which a service is oriented or who are intended to benefit from programme measures (usually the target groups), are recorded. Furthermore, the impacts on social groups that do *not* belong directly to the *target groups*, but among which effects are nevertheless to be expected, are also measured. In addition, the impacts in the *social subsystems* or *policy fields* in which the interventions take place are measured, as well as in fields that are not the target of the interventions, but which are related to them.

In accordance with this approach, it is not sufficient to merely establish whether the intended *target groups* are *reached*, but it should also be examined whether other social groups are affected – unintentionally – by the service provision or intervention measures, either positively or negatively (e.g. through exclusion, a worsening of their situation etc.).

The question of whether target groups are reached, along with the issue of whether and to what extent the *target groups benefit* from the services offered or programmes carried out, is of central importance for many non-profit organisations. It should also be noted whether target groups (potential service recipients) know of the programme on offer, and are aware of, and utilise, their entitlement to the service. It may, for example, be the case that somebody does not wish to expose himself or herself as a social welfare recipient, or that someone finds the procedure at the employment agency demeaning and thus foregoes his or her entitlements. Or within a development project, the intended target group (e.g. elementary school leavers) may be replaced by a different one (e.g. high-school graduates), due to the training programme on offer being too demanding for the actual target group. A company may not be too concerned with who buys its products. If it turns out, for example, that high-school graduates rather than elementary school leavers respond to the offer, but that all business goals (turnover, profit, market position) are otherwise reached, in principle there is no imperative need for action. In the case of non-profit organisations the situation is different, though: for their service provision it is crucial that the 'right', i.e. the aimed-for target group, which has been identified as being in need, is also indeed the beneficiary.

Furthermore, in contrast to companies for whom the market determines supply and demand, in the case of many services on offer from non-profit organisations, all persons defined as belonging to the target group are 'eligible for benefit'. Thus, whether they are reached, or do not know anything of the service offered, or do not take advantage of it, due to certain underlying conditions (e.g. social shame, pressure, time and effort etc.), or whether others tend to benefit from the services offered, are important issues in an evaluation.

The *scope of impact* of services offered or programme measures implemented is another central assessment criterion, as it enables the establishment of the extent to which services offered have been utilised or innovations disseminated. Here the question arises of how many people (or organisations) benefit and/or whether system-changing impacts can be identified.

This can be illustrated with an example: a business start-up programme offers courses that impart innovative techniques and strategies for founding new companies. This programme is deemed successful if the persons trained actually use this knowledge to found new firms, ones that prove their ability to survive in the market over more than just the short term (sustainability). If non-participants of the course should also acquire this knowledge (e.g. by studying the course documents, copying the strategies of the persons trained), the scope of the programme's impact widens. So-called 'multipliers' are thus sometimes given targeted training, so that they pass on their knowledge and others profit from it, too. The greater the extent to which new techniques, procedures and knowledge are passed on, then, the more these 'innovations' are dispersed and lead to *'diffusion'*. In many projects and programmes, e.g. in the field of development cooperation, this is exactly the effect that is targeted. Farmers may apply new, more efficient cultivation methods, artisans may use new production methods, and small firms may boost their sales with novel marketing activities etc. The more the intended 'innovations' spread, the more people apply and derive benefit from them, and thus the broader is the scope of impact of such programmes.

With regard to the measuring and evaluation of *external impacts*, the following aspects should thus be considered:

- *Goal acceptance among target groups*
  is present if the intended target groups actively support the programme concept and its goals.
- *Target group attainment*
  has been achieved if the intended target groups are reached by the services rendered or measures implemented.
- *Target group utility*
  is present if the needs and demands of the target groups are met, and they are satisfied with the provision.
- *Diffusion*
  is present, firstly, if outputs and their resulting impacts not only benefit the immediate target groups, but also envelop additional population groups, i.e. if impacts arise beyond the target groups. Secondly, diffusion can also be established if outputs or impacts spread within the intended policy field (social subsystem), or even beyond.

As in the case of internal impacts that arise within the executing agency, an overall balance can also be compiled of external impacts. This is done by differentiating all observed changes (the gross outcome) based on whether they are attributable to programme interventions (in which case they are net, or programme, effects) or are the result of other factors. Intended programme impacts correspond to the programme goals. The effectiveness of a programme is determined by the extent to which the goals it targeted have been achieved.

(5) Sustainability

The concept of *sustainability* can, as shown in chapter 3.6, be applied at at least two different levels. At the *macro level* it is used to refer to concepts that attempt to reconcile *economic, social,* and *ecological variables.* Diverse concepts now exist in which these dimensions are operationalised in very different ways. The intention here is not to add a new facet to this multiplicity of theoretical concepts. Instead, the significance these three dimensions have for the implementation of programmes or for the service provision of non-profit organisations is determined in a pragmatic way.

An *economic variable* important for the quality appraisal of business enterprises is *efficiency*, which relates input to output. In the case of non-profit organisations, there are two reasons why this dimension is hard to measure. Firstly, input and, above all, output often cannot be quantified, and secondly, service prices are not regulated via markets. While input can often still be measured in quantitative terms and even in monetary units in the case of non-profit organisations - in the form of resources invested - this is frequently no longer possible in determining output and outcomes, meaning that only qualitative information can be resorted to. This can be illustrated with an example already used in this chapter.

Input: The funding increases of X million have led to the employment of Y more teachers in the school system.

Output: The number of classes arranged and children taught has thus risen from X to Y.

Outcome/impact: The (potential) outcomes caused by this can indeed be characterised qualitatively (e.g. an improvement in education standards at an individual and societal level), but the resultant economic effects can scarcely be specified in monetary terms.

The appraisal of the relationship between input and output, or between expenditure and income, is especially difficult to formulate if prices are not regulated by markets, e.g. because no free markets exist, with prices determined 'politically'. These determinations of course have a direct influence on income, and thus on the cost/income ratio.

While profit-oriented companies calculate and evaluate the price of a product or service before its introduction into the market, in order to establish whether it can be offered cost-effectively or profitably, the situation is different in the case of many services provided by non-profit organisations. What 'price' is appropriate for the support of social welfare recipients, or the question of how much the training of a university graduate should cost, or how expensive the placement of an unemployed person should be, is not regulated by markets. The price is not dependant on the decision of customers as to how much they are prepared to pay for a certain service; it is determined in other ways. In democratic societies, it is ultimately authorised decision-making bodies that decide what amount of funding is allocated to state-run services.

Although efficiency can often only be ascertained with difficulty in the non-profit sector, and not through the use of quantitative economic data alone, cost-benefit, cost-performance and cost-effectiveness analyses should be carried out all the same, even if only to a limited extent, in order to at least get an idea of the relationship between cost and output. This is the only way of estimating what outlay is necessary for the attainment of particular results or specific outcomes. Knowledge about the cost-performance or cost-effectiveness ratio is of great significance for the appraisal of programmes or services, as well as for the decision on their implementation or continuation, even if ultimately political, normative, ethical, or other valuation standards are also called upon. Moreover, the ascertainment of programme efficiency facilitates an examination of whether the outputs and impacts established can be achieved more economically in a different way.

Socio-political relevance can serve as a *social variable* for the sustainability of programmes or services of non-profit organisations, as it represents a central assessment criterion for tax-financed public institutions as well as non-profit organisations that are financed by donations or contributions.

In contrast to business enterprises, for whom socio-political criteria play only a small role in quality considerations (e.g. in EFQM: 6% of all criteria points), and for whom price and customer wants are governed by markets, non-profit organisations have to decide for themselves what funds should be employed for what measures and programmes, and what 'prices' should be requested for them.

While the demand for a commercial product is governed by the purchase decision of the customer, the need for a publicly-financed measure is determined democratically or directively. At best, the market of opinions and interests plays a role, in which various stakeholders, associations, parties, and lobbyists enjoy different weightings. Decision about the allocation of resources and performance of tasks are not made by customers, the buyers of a service or its claimants/recipients, but by political actors who (rather than the customers) have to legitimise them.

Particularly if there is no market or price mechanism, it is all the more important to examine the socio-political relevance of services or programme measures in relation to alternative uses of the resources employed and outcomes that could potentially be achieved.

Ultimately, the decision on what resources to use for what purpose, and how the impacts measured are to be assessed, is always a *normative* one. As long as the measurement of impacts does not go beyond a mere target/actual comparison - and thus remains an assessment of goal attainment – it, too, barely contributes towards objectifying this normative discussion. Only an open approach that encompasses unintended impacts and side-effects is capable of challenging the approach defined normatively at the start of the project or programme, and widening the perspective to take in new problems and objections against the procedure. Even though the assessment of effects achieved is ultimately subject to subjective appraisals, and a general consensus on the social relevance of measures and impacts is almost possible to achieve, a matter-of-fact measurement of impacts by outsiders using scientifically-recognised procedures can contribute significantly to objectifying the discussion, and thus to finding a compromise. Ultimately, the acceptance of the pursuit of profit and the continual increasing of efficiency as primary economic aims also represents a normative convention of capitalist society, which was opposed and even vehemently fought against by large sections of humanity up until very recently.

Closely related to the discussion about the *social limits* to unchecked economic development with no control through human intervention is, since the early 1970s at the latest, the issue of *ecological limits*. It is indisputable that, for all its technological possibilities, the human race has so far not been able to survive without the natural resources of planet Earth, and that this will certainly not change in the foreseeable future. However, the question of how much weight can be attached to strains on the ecosystem caused by human activities, what the effects of these activites are on it, and whether they should be tolerated or not, has until now by no means been answered unequivocally and conclusively. More recent measurement procedures, such as the "ecological footprint"[116], are certainly not uncontroversial, and the complex causal relationships in the ecosystem are far from having been comprehensively explored.

So, with regard to the sustainability of non-profit organisations' programmes or services, their *'environmental compatibility'* must by all means be considered as an *'ecological variable'*. Purely technically-oriented approaches such as "environmental impact assessment" are only of limited help here, even though they have become standard procedure in planning processes. Of late, the focus has been on integrative methods, which, under the guise of, for example, "strategic impact assessment", "social impact assess-

---

116 The *'ecological footprint'* concept is an attempt to ascertain the land and water area required for lastingly maintaining current living standards and lifestyles. These calculations incorporate, for instance, the area required for the production of foodstuffs and clothing, for the disposal of waste, and for the sequestration of carbon dioxide released. The sum total of the use of land and water space by all people is related to the actual total area of the Earth. Through disaggregation (assuming equal distribution), the 'footprint' can even be calculated for individuals, regions, countries or continents, and compared with others. The concept was developed by Mathis Wackernagel and William E. Rees (Wackernagel & Rees 1997), and has come to be supported by many NGOs (e.g. the WWF, which also supports the "Global Footprint Network" founded by Wackernagel: www.footprintnetwork.org). The major advantages of this indicator are its ease of interpretation, its relatively simple calculation, and the variety of possible comparative calculations. Its weaknesses are its static calculation of area required, its non-consideration of the multiple use of areas, and its bias towards Western culture (for information on the scientific discussion, cf. e.g. Chambers et al. 2000; van Kooten & Bulte 2000; van den Bergh & Verbruggen 1999, Lewan & Simmons 2001; Wackernagel et al. 2002).

ment", or "sustainable impact assessment", bring various dimensions together in ex-ante appraisals (cf. Kirkpatrick and George 2003; George and Kirkpatrick 2003). Experiences from the field of development cooperation have shown, however, that even such extensive refinement of planning procedures cannot ultimately replace the creation of suitable continuous monitoring and control instruments, which guarantee early reporting of (undesirable) developments to decision-making bodies.

Even though natural scientific methods are relatively advanced in comparison to those of social and economic science, even in this field such monitoring of impacts can only serve to objectify the normative discussion, but not to fundamentally decide it. Thus, for example, the question of whether society should follow a "sufficiency" strategy[117], characterised by non-consumption and self-limitation, can be equated with the question of to what extent nature is worth protecting and should be considered a good on a higher plane than individual self-interest. The debate about "weak" versus "strong sustainability" (cf. Pfister and Renn 1997), in which a strict ecological orientation of all economic activity is set against faith in the future substitutability of depleted resources, can be assessed in a similar way. If mankind were to follow the concept of "strong sustainability", it would no longer be allowed to use crude oil, for example. On the other hand, the use of this re-

---

117 *Sufficiency* refers to strategies that are oriented towards reducing resource consumption and demand for goods. The term is often used in environmental research, as distinct from efficiency (i.e. resource productivity) and consistency (i.e. the maintenance of ecological balance). The differences can be illustrated using an example as follows. The efficiency strategy demands from the car industry a reduction in petrol consumption relative to performance achieved, but not, however, an absolute reduction in the petrol consumption of all vehicles produced. The sufficiency strategy, on the other hand, expects a trend towards decreased consumption, which, if resource productivity were to stay the same, could also be achieved through lower vehicle performance. According to the consistency strategy, both approaches are wrong, as combustion engines continue to consume non-renewable resources. It demands the introduction of new motors, such as those with hydrogen-drive, for which a closed ecological cycle can be created.

The sufficiency strategy has come in for criticism, due especially to the radical demands of some of its exponents for a "new asceticism" (cf. e.g. Cramer 1997), and is often seen as "backward" and "anti-progress". However, more moderate exponents, such as the Wuppertal Institute for Climate, Environment and Energy in Germany (cf. Linz 2004, Bund & Misereor 1996), associate the sufficiency strategy with, on the one hand, management concepts aimed at reducing inputs whilst retaining product quality (i.e. resource-saving behaviour for increasing profits in the production field), and, on the other hand, with the concept of 'quality of life' (i.e. the theoretical possibility of demand satiation and accompanying satisfaction – in contrast to the notion of 'Homo economicus', which is based on assumptions of infinitely growing demands accompanied by constant dissatisfaction (on the concept of quality of life, cf. Glatzer & Zapf 1984)). In this sense, sufficiency seeks adequate satisfaction of needs, and a process of optimisation through a reduction in the outlay necessary for achieving this state of satisfaction; i.e. it is concerned with higher 'quality of life', and not 'abstinence' or the 'renunciation' of needs.

source, currently continuing to grow in an unchecked fashion, can easily be justified as "weak sustainability", posing the question of what is actually supposed to be novel in such an approach. Ultimately, ecological measures, just as economic and social ones, are in no way compulsory, logically-derivable imperatives, but rather conscious, normative decisions by people, that can at best be made in a factual manner on the basis of the existing, ever-increasing pool of knowledge on the impacts of measures.

In summary, it can be stated that *macro-level sustainability* is determined by *three variables*, which are operationalised in the following way:
- *Efficiency*
  is present if all intended outcomes are achieved with the deployment of as few resources as possible.
- *Social relevance*
  is present if the impacts that arise from services rendered are classed as socio-politically relevant and beneficial.
- *Environmental compatibility*
  is present if resources used to provide services are handled in an environmentally-friendly way, and if services rendered and resulting impacts are environmentally benign.

In order to be able to realise the desired future state of a society in which economic, social and ecological aims are in harmony with one another, there is a need, as has been emphasised, for political strategies and programmes that contribute to sustainable development. Here the question arises of whether measures only have an effect for as long as they are supported with funding, or whether structures can be created and changes in behaviour brought about that permanently alter a problem situation.

This can be illustrated using an example: assume that an incentive programme is intended to serve the integration of disabled apprentices. As long as funding is provided, the programme works flawlessly. However, if there is no success in bringing about a change in attitudes among companies (target groups) – with them recognising, for example, that disabled persons can fulfil the job requirements too – then employers will cease to take on disabled workers following termination of the support, with the programme proving unsustainable.

A further example, taken from the environment sector, underlines this problem: within the framework of a support programme implemented by the German Environmental Foundation, the creation of environmental consultation structures in local authorities and associations was financed. As shown by an evaluation, these structures have outlasted the cessation of support, and continue to be used for their original purpose (cf. Stockmann et al. 2000).

Sustainability only arises if organisational structures are formed and behavioural changes brought about that outlive the ending of support. In order to determine the *sustainability of programmes*, a sophisticated, multidimensional concept has been developed here, which is used to assess sustainability at the programme level. According to this concept, programme sustainability exists if the various dimensions of sustainability (programme-, output-, system- and innovation-oriented sustainability) are achieved (cf. chapter 3.6 fig. 3.10).

In summary, the *set of evaluation guidelines* comprises the following *areas of inquiry and assessment*:

(1) Information about the programme (especially its concept, aims, resources) and its environment (especially its field of practice/policy, target groups)

(2) The planning and implementation process of a programme throughout its life-cycle (preparation/planning, implementation, termination of support, aftercare support)

(3) The competence of the organisation implementing the programme or rendering the service, based on goal acceptance, personnel, organisational structure, resources, technology, as well as changes in these parameters over time (internal impacts)

(4) The type and magnitude of changes in external impact fields (those outside of the executing agency), especially goal acceptance among target groups, target group attainment, target group benefit, diffusion (external impacts)

(5) Sustainability

- At the macro level: the way and degree to which a programme (or service offered by an organisation) achieves the economic, social and ecological dimensions of sustainability, measured by efficiency, socio-political relevance and environmental compatibility

- At the programme level: dimensions of sustainability achieved, characterised as programme-, output-, system- or innovation-oriented sustainability.

While sustainability at the macro level can be assessed at any time using the three criteria specified, programme sustainability can only be measured explicitly following the termination of support. It refers, by definition, to the phase of the programme subsequent to support, and can therefore only be established through ex-post evaluations. Conclusions as to programme sustainability that are gleaned from life-cycle data prior to the cessation of support at best represent forecasts of future, expected sustainability.

Comparison of evaluation criteria used for assessing programmes

Before the set of evaluation guidelines is formulated in full on this basis, we should examine what criteria are identified or used for the evaluation of programmes in the literature and by major programme-implementing organisations.

An important actor is the Development Assistance Committee (DAC) of the Organisation for Economic Cooperation and Development (OECD), with which many national organisations align themselves, and which employs the following criteria for programme evaluations.[118]

Relevance: The extent to which the aid activity is suited to the priorities and policies of the target group, recipient and donor.

Effectiveness: A measure of the extent to which an aid activity attains its objectives.

Efficiency: Efficiency measures the outputs – qualitative and quantitative – in relation to the inputs. It is an economic term which signifies that the aid uses the least costly resources possible in order to achieve the desired results. This generally requires comparing alternative approaches to achieving the same outputs, to see whether the most efficient process has been adopted.

Impact: The positive and negative changes produced by a development intervention, directly or indirectly, intended or unintended. This involves the main impacts and effects resulting from the activity on the local social, economic, environmental and other development indicators. The examination should be concerned with both intended and unintended results and must also include the positive and negative impact of external factors, such as changes in terms of trade and financial conditions.

Sustainability: Sustainability is concerned with measuring whether the benefits of an activity are likely to continue after donor funding has been withdrawn. Projects need to be environmentally as well as financially sustainable.

Very similar criteria are put forward by Bussmann, Klöti and Knoepfel (1997: 100 ff.) for assessment within political evaluation:

- Output
- Impact
- Effectiveness
- Outcome
- Efficacy
- Cost-effectiveness (efficiency).[119]

---

118 http://www.oecd.org/document/22/0,2340,en_2649_34435_2086550_1_1_1_1,00.html (November 2000).
119 Cf. also Shadish et al. 1991; Knoepfel et al. 1997: 98 ff.; Rossi, Freeman & Lipsey 1999: 22 ff.

Posavac and Carey (1997: 42 ff.) formulate their criteria as questions:

- Does the program or plan match the values of the stakeholders?
- Does the program or plan match the needs of the people to be served?
- Does the program as implemented fulfill the plans?
- Do the outcomes achieved match the goals?
- Is there support for the program theory?
- Is the program accepted?
- Are the resources devoted to the program being expended appropriately?

Vedung (1999: 223) applies four assessment criteria for the evaluation of state interventions:

- Effectiveness	=	degree of goal attainment of outcomes, irrespective of cost
- Productivity	=	output relative to cost
- Efficiency (cost-benefit)	=	monetarised value of programme impacts relative to monetarised programme costs
- Efficiency (cost-effectiveness)	=	objectively expressed programme impacts relative to monetarised programme costs

If we compare the criteria obtained here on the basis of theoretical deliberations with those used in programme evaluations, it becomes clear that some are identified frequently and others seldom or not at all (cf. fig. 3.12). The assessment criterion mentioned most often is *goal attainment (effectiveness)*, which often also encompasses *target group attainment* and the *scope of effectiveness* in its definition. Evaluations that focus on this criterion are very strongly goal-oriented. As will be shown in the next chapter, this kind of approach differs from the concept favoured here, under which observed impacts are recorded first of all using the set of evaluation guidelines, and only then is it assessed whether the changes detected are the result of programme impacts or the effects of other factors, with the degree of goal attainment (effectiveness) then ultimately being determined.

The assessment criteria *output, outcome, impact* and *efficiency* (economy, cost-benefit ratio, cost-effectiveness ratio) are also mentioned frequently. However, the terms used are not always based on identical definitions.

Target group factors (such as programme acceptance, target group requirements, conformance of the programme with the values of stakeholders) and the *issue of resources* are seldom dealt with (cf. Posavac & Carey 1997). *'Customer satisfaction'*, a central issue in the quality management discussion, is largely omitted, even though in the field of evaluation too it is deemed necessary to use the satisfaction of target groups (users) as an assessment criterion: "Although client satisfaction alone is not sufficient as a measure of quality, it is universally accepted as one of several necessary outcome measures"[120] (Royse et al. 2001: 192).

While *efficiency*, which here is identified as a component of *macro-level sustainability*, is often used (even though it is given differing definitions), *socio-political relevance* is rarely mentioned, and *environmental compatibility* not at all. The DAC does use the concept of *relevance*, but in a very narrow sense, only using it to refer to the degree "to which the aid activity is suited to the priorities and policies of the target group, recipient and donor".[121]

Programme-level sustainability is (among the selection made here) likewise only employed as an assessment criterion by the DAC, and, in respect of the sustainability typology developed in this book (cf. chapter 3.6, fig. 3.10), refers only to the first dimension.

As an *intermediate conclusion* from this comparison, it can be stated that the assessment criteria typically employed in programme evaluations are all included in the list of criteria derived in this work. Moreover, certain individual criteria are defined in a more differentiated way, with new ones added to them. So, the criteria used here are compatible with those frequently encountered in programme evaluations, serve to complement them, and, to some extent, go beyond them.

Another important finding of this comparison is that the criteria typically used in programme evaluations only correspond to the impact fields characterised here as 'external'. Criteria for assessing the planning and implementation process (management process), and the competence of programme-implementing organisations, on the other hand, are not to be found. In this sense, the evaluation design developed here is distinguished by its *holistic approach*. It *encompasses criteria for assessing the organisational and situational context conditions of a programme, as well as the internal and external impacts brought about by intervention measures.* This produces the following *advantages*:

(1) The holistic approach provides the possibility of achieving *as complete a coverage as possible* of all relevant impact fields.

(2) Through the characterisation of programme interventions and the assessment of organisational and situational context conditions, the chance of *being able* to correctly *attribute causes* also *increases*.

(3) Due to the *high flexibility* of the evaluation design with regard to various fields of application and evaluation tasks, it is particularly suited to non-profit organisations, which are active in very diverse fields of policy and practice, and have a broad range of different aims and functions.

---

120 Cf. footnote 53.
121 Cf. also Rogers (1995: 11), who distinguishes between "earlier adopters" and "later adopters".

Figure 3.12: Assessment criteria for evaluation

DAC, 2005	Bussmann et al., 1997	Posavac & Carey, 1997	Vedung, 1999	Stockmann, 2008
Impact	Impact			Impacts
	Outcome	Outcome		Programme outcomes
	Output			
Effectiveness	Effectiveness Efficacy	Effectiveness	Effectiveness	Effectiveness
		Goal and programme acceptance among target groups		Goal acceptance
		Consistency with target group values and require-ments		Relevance to target group Benefit to target group Target group attainment
				Diffusion
Efficiency	Efficiency	Efficiency	Efficiency: cost-benefit and -effectiveness ratios, productivity	Efficiency
Relevance				Socio-political relevance
				Environmental compatibility
Sustainability				Programme-level sustainability

3.7.3 Quality criteria

Although the various *criteria* for assessing programmes mostly do not lead directly to the establishment of the quality of the programme, they can nevertheless be *used for quality appraisal*. Ultimately, the determination of the value or utility of an intervention is the aim of every programme evaluation (cf. Rossi, Lipsey & Freemann 2004: 208; Vedung 1999: 213; Mertens 1998: 219). Such a *determination of value or benefit* can, then, also be used as a *gauge of the quality* of a programme, measure, or service offered. In such a case, *evaluation criteria* are *simultaneously 'quality criteria'* too (e.g. in the case of Vedung 1999: 223). If this perspective is taken, then the theoretically-derived assessment criteria for programme evaluation can be compared with the criteria used in business management quality concepts.[122]

In what has become a classic distinction, which can be traced back to Donabedian (1980: 80), *three dimensions of service quality* are identified (cf. Eversheim et al. 1997: 36, Eversheim 1997: 10 f., 2000: 10 f.; Raidl 2001: 33 ff.):

- *Structural quality*
  refers to all temporally stable conditions that put an organisation in a position to provide a service (e.g. buildings, technical equipment, personnel).
- *Process quality*
  describes the procedure of service provision, i.e. all activities that take place in the course of services being rendered, including in dealings with customers.
- *Outcome quality*
  refers to the achievement of service aims and customer satisfaction with service provision.

In a further categorisation, attributable to Garvin (1984: 25 ff.), *five quality dimensions* are distinguised, which go beyond the distinction made by Donabedian (1980: 80) (cf. also Oppen 1995: 43 ff.; Schubert & Zink 1997: 3 ff.; Schedler & Proeller 2003: 69 f.):

- *Product-related quality*
  is determined by individual features of the product itself.
- *Customer-related quality*
  is measured by whether the product corresponds to customer demands (customer satisfaction).
- *Value-related quality*
  indicates whether a product or service is worth its price, by relating input to output (efficiency).
- *Political quality*
  is measured by the political benefit that a product or service creates. A distinction is made between the objective benefit to society (e.g. improvement in living standards, security) and the social benefit (e.g. social peace, community cohesion).
- *Process-related quality*
  is determined by the degree of dependability of processes (few errors), as well as by their optimisation (speed, efficiency), and also encompasses the standards-compliant and correct rendering of a service.

Below, we shall briefly examine to what extent the quality dimensions developed by Donabedian and Garvin differ from the evaluation criteria used here. Figure 3.13, which portrays the different characteristics in summary form, may serve as an orientation aid.

---

122 The criteria used in TQM models such as EFQM ('enabler' criteria and results criteria) do not constitute quality criteria, as these models are not concerned with measuring quality against certain selected criteria, but rather with creating it in a processual way.

In the business management quality discussion, *process quality* refers to the procedure of service provision (Donabedian 1980: 80), or to the processes and their optimisation that ensure the standards-compliant and correct rendering of a service (Garvin 1984: 25 ff.). *Structural quality* encompasses all temporally stable conditions that enable a company to render a service (Donabedian 1980: 80).

In the evaluation design developed in this book, these two aspects are also dealt with, but are divided up analytically in a different way. On the one hand, the planning and implementation (management) process of intervention measures or programmes is assessed – which could be referred to as *'planning and implementation quality'*. On the other hand, the competence of the programme-implementing organisation is assessed, as it is assumed that a capable organisation is necessary for effective implementation (i.e. that is oriented towards achieving maximum target-oriented outcomes). An appraisal of its structures and processes is required in order to establish this.

As programme interventions can target both the executing agency (implementing organisation) and, beyond this, external impact fields, impacts are to be expected both within the executing agency (referred to here as internal impacts) and in external impact fields (e.g. among target groups, in policy fields etc.). It is therefore sensible to distinguish between *'internal impact-based quality'*, with respect to the competence of the executing agency and the impacts triggered within it, and *'external impact-based quality'*, if external impacts are being assessed. In the latter case, it should be ascertained and assessed, among other things, to what extent target groups accept and support the programme, whether and to what degree they are reached by the programme measures, what benefit is produced, whether the demands of audiences (users) are met and how satisfied they are with the services or programme offered, and what diffusion effects have arisen among target groups and in policy fields. Furthermore, the recorded impacts are examined with regard to whether they are of an intended or unintended nature, and what goals have been attained. The *sustainability* dimension of programmes and measures, crucial for the work of non-profit organisations, does not appear in the quality concepts of Donabedian, Garvin et al. Under the evaluation design developed here, the impacts caused within the executing agency, and in the fields of practice, policy and beyond, are assessed using a multidimensional sustainability model.

In the private sector quality debate, the assessment dimensions are focused on the *quality of results* (Donabedian 1980: 80) and *product- and customer-related quality* (Garvin 1984: 25 ff.). That is to say, they are concerned to a far greater extent with direct goal attainment and customer satisfaction. Evaluations, in comparison, not only cover a far broader, more complex range of outcomes, but also include unintended effects in all areas of assessment.

The quality dimensions efficiency (ratio of input to output) and relevance (usefulness to society) are employed in both Garvin's (1984) model and the evaluation design developed here. The dimension of environmental compatibility is also included here, and together these three dimensions operationalise the three pillars of sustainability, as an economic, social and environmental variable.

Figure 3.13: Assessment dimensions in quality and evaluation concepts

| Quality criteria | | Evaluation criteria (Stockmann) |
Donabedian	Garvin	
Process quality	Process-related quality	Planning (programme design) Control (implementation)
Structural quality	-----	Competence of the programme-implementing organisation Internal impact balance
Results quality	Product- and customer-related quality	Goal acceptance among target groups Target group attainment Benefit Diffusion External impact balance
-----	-----	Programme sustainability
-----	Value-related and political quality	Efficiency Social relevance Environmental compatibility

Whilst value-related quality (efficiency) is dominant in business management quality dimensions - in order to determine whether a product or service is worth its price - and the cost-performance or cost-effectiveness ratio is thus extensively examined, political quality (or social relevance) plays a rather secondary role. In the evaluation of non-profit organisations, exactly the reverse is often the case.

It can thus be stated that, as the highest and most widespread aim of evaluation is the determination of the value or benefit of a measure or programme, the criteria used for evaluation can, at the same time, be employed to assess service or programme quality. Analogous to the quality dimensions developed by Donabedian, Garvin at al., the evaluation criteria derived here can be condensed into *four quality dimensions* (cf. fig. 3.14).

(1) Planning and implementation quality is determined by – as set out above – the extent to which, during the planning phase, the problem situation and target group requirements have been 'correctly' identified, and to which a programme has been developed that is appropriate for dealing with the problem and takes into account stakeholder interests and the given context conditions. Another contributory factor is whether, during the implementation phase, planning errors and implementation problems have been identified in good time, with prompt management interventions following.

(2) Planning and implementation quality has a direct influence on internal and external impact fields. A competent 'executing agency' is necessary for programme implementation. The strengthening of this organisation may, in some cases, be a programme aim. But, regardless of this, impacts are certain to arise within the implementing organisation merely through its carrying out the programme. The extent to which the executing agency is up to the task, and what changes have occurred over time (internal impact balance), can be assessed based on the organisational evaluation criteria specified (goal acceptance, personnel qualification, organisational structure, resources, technology), and combined under the heading *'internal impact-based quality'*.

(3) 'Planning and implementation quality', as well as 'internal impact-based quality', have an influence on external impact fields, i.e. the fields of policy and practice in which a programme produces impacts. The extent to which *'external impact-based quality'* has been achieved is assessed using the evaluation criteria target group acceptance, target group attainment, benefit that has arisen among the target groups and beyond, and diffusion effects, and is evaluated based on a subsequent impact balance that also incorporates the degree of goal attainment (in external impact fields).

(4) The fourth quality dimension comprises, firstly, *programme-level sustainability*, which is influenced by the effects on internal (executing agency) and external impact fields. It is assessed using the multidimensional sustainability concept developed here. This quality dimension also includes *macro-level sustainability*, which is made up of three variables, and can also be referred to as *economic, social and ecological sustainability*. Whilst the criteria specified previously can largely be assessed based on empirical data, the quality dimension 'macro-level sustainability' contains a strongly normative element of judgement. The appraisal of the *efficiency, socio-political relevance* and *environmental compatibility* of non-profit sector products and services can – as has been discussed in detail – only be carried out with the aid of abstract moral concepts, political principles, or societal laws and regulations.

The quality along each dimension is assessed more positively, the higher the individual assessment criteria are rated:

- The more target group- and problem-oriented, flexible etc. the nature of planning and implementation (cf. chapter 3.7.2), the more positively *planning and implementation quality* is assessed.
- The more competent the executing agency (measured using the selected organisational parameters), and the more positive the internal impact balance, the more highly *internal impact-based quality* is rated.
- The greater the goal/programme acceptance among target groups, the greater the benefit of and satisfaction with the service and programme provision, the greater the diffusion among audiences and within the programme-related fields of policy and practice, and the more positive the external impact balance, the more highly *external impact-based quality* is rated.

- The higher the efficiency, socio-political relevance, and environmental compatibility, the more positively the *quality of macro-level sustainability* is assessed. The *quality of programme-level sustainability* is determined using the multidmensional sustainability concept.

Figure 3.14: Quality dimensions for the assessment of the outputs and impacts of (non-profit) organisations

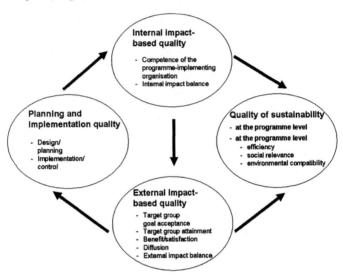

As a basic summary, the following *causal relationships* exist between the *four quality dimensions*:
- The higher the quality of planning and implementation, the higher the *internal impact-based quality*, as any performance deficits in the executing agency are removed.
- The higher the internal impact-based quality, the higher the *external impact-based quality*, as it is assumed that a capable executing agency is necessary for effective programme implementation.
- The higher the internal and external impact-based quality, the higher the *sustainability of the programme*, as it is assumed that the likelihood of achieving sustainability rises if an effective executing agency is present, if target groups value the programme/service provision highly, use it and are satisfied with it, and if the target groups are reached and high diffusion effects facilitate as wide and deep a dispersal as possible.

- The higher the internal and external impact-based quality, the higher the *macro-level sustainability*, as an effective executing agency is required for the efficient rendering of services or implementation of programmes, and because social relevance and environmental compatibility are dependent upon target group acceptance, the rate of use, satisfaction with the provision, and dissemination within the relevant policy fields.

If we compare the quality dimensions formulated by Donabedian, Garvin et al., as well as the criteria/standards used within the scope of TQM (EFQM) and ISO certification, with those used in programme evaluation, it is noticeable that, *under business management approaches, primarily internal criteria relating to the organisation and its structures and processes are employed. Under programme evaluation, on the other hand, primarily those criteria that relate to 'external' impact fields are employed.* Quality dimensions such as 'impact quality' or 'customer-related quality', which, in a broad sense, represent 'external impacts', encompass only a narrow range of interests. Whilst ISO deals almost exclusively with internal organisational processes, under EFQM 'social results' are appraised, even though they are only given a marginal weighting. Within Garvin's model of quality, the appraisal of 'political quality' at least represents the inclusion of one socially relevant parameter.

Figure 3.15: Causal relationships among quality dimensions

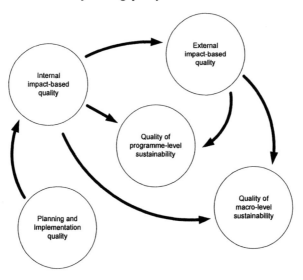

With regard to programme evaluation criteria, it has already been pointed out that these barely incorporate internal dimensions relating to the organisation or programme (service provision), but rather concentrate almost exclusively on the evaluation of 'external' areas of activity.

The evaluation model developed here merges the two perspectives by theoretically deriving five areas for assessment, which have, moreover, proved themselves empirically in numerous evaluation studies. On top of the programme and its situational context, the following are also assessed: the planning and implementation (management) of a programme (or service); internal quality dimensions, i.e. those relating to the executing agency (internal impact fields); external parameters, i.e. those relating to fields of practice/policy and target groups (external impact fields); and macro- and programme-level sustainability. So, the design developed here *integrates internal and external areas of assessment*, and thus represents a *holistic approach*.

If we compare the four quality dimensions formulated in this work with those developed by Donabedian, Garvin et al., it also becomes clear that the focus of the latter is on product-, customer- and value-/economy-related quality. This is in line with the contextual conditions and tasks of companies operating on the free market. The quality dimensions defined within the framework of the evaluation approach developed here, on the other hand, are much more strongly oriented towards intended and unintended impacts triggered, which are recorded in a sophisticated way and on a wide scale, and are then related to each other. In addition to a comprehensive examination of changes to the executing agency based on theoretical organisational criteria, which are also relevant to business management analyses, the analysis of external impact-based quality goes way beyond a product- or customer-based approach.

Whilst programme-level sustainability has no equivalent in the business management quality dimensions, the dimensions of efficiency and relevance, but not environmental compatibility, are in fact given consideration. However, efficiency is attributed with a high, and relevance rather a lesser, degree of importance.

It can thus be stated that the *evaluation criteria* derived from the evaluation approach developed in this book, and the *quality dimensions* formulated from them:

(1) Incorporate the assessment criteria commonly used in programme evaluations, which relate primarily to external areas of evaluation.
(2) Contain internal criteria relating to the implementing organisation, as can be found in business management approaches too, but without their narrow restriction to internal processes.
(3) Correspond to the contextual conditions, management requirements, and quality demands of non-profit organisations.

The conclusion is thus reached that the evaluation approach developed here is particularly suitable for the *measurement and assessment of the output and impacts* of non-profit organisations, because:

(1) The criteria compiled here, in contrast to programme evaluation, do not merely focus on 'external' assessment factors concerned with the field of policy, goal attainment, target groups etc.
(2) Unlike under business management approaches, the focus is not only on the use of 'internal' assessment factors (quality dimensions).
(3) It not only encompasses business-oriented dimensions, as employed to determine the quality of products and services of profit companies; but rather the criteria are derived based on universal considerations of organisational theory, that are, in principle, valid for organisations of any kind.

4 Evaluation Methodology and Application

4.1 Overview

At the centre of this chapter is, firstly, the development of a set of evaluation guidelines. This is based on the subject areas and criteria identified in the previous chapter, and serves the examination and assessment of structures and conditions, as well as of changes in these over time. Secondly, the basic principles necessary for applying the set of guidelines will be set out.

The *set of evaluation guidelines (chapter 4.2)* constitutes the core of the evaluation concept developed here, which follows an impact-based approach. This means that, in contrast to classic target/actual comparisons, the focus is not on goal attainment, but rather on the search for empirically observable changes in a programme's environment. The evaluation guidelines serve to structure and give direction to the collection of information. Building on the three theoretical approaches – the life-cycle model, and the theoretical conceptions of organisations and innovation/diffusion – as well as on the multidimensional sustainability model, a *sample set of evaluation guidelines* will be produced. In general, such sets of guidelines can be developed for all measures, projects, programmes or institutionalised service provision by organisations, and applied to all phases of their life-cycle within both formative and summative evaluations. Using this 'prototype' as a starting point, the analytical questions that are classified within it according to subject area are to be supplemented, expanded and adjusted.

Chapter 4.3.1 outlines how to proceed in carrying out the *information search*. In accordance with the impact approach, the starting conditions and observed changes over time are recorded, compared with intended goals, and, finally, examined with regard to their cause (causality). The primary advantage of this approach is that it avoids a premature narrowing of the perspective to focus just on goals and their attainment, and thus reduces the risk of unintended impacts being neglected.

Each *subject block* of the set of evaluation guidelines features a series of *central questions*, which serve to ascertain the starting conditions and changes that have occurred over time. In order to condense the information obtained, each subject block ends with an '*appraisal line*', which incorporates all quantitative and qualitative data that have been collected. This approach facilitates comparisons over time or, in the case of meta-analyses, between programmes too, and makes it possible to create programme profiles, with which programme development can be depicted in compressed form (*chapter 4.3.2*).

The subject blocks of the analytical framework contain a multitude of phenomena that are not directly measurable (e.g. goal acceptance, employee qualification, employee satisfaction). In order to nevertheless obtain data on these non-directly depictable phenomena, empirical social research employs '*indicators*'. What these are, what requirements they are supposed to fulfil, how they are designed, and what should be borne in mind when dealing with them, is set out in *chapter 4.3.3*. Especially if a monitoring and evaluation system is to be developed, in order to provide programme managers with a continuous stream of management-relevant data, then the creation of an indicator database is necessary. For this purpose, data are collected at regular intervals and stored. The structure of the database is aligned with the subject areas of the set of evaluation guidelines. For each of the central questions listed there, appropriate indicators should be developed for data collection.

The question of 'how' to go about measuring is dealt with in *chapter 4.4*. In principle, all *test designs and data collection methods* well-known in empirical social research can be used for evaluation research, but not all of them are equally suitable for the evaluation of impacts. In *chapter 4.4.1*, the designs most relevant for impact evaluations are presented, and their benefits and drawbacks discussed. The selection of a test design that is appropriate for the evaluation problem at hand is especially important for the clear determination of net impacts, since if the scope and magnitude of impacts that emanate from a programme are underestimated, there is a danger of the programme being curtailed or even completely phased out. If, on the other hand, programme effects are overestimated, there is a converse risk of money being invested in a programme that is not at all, or only barely, effective. *Selection of the test design* is thus of crucial significance, especially for *causal analysis*.

The *collection methods* with which data can be obtained to ascertain the impacts and detection of causal relationships are the subject of *chapter 4.4.2*. First of all, the methods are presented which are most important in evaluation, followed by an explanation of why a 'multi-method approach' is generally preferable. Through the application of various quantitative and qualitative methods, the aim is to compensate for the weaknesses of one data collection tool with the strengths of another. It is important in all cases – as with test designs – that evaluators are aware of the methods that can potentially be employed, and of their different strengths and weaknesses, so that they can select and apply a combination suitable for the evaluation problem at hand.

As evaluations take place in a *social context*, evaluators require not only a high degree of methodological competence, but also the ability to find their way around the complex evaluation environment, which is usually characterised by divergent stakeholder interests. As emphasised earlier on, evaluation differs from basic research in a number of respects. Not only in the sense that evaluation should always create value, and frequently constitutes contract research, but also because it takes place in a political environment, and thus quickly becomes a political issue itself. What needs to be considered in this context, and what standards are to be adhered to, is dealt with in *chapter 4.5.1*.

The various interests and perspectives of stakeholders can best be considered and integrated within the framework of a *participatory evaluation approach*. This facilitates not only the increasing of stakeholder acceptance of the performance of the evaluation and, in the long term, of the implementation of its results, but also the optimisation of the evaluation design. Through the interaction of evaluators (methodological experts) and persons responsible for programme implementation (subject matter experts), or those otherwise involved with or affected by the programme (target groups in particular), methodological knowledge and insider knowledge can be combined. This can then be used to develop an evaluation design that not only meets the information requirements of clients and those responsible for the programme, but also incorporates the perspectives and views of other stakeholders (especially target groups). Such a participatory evaluation model is presented in *chapter 4.5.2*.

Before an evaluation can be carried out, the individual *stages* need to be planned in as much detail as possible. This is the subject of *chapter 4.6*, in which the process sequence of evaluation is roughly outlined, with the focus on practical advice as to how to approach it. Here too, the explanation is necessarily limited to a number of fundamental observations.

Overall, chapter 4 is set out in such a way as to describe in detail the development of the set of evaluation guidelines, as well as the management of the application and assessment procedure, as these represent the core of the evaluation concept developed in this book (chapter 4.2 and 4.3). With regard to the 'methods of evaluation' (chapter 4.4), on the other hand, it is sufficient to simply present an overview, as there is extensive and multifaceted literature on this subject which can be referred to during application. This is also true of the 'social context of evaluation' (chapter 4.5) and the 'process of evaluation' (chapter 4.6), but the evaluation concept developed here, along with the participatory approach to evaluation planning and implementation, necessitate some additional knowledge, which will be discussed with the support of practical experiences.

4.2 Evaluation guidelines

As has been stressed a number of times, the evaluation concept developed in this book is of an impact-based nature. The set of evaluation guidelines developed is thus primarily concerned with the *measurement and assessment of impacts* produced by an organisation's service provision, or by the programme or measures that it implements. To this end, however, it is also necessary to examine the structures, processes and conditions under which impacts arise. Only by doing this is it possible to carry out a subsequent causal analsysis.

Evaluations often concentrate heavily, or even exclusively, on *goal attainment*. Yet this represents – as explained in chapter 3.2 – only a subset of all programme impacts, namely the intended ones. The role that the aims of a programme should play in impact evaluation is, however, contentious.

As shown by the comparison of evaluation criteria that are applied (undertaken in chapter 3.7.2 (fig. 3.12)), the assessment of the effectiveness of a programme is of central significance. One of the most important issues as regards impacts is therefore: "To what extent is the programme successful in achieving its goals?" (Weiss 1974: 47). Here, the goals of a programme become, in a similar way to in the case of the comparison of standards with reality, the benchmark of the empirical analysis (cf. Mayntz 1980c: 4). Within the *classic goal model of evaluation research*, the degree of actual goal attainment is determined only along the intended goal dimensions, using a target/actual comparison (cf. Hellstern & Wollmann 1980a: 7; Lange 1983: 260; Wollmann 1994: 174).[123] This is done by ascertaining the programme goals, translating them into measurable indicators of goal attainment, collecting data on the indicators among the target groups, and comparing these data with the goal criteria (cf. Weiss 1974: 47; Meyers 1980: 110 ff.; Rossi et al. 1988: 21 ff.).

A prerequisite for a *results evaluation* of this nature is thus the existence of specified programme aims that are able to be operationalised. However, this can present a number of *problems*:

- Programme goals are often only vaguely formulated, being very abstract in their nature. Weiss (1974: 48) thus notes that: "At times the official goals are merely a long list of empty, and sometimes irreconcilable, platitudes (cf. also Derlien 1976: 21; Grabatin 1981: 23; Brandtstädter 1990b: 221; Vedung 1999: 54).
- Official goals may diverge from those actually pursued. Goal specifications are often only part of a political rhetoric of legitimation, which bear little resemblance to actual programme processes (cf. Etzioni 1971: 34; Weiss 1974: 48; Brandtstädter 1990b: 221; Vedung 1999: 55).
- Goals tend to undergo change over time, leading to a danger of assessing goal attainment based on goals that are no longer relevant (cf. Hall 1980: 537; Lange 1983: 263).
- Multiple actors are involved with the implementation of a programme, and they may all pursue different (sometimes even contradictory) goals. The question thus arises of what goals the achievement of results should be measured against (cf. Weiss 1974: 48; Bussmann et al. 1997: 47).
- If goal dimensions are taken as the starting point of an investigation, there is a risk that unintended effects get systematically neglected (cf. Lange 1983: 263; Weiss 1974: 56 ff.).[124] Yet it is precisely these effects that may prove to be decidedly interesting and

---

[123] If only intended changes (= goals) are empirically measured, this is referred to as *performance control*.
[124] For information on the unintended consequences of activities, cf. also Halfar 1987; Schwefel 1987a, b, c; Lachenmann 1987.

significant (cf. Brandtstädter 1990b: 221; Sherrill 1984: 34; Lachenmann 1987: 319; Posavac & Carey 1997: 25).[125]

Because of these problems with goal-oriented evaluation, a number of evaluation researchers consider it "unwise for evaluation to focus on whether a project has 'attained its goals'" (Cronbach et al. 1981: 5). It should be borne in mind that: "Evaluators who know the goals of the program might unintentionally focus on information that supports the goal and not observe how the program is actually administered or assess the total impact on the program's clients"[126] (Posavac & Carey 1997: 25). Scriven (1991: 180) thus recommends: "In the pure form of this type of evaluation, the evaluator is not told the purpose of the program but does the evaluation with the purpose of finding out what the program is actually doing without being cued as to what it is trying to do".

Scriven (1967, 1980, 1983, 1991) is also of the opinion that the specification of goals necessarily leads to the incomplete ascertainment of programme consequences, which moreover reflects the interests of just a small group of stakeholders, and he thus proposes the performance of 'goal-free' evaluations (cf. also Lachenmann 1987: 319, Cook & Matt 1990: 19). This *'goal-free approach'* was also a reaction "to what was seen as a slavish acceptance of the objectives-based approach to impact evaluation" (Owen & Rogers 1999: 269). It was thus recommended that the specified or intended goals of a programme be disregarded: "The purpose is to examine all program effects, rather than limiting the investigation to outcomes which reflect program objectives" (ibid.). Goal-free evaluation is seen as offering the following advantages (cf. Scriven 1991: 180):

- The costly, time-consuming, complex definition and weighting of programme goals is dispensed with.
- Goal-free evaluation disrupts ongoing programme implementation to a lesser extent, as actors need not account for programme aims.
- The social, perceptual and cognitive influencing of evaluators is less likely, as they have less contact with programme managers and staff.
- It is reversible, i.e. it can give way to a goal-oriented evaluation at a later stage; yet the opposite of this is not possible.

However, since *all programmes and services exhibit* a certain, though not always explicitly formulated, *value and goal orientation* (cf. Brandtstädter 1990b: 221), the idea of completely "goal-free programmes or goal-free evaluations would be extremely naïve" (Weiss 1974: 22). Owen and Rogers (1999: 269), among others, also refer to this point:

---

125 The goal approach is also criticised for not giving consideration to why a programme is successful or otherwise (cf. Weiss 1974: 48), or whether a programme could have achieved its aims more effectively (cf. Brandtstädter 1990b: 221). Moreover, the objection is made against it that not all evaluation criteria can be derived from the goal system (cf. Budäus & Dobler 1977: 69; Weiss 1974: 48).

126 Cf. footnote 53.

"Practically, the notion of deliberately ignoring the intentions of a programmatic intervention borders on the bizarre. Commissioners and clients are almost always interested in whether program objectives have been met, and the evaluator would need to go to extremes to ignore information about how the program is meant to operate".

Issues of *goal attainment and assessment* can thus hardly be excluded from the scope of activity of an impact-based evaluation, but it should certainly not focus on these exclusively. This could potentially lead to important effects remaining disregarded, dramatically influencing conclusions as to the success, effectiveness and sustainability of a programme (cf. Shadish 1990: 166).[127]

As the focus in this book is on the impacts produced by a service or programme, a sole orientation towards specified goals is not sufficient, for the reasons given. Instead, an *impact approach* is preferred, which aims, in a hypothesis-driven way, to ascertain empirically as many (intended and unintended) impacts as possible. Only then is it determined whether these impacts correspond to programme goals and, in addition, whether they are the consequences of programme interventions. The *hypothesis-driven search* is *structured by* the *set of evaluation guidelines*. These guidelines are based on the theoretical considerations presented in chapter 3, and apply the assessment criteria developed there. They serve to examine existing structures and conditions, as well as any changes detected over the course of support and possibly beyond. The issue of whether the changes observed are attributable to programme measures or other causes is also dealt with.

To this end, in addition to the programme and its environment and the intervention process itself (particularly its planning and implementation), the programme-executing (service-performing) agency and external impact fields are also examined. A distinction is made between impacts produced by the programme interventions, planned or unplanned, within the executing agency (internal impacts), and those that go beyond the executing agency (external impacts). The set of evaluation guidelines concludes with an assessment of programme quality, carried out using the *four* quality dimensions developed. If the evaluation is of an ex-post nature, programme-level sustainability can also be established. The evaluation guidelines are indeed oriented towards theoretical requirements, but are

---

127 If the *value of a programme* is to be assessed, in addition to the assessment of the *effectiveness* and *sustainability* of the programme, an *efficiency assessment* must also be carried out. Whilst impact analysis attempts to discover whether a programme achieves its aims, and what impacts have arisen due to the programme, an efficiency assessment estimates the cost-benefit ratio with regard to resources employed and results. This involves ascertaining what costs have been incurred by whom , and to whom what benefits have accrued. A programme is deemed efficient if maximum benefit has arisen with minimum resource deployment (cf. Hellstern & Wollmann 1984: 25; White 1986: 18; Rossi 2004: 343 ff.).

designed based on *technical data collection logic*. The basic structure of the set of guidelines is depicted in fig. 4.1.

(1) Programme and environment

The first section of the set of guidelines is concerned with the *description of measures or programmes* and their *intervention environment*. Specifically, the programme goals, programme and innovation concept, and human, financial and technical resources should be characterised. When *describing goals*, the various goal levels and stakeholders should be taken into account. For example, the extent to which the individual goals are compatible with each other, what goal conflicts may exist, etc. should be analysed. The analysis of the *programme concept* should deal primarily with the implicit 'programme theory'. Here it should be examined on what analytical levels (individual, organisational, systemic) and along what dimensions (behaviour, processes, structures) impacts are to be produced (cf. chapter 3, fig. 3.1), what cause-effect relationships are assumed, and how environmental and risk factors are assessed. Another important element is the description of the *innovations* themselves that are to be introduced through the programme interventions, as well as the appraisal thereof with regard to existing structures and systems.

As explained earlier, the set of guidelines is intended to implement an impact-based evaluation approach. The guidelines sections "programme and impact concept" therefore enjoy particular significance - for the measurement and assessment of impacts, and subsequent causal analysis. In addition to deriving the cause-effect, innovation and diffusion hypotheses on which the programme is either explicitly or implicitly based, specific cause-effect hypotheses should also be formulated on the basis of the three theoretical approaches presented (the life-cycle model, organisational theory, and the innovation/diffusion model), irrespective of whether these are already explicitly or implicitly contained within the programme and innovation concept. Firstly, this avoids important programme considerations and intended aims not being given sufficient attention. And secondly, the formulation of hypotheses independent of actual programme goals (based on theoretical relationships) should ensure that unplanned impacts (from the point of view of the programme) are not overlooked. Moreover, this serves to make the examination of cause-effect relationships easier.

In order to achieve programme goals – the implementation of which is set out within the framework of the conceptual design – human, financial and technical *resources* are required. It should thus be assessed to what extent budgeted and available resources are adequate for goal attainment.

Figure 4.1: Evaluation guidelines structure

1.	Programme and environment
	Programme description
1.0	Programme data
1.1	Programme concept
1.2	Innovation concept
1.3	Resources
	Environmental/contextual conditions
1.4	Country characterisation
1.5	Field of practice/policy (social subsystem)
1.6	Target group description (audiences, users)
2.	**Programme process**
2.1	Preparation/planning
2.2	Programme management
2.3	Preparation for termination of support
2.4	Aftercare support
3.	**Internal impact fields (executing agency)**
	Organisational competence of the agency
3.1	Goal acceptance within the implementing organisation and, where applicable, the executing agency (e.g. sponsor)
3.2	Personnel
3.3	Organisational structure
3.4	Financial resources
3.5	Technology: technical infrastructure
3.6	Technology: organisational agenda/concept
3.7	Balance: Internal programme impacts
4.	**External impact fields (target audiences, fields of policy/practice)**
4.1	Goal acceptance among target groups
4.2	Target group attainment
4.3	Benefit to target groups
4.4	Target group-spanning impacts
4.5	Impacts in the policy field of the programme
4.6	Policy field-spanning impacts
4.7	Balance: External programme impacts
5.	**Programme quality**
5.1	Planning and implementation quality
5.2	Internal impact-based quality
5.3	External impact-based quality
	Sustainability:
5.4	At the programme level
	At the macro level
5.5	Efficiency
5.6	Socio-political relevance
5.7	Environmental compatibility

© Reinhard Stockmann 2005

For the assessment of the parameters of the measure or programme that are listed in the set of guidelines, knowledge of *environmental conditions* is required. Even though these two areas of evaluation can only be dealt with analytically one at a time, the evaluation and assessment of the individual fields is only possible by taking a combined perspective. Depending on the type of programme in question, particularly if it involves developing countries, knowledge of national and regional conditions is essential.

With all programmes, the *field of practice* or *policy* in which the programme interventions occur (e.g. a country's health or vocational training system) should be analysed. In doing so, all fields in which programme impacts are expected should be given consideration, if possible. For instance, within a vocational training programme, it is to be assumed that impacts will arise in the general education system (in order to lay the foundations for the transition of pupils into the vocational training system), in the vocational training system itself as the primary policy field, and in the employment system (in which the graduates of a certain vocational training programme should find a job that matches their training).

Every programme and service is directed towards certain *target groups (audiences)*. It is necessary to accurately describe these target groups, as it should later on be determined whether they are reached at all by the programme measures, whether the service fulfils their needs, what benefit they derive from it, and whether they are satisfied with it etc.

In this section of the set of guidelines, the following specific issues and circumstances are to be investigated and assessed:

Programme description
(1.0) Programme data
- Programme title
- Programme type
- Policy field/field of practice/social subsystem (e.g. health/education/economic system)
- Executing agency structure (characterisation of the implementing organisation and, where applicable, its 'political' parent agency)

(1.1) Programme concept
- Description of goals and intended impacts
- Intervention measures with which programme goals are to be realised
- Analytical levels (individual, organisational, systemic) and dimensions (behaviour, processes, structures) on which impacts are to be produced
- Description of implicit programme theory, as well as of the relationships assumed to exist between measures (interventions) and impacts
- Assessment of the goal system and programme theory with regard to freedom from contradiction, clarity, chances of implementation considering environmental/risk factors (cf. guidelines section 1.2), and problem adequacy (are goals appropriate for the problem at hand?)

- Cause-effect hypotheses that can be formulated based on the three theoretical approaches conceived here (the life-cycle model, and organisational and innovation/diffusion theory). Description of the impacts that are to be expected on the basis of these. Have the most important cause-effect relationships been given consideration in the implicit programme theory?

(1.2) Innovation concept
- Description of the reforms (innovations) that are to be introduced, in accordance with fig. 3.6 (product/service innovations, procedural, organisational/structural, personnel innovations)
- Specific characteristics of the innovation (cf. chapter 3, fig. 3.8) from the perspective of potential users (relative benefit, compatibility, complexity, testability, observability, stage of maturity)
- Assessment of the chances of diffusion, considering the specific characteristics of the innovation (see above), the competence of the executing agency (cf. guidelines section 3), and external conditions (environmental factors such as values, norms, traditions, laws, ecological environment etc.) (cf. guidelines sections 1.4 & 1.5)

(1.3) Resources
- Means of financing the programme, divided up amongst the various executing entities and actors (e.g. government department, implementing organisation, target groups etc.)
- Deployment of human resources (e.g. paid and voluntary employees)
- Technological resources (e.g. technical equipment)
- Expenditure of time (e.g. length of the support programme)

Environmental/contextual conditions
(1.4) Country characterisation
- Description of socio-political, economic, cultural, ecological, and other situational conditions relevant to the programme (service on offer)

(1.5) Field of practice/policy (social subsystems)
- Description of the policy fields (social subsystems) in which programme impacts are to be expected, focusing on circumstances relevant to the programme:
  - Particularly the actors in the policy field (non-profit organisations, companies), cooperation, networks etc.
  - Underlying normative, legal, traditional etc. conditions of the policy field (also with regard to the introduction of the innovation)

(1.6) Target groups (audiences, users)
- Definition and description of the target groups that are intended to derive benefit from the programme, specifying relevant variables, especially:

- Socio-economic structure, age, gender, and other sociodemographic variables
- Values, norms, traditions of the target group
- Target group expectations of the programme
- Identification of divergent interests and potential conflicts among the target groups
- Relevance of the programme to the target groups
- Description of groups that are not target groups, and are thus excluded from the programme/service

(2) Programme process

The second section of the set of evaluation guidelines deals with the programme process. As explained in chapter 3.3 and 3.7.2, the nature of the programme process - the quality of planning and implementation - has an effect on service provision, on programme effectiveness etc. The starting assumption here is that programmes that consider target group needs and demands, as well as relevant organisational and situational conditions, in planning and implementation, are more likely to achieve set goals and intended impacts than those that are not adequately planned and managed.

In order to carry out an *assessment of the programme process*, then, above all the *preparatory planning* of the programme is to be analysed, along with the individual implementation steps. In addition to the nature and quality of programme planning and control by the various actors involved, the *preparation* of the particularly sensitive *programme/support end* phase, along with possible *aftercare support* by the sponsor, constitute important areas of examination. Depending on what phase of the programme process the evaluation relates to, and what analytical perspective it takes (cf. chapter 2, fig. 2.9), either the planning phase or individual implementation phases may be at the forefront of considerations. In the case of ex-post evaluations, i.e. those carried out only after support has been terminated - usually to analyse programme sustainability - all phases of the programme process are relevant.

Specifically, the following issues should be dealt with:

(2.1) Preparation/planning
- Planning steps performed (feasibility study, workshops etc.)
- Analyses carried out during the preparation phase (including problem/situation analysis, goal analysis, target group/stakeholder analysis, analysis of implementing agencies, need analysis, micro- and macroeconomic analysis)
- Consideration of factors that ensure the sustainability of the programme beyond the termination of support
- Involvement of the most important stakeholders

Implementation

(2.2) Programme management
- Adjustment of programme planning during the various implementation steps to take account of implementing agency/contextual requirements
- Existence of a well-functioning quality management/monitoring/evaluation system that supplies management-relevant data which are also utilised
- Collaboration between implementation partners
- Involvement of all stakeholders important for programme implementation

(2.3) Preparation for termination of support
- Development of a realistic goal system for the post-support phase
- Gradual reduction of support resources
- Involvement of important stakeholders

(2.4) Aftercare support
- Measures implemented to provide aftercare support for the programme; with what aim, by whom, with what degree of success?
- Performance of an ex-post evaluation, other forms of follow-up monitoring, incorporation of the results into the implementing organisation's knowledge management system

(3) Internal impact fields (executing agency)

In the third section of the set of evaluation guidelines, the *organisational competence* of the programme-implementing and/or service-rendering organisation – referred to here as the *executing agency* or *implementing organisation* – is analysed. The executing agency not only forms the structural requirements necessary for service provision/programme implementation, but its structural parameters may themselves be the target of change. The structure of this section is aligned with the theoretical organisational parameters listed in chapter 3.4 (goals, personnel, organisational structure, financial resources, technology) (cf. in particular chapter 3.4.1, fig. 3.4, and chapter 3.7.2). With the *goals* of the programme having already been dealt with in section (1.1) of the analysis guidelines, the objective is now to determine whether the goals and programme concept meet with acceptance within the implementing organisation or (if present) within the political executing agency (or sponsor), e.g. government department or charity. An important outcome of numerous evaluation studies has been that, without *acceptance*, measures and programmes are not enduringly successful or effective. A great deal of attention is thus given to the measurement and assessment of the acceptance of programme goals and the programme concept.

As has already been explained in detail, measures and programmes cannot be successfully implemented if they are lacking *qualified personnel*, a *well-functioning* (formal and informal) *organisational structure*, sufficient *financial resources*, and appropriate *technology*. With regard to technology, a distinction is made between *technical equipment*, which must be suitable for implementing programme measures or rendering the service, and the *content-based concept* of an organisation in terms of managing product and service provision. Here it should be examined, firstly, whether the goals and concept of a programme are consistent with the agenda/concept of the organisation as a whole. And secondly, it should be assessed whether, and to what extent, an executing agency has the innovation potential to adapt its own agenda, as well as the support programme, to conditions that change over time, so that innovation inertia is avoided (cf. chapter 3.5.1).

Section 3 of the guidelines concludes with a *summary assessment* of all internal programme impacts identified. For this, the intended and unintended *impacts* are viewed from a holistic perspective (cf. chapter 3.7.3, fig. 3.14). The approach adopted here is presented in chapter 4.3.

The following specific areas of analysis (subject blocks) are to be dealt with:

(3.1) Goal acceptance
within the implementing organisation and the parent executing agency (political institution, sponsor); (sponsor and implementing organisation are sometimes one and the same).
- Degree of knowledge about the programme (its aims, activities, stakeholders, impacts etc.) among managers
- Management assessment of the programme
- Relative importance of programme goals in the overall context of organisational aims
- Support for the programme (resources, commitment etc.)

(3.2) Personnel
- Skills
- Recruitment, employee turnover
- Personnel training

(3.3) Organisational structure
- Makeup of the organisational structure (using e.g. organisational charts, job charts, job descriptions)
- Functional capacity of separate organised subsystems (e.g. production, administration)
- Work scheduling, coordination
- Decision-making structure, responsibilities
- Internal information flow and cooperation (formal and informal)
- Information flow and cooperation with external partners, organisations, actors
- Integration in a network
- Functionality of the quality management/evaluation system

(3.4) Financial resources
- Budget of the implementing organisation
- Existence of medium- and long-term financing plans
- Financing of the executing agency (who provides what amount of funding?)

(3.5) Technology: technical infrastructure
- Description of technical equipment
- Standard of equipment relative to the demands of the programme concept
- Condition of technical equipment
- Rate of utilisation of technical equipment

(3.6) Technology: organisational agenda/concept
- Description of the content-based agenda for managing service provision and implementing organisational aims
- Ability to adapt the organisational agenda to changing external conditions
- Ability to develop and implement innovations

(3.7) Internal programme impacts
- Which of the changes listed in the guidelines under points (3.1) to (3.6) (= the gross outcome) are attributable to programme interventions (= programme/net effects)? What is to be rated positively, and what negatively?
- Which programme impacts were intended (= programme goals), and which were not?
- Which targeted (planned/intended) goals have been achieved (effectiveness) (= goal attainment in accordance with a target/actual comparison)?

(4) External impact fields (audiences, fields of policy/practice)

In the fourth section of the framework, effects that go beyond the executing agency are examined (external impacts). This comprises impacts among audiences of the programme (target groups, users), among non-target groups, and in the policy fields in which programme impacts are to be triggered.

As the spread of programme innovations depends to a large extent on their *acceptance among target groups*, the first thing to establish is whether, and to what extent, target groups actively support the programme concept and its associated goals, measures, and innovations. Then it can be ascertained whether, and to what degree, *intended audiences* are reached (degree of diffusion within the target group), what *benefit* they derive from the programme measures, and how satisfied they are with the programme/service. In addition to this, it should be established whether *users other* than those originally intended are able to benefit from the service or programme (degree of diffusion outside of the target group).

Of particular significance is the issue of the impacts that arise in the policy field in which the programme interventions take place. It should also be established whether or not changes have occurred in neighbouring sectors.

Section 4 of the guidelines concludes with a *summary assessment* of all external programme impacts identified. For this – as in section 3 – all intended and unintended *impacts* are subjected to a holistic assessment.

In order to identify external impacts and subject them to an overall balance, the following areas of analysis are to be dealt with:

(4.1) Goal acceptance among target groups
▪ Assessment of the programme, its goals, measures and intended impacts by the (where applicable various) target groups
▪ Involvement of target groups in the design and implementation of the programme, through financial and human contributions (e.g. in meetings, workshops, through the development of their own proposals and ideas)
▪ Further development of the programme innovations

(4.2) Target group attainment
▪ Description of goal attainment among the chosen target groups
▪ Degree of goal attainment (proportion of the target group reached)
▪ Degree of diffusion (proportion of the target group that has adopted the innovations introduced)
▪ Accessing of target groups (through what measures?)

(4.3) Benefit to target groups
▪ Benefit of the programme to target groups
▪ Disadvantages for target groups arising from the programme
▪ Have target group expectations and demands been met?
▪ Target group satisfaction with the programme/service
▪ Effects on living conditions and other spheres of life relevant to the programme (e.g. participation and solidarity behaviour, organisational ability, self-help skills etc.)

(4.4) Target group-spanning impacts
▪ Description of other groups that also benefit from the programme/service
▪ Disadvantages for non-target groups arising from the programme
▪ Groups that have adopted innovations emanating from the programme
▪ Accessing of further user groups (through what measures?)
▪ Further development of the programme innovations

(4.5) Impacts in the field of policy/practice (social subsystems)
▪ Descriptive level of the diffusion effects that have arisen within the policy field (social subsystem) in which the programme was implemented (product, procedural, organisational/structural, personnel innovations)

175

- Degree of diffusion of the programme innovations in the policy field (e.g. through the adoption of policies by other organisations)
- Description of system-shaping impacts (e.g. through the changing of legal regulations and laws, the creation of new institutions, system alterations, the founding of new organisations etc.)
- Description of other impacts that can be observed in the policy field

(4.6) Policy field-spanning impacts
- Diffusion effects that have arisen in relevant policy fields related to the one in which the programme was implemented
- Impacts that have arisen in other social subsystems relevant to the programme (e.g. social, economic, ecological, cultural, political impacts)

(4.7) External programme impacts
- Which of the impacts listed in the set of guidelines under points (4.1) to (4.6) (= the gross outcome) are attributable to programme interventions (= programme/net effects)? What is to be rated positively, and what negatively?
- Which programme impacts were intended (= programme goals), and which were not?
- Which of the targeted (planned/intended) goals have been attained (effectiveness) (= goal attainment in accordance with a target/actual comparison)?

(5) Programme quality

In section 5 of the set of evaluation guidelines, the quality of a programme, measure or service is assessed. This involves repackaging the data collected within sections one to four of the guidelines, and using it for the appraisal of the various quality dimensions (cf. chapter 3.7.3, particularly fig. 3.14).

The assessment of *planning and implementation quality* is based largely on information from section two of the guidelines, and the assessment of *internal and external impact-based quality* on information from sections three and four. *Programme-level sustainability* is appraised using the multidimensional sustainability concept developed in chapter 3.6. The dimensions chosen here as the three *macro-level sustainability* variables – *efficiency, socio-political relevance,* and *environmental compatibility* – can (as discussed in chapter 2.2) often be measured only with great difficulty, meaning that social values and norms ultimately have to be drawn upon when assessing them, which themselves are subject to change over time.

In examining the various quality dimensions, the following criteria should be assessed:

(5.1) Planning and implementation quality

The following points of the set of evaluation guidelines should be given particular attention in carrying out the assessment:	
(2.1) Preparation/planning	*(2.3) Preparation for termination of support*
(2.2) Programme management	*(2.4) Aftercare support*

- Assessment of the overall quality of programme planning and implementation
- Consequences of programme quality for the internal and external, intended and unintended impacts produced

(5.2) Internal impact-based quality

The following points of the set of evaluation guidelines should be given particular attention in carrying out the assessment:	
(1.1) Programme concept	*(3.4) Financial resources*
(1.2) Innovation concept	*(3.5) Technology: technical infrastructure*
(1.3) Resources	
(3.1) Goal acceptance	
(3.2) Personnel	*(3.6) Technology: organisational agenda/concept*
(3.3) Organisational structure	*(3.7) Internal programme impacts*

- Assessment of the overall competence of the executing agency
- Intended and unintended impacts of the programme interventions that have altered the competence of the executing agency
- Consequences of the competence of the executing agency for external impact fields

(5.3) External impact-based quality

The following points of the set of evaluation guidelines should be given particular attention in carrying out the assessment:	
(1.4) Country characterisation	*(4.3) Benefit to target groups*
(1.5) Field of practice/policy	*(4.4) Target group-spanning impacts*
(1.6) Target groups (audiences, users)	*(4.5) Impacts in the field of policy/practice*
(4.1) Goal acceptance among target groups	*(4.6) Policy field-spanning impacts*
(4.2) Target group attainment	*(4.7) External programme impacts*

- Intended and unintended impacts with regard to:
  - Target group attainment and degree of diffusion among target groups
  - Benefit to target groups
  - Target group-spanning diffusion effects
  - Diffusion effects in the field of policy/practice targeted by the programme and ...
  - In neighbouring policy fields

(5.4) Sustainability at the programme level

> *The sustainability of a programme can only be assessed once support has ended. Sections (3) and (4) of the set of evaluation guidelines are of particular relevance to this assessment.*

In order to create a sustainability profile (cf. chapter 3.6), the following questions should be answered:

- Does the target group/executing agency carry on the innovations (reforms) out of self-interest and for their own benefit?
- Have other groups/organisations adopted the innovations out of self-interest and for their own benefit on a lasting basis?
- Do the innovations lead, via processes of diffusion, to an increase in the performance of the system as a whole (e.g. health/education/economic system)?
- Does the target group/executing agency have innovation potential, allowing it to react to changed environmental conditions flexibly and appropriately?

Consequences of planning and implementation process quality and executing agency competence for sustainability

Sustainability at the macro level (economic, social and environmental quality)

(5.5) Efficiency

> *The following points of the set of evaluation guidelines should be given particular attention in carrying out the assessment:*
>
> | | |
> |---|---|
> | *(1.3) Resources (input)* | *(4.4) Target group-spanning impacts* |
> | *(3.7) Internal programme impacts* | *(4.5) Impacts in the field of policy/practice* |
> | *(4.2) Target group attainment* | *(4.6) Policy field-spanning impacts* |
> | *(4.3) Benefit to target groups* | *(4.7) External programme impacts* |

- Ratio of input to output
- Ratio of input to outcome
- Ratio of input to internal and external impacts

(5.6) Socio-political relevance

The following points of the set of evaluation guidelines should be given particular attention in carrying out the assessment:	
(1.0) Programme data	*(4.2) Target group attainment*
(1.1) Programme concept	*(4.3) Benefit to target groups*
(1.2) Innovation concept	*(4.4) Target group-spanning impacts*
(1.4) Country characterisation	
(1.5) Field of practice/policy	*(4.5) Impacts in the field of policy/practice*
(1.6) Target groups	*(4.6) Policy field-spanning impacts*
(3.7) Internal programme impacts	*(4.7) External programme impacts*
(4.1) Goal acceptance among target groups	

- Assessment of the programme and the impacts triggered by it with regard to socio-political relevance, as measured by:
    - The socio-political values prevalent in a country (such as social justice, equality of opportunity, emancipation, democracy etc.)
    - The socio-political goals of the government of a country
    - The aims and agenda of political programme-executing agencies and implementing organisations
    - The expectations, needs, and demands of target groups

(5.7) Environmental compatibility

The following points of the set of evaluation guidelines should be given particular attention in carrying out the assessment:	
(1.1) Programme concept	*(3.5) Technology: technical infrastructure*
(1.2) Innovation concept	
(1.4) Country characterisation	*(3.7) Internal programme impacts*
(1.5) Field of practice/policy	*(4.7) External programme impacts*

- Assessment of the programme and the impacts triggered by it with regard to environmental compatibility, considering:
    - The extent to which resources are conserved in the production of goods and services
    - The extent to which solutions avoid damage to the environment
    - The use of ecologically innovative solutions
    - The overall level of negative ecological impacts

179

The set of evaluation guidelines presented here represents a *basic framework* that can be used for the development of guidelines specific to certain fields of practice/policy. In contrast to ISO and EFQM, which do not offer sector-specific versions, preferring instead to emphasise the universality of their applicability, here it becomes clear that evaluation guidelines need to be adapted in accordance with the precise nature of the task, the specific conditions of the evaluation, and the nature of the field of policy/practice.

Empirical experiences gained over the last 15 years using earlier forms of this set of guidelines, which itself has passed through a process of development, have shown that, building on this basic framework, *sets of evaluation guidelines can be established for any type of programme, measure or service provision, in any phase of the political process* (cf. chapter 2, fig. 2.10). *The topics specified in the set of guidelines can be dealt with prospectively within ex-ante evaluations, investigatively within formative evaluations, or in a reflective manner within summative evaluations.* Sets of guidelines have not only been developed for *diverse fields of policy/practice* (e.g. development cooperation, the environment, education, vocational training, health, rural development, water and sewage etc.), but have also been employed in *all regions of the world* for *all forms of impact-based evaluation.*[128]

When developing guidelines specifically for certain policy fields, depending on the nature of the task, a different *focus* can be adopted with regard to the specification of topics and the information search. In the case of a summative evaluation, carried out for an ongoing or completed programme, the analysis of impacts and causal analysis (causal attribution), for example, may be at the forefront of considerations. The emphasis should then be less on undertaking as precise and detailed a description and assessment of the programme and its planning and implementation process as possible, and more on establishing and analysing internal and external impacts. Depending on interest, internal impacts may receive more attention than external ones, or vice versa. The former may be the case if, for example, aspects concerning the support of the executing agency have played a major role, with the aim of increasing its competence; the latter if the main objective has been to improve the situation of the target groups and/or to change the conditions of a system in a certain policy field.

In the case of a formative evaluation, on the other hand, process aspects should receive more emphasis. Of primary significance for an ex-ante evaluation is the detailed analysis of programme conditions and the situational context, as well as of target groups that are to benefit from the programme and the executing agency through which it is to be implemented.

---

128 Cf. e.g. Heinrich & Meyer 2005; Stockmann 2005b, 2004a & c, 2002b, 2001a & b, 2000a, b, c & 1996; Caspari 2004; Stockmann, Krapp & Baltes 2004; Baltes, Krapp & Stockmann 2004; Meyer et al. 2003; Ludwig & Koglin 2003; Stockmann et al. 2001 & 2000; Stockmann, Meyer, Kohlmann, Gaus & Urbahn 2001; Stockmann, Caspari, Kevenhörster 2000; Stockmann, Meyer, Krapp & Köhne 2000; Caspari et al. 2000.

However, when developing task-specific guidelines and ones tailored to certain political fields on the basis of the framework presented here, it should be noted that the idea is *merely* to *determine* the *focus*, with, for example, a more refined range of questions being drawn up for certain subject blocks (guidelines sections) than for others. But *no subject block should be omitted from an evaluation!* Even if no statements can be made as to a programme's effectiveness or sustainability, for example, due to its stage of development, such questions should be dealt with prospectively (what is to be expected?), so that even during the planning phase of a programme these aspects are not forgotten. Important foundations, e.g. for the future effectiveness or sustainability of a programme, are laid during the planning phase. Conversely, an ex-post evaluation cannot forego the recording of programme and environmental data, as these are necessary for the determination of impacts and their causes.

The range of subjects of the set of guidelines complies with the preceding theoretical considerations, which is a further reason why individual subject blocks cannot simply be dispensed with. They represent the operationalisation of the various theoretical deliberations, are related to one another, and are particularly essential for carrying out causal analysis. This very aspect of the evaluation design developed here is what distinguishes it from a model such as EFQM, in which criteria are defined and weightings applied without any theoretical rationale, simply based on plausibility considerations.

In the appendix, an *example set of guidelines* is documented, which has been developed on the basis of the framework presented here. It is a *set of guidelines for evaluating development cooperation programmes and projects*, and can – depending on the focus of the information search – be used either for more formative, or more summative, purposes. It can thus be applied during all phases of the political process.

4.3 Application and assessment procedure

4.3.1 Process perspective

The data necessary for the description and assessment to be carried out within the various guidelines sections are collected with the help of a range of methods, which will be examined later on. When gathering data it should be ensured that the central questions arranged within the respective subject blocks are dealt with in a *process-oriented* manner.

Impacts represent changes (cf. chapter 3.2), and in order to establish them, data that have been collected at at least two different points in time are required. As will be shown later on, in chapter 4.6, in which the various test designs for evaluating impacts are presented, measurement accuracy increases with the number of data collection time-points. This means that changes that have occurred during and after the course of the programme can be traced more easily, the more data points there are. What is more, this also increases the probability of being able to undertake realistic cause-effect attribution.

Depending on whether the evaluation in question is of an ex-ante, ongoing, or ex-post nature, different time-points are examined (cf. fig. 4.2). In the case of ex-ante evaluations, the time-point of the evaluation (t0) is even before the beginning of the programme (tB). During the course of the programme, multiple evaluations can of course be carried out (t1-tn). So-called concluding evaluations take place at the time of the termination of support (tS), whilst ex-post evaluations are carried out some time (months or years) after the support end (tE).

Figure 4.2: Evaluation time-points

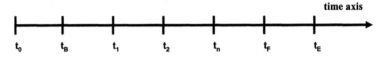

t_0 = ex-ante evaluation
t_B = evaluation at the beginning of programme support
t_1-t_n = evaluation time-points during implementation (on-going)
t_F = concluding evaluation at support end
t_E = ex-post evaluation after support end

Each evaluation should consider the results of previous evaluations, and use their data as points of reference to facilitate the identification of changes.

It is often the case that no ex-ante evaluations, in the form of planning or baseline studies that document the starting position at the beginning of the programme, are available. Under such circumstances, the benchmark data needed for the assessment of changes are lacking, and can then only be collected retrospectively. The problems associated with this will be explored in chapter 4.6. It can generally be observed that, in the case of formative evaluations, data must be gathered and appraised as rapidly as possible, so that results can be used in the management process. Even more important is that data are collected continually throughout the course of the project, which is the task of monitoring (cf. chapter 2.3.3). The more extensively the required data are collected by continual monitoring, the easier periodical evaluations are to carry out. The set of guidelines can also be used for establishing monitoring systems, an issue which will be dealt with later on.

Adhering to the *process perspective*, the following *procedure* should be observed:
Within an initial review of the situation (feasibility/baseline study), information is collected on the respective subject blocks of the set of guidelines. This forms the comparison data for the subsequent evaluation, in which it is also established what changes have oc-

curred in the interim period. Under further evaluations, the data from all previous evaluations serve as a basis for comparison. Ideally, all changes that occur between evaluation time-points should be detected (although clearly this idealistic demand cannot be met in practice).

As explained earlier on, the set of evaluation guidelines developed here is oriented towards measuring and assessing impacts, and does not follow the classic goal approach. This means that, within every evaluation, irrespective of specific programme and service aims, all subject blocks of the set of guidelines are to be addressed. This still applies even if the improvement of the qualification structure of personnel, for example, or the enhancement of the structure of the executing agency do not even constitute programme aims. As improvements or deterioration in these evaluation areas can have an influence on programme/service impacts, such changes over time should be documented.

In contrast to classic target/actual comparisons, goal attainment is not at the centre of the evaluation, but rather the search for impacts that occur in the environment of a programme - within the implementing organisation (executing agency), among target groups, and in the policy field in which the programme is intended to trigger effects etc. The evaluation guidelines serve to structure and give direction to the information search, helping to avoid a premature narrowing of perspective to focus merely on intended outcomes.

Figure 4.3: Types of impact - example 1

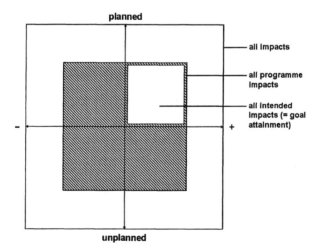

Figure 4.4 represents the special case in which a programme has produced 100% positive impacts, all of which were planned. In this situation, 100% goal attainment (hatched

area) can also automatically be established. No 'planned' (accepted) negative programme impacts or unplanned (positive or negative) programme impacts have arisen at all.

Causal analysis usually represents the most difficult task of evaluations. It will often not be sufficient to assess the data collected within sections (3) and (4) of the set of evaluation guidelines with regard to causal relationships. Rather, well-founded statements can only be formulated on the basis of separate cause-effect analyses that utilise appropriate methodological procedures (cf. chapter 4.4.1). For the analysis of relationships, the implicit programme theories derived within the scope of the programme and innovation concept (guidelines sections (1.1) and (1.2)) are used, as well as the hypotheses developed on the basis of the three theoretical approaches (the life-cycle model, and organisational and innovation/diffusion theory).

Figure 4.4: Types of impact - example 2

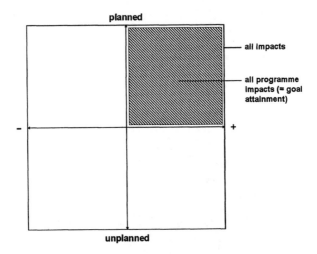

Instructions for following a process-oriented approach:
✓ The set of evaluation guidelines can be used for formative and summative evaluations, for all phases of the programme process. On the basis of the basic framework outlined here, a set of guidelines is to be developed that corresponds specifically to the relevant policy field and nature of the task at hand (see appendix for a set of guidelines for evaluation in the field of development cooperation).
✓ All subject blocks of the set of guidelines are to be dealt with in an evaluation. None should be omitted, as they represent the operationalisation of the various theoretical

considerations, are interconnected, and because the data are required for causal analysis.

✓ Depending on whether the evaluation is of an ex-ante, ongoing, or ex-post nature, data collection time-points vary (cf. fig. 4.1), meaning the procedure needs to be modified accordingly. In the case of an ex-ante evaluation, for example, of course neither the assessment of implementation nor the measurement of impacts can be carried out. In this situation, the corresponding subject blocks are to be dealt with prospectively: what should be borne in mind for the management of the programme; what impacts are to be produced in the respective areas? Changes (relative to the planning or baseline study) can only be observed within a subsequent evaluation.

✓ To be able to establish changes in a condition, it must be measured at several (at least two) points in time. If no comparison data are available from planning or baseline studies, they should be ascertained retrospectively. In all evaluations, the results of previous evaluations are to be taken into account. The more data points prior to, during, and subsequent to the programme there are, the more reliable the pool of data for the documentation and assessment of impacts that arise, as well as for the examination of relationships.

✓ Programme planning and management, the termination of support, and aftercare support can each be assessed at just one point in time. Only if a number of ongoing evaluations are performed during programme implementation is the aspect of management evaluated at more than one time-point. The state of affairs at the time of planning and implementation should be applied as the benchmark for assessment.

✓ In contrast to classic goal-oriented target/actual evaluations, here the orientation is not towards goals, but rather impacts observed. In order to cover as wide a range of intended and unintended impacts as possible, all changes detected – regardless of goals – are documented, structured and assessed using the set of evaluation guidelines.

✓ It is important when deriving empirical 'situations' at various points in time that this does not become mere description, but that changes (impacts) observed are always considered in a process-oriented manner.

✓ An overall balance should be produced in each case for the classification of internal and external programme impacts. Here it should first be examined which impacts observed are attributable to the programme interventions (= programme impacts), and which of these are to be rated positively and which negatively. It is then established which of the programme impacts observed were intended (= programme goals) and which were not. Finally, which, and how many, of the targeted goals have been achieved can be evaluated (= goal attainment).

✓ For the analysis of causal relationships, and to deal with the question of which impacts are attributable to programme interventions, the programme theories derived within the context of the programme and innovation concept, as well as the hypotheses developed on the basis of the three theoretical approaches (the life-cycle model, and organisational and innovation/diffusion theory) are used.

> ✓ To be able to make well-founded statements about causal relationships, separate cause-effect analyses that make use of appropriate methodological procedures are often necessary (cf. chapter 4.4.1).

4.3.2 Assessment procedure

Each subject block of the set of evaluation guidelines consists of a series of central questions. In order to answer these, various empirical data collection methods are employed, which are dealt with in chapter 4.4.2.

The guidelines serve to give direction to the information search, and to structure the material collected. As a significant objective of evaluation is to make comparisons, in order to detect changes over time, a problem is presented by the need to further reduce the diversity of the data in order to make them more manageable to this end. To achieve this, the quantitative and qualitative information collected via the central questions of a subject block are condensed into a summary appraisal.

This *appraisal* is carried out using a *10-level scale*, which is attached to the end of each subject block. The procedure for this involves putting all information gathered into a 'funnel', so to speak, and compressing it. Each 'funnel' is formed by the questions specified in the relevant subject block of the evaluation guidelines, which, for every data collection time-point, are bundled together to create an appraisal figure. Each *scale rating* represents the *highest possible form of compression* of findings presented. In principle, this appraisal need not necessarily be done quantitatively; a purely qualitative summary judgement at the end of a subject block is also possible. However, the conversion of this appraisal into a figure offers the *advantage* of making comparisons over time and between different programmes markedly easier. This advantage proves to be all the more significant, the longer the time series and/or the larger the number of programmes that are to be compared with each other. If the scale values along one dimension, for a certain subject block, are plotted, e.g. for two points in time, they not only provide information about the respective appraisals, but the distance between the appraisal ratings also sheds light on the changes, i.e. on the impacts that have arisen over time. A further advantage of this is that, as well as changes in individual dimensions, the direction of these changes can also be identified.

An *example* will now be used to illustrate what has been discussed up to now.

Under section (3.1) of the set of evaluation guidelines, various structural parameters of the executing agency are assessed, one of which is "goal acceptance within the implementing organisation". In order to assess this, the following central questions were formulated, which may be modified to fit the nature of the evaluation task and the policy field of the programme (cf. the example set of guidelines in the appendix):

- What knowledge does the management of the executing agency have of the programme (its aims, activities, stakeholders, impacts etc.)?
- How is the programme assessed by managers?

- What relative importance do programme goals have in the overall context of organisational aims?
- What support is afforded to the programme (resources, commitment etc.)?

The answers to these and, where applicable, further questions that have been added on, can be used as 'indicators'[129] to establish how great the acceptance of the programme within the executing agency is. It is then assumed that acceptance is high if the management is well-informed about a programme and rates it as important for the executing agency, if programme goals are seen as being at least compatible with the aims of the organisation, and if all necessary resources for the implementation of the programme are available. A further 'indicator' of high acceptance may, for example, be advocacy of the programme by management in public, or instructions to cooperate closely with the programme department within the organisation and to adopt the innovations introduced by it. The development of ideas and suggestions for improving the programme innovations etc. would also be a sign of high acceptance.

Although the development of 'indicators' is based on the central questions outlined within the respective subject blocks, it constitutes a creative act within each separate evaluation, as the characteristics of a programme and its policy field, as well as the nature of the evaluation task, must be taken into account. At the end of this 'assessment block', an overall appraisal of the "goal acceptance within the executing agency" is carried out, and transferred into the 'appraisal line'. This appraisal, performed at two evaluation time-points, could, for example, appear as follows:

Goal acceptance within the executing agency

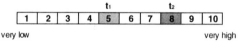

This example result can be interpreted as meaning that goal acceptance within the executing agency was not yet very pronounced at evaluation time-point t1 (possibly the beginning of the programme), but that the support programme was instead initially viewed with caution. At time-point t2, it can be established that acceptance of the programme within the executing agency has distinctly increased.

The compression of data into an appraisal figure for each data collection time-point entails considerable *haziness*. Thus, in answering the central questions for the assessment of "goal acceptance within the executing agency", questions inevitably arise, such as what exactly is to be understood by "executing agency", how should the various appraisals of individuals or groups within the executing agency be treated, what significance should be attached to management, etc.? No detailed assessment regulations can be defined for this, however; these questions can only ever be dealt with on a case-to-case basis. Otherwise, the set of evaluation guidelines would be stiffened by a corset of requirements, denying

---

129   See the next subchapter for information on the concept of indicators.

the evaluator any kind of flexibility, which is necessary to be able to carry out assessments that fit the nature of the task and the situation.

Another issue relates to the *weighting* of the various central questions, or 'indicators', that are combined to form a subject block (e.g. acceptance within the executing agency). For this it must be determined what significance is to be attributed to the respective indicators. In the example selected here, it would need to be decided whether the "degree of knowledge about the programme among management" identified is of equal significance (should be weighted equally) in the overall assessment - depicted in the 'appraisal line' - to the (rhetorical) "assessment of the programme by managers" or the actual "support for the programme". This weighting process can be carried out intuitively within the scope of an evaluation, or can be defined in detail in advance. In any case, weightings performed should be documented verbally and, within scientific evaluations, also in quantified form.

As numerous experiments with weighting factors show, however, their significance should not be overestimated. Only when using extreme weightings do differing overall appraisals result. This will now also be demonstrated using the chosen example.

The *appraisal format* may appear as shown below:

Example 1: no weighting

	Appraisal	Weighting	Final rating
- Degree of knowledge about the programme among management	7	1	7
- Assessment of the programme by managers	9	1	9
- Relative importance of programme goals in the context of overall organisational aims	8	1	8
- Support for the programme	7	1	7
Σ	31	4	31
$\overline{X}_{t_1}$			7.75

Goal acceptance within the executing agency

1	2	3	4	5	6	7	8	9	10

very low   very high

Example 2: moderate weighting

	Appraisal	Weighting	Final rating
- Degree of knowledge about the programme among management	7	2	14
- Assessment of the programme by managers	9	1	9
- Relative importance of programme goals in the context of overall organisational aims	8	2	16
- Support for the programme	7	3	21
Σ	31	8	60
$\overline{X}_t$			7.5

Goal acceptance within the executing agency

| 1 | 2 | 3 | 4 | 5 | 6 | 7 | 8 | 9 | 10 |

very low   very high

Example 3: extreme weighting

	Appraisal	Weighting	Final rating
- Degree of knowledge about the programme among management	7	3	21
- Assessment of the programme by managers	9	1	9
- Relative importance of programme goals in the context of overall organisational aims	8	4	32
- Support for the programme	7	10	70
Σ	31	18	132
$\overline{X}_t$			7.33

Goal acceptance within the executing agency

| 1 | 2 | 3 | 4 | 5 | 6 | 7 | 8 | 9 | 10 |

very low   very high

This example illustrates that, even with an extremely uneven distribution of weightings, the overall average (arithmetic mean, X) is barely affected. If the number of indicators (in this case only four) grows, this deviation becomes even smaller.

189

Weightings within subject blocks are only necessary if making the separate indicators (central questions) equal is deemed theoretically inappropriate. However, there is no theory available with which an exact weighting could be derived. In this sense, the weighting of individual central questions represents 'well-informed arbitrariness' (Dahrendorf). Weightings and appraisals different to those chosen are thus always conceivable.

In order to reduce the degree of subjective judgement, all *appraisals* should be carried out by at least *two evaluators*, each separately from others, and then subsequently examined with regard to their degree of conformity. If appraisal figures differ, the discrepancies can be settled either by calculating the average, or consensually, taking all arguments into consideration. Weightings and appraisals should be *made transparent* in all cases.

Experience with thousands of appraisals carried out in this way has shown that problems hardly ever arise in practice. Deviations tend to be minimal, and can easily be settled by evaluators in a consensual manner.

In an evaluation based on the set of guidelines, the following *procedure* is followed: for each central question (developed beforehand) per subject block, quantitative and qualitative data are collected and structured accordingly. The information is entered into the subject blocks to correspond to the central questions. To conclude, a qualitative overall appraisal is carried out, which is defined quantitively as an appraisal figure, and this is then entered into an 'appraisal line'.

The primary *advantages of this assessment procedure* relative to purely subjective appraisals are that:

- Assessment criteria and their weightings are disclosed
- An array of quantitative and qualitative data are collected for assessment, in order to create as broad an empirical foundation as possible
- The appraisals, carried out on the basis of documented findings and rationale, are intersubjectively verifiable, at least to some extent.

It should be particularly emphasised that the appraisals performed do *not* claim to provide *'true' values*. Much more important than the absolute value (e.g. 7 or 8) is the relative positioning on the appraisal scale, and the change that occurs over time.

The subject blocks (analytical fields) documented in the set of evaluation guidelines are developed via central questions, and conclude in each case with an 'appraisal line'. The central questions need to be specified in more detail to correspond to the nature of the evaluation task at hand, the type of programme, and the policy field. The list of assessment criteria, which is of course derived analogously from the subject areas depicted in chapter 4.2, is presented in fig. 4.5.

The summary assessment criteria of each subject block can be used to create a *programme profile*, in which all of these criteria and their appraisal at all evaluation timepoints are listed one below the other. This form of representation allows all changes (impacts) in the programme and its environment, within the executing agency (internal impacts) and its environment (audiences, field of policy/practice), as well as the assessment of programme quality, to be depicted.

Figure 4.5: Assessment criteria

1.	**Programme and environment**
1.1	Logic of programme concept
1.2	Conformity of the programme innovation
1.3	Availability of resources
1.4	Country-specific contextual conditions for programme implementation
1.5	Policy field-specific contextual conditions for programme implementation
1.6	Relevance of the programme to target groups
2.	**Programme process**
2.1	Quality of programme preparation/planning
2.2	Quality of programme management
2.3	Quality of preparation for the termination of support
2.4	Quality of aftercare support
3.	**Internal impact fields (executing agency)**
3.1	Goal acceptance within the implementing organisation and, where applicable, within the parent executing agency
3.2	Level of qualification of implementing personnel
3.3	Effectiveness of the executing agency's organisational structure
3.4	Financial capacity of the executing agency
3.5	Technical standard and condition of the executing agency's equipment
3.6	Innovation potential of the executing agency
3.7	Internal impact balance
4.	**External impact fields (audiences, fields of policy/practice)**
4.1	Goal acceptance among target groups
4.2	Degree of diffusion within target groups
4.3	Benefit to target groups
4.4	Target group-spanning diffusion effects
4.5	Diffusion effects within the policy field
4.6	Diffusion effects in neighbouring policy fields
4.7	External impact balance
5.	**Programme quality**
5.1	Planning and implementation quality
5.2	Internal impact-based quality
5.3	External impact-based quality Sustainability
5.4	At the programme level At the macro level
5.5	Efficiency
5.6	Socio-political relevance
5.7	Environmental compatibility

In this way, the state of the programme across all assessment dimensions can be ascertained at a glance. If data for further evaluation time-points are added, the *progress of the programme over time* can also be reviewed. It can thus easily be identified whether positive (increasing scale values) or negative (decreasing scale values) changes have come about between data collection time-points. In addition, *'target marks'* can also be plotted on the scales, i.e. values that are to be reached within the framework of programme implementation. It is not necessary to specify the highest possible number of points for all assessment dimensions (maximum 10). It may, for example, be sufficient for a certain programme if financial capacity and the technical standard of equipment only reach point 7 or 8, whilst in terms of goal acceptance, on the other hand, maximum points are targeted. In the case of a different programme, socio-political relevance may be of such significance that lower appraisals of efficiency and of the competence of the executing agency are accepted, because, for example, there are currently no apparent possibilities for markedly improving these. The 'target marks' of a programme can thus be set at very different points. The appraisal ratings at the respective evaluation time-points then indicate how far the programme is from these 'target marks', and whether, over time, it is moving towards or away from them.

The *programme profile* tool thus represents the *highest level of compression* of information obtained through evaluations and the assessments based upon it, providing an *at-a-glance* depiction of *programme development*.

Figure 4.6 presents a fictitious example of such a programme profile, in which appraisals of the individual dimensions are shown at two points in time (t1 and t2). The difference between t1 and t2 represents the changes over time. If the value of t2 is greater than that of t1, the situation has improved; if the opposite is the case, the situation has worsened. Target marks (T), which are to be achieved within the course of the programme, are also plotted. If the values of T or t1/t2 are equal to or greater than T, this target has already been reached.

The *example* depicted in fig. 4.6 is based on a *vocational training programme* in country X, which is supported by German funds within the scope of development cooperation. Up to now, two evaluations have taken place. At the beginning of the project a baseline study (ex-ante evaluation) was carried out in order to examine and assess the initial state of affairs (t1). The second evaluation (ongoing) was performed after support had been provided for more than two years (t2), with the objectives of documenting the level of progress up to that point and supplying the programme management with data relevant to decision-making.

The values plotted[130] in the programme profile could be interpreted as follows:

Programme and environment:
The *programme concept* is credited with having a high degree of logic, which means, for example, that the goals and theory of the programme are largely deemed to be consistent, clear, and appropriate for the relevant problem situation, that the most important cause-effect relationships have been considered and properly derived, that, taking existing risk factors into account, there is a realistic chance of implementation, etc. In short: the programme concept is convincing. As regards the *innovation concept*, the reforms to be introduced are certified as conforming to the inner and outer conditions of country X and the policy field (the vocational training system). As the government of the partner country is positive about the concept, it provides extensive *resources*, which are supplemented by the development funds from the donor country.

Country- and policy field-specific contextual conditions are seen as being favourable, whilst *relevance to target groups* is rated extremely highly. As regards the vocational training programme, the objective may be to replace the current academic vocational training system, afflicted with numerous deficiencies (such as low practical relevance, low output, low demand orientation), with a dual system, within which a portion of training is in future undertaken in a firm and the other part in school, and for which industry and government assume mutual responsibility. As country X has a rich tradition of trades, with the idea of on-the-job training already well established, starting points exist for the new combination of practical and academic training. External conditions, such as values and norms (tradesmen enjoy a relatively high social standing) and legal regulations, are also consistent with the programme. One thing that proves to be difficult is that fact that, in country X, state actors (e.g. the education ministry) and private companies have until now hardly collaborated, and have reservations about each other. Moreover, there are scarcely any organisational associations representing private enterprise that could serve as a contact person for the state, with existing business associations showing no interest in issues of training.

The *relevance of the programme* is not doubted by any of the stakeholder groups. Training is in urgent need of improvement if business productivity is to be enhanced and international competitiveness increased. The programme is primarily aimed at school leavers, for whom it is intended to represent an alternative (to unemployment or further schooling and higher education).

The similarity of appraisals at both evaluation time-points (which can be recognised by the heavily overlapping circles) illustrates that these ratings in the area of the programme and its environment have not changed over time.

---

130 If longer time periods are evaluated (e.g. within an ex-post evaluation), appraisals can also be undertaken at two or more points in time.

Figure 4.6: Example of a programme profile

Assessment criteria	Appraisal scale
	1 2 3 4 5 │ 6 7 8 9 10

Programme and environment
- Logic of programme concept — t1: 8, t2: 8
- Conformity of the programme innovation — t1: 8, t2: 8
- Availability of resources — t1: 9, t2: 9
- Country-specific contextual conditions — t1: 6, t2: 7
- Policy field-specific contextual conditions — t1: 6, t2: 7
- Relevance of the programme to target groups — t1: 10, t2: 10

Programme process
- Quality of programme prep./planning — t1: 7
- Quality of programme management — t1: 8
- Quality of preparation for the termination of support
- Quality of aftercare support

Internal spheres of activity (executing agency)
- Goal acceptance within the executing agency — t1: 7, t2: 8, T: 10
- Level of qualification of implementing personnel — t1: 7, t2: 8, T: 9
- Effectiveness of the organisational Structure — t1: 5, t2: 6, T: 8
- Financial capacity of the executing agency — t1: 4, t2: 5, T: 7
- Technical standard of equipment — t1: 4, t2: 6, T: 8
- Innovation potential of the exec. agency — t1: 5, t2: 6, T: 8
- Internal impact balance — t2: 7, T: 9

External spheres of activity (audiences, policy fields)
- Goal acceptance among target groups — t1: 10, t2: 10, T: 10
- Degree of diffusion within target groups — t2: 3, T: 7
- Benefit to target groups — t2: 8, T: 9
- Target group-spanning diffusion effects — t2: 2, T: 7
- Diffusion effects within the policy field — t2: 2, T: 6
- Diffusion effects in neighbouring policy fields — t2: 2, T: 6
- External impact balance — t2: 4, T: 7

Programme quality
- Planning and implementation quality — t2: 7, T: 10
- Internal impact-based quality — t2: 6, T: 9
- External impact-based quality — t2: 4, T: 8
- Sustainability at the programme level — T: 8
- Efficiency — t2: 1, T: 8
- Socio-political relevance — t2: 9, T: 10
- Environmental compatibility — t2: 9, T: 10

Key: time-point t1: ○   time-point t2: ●   target mark T: Ⓣ

Programme process:
The programme is currently at the start of its third year of implementation. *Planning*[131] did not go as well as would have been hoped. Although a thorough baseline study (feasibility study) was carried out, examining all significant aspects of the support programme, important stakeholders were not able to be involved due to time constraints. Attempts were made to rectify this during the *implementation phase.* Collaboration between participants is indeed working, but there is still room for improvement. It is assessed as positive that a monitoring system was created right at the beginning, which provided relevant data for the second evaluation and is used for quality management.

Internal impact fields:
The programme profile indicates that the implementing organisation was initially very receptive to the programme, yet nevertheless viewed it with scepticism. Over time this scepticism was successfully reduced, and *goal acceptance* is rated highly overall, although the target mark (T)[132] has not yet been reached. This is set at an especially high level here (at the maximum value, 10), as the well-founded belief is prevalent that, in the long run, the introduction of a cooperative training system will not prove to be sustainable without its absolute acceptance within the executing agency.

Although the *level of qualification of implementing personnel* is somewhat better than the average in other technical schools in the country, it is nevertheless not sufficient. During the first phase of implementation, the programme took care of the further qualification of personnel to a greater degree, and was clearly successful in doing so.

The *organisational structure, financial capacity, technical standard of equipment,* and *innovation potential* continue to constitute weak points of the executing agency. The biggest improvements made during the support period relate to *technical equipment,* with extensive deliveries from the donor country having been arranged. The *organisational competence* of the executing agency, on the other hand, improved less during the support period, and there is still a considerable amount to be achieved in this area by the time support ends (target mark). As bureaucratically rigid structures can only be made more effective with great difficulty, though, persistence and endurance are required here. It should be monitored closely over time whether the target mark can actually be reached or not. In terms of the *executing agency's financial capacity*, the situation is no better. Al-

---

[131] The appraisal of planning always relates to the time before the actual programme begins, meaning that, as a rule, only one appraisal time-point is required. Replanning during implementation is considered programme management. This can be appraised at multiple points in time, especially in the case of longer programmes. Preparation for the termination of support is a very short phase, for which a one-off appraisal is sufficient. The same is also usually true of aftercare support.

[132] The target mark (T) can define the value aimed for at the end of the support for a programme. In the case of longer-lasting programmes, multiple target marks (phase targets) may also be specified for different points in time.

though there are currently a substantial amount of resources available thanks to the provision of support, overall the executing agency is in a somewhat poor situation as regards funding. Even though a relatively low target level (T = 7) has been set for this appraisal dimension, a huge effort is still required to achieve this. If government financing of the schools cannot be increased, one option would be to create sources of self-financing (such as exam fees, paid work etc.). Due to its limited overall organisational competence and financial capacity, as well as to the fact that the level of qualification of implementing personnel has only recently been increased, the *innovation potential* of the executing agency remains slight. An improvement in these other parameters, however, would also be expected to produce enhanced innovation potential.

The *internal impact balance* can only be worked out at one point in time (t2), as at the time of the baseline study no impacts were yet possible. The appraisal in the programme profile implies that many of the changes observed are attributable to the programme interventions, and that the positive effects far outweigh the negative ones.

External impact fields

In the area of *external impact fields,* too, in most cases only one appraisal time-point is possible within the programme example chosen here. It should also be borne in mind that, in the case of many assessment parameters, at the evaluation time-point (t2), after two years of support, only a few diffusion effects would have had a chance to occur. The realisation of diffusion effects is primarily a task concerning later programme phases. In doing so, the extent to which the appraisals of the individual dimensions approach the specified target marks should be examined in as much detail as possible.

In this fictitious example, the programme is rated very highly and supported by its direct *target groups* (trainees and employers). This may mean, for example, that many firms are prepared to provide apprenticeship places for cooperative training, and to participate in joint management bodies, and that a lot of school leavers decide to pursue this type of training, meaning that the best qualified ones can be selected.

The *degree of diffusion within target groups* is still low, due to little time having elapsed, but it can nevertheless be observed that the chosen target groups are being reached. The target mark has been set at T = 7 for the support end. This means that the programme will be deemed a success, and its sustainability seen as being secured, if around 70% of firms and the majority of school leavers participate in this form of training. The evaluation was accompanied by an initial analysis of the destination of graduates of the scheme. In the fictitious example, it is assumed that the first training cycle has been completed. The survey of graduates showed that a considerable number of them were taken on by the firms in which they were placed, that their income situation had improved etc. A survey of the firms also delivers positive appraisals. In future, it should be monitored in detail whether the *benefit* for the two main target groups (school leavers and companies) remains high, or even increases yet further (e.g. by graduates making a successful career for themselves, companies boosting their productivity and competitiveness etc.).

196

With regard to *target group-spanning impacts*, it is most notable that the families of graduates also benefit from their occupation. Outweighing this, however, is the fact that job entrants that have undergone purely academic training are now at a disadvantage compared to cooperatively trained graduates. As the purely academic training system is intended to be replaced by the dual system, this negative effect can be expected to decline as the new system spreads, because, in the ideal case, there will then no longer be any graduates that have undergone purely academic training.

Diffusion effects within the policy field (vocational training system) are still low. The aim, however, is that when support has ended, a large proportion of vocational training in selected occupations will be fundamentally of a dual nature, i.e. it is hoped that vocational training undergoes a systematic change.

Diffusion effects in neighbouring policy fields can barely be detected thus far, but are nevertheless expected, particularly in the employment system, within which dual training is to be recognised and rewarded - on the job market and by businesses.

Up to now, only a few changes have occurred in external *impact fields*. Impacts that have been ascertained are largely attributable to the programme interventions. The appraisal scale, as in the case of internal impact fields, depicts the net impacts achieved.

Programme quality:
On the basis of the progress of the programme assumed in this example, it is not yet possible to perform well-founded appraisals for all quality dimensions.

With regard to *planning and implementation quality*, it can be stated that, although planning was not optimal, it was rated positively overall, largely thanks to the thorough baseline study. During implementation, the stakeholders neglected during the planning phase were also able to be better integrated. Overall, the quality of the programme process is rated as 'good'.

Internal impact-based quality can, given the currently assumed programme status, at best be rated as moderate. Although goal acceptance is very high within both implementing organisations, whilst the level of qualification and standard of technical equipment especially have already been improved considerably thanks to the programme measures, organisational parameters that are more difficult to influence (such as organisational structure, finances, innovation potential) have thus far barely changed at all for the better.

In order to achieve satisfactory *external impact-based programme* quality, a further lengthy period of support is necessary, with the difference between the target mark and the current rating still very considerable. This is primarily attributable to diffusion effects only being expected to arise during later programme phases.

Sustainability at the programme level can only be assessed ex-post, following the termination of support. *Macro-level sustainability*, on the other hand, can be assessed at any time. At the end of the second year of support, the ratio of input to output (or outcome) (efficiency) still appears very unfavourable, with high personnel and cost outlay only producing a low yield. There are still just a small number of graduates, and intended impacts remain modest.

As far as *socio-political relevance* is concerned, on the other hand, the situation is very different. Right from the commencement of support, this has been distinctly high, with the programme making a significant contribution to the implementation of the socio-political aims of the partner country, as well as the organisational objectives of the executing agency, and meeting the expectations, needs and demands of employers and school leavers (both target groups).

As the vocational training programme also deals with environmental issues in its curricula, and it is to be expected that this will produce ecological improvements in relevant occupations (e.g. car mechanic, plumber), the *environmental compatibility* of the programme is rated very highly.

This gives a rough idea of what the reasons behind the appraisals depicted in the programme profile may be, which in this case serve merely as examples. The point, though, is to illustrate that the *programme profile*, as the highest level of compression of assessments carried out on the basis of all monitoring and evaluation data gathered, represents a *useful management aid for quality development*. It can depict changes (impacts), and their direction over time, at any number of measurement time-points, and signal whether the programme is evolving in the desired way (meeting target marks) within the scheduled time framework.

Instructions: assessment procedure and programme profile

✓ The quantitative and qualitative data (information) collected for each subject area of the set of evaluation guidelines is structured and assessed based on the central questions. Various methods of data collection are employed (cf. chapter 4.4.2).

✓ The individual assessments are 'condensed' into an appraisal figure per subject block for each data collection time-point, using a 10-level scale, where 1 is the lowest and 10 the highest rating.

✓ The appraisal figure does not constitute a 'true' value, but rather an extremely abridged quantitative appraisal that represents all the quantitative and qualitative assessments of a subject block.

✓ As certain central questions within a subject block may, depending on the programme, be more important than others, the individual questions can also be weighted to reflect their greater significance. The weightings should then be disclosed.

✓ Appraisals need to be plausibly justified and backed up empirically by the data in a logical manner, as well as being intersubjectively verifiable.

✓ In order to reduce the degree of subjective judgement, all assessments should be carried out by at least two evaluators, with discrepancies settled either consensually or through averaging.

✓ The appraisal lines at the end of each subject block can be used to create programme profiles. For this, all scale ratings are depicted in diagrammatic form.

> ✓ Based on the gaps between separate appraisal time-points, the development of the process can be mapped along a certain dimension, as well as for the programme as a whole across all dimensions.

4.3.3 Indicators

Definition and types of indicators

As has already been explained, the set of evaluation guidelines can not only be used for ex-ante evaluations (feasibility, planning and baseline studies), as well as for evaluating ongoing and completed programmes; it can also be used for the *creation of a continuous monitoring system*. To this end, appropriate indicators are to be developed for each subject block, based on the central questions of the set of guidelines. An *indicator database* can thus be compiled, in which all data collected for the various indicators at different points in time are stored.

What *indicators* are, how they are developed, and what should be observed in doing so, will now be briefly dealt with.[133] Just like the concept of 'evaluation', the notion of *'indicators'* is not familiar to most people. Yet they use indicators very frequently in their daily lives, albeit under different names, such as characteristic, circumstance, indication, or even rate, proportion, average etc. The latin origin of the word 'indicator' is indicare, which means to indicate. The Duden dictionary of foreign words thus defines an indicator as a "circumstance or characteristic that serves as a [demonstrative] indication of, or clue to, something else". Indicators depict a situation, display something, reveal something, such as about the general condition or performance potential of the economy, the level of satisfaction in society, or the development of a company. The German dictionary of sociology describes indicators as "a variable that can be established (e.g. through surveillance or questioning) by direct empirical measurement, which gives information about something that itself is not directly measurable" (Hartmann 2002), thus giving a hint as to how data required for compiling indicators are obtained.

According to these definitions, *an indicator makes a non-directly measurable phenomenon visible through the application of empirical methods*. Indicators very often describe something (e.g. satisfaction with a service, modes of use, the condition of a device etc.), display performance (e.g. speed, examination marks, production figures etc.), or measure something (e.g. petrol consumption, energy consumption, pollutant discharge etc.). They are always intended for a certain form of use, and can thus be classified according to what *purpose* they serve. A distinction is made between:

---

133 This portrayal draws on the CEval working paper no. 10 "Was ist Evaluation?" ("What is Evaluation?"), by Wolfgang Meyer.

(1) Input indicators
which show the resources and expenditure deployed towards goal attainment (investments, e.g. the number of personnel employed, financial capital in euros, time in days etc.).

(2) Output indicators
which show the concrete (material) impacts of measures implemented (results, e.g. metres of road built, the number of young persons trained, consultations carried out).

(3) Outcome indicators
which relate to impacts that correspond to goals, i.e. to the immediate benefit achieved through results with regard to goal attainment (benefit, e.g. for road users, persons trained, persons advised etc.).

(4) Impact indicators
which measure effects that go beyond the actual goals and target groups, particularly unintended effects, as well as the durability of impacts (e.g. implications for the environment, for persons trained in other ways, those not in receipt of advice etc.).

Another significant property of indicators is that they *facilitate comparisons*. These are particularly important over time, using time series, for example, in order to identify changes. Comparisons can also be made across different entities (systems, organisations, individuals, products etc.). In order to compare units of differing size with each other (e.g. a school with 100 and one with 200 pupils), indicators are often expressed as an (arithmetic) fraction, with the denominator comprising the size factor. School-leaving examination figures, for example, are calculated by dividing the number of successful pupils by the total number of pupils. Indicators are also often used to measure (actual) performance against a target value, e.g. to measure the number of pupils educated in one year against the number that had been targeted, or the reduction in the failure rate against a specified minimum value. The indicator can be expressed as a fraction (e.g. the proportion of graduates that have found work within a certain time period), or as the percentage difference between the standard and the actual value (e.g. the percentage of goals achieved). Yet absolute numbers can also be used as indicators for undertaking comparisons with standards, e.g. if the number of training courses actually abolished is to be compared with targets.

Some indicators can be formed very simply, e.g. using a numerical value, whilst others require extensive theoretical consideration first. Weight, for example, as an indicator of the heaviness of an object, can be measured in grams, the length of an object in centimetres. Things become more complicated, however, in the case of the indicator 'income', for instance. Although this too can be measured quantitatively (in monetary units), it must first of all be established in what currency, at the prices of which base year etc. this should be done. It also needs to be clarified for what (what construct) income is to be taken as an indicator. It could be used to indicate affluence, prosperity, or to depict social inequality. The reputedly straightforward indicator 'education' is not at all easy to ascertain either. It can, for example, be measured in school years completed and/or exam certificates obtained. The situation becomes even more compex if a social-scientific construct such as 'status' (the social rank of an individual) is to be determined. Usually, a combination of indicators, such as income, education, and job, is employed in such a case.

These examples further highlight the fact that indicators can have different *'levels of measurement'*. In the social sciences, the notion of measuring is dealt with very liberally, with even classification, i.e. the allocation of objects to certain categories, treated as a measurement process.

An indicator can thus be formed, for example, by classifying objects according to whether they are 'light' or 'heavy', 'short' or 'long', and subjects according to whether they have a 'high' or 'low' income, through categorising features according to an organising principle. It should be noted that this organising principle, as well as the type and number of categories used, is the result of individual decisions. For example, income, divided into the categories 'high' or 'low', can be used as an indicator of affluence, yet this indicator could also incorporate three or more categories, e.g. 'high', 'middle' and 'low' income. Or, as income can easily be measured quantitatively in monetary units, the indicator could also be recorded directly on the basis of a numerical value, which would represent a transition from a qualitative to a quantitative indicator. The indicator 'income' for the phenomenon 'affluence' would then not only have been recorded qualitatively (high/low or rich/poor), and subsequently put into a ranking order (high/medium/low), but also expressed quantitatively as a metric unit (money). In accordance with these three levels of measurement, *three types of scale* are distinguished in the social sciences, each with specific characteristics: nominal, ordinal and interval (metric) scales (cf. Krämer 1994: 13 ff.).

Whilst a higher scale level means that an indicator has greater *information content*, it also places higher *metrological requirements* on data collection. That is to say, quantitative indicators with metric scales have greater information content, as they also shed light on the ranking order and intervals between objects. This information gain, however, must be 'bought' with accordingly higher expenditure on data collection. Conversely, qualitative indicators save on this added expense within the scope of data collection, but then move the task of forming ranking orders or identifying intervals between units to the analysis phase.

Whether numerical values are used or not says nothing about the *quality of a measurement*, and only this determines the quality of results. Conversely, of course, qualitative statements are not 'qualitatively better' than quantitative ones simply because numerical values are avoided. The fact that numerical values '(over-) simplify reality' does not mean that a verbal description expresses the circumstances more correctly. Detailed comments and extensive quotations (the 'decimal places' of qualitative social research) likewise do not necessarily imply greater measurement precision.

Requirements of indicators

Wolfgang Zapf (1977), one of the founding fathers of social indicator research, once pointed out that the *construction of good indicators* is first and foremost a question of so-cial-scientific imagination. As there are still no universal rules for the creation of indicators, this statement retains its validity today. A good indicator must meet theoretical, methodological, practical and social *requirements*:

(1) Theoretical requirement
The relationship between the circumstance measured by an indicator and the immeasurable construct must be clearly identifiable, i.e. the indicator must measure that which is to be depicted (validity). The better an indicator can be theoretically justified and operationalised, the better it can depict the immeasurable construct. It can reasonably be argued, for example, that the number of years spent in school and higher education, or educational attainment, can be employed as indicators for the construct 'education'. What is more, these indicators can also be easily measured.

(2) Methodological requirement
The quality of a measurement, and thus the methodological quality of an indicator, is determined by whether it reliably measures that which it is intended to measure. So, even if repeated measurements are taken, the same result is obtained (reliability). In addition, a measurement procedure should be objective, i.e. regardless of who carries out data collection, the result is the same (objectivity).

(3) Practical requirement
A good indicator is distinguished by being able to be measured as accurately as possible with justifiable expense. The aim is to obtain as much valid, reliable information as possible with minimal expenditure.

(4) Social requirement
Indicators must be socially accepted, so that the measurement results are recognised as a basis for decision-making. Here it is assumed that results only enter decision processes if participants have confidence in the indicator concept and trust the information obtained in this way.

The development of indicators is therefore not only a technical procedure, but also a social process in which the most important stakeholder groups should be incorporated. It has proven to be successful if *methodological experts*, who have the technical knowledge for constructing indicators, collaborate with *subject matter experts*, who are familiar with programme- or service-related issues. This not only ensures that indicators best meet theoretical and methodological demands, but also that they are adapted in accordance with specific organisational, political, sociocultural or regional conditions, and are accepted by all parties involved. In order to design 'good' indicators, it is thus essential to have not only 'social-scientific creativity', but also methodological competence, thorough specialised (content) knowledge, practical experience, and social aptitude.

Indicators are sometimes also furnished with *'target figures'*, which are intended to make clear at what value a set aim is accepted as having been achieved. These target marks are not part of the indicator, but rather threshold values, however defined, which have to be justified. The indicator value, on the other hand, is empirically obtained.

Choice and number of indicators

As indicators always constitute (to a greater or lesser extent) imperfect 'aids' for measuring immeasurable phenomena, the *number of indicators* used is closely linked to the requirement of the *measurement accuracy* of the (non-directly measurable) theoretical construct. The following can be said to be true: the worse the selected indicators are at measuring a dimension of the theoretical construct, the more indicators must be employed in order to be able to depict it reasonably adequately. Conversely, the opposite is also true: the better an indicator is at fulfilling its function, the less the extent to which further indicators are required to safeguard ('validate') results. In developing indicators, the limits of the practically feasible are often reached, as not everything that seems theoretically desirable can always also be implemented. Human and financial resources, along with time, are restrictions that need to be considered when devising indicators. As a rule, the temptation to strive for perfection in the choice and construction of indicators should thus be resisted. With regards to their selection, there is a danger that too many indicators are adopted. Many aspects appear important, but it should be borne in mind that the data collection for each indicator usually involves considerable time outlay. When forming indicators, the constant query should not only be whether the indicator promises valid and reliable results, but also whether it can be measured with justifiable expense. A good *guiding question for selecting indicators* is the following one: "*Who* needs *what* information, *when*, by *whom*, *how*, for *what*, and *how much* does it cost?" (cf. fig. 4.7).

Furthermore, it should not be forgotten that, no matter how good the choice of indicators, this does not lessen the importance of their *interpretation*, which is always dependent on contextual conditions. A gross domestic product (GDP) of 970 US$ per capita in PR China, for example, is to be assessed differently to a similar amount in the USA. As both quantitative and qualitative indicator values always require interpretation, it is all the more important that individual development steps are documented and made transparent, so that the quality of the indicators and corresponding data can be judged. Only then is an interpretation of the data intersubjectively verifiable.

Procedure

In order to meet the theoretical, methodological, practical and social requirements of the construction of good indicators, what has proved most successful – based on experiences in numerous evaluations and research and development projects – is to develop the indicators together with the personnel of the executing agency and/or other stakeholders.

This is approached by firstly explaining, within the framework of a workshop, the sense and purpose of a monitoring and/or evaluation system, for which the indicator database is to be developed.

Next, an introduction to indicator development takes place, in order to then eventually apply the technical rules for generating indicators on a collective basis, within a social process. The set of evaluation guidelines serves as the foundation, specifying subjects (areas of analysis), central questions, and summary appraisal criteria for each subject block. In developing indicators, 'methodological' and 'subject matter' experts cooperate with each other. An indicator framework was developed in this way in Egypt, for instance, for the creation of a monitoring and evaluation system, in order to oversee the introduction of a dual vocational training system. The framework was put together in conjunction with the domestic executing agency and various stakeholders. Consequently, it does not represent an ideal-typical framework, but rather reflects the real situation, i.e. it contains some indicators that, measured against the standards listed here, do not always fulfil all requirements.

Figure 4.7: The 7 central questions for selecting indicators

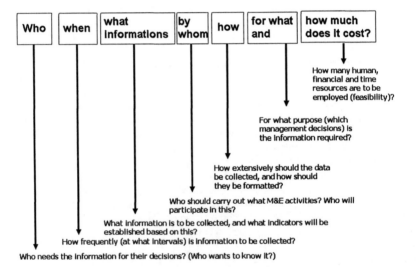

When developing indicators in practice (and not in laboratory-like situations), compromises have to be made between the four central requirements (theoretical, methodological, practical and social). Not everything that may be theoretically desirable, methodologically realisable, and practically feasible can be implemented, due to the expense. And even if these three requirements can be met, there may be political or social reasons why an indicator that is in principle 'feasible' cannot be used.

The *indicator framework documented in the appendix* has been used for over three years for decision-making processes within the framework of a monitoring and evaluation system. Data are collected, assessed, and prepared for decision-makers on a continuous basis by implementing personnel, with no external assistance, using various collection methods and information sources. As the data have already been gathered at different points in time, programme development can, as shown in the programme profile in chapter 4.3.2, be traced and made transparent along the various appraisal dimensions.

Procedure:
- ✓ It can be stated that indicators serve the purpose of making non-directly measurable phenomena visible through the use of empirical methods.
- ✓ Indicators can be used to ascertain inputs, outputs, outcomes, or impacts, with the aid of various levels of measurement (nominal, ordinal or interval scale level).
- ✓ Whether an indicator is specified qualitatively or quantitatively is not as important as that it, first and foremost, provides a valid measurement of what it is supposed to depict, i.e. that it is selective, and enables as precise a classification and allocation of circumstances observed to the chosen categories as possible. Furthermore, it is of crucial importance that the indicator is reliable, i.e. that circumstances monitored over time are always allocated to the same categories. Indicators should also be objective (i.e. independent of the person measuring them), as well as practicable (i.e. measurable with justifiable expense) and socially accepted, so that the results are used for decision-making processes.
- ✓ The development of indicators constitutes a complex undertaking, within which methodological competence should be combined with knowledge of programme content. In addition, the various interests of different stakeholders are to be taken into consideration.
- ✓ When formulating indicators, the first procedure is to clarify what circumstance they are to depict. Indicators are then selected, and examined in terms of their informational value and the extent to which they can be operationalised. Subsequently, it should be established with what degree of accuracy (scale level) the indicators will be measured, and with what methods data collected, before the measurement and analysis are then performed.

4.4 Evaluation methods

4.4.1 Test designs for the evaluation of impacts

Now that the set of evaluation guidelines has been developed and its application explained in the previous subchapters, the way that the data necessary for evaluation can be obtained will be explored here. Impact analyses have to deal with two central problems, the first of which is the *problem of identifying and measuring impacts*. Here the question arises of how the planned and unplanned impacts of a programme or service can be ascertained as accurately and completely as possible. Impact analyses also have to deal with the *problem of identifying causal relationships* between programme interventions (as independent variables) and impacts detected (as dependent variables), given the prevailing conditions and opportunites for action. The issue here is how cause factors of impacts can be determined as clearly as possible, and competing explanations ruled out (cf. Hellstern & Wollmann 1984: 25; OECD 1986: 34; White 1986: 4; Staudt et al. 1988: 32; Diekmann 1995: 309 ff.; Kromrey 2002: 82 ff.; Rossi, Lipsey and Freeman 2004: 233 ff.). The *quality of a research design* therefore depends on the extent to which (if possible all) relevant impacts can be identified and causality problems solved.

As already explained in chapter 3.2, the theoretical/methodological challenge is to separate the *net effects*, i.e. those actually triggered solely by the interventions, from other impacts (the effects of other factors and design effects). In principle, *all test designs* in the repertoire of empirical social research can be employed for this purpose. When choosing a design, every evaluation is confronted with the problem that, whilst on the one hand, statements should be made that are as accurate as possible, on the other hand, the specific conditions present (time, financial resources, readiness to cooperate etc.) only rarely enable the application of an optimal design. However, this situation should not lead to design alternatives being rashly discarded simply because they are not sufficiently familiar, or because (reputedly) simpler – 'more convenient' – designs are preferred.[134]

It is beyond the scope of this book, though, to present all potential impact evaluation designs and discuss their benefits and drawbacks.[135] More detailed explanations would quickly exceed the bounds of this chapter, and necessitate a volume devoted exclusively to methods. Instead, an attempt will be made to provide an *overview*, and to highlight the *diversity of the range of methods available*. The focus here is on the identification of some important methodological issues and relationships, which should – if at all possible – be observed in an evaluation. A detailed description of the application of the designs and methods presented will be foregone, due to space constraints, as will the tempting

---

134 Regrettably, it is not infrequent for evaluations to be carried out with the bureaucratic attitude reflected in the line "that's the way we've always done it". More complex designs often do not enjoy much popularity, either among clients or contractors.

135 Cf. the relevant specialist literature, e.g. Schnell, Hill, Esser 1999; 2005; Kromrey 2002; Diekmann 2004; Rossi, Lipsey and Freeman 2004.

opportunity to report on the rich array of practical experience gleaned from numerous evaluations.

The examination of the impacts of interventions requires firstly that a programme has been in place for some time, so that effects can already be detected. Secondly, hypotheses are necessary to guide the investigation, which are based on either the relationships supposed or explicitly formulated within the programme theory, or on separate considerations that utilise appropriate theoretical models. In order to examine the attainment of programme aims, clearly-defined goals are also necessary.

The detection of assumed relationships is carried out with the help of observable *indicators*. The test set-up or 'research design' determines in what way (how, when, where, how often) the empirical indicators are to be measured. The *research design* is *crucial* in terms of the degree of certainty with which the question of the relationship between cause and effect can be answered (cf. Schnell, Hill, Esser 1999: 203).

Common to all impact analysis designs is that they are based on *comparisons*. To this end, two groups are usually formed: one in which the planned intervention occurs (referred to as the experimental group), and one in which no intervention is carried out (the control group). The comparison of the two groups indicates the effect of the stimulus (the intervention). The primary *aim* in *choosing a design* is to exclude competing explanations and 'confounding variables', in order to be able to prove the cause-effect relationship as convincingly as possible. *'Confounding factors'* may be linked to the method, e.g. to *biased samples*. This is the case if the experimental and control groups not only differ with regard to the intervention, but also in terms of other features, which may equally have produced the impacts. The use of differing measurement instruments (e.g. modified tests, differently formulated questions, inconsistent answer options etc.), or a (possibly unintentional) difference in evaluator behaviour between the experimental and control groups can also lead to an impairment of measurement results.

The factors identified above are - based on Campbell and Stanley (1963) – referred to as factors that influence *'internal validity'*. Internal validity is present if the intervention is indeed responsible for the variation in the dependent variable (impact). If, however, the impact has been caused by one or more confounding factors, then there is said to be no internal validity. If both confounding factors and the intervention are responsible for the change in measurement readings, there is a 'confounding' of effects, and the internal validity is similarly damaged.

'External validity' (also called ecological validity) refers to the possibility of transferring results to other (groups of) people and contexts. External validity is not present if an experimental situation differs so fundamentally from the real day-to-day one that, although internally valid effects can be verified, in a day-to-day context they cannot. Such effects, also referred to as 'reactive' effects, can also occur if experimental subjects are sensitised to a stimulus within a pretest, which can serve to lessen or strengthen the influence of the stimulus (the intervention).

There are a range of techniques for eliminating or controlling these *confounding variables*:

(a) Random controls
The most important and 'safest' procedure is that of randomisation (random allocation), within which people are allocated 'randomly' to the experimental or control group. So, every person has an equal chance of ending up in one of the two groups via a random procedure (e.g. coin toss, drawing of lots, random numbers etc.).

(b) Matching
This procedure attempts to allocate people who are similar in terms of certain characteristics to the experimental and control group. That is to say, for every person in the experimental group, an 'equivalent' partner (match) is identified, who is not subjected to the intervention. This 'parallelisation' creates a contrived (but nevertheless actually existing) control group (cf. Rossi, Lipsey and Freeman 2004: 275).

(c) Statistical controls
Statistical controls are often employed in addition to random controls, and particularly in the case of matching, in order to establish whether the experimental and control groups are indeed alike in terms of all important features. A statistical control group is formed by trying to generate a statistical copy of the experimental group with regard to all relevant characteristics.

In contrast to matched control groups, which are chosen prior to data collection based on certain features that mean they mirror the experimental group as closely as possible, the statistical 'control group' is not formed until after data has been gathered. As the comparison group thus only comes into existence in the data analysis phase, this process is referred to as 'statistical' control.

Whether matched or statistical controls are used in impact analyses depends primarily on the relative proportion of participants/non-participants in the parent population. For example, it would make little sense to seek the participants of an environmental advice programme using a general population survey, as these people would barely be captured, even in the case of a huge sample. In order to ascertain the impacts of programmes with a relatively narrowly defined target group, this procedure would be barely feasible. Matched controls would thus be preferable in such cases.

(d) Reflexive controls
Under this form of control, the experimental group becomes its own control group, by observing the measurement readings of the participating experimental units before and after the intervention. The term 'reflexive' is intended to express that, within such a design, the experimental group provides its own control data, with no separate comparison group. If reflexive controls are employed, is must be assumed "that no changes in the tar-

gets on the outcome variables have occurred in the time between observations other than those induced by the intervention" (Rossi, Freeman and Lipsey 2004: 290). Based on this assumption, differences between measurement readings prior to and following the intervention are interpreted as net effects.

Although this technique has the advantage that differences in demographic composition are ruled out, as the group is always the same one, it has the crucial drawback that it can no longer be clearly concluded whether the observed change in measurement readings is actually attributable to the intervention. The higher the number of measurement readings, the greater the degree of certainty of statements about the effects of the intervention, especially if there are a lot of measurement time-points prior to the introduction of the intervention, as a 'trend' then becomes better visible, depicting what would have happened if there had been no intervention. At the same time, though, the collection of data at as many different points in time as possible also represents a serious problem. The further the measurement time-points go back in time before the intervention (which has a positive influence on the calculation of a trend), and the longer the programme lasts, the older the experimental subjects become, meaning age-related effects can arise. Moreover, endogenous and exogenous factors, as well as historical events, can have an additional influence on the target variables (indicators) during this time, distorting the estimation of net effects.

(e) Generic controls
For individual phenomena and processes of social life, there are generally recognised, empirical statistical values, which serve as so-called generic controls. This means that intervention effects within the experimental group can be compared with typical changes in the population as a whole. Statistical values such as mortality and fertility rates, indicators that characterise the labour force etc. are drawn on to estimate what would have happened without the intervention. Differences between measurement readings following the intervention and the statistical values are interpreted as the net effect. The statistical values replace, as it were, the control group. However, as such statistical values only exist for a few social fields, and even where they do exist only in a very coarse form, generic controls can not often be employed. Rossi, Freeman and Lipsey (1999: 332) recommend: "Generic controls should be used only when other types of controls are not available, and then only with the utmost caution".

(f) Shadow controls
Shadow controls also constitute a very uncertain form of control. Here, the impacts among the (groups of) persons subjected to an intervention are compared with that which would have been expected 'normally', i.e. without the intervention. For such an assessment, experts, programme managers and/or participants are called upon. Rossi, Freeman and Lipsey (1999: 356) use the term "shadow controls" for this: "...a name chosen to reflect their role as a benchmark for comparison as well as their usual lack of a substantial evidential basis". Despite their low 'degree of certainty', shadow controls are, for a range

of reasons, used again and again. This is, on the one hand, because they are seen as an alternative to reflexive controls, but primarily beause they cost so little, or simply because they have always been employed.

The *quality of a design* is measured in particular by the degree to which alternative explanations and confounding variables are successfully eliminated. The various research designs have differing levels of aptitude for achieving this. All of them exhibit strengths and weaknesses, meaning that statements about net impacts can never be made with absolute certainty, but rather always with a certain probability or plausability. Figure 4.8 provides an overview of the most important impact analysis designs.

Figure 4.8: Typical research designs for impact analyses

Design		Selection of experimental units	Type of control group	Data collection time-points
I.	'Real' experiments/ field experiments	Random selection	Random controls, often additional statistical controls	Minimum: only after the intervention. Usually before and after; often multiple measurements during the intervention
II.	Quasi-experiments	Uncontrolled selection	Matched and/or statistical controls	Minimum: only after the intervention. Usually before and after. Often multiple measurements during the intervention
III.	Cross-section analyses	Uncontrolled selection	Statistical controls	Only post-measurements
IV.	Pretest-posttest analyses	Uncontrolled selection	Reflexive controls	Minimum: pre- and post-measurement
V.	Retrospective pretest/posttest analyses	Uncontrolled selection	Retrospective reflexive controls	Post-measurements with retrospective measurements of the starting situation
VI.	Panel analyses	Uncontrolled selection	Reflexive controls	More than two measurements during the intervention
VII.	Time series analyses	Uncontrolled selection	Reflexive controls	Multiple measurements before and after the intervention
VIII.	Judgemental approach	Uncontrolled selection	Generic and/or shadow controls	Only post-measurements

Source: based on Rossi et al. 1988: 113; Rossi, Freeman and Lipsey 1999: 261.

Experiments and quasi-experiments

There is scarcely any doubt that an experimental design is the ideal arrangement for testing causal hypotheses (cf. Diekmann 1995: 290; Schnell, Hill, Esser 1999: 214 ff.; Rossi, Lipsey and Freeman 2004: 233 ff.), as only a 'real' experiment accommodates the technical *requirements for examining a causal relationship*. These are:

- The chronological order of measure and impact
- The linking of measure and impact
- The control of external variables through randomisation and/or matching when measuring the relationship between measure and impact, or through the incorporation of all conceivable external variables (cf. Campbell 1969: 409 ff.).

Therefore, especially in the early years of evaluation research, *experimental designs* were favoured. In the light of the complexity of research problems, and the necessity of producing external validity as well as ensuring the internal validity of the test set-up, it has not been possible to use the creation of laboratory situations to strive for complete control of external factors, as, although they exhibit high internal validity, externally they are barely valid. So, instead, *field experimental designs* have been preferred (cf. Weiss 1974: 88 ff.; Rossi et al. 1988: 125 ff.).

Within this type of design, an attempt is being made to systematically control the conditions of a field situation, and to manipulate the variables relevant to the experiment. Through field experiments, the aim is pursued of transferring the logic of classic experiments to test set-ups in the social sphere. In real-life social situations, however, there are a whole range of reasons why this is never fully possible (cf. Kromrey 2002: 96 ff.).

Although experimental designs ('real' experiments and field experiments with randomisation) appear superior to other types of test design in measuring impacts, and are characterised as the most rigorous method of determining the net effects of a programme (cf. Campbell 1969: 409 ff.), they entail a number of *problems*:

- Due to theoretical and empirical restrictions, the number of explanatory factors incorporated is, in principle, incomplete.
- As field experiments, too, are dependent on the interaction between researcher and experimental subjects, researchers and their data collection instruments trigger changes in the test situation, which are attributed to the intervention measures, and these need to be separated from the effects (cf. Thompson 1990: 379 ff.). A straightforward control group is not sufficient to safeguard against this, and the only solution is the elaborate Solomon four-group design, which can scarcely be implemented in the field (cf. Campbell & Stanley 1963: 178).
- As the collaboration of experimental units occurs on a voluntary basis, there is a danger of self-selection of participants on the basis of certain features, which can lead to distortion of the representativeness of persons involved.
- Project interventions and their effects are so complex that recreating test conditions is only possible with great difficulty, and distortions in test conditions in the case of repeated measurements can produce slightly different results (cf. Campbell 1969: 409

ff.; Weiss 1974: 90 ff.; Lange 1983: 264 ff.; Bamberger 1989: 223 ff.; Diekmann 1995: 303 f.; Schnell, Hill, Esser 1999: 214 ff.; Rossi et al. 1999: 301; Kromrey 2002: 92 ff.; Rossi, Lipsey & Freeman 2004: 237 ff.).

In evaluation practice, experimental designs do not seem to have met the expectations placed upon them. Many analyses carried out within the scope of the "Great Society program" in the 1960s and '70s were not able to detect any *significant programme effects using experimental designs*: "...one could never demonstrate statistically that a program made a difference" (Deutscher & Ostrander 1985: 24). The consequence of this was "that more often than not evaluation research could be employed as a rationale for eliminating a program" (ibid., cf. also Shadish 1990: 160). In pedagogical research, too, complaints were made that "many quantitative experimental evaluations did not find any significant effects" (Wittmann 1985: 182). In trying to provide statistically significant results and strengthen internal validity, designs became more and more elaborate, and required more and more time and money, leading to the view gradually becoming established that: "This 'ideal' evaluation approach proved to be overly sophisticated, costly, and unpractical for the evaluation of most development projects." (Binnendijk 1989: 209).[136]

In addition to the problems with experiments already discussed, *objections* are also made against this method *in principle*:
(1) One of the most significant criticisms of the *experimental design* is that it is *not suitable for the analysis of complex phenomena* (cf. Mayntz 1985: 74). According to Grupp (1979: 150), the crucial difference between straightforward and complex problems is that the former are limited to just a few parameters, with the remaining section of reality masked out. Experimental designs are seen as being tailored to this type of issue, for a golden rule of experiments is that it is inexpedient to vary more than one parameter at a time, in order to avoid confusion. This means that the number of parameters examined in an experiment must be small. Aggregate phenomena, such as organisations, political decision-making processes, and programmes, constitute complex phenomena, however, that are defined to a much lesser degree than simple ones, involve many parameters, are concerned with complex impacts, and demand knowl-

---

136 Just as it cannot be completely ruled out that all programmes investigated really were not able to achieve any significant effects, it can also not be ruled out that the lack of empirical evidence of impacts is attributable to methodological deficiencies. A definitive judgement cannot be made here. Some interpret the lack of evidence of significance as a failure of the programmes (cf. e.g. Rossi 1978; Rossi & Lyall 1976; Rossi, Berk & Lenihan 1980), whilst others take the view "...that the failures of programs reflect the failures of evaluation methods" (Chen & Rossi 1980: 107, cf. also e.g. Weiss & Rein 1969; Scriven 1972). The lack of effects has also been attributed to, among other things, the use of relatively crude procedures, such as the common method of assessing differences in mean values between treatment and comparison groups (cf. Shadish 1990: 163; Wittmann 1985: 194).

edge of all the effects of a given action, including its remote side-effects (cf. Mayntz 1985: 74 f.; Diekmann 1995: 303).

(2) A further criticism is that *the experimental design* is *not at all suitable for the measurement of social change, because of its ahistoric nature.* Yet this is exactly what most social programmes intend to achieve, and should be measured: "In its steadfast commitment to an unchanging design and its insistence on limiting evidence to the results of the experiment itself, it is not appropriate for the evaluation of many social programs" (Deutscher & Ostrander 1985: 24). Guba and Stufflebeam (1968) argue that, under the experimental method, the control of so many conditions leads to the creation of an artificial programme world, which can no longer be transferred to the real world.

(3) Moreover, the *dominant orientation towards internal validity* has come in for increasing criticism. Brandtstädter (1990b: 218), for instance, notes that the internal validity of an experiment is less dependent on structural design features, and more on "how strong the theory employed to explain findings is in comparison to competing explanatory arguments". That is to say, even designs that are 'weak' in terms of experimental logic can by all means possess high internal validity if there is only one plausible explanation for observation findings. Conversely, a 'real' experiment achieves only weak internal validity if there are equally plausible, competing explanations for the occurrence of the findings. Similar reservations are also expressed about the aspect of external validity, or the generalisability of a finding, "which can be judged based on structural design features to just as small an extent as internal validity" (ibid.). Furthermore, it is pointed out that laboratory experiments by no means offer a guarantee of internally valid results. Measurement effects, experimenter effects, and other influences have been successfully demonstrated by numerous tests, including in laboratory experiments, despite the given control options. Equally, field experiments are not valid simply because they are carried out 'in the field', as this too involves interfering in the 'natural' lived-in world and, at least situationally, changing it. This too can produce distortions (cf. Schnell, Hill, Esser 1999: 217).

(4) Limitations to the application of experiments also result from *professional ethics and the law.* For example, appropriate control groups cannot be formed if certain programmes reach all or most members of a specific population, or if the use of a certain programme is not voluntary, but rather compulsory for all (cf. Weiss 1974: 90). Furthermore, design-related manipulation of people is out of the question in cases where programmes cover genuine needs, meaning it would be immoral to consciously allocate them to a (control) group (cf. OECD 1986: 37; Bamberger 1989: 235; Diekmann 1995: 303 f.; Rossi et al. 1999: 301; Rossi, Lipsey & Freeman 2004: 259 f.).

If the experimental design cannot be employed, for methodological or technical reasons, or due to issues of research ethics, *quasi-experiments* are often resorted to, which can be referred to more simply as "experiments without randomisation" (Diekmann 1995: 309). That is to say, quasi-experiments are based on experimental logic, but without being able to fulfil all conditions of classic experiments. A fundamental difference to experiments is

213

that the apportionment of experimental and control groups is not possible through random selection, but rather matched and/or statistical controls are employed instead.

The *quasi-experimental test set-up* with comparison groups is *particularly suitable* for the tasks of impact-based *evaluation research* (cf. Kromrey 2002: 100; Diekmann 1995: 320), even though, due to the lack of randomisation, one cannot be completely sure whether potential effects of external variables have been successfully neutralised. However, this is not just the main problem with quasi-experimental designs, but rather, of course, with all non-experimental research concepts.

Control groups can only be formed if not all test persons are covered by a programme or service. Particularly in the case of programmes involving legal entitlement, or with a long tradition or duration, where everyone is a beneficiary of such measures, it can be difficult or even impossible to find people who do not have an interest in them. An example of this would be an evaluation that distinguishes between children that watch TV and those that don't, or an investigation in which 6- to 14-year-old children who attend school are to be separated from those that do not, or a study of social welfare recipients that differentiates between those that accept support and those that (despite entitlement) decline it. Even if enough people were to be found that do not watch TV, or do not go to school although they are required to, or who forego their social welfare benefits even though they are eligible for them, it can be assumed that a control group formed in this way would scarcely serve as a 'parallel' comparison group, as it will exhibit characteristics different to those of the experimental group.

Under such circumstances, it is not possible to create control groups. However, often they are done without for other reasons, in particular because they are seen as being too time-consuming or expensive. Many donor organisations in the field of development cooperation, for example, resist the setting up of control groups: "It often seems preferable to use the money budgeted on the survey to extend the project's benefits rather than study non-recipients" (OECD 1986: 37). This view is still held in many state and non-state development organisations.

Cross-section analyses

If even the conditions necessary for a quasi-experiment are not present, an attempt can be made to ascertain the social reality after the event using so-called *'ex-post facto designs'*, under which all variables to be measured are surveyed at one point in time (cf. Schnell, Hill, Esser 1999: 218 ff.).

Cross-section analyses are classified as this type of design. Their test set-up consists of random samples or complete surveys at just one time-point. Typically, a sample is taken of the target population, covering people that have participated in a programme as well as those that haven't. The measurement readings of the target variables (in which impacts should be detected) of both groups are then compared with each other (post hoc). Other characteristic values are held constant with the help of statistical controls. As cross-section analyses only undertake measurements at one point in time, retrospective questions are used in an endeavour to obtain information about earlier time periods.

Cross-section analyses also take advantage of the fact that programmes are sometimes implemented in different regions in a slightly modified form. These variations in programme configuration are used to detect effects of the programme. By measuring the magnitude or extent of programme interventions ('program dosage'), and then contrasting it with the impacts of the programme on various target dimensions, the effects of these variations can be measured, with all other important dimensions kept statistically constant (cf. Rossi, Freeman and Lipsey 1999: 267).

Cross-section designs have the *advantage* of being, as a rule, quick to implement and relatively economical. *Problematic* – as in the case of all ex-post facto set-ups – is the issue of the causal order, which stems from collecting all data simultaneously at one point in time. This leads to the possibility of alternative explanations. It may be, for example, that watching films with aggressive content causes aggressive behaviour, but it may also be that the opposite is the case. Moreover, the control of external variables is considerably more difficult to ensure than in the case of experiments. So, it may be that other variables, and not the independent variable, are responsible for changes observed.[137]

Pretest-posttest analyses

Particularly popular within evaluations is the *pretest-posttest design*, under which indicators are measured before and after the introduction of an intervention. The difference between the measurement readings should provide information about the net effect of a programme. Here it is assumed that pretest and posttest measurement readings would have been identical if there had been no intervention, meaning that the differences recorded represent gross and net effects simultaneously. Although at first glance this design may appear very convincing, a closer look reveals that pretest-posttests analyses are among the designs *least suitable* for measuring impacts. Because there is no control group, with the experimental group acting as its own control group, the detachment of programme impacts from those resulting from confounding variables is almost impossible. Net impacts can thus not be estimated properly at all. A further complication arises if, instead of per-

---

137 A distinction is made between 'antecedent variables' and 'intervening variables'. The former precede the independent variable, which would be the case, for example, if style of upbringing is strongly correlated with both film consumption and aggressiveness, but that the originally strong relationship between film consumption and aggressiveness disappears when considering style of upbringing at the same time. The latter are external variables that occur between the independent and dependent variable in chronological terms. In the example of film consumption and aggressiveness, frequency of conflict with partner and friends could be such an intervening variable. Lastly, there is also the possibility of a 'hidden relationship', a seemingly non-existent correlation. This would be the case, for example, if no correlation is evident at first between film consumption and aggressiveness, but one becomes apparent if the external variable self-confidence is taken into consideration, which had served to 'hide' it (cf. Schnell, Hill, Esser 1999: 223 f.).

forming pretest measurements, target group members are questioned retrospectively some time after the beginning of programme support about the situation prior to the intervention. Clearly, due to memory gaps, the tendency to harmonise etc., considerable distortions can result from this.

Panel analyses

The validity of ex-post facto designs – such as cross-section analyses – is seriously limited by the one-off, simultaneous measurement of all relevant variables. However, the problem of the causal order of variables associated with this design can be alleviated through the repeated application of the design. Such tests are called – in contrast to cross-section analyses, which only involve one measurement – 'longitudinal analyses'. If *the same variables, operationalised in the same way,* are measured *among the same people at different time-points,* this test set-up is described as a *'panel'*. Panel studies thus represent an extension of the pretest-posttest design. If data are collected at two or more time-points (t1, t2...tn) (also known as 'survey waves'), it can be established by comparing the readings from the first, second, and further measurements whether, and how, the variables have altered, and what statistical relationships exist between the variables (measured at t1) and the supposed dependent variables (measured at t2). The primary *advantage* of panel studies is thus that independent and dependent variables can be related to each other with a time delay. For the analysis of relationships, multivariate analysis techniques are employed (cf. Schnell, Hill, Esser 1999: 226 ff.).

Panel designs are much more suitable for impact analysis than, for instance, cross-section or pretest-posttest analyses, as the additional measurement time-points facilitate a significantly better estimation of the nature of the impact of an intervention.

Time-series analyses

For a diverse array of social phenomena, extensive *time series* exist (e.g. birth rates, divorce rates, economic growth etc.). Many institutions and administrative bodies also collect data on occurrences or conditions (e.g. the number of university applicants, drop-outs, graduates, the number of licensed cars, church-leavers etc.). Such data, collected regularly (e.g. monthly, quarterly, annually) by official statistics agencies, social-scientific surveys, public and non-public bodies, can be used to form time series, which may be employed for 'purposes of control'. That is to say, these data provide a relatively secure basis for estimating how the target variables would have developed without the intervention measures. More precisely, this is usually approached by carrying out a series of measurements on aggregated experimental units before an intervention or significant programme modification has been implemented. These data are used to calculate a 'trend', which enables a forecast of what would have happened had there been no intervention. This 'trend' is then compared with the measurement readings obtained subsequent to the introduction of the intervention. Based on the difference between the 'trend' calculated over the long-term and the values recorded following the intervention, conclusions are drawn as to the net effect of the intervention. Random fluctuations can be controlled with the help of inferential statistical test procedures.

The biggest *problem* with time-series analyses is that multiple measurement timepoints (30 are recommended) are required prior to the intervention measure coming into force in order to generate a trend (projection). Time-series analyses are therefore usually limited to the examination of official statistical data, or data that are provided via regularly performed surveys. Rossi, Freeman and Lipsey (1999: 268) favour this model if no control groups can be formed: "Time-series designs are the strongest way of examining full-coverage programs, provided that the requirements for their use are met".

Judgemental approach

The *most economical*, but also by some distance the *least reliable and most imprecise design* for determining programme impacts is the *judgemental approach*. Here, the judgements of experts, programme administrators, and participants are called upon to assess net impacts. Under this model, experts are assigned with the task of inspecting the effects of a programme. This usually occurs through a visit to programme-implementing organisations, whose employees are then questioned. This form of impact 'measurement' is described by Rossi, Freeman and Lipsey (1999: 269) as "the shakiest of all impact assessment techniques".

Sometimes such judgements are also made by programme managers themselves. It should come as no surprise that this usually leads to programme effects being portayed more positively than the empirical evidence suggests, as the administrators of a programme have an obvious interest in letting their work be seen in as favourable a light as possible.

Such appraisals sometimes also include the judgements of participants on the effectiveness of programmes. Questioning the *audiences* (users or affected parties) of a programme sounds particularly plausible, as who should be more familiar with the impacts of a programme than those that know the object of analysis from first-hand experience? The users of a service or persons affected by a measure may thus be deemed the 'real' experts. Rossi, Freeman and Lipsey (1999: 269), though, argue: "However, it is usually difficult, if not impossible, for participants to make judgments about net impact because they ordinarily lack appropriate knowledge for making such judgments".

Kromrey (2002: 103) goes even further with his criticism of this method, pointing out that the judgements obtained "neither have the status of appraisals in the sense of 'technological' evaluations, nor that of appraisals of neutral experts". Rather, they are "individually biased value judgements of people in a particular relationship – as a user, affected party – with the object of analysis". Kromrey thus proposes that, in this case, "acceptance surveying" rather than evaluation is referred to. The notion of *'participant satisfaction'* appears even more suitable. Although this is an important feature for the assessment of programme quality, as explained in chapter 3.7, it is by no means a substitute for impact analysis.

So, the completion of participant surveys by students, for example, is not a suitable way of evaluating the impacts of different 'teaching styles'. They make even less of a contribution towards assessing such complex chains of effect as those triggered by development projects. Nevertheless, these procedures, passed off as evaluation, enjoy particular popularity in contexts as diverse as universities and developing countries, as well as in other policy fields. Perhaps this is not least due to the fact that they often represent 'token activities': evaluations are indeed to be performed, but must cost as little as possible. The method of questioning participants, i.e. the alleged 'real' experts, sounds attractive, as it is easy to carry out, economical and always produces results.

However, it should be borne in mind that wrongly-applied methods, or those used for the wrong purposes, lead to serious *misinterpretations*, and can thus have *fatal consequences* for the *management decisions* based thereon, particularly if the evaluations in question have ramifications for the allocation and distribution of financial resources, or even for the continuation or cessation of programmes.

'Evaluations' based solely on participant or target group surveys should therefore be judged with extreme scepticism. This is especially true if evaluation designs for impact analysis are developed on this basis, and are referred to under the pretence of *'participatory approaches'* as being superior to other, traditional (scientifically-based) methods. An example of this is Neubert's (1998: 93) method of "social impact analysis", whose evaluation design is based "basically on matched 'pretest-posttest comparisons' of the reality of life in the project region", in order to not only be able to identify changes, but also their causes. The primary data source is "the systematised memories of the target group", which are unearthed "within group discussions based on PRA methodology[138] with representatives of the target group" (Neubert 1998: 51).

In conclusion, it can be stated that the choice of a test design appropriate for the evaluation problem/task is of particular importance. Data obtained through monitoring and evaluation should create value, e.g. should provide programme management with the information it requires to make rational decisions. It is therefore important to ensure that the data gathered through an evaluation are reliable and valid. The *methodological weaknesses* associated with the respective designs, and the *degree of certainty* (probability) with which certain statements are formulated, need to be made transparent. There are situations in which only an expert judgement or impact appraisal by the programme administrator is feasible, and in such cases the associated limitations must be made clear. Otherwise there is a *danger* that methodologically-demanding designs are no longer even deployed, because – as the simplistic models suggest – things can be done much more straightforwardly and economically.

There is also a *risk* that management decisions are made on a supposedly secure informational basis, which can produce disastrously undesirable developments. One should thus not be too hasty in agreeing with Rossi, Freeman and Lipsey (1999: 269) when they

---

138   PRA = Participatory Rural Appraisal. Cf. the critical comments of Caspari 2004: 101 ff.

argue that "some assessment is usually better than none". Sometimes no evaluation seems to be better than a poor one.

The German Evaluation Society (DeGEval)[139] has developed a range of standards for ensuring the quality of evaluations (cf. http://www.degeval.de (German language website); standards@degeval.de). In addition to utility, feasibility and propriety standards (cf. the following chapters, 4.5 and 4.6), nine *accuracy standards* are listed, in order to safeguard the *scientific nature* of an evaluation. They are intended to contribute towards ensuring "that an evaluation produces and discloses valid and useful information and findings pertaining to the evaluation questions" (ibid.). To achieve this, a scientifically precise approach is recommended, beginning with the characterisation of the evaluand and its context (cf. subject block (1) of the set of evaluation guidelines in chapter 4.2, "programme and environment"). In order to obtain valid and reliable information, the quality criteria of quantitative and qualitative social research apply, and their methods should be applied. In this sense, the *accuracy standards* are oriented towards the professional rules prevalent in empirical social research. In developing the evaluation concept (chapter 3) and the set of evaluation guidelines derived from it (chapter 4.2), as well as in the application and assessment procedure explained in chapter 4.3, the DeGEval standards were taken into consideration. These standards are set out in detail below:

A1 – Description of the Evaluand
The evaluand should be described and documented clearly and accurately, so that it can be unequivocally identified.

A2 – Context Analysis
The context of the evaluand should be examined and analyzed in enough detail.

A3 – Described Purposes and Procedures
Objects, purposes, questions, and procedures of an evaluation, including the applied methods, should be accurately documented and described, so that they can be identified and assessed.

A4 – Disclosure of Information Sources
The information sources used in the course of the evaluation should be documented in appropriate detail, so that the reliability and adequacy of information can be assessed.

---

139 The German Evaluation Society (Gesellschaft für Evaluation (e.V.)) was founded in 1997, and among its aims is to promote the understanding and utilisation of evaluation and of its contribution to public opinion formation in Germany. For this purpose, its task is to develop and disseminate professional evaluation standards, to improve the exchange between evaluators, and to support education and training in the evaluation field, research into evaluation, and international exchange with other evaluation societies. Cf. http://www.degeval.de (German language website).

A5 – Valid and Reliable Information

The data collection procedures should be chosen or developed and then applied in a way that ensures the reliability and validity of the data with regard to answering the evaluation questions. The technical criteria should be based on the standards of quantitative and qualitative social research.

A6 – Systematic Data Review

The data collected, analysed, and presented in the course of the evaluation should be systematically examined for possible errors.

A7 – Analysis of Qualitative and Quantitative Information

Qualitative and quantitative information should be analyzed in an appropriate, systematic way, so that the evaluation questions can be effectively answered.

A8 – Justified Conclusions

The conclusions reached in the evaluation should be explicitly justified, so that the audiences can assess them.

A9 – Meta-Evaluation

The evaluation should be documented and archived appropriately, so that a meta-evaluation can be undertaken.

Procedure:
- ✓ The selection of a test design that ensures the clearest determination of the net impacts of a programme or service as possible is of great importance. If an evaluation underestimates the extent and magnitude of impacts produced by a programme, the latter runs the risk of being curtailed or even completely discontinued. If, on the other hand, an evaluation overestimates programme effects, large amounts of funding may potentially be invested in a wholly or largely ineffective programme. A great deal of responsibility is thus incumbent upon the evaluation.
- ✓ In choosing a test design, scientific and client requirements must be balanced. On the one hand, evaluations should supply results that are as valid and reliable as possible, yet on the other hand, these should in most cases be provided as economically and, most importantly, as quickly as possible, so that they can also be used in decision-making processes.
- ✓ As shown, there are a range of test designs, each with differing suitability for eliminating or controlling confounding variables, i.e. variables that could equally be responsible for the effects detected, so that net effects - impacts that are solely attributable to programme interventions - can be substantiated with a high level of certainty.
- ✓ Experimental designs seem to be best qualified to fulfil this task, because (1) the stimulus (the intervention) can be deliberately introduced and varied within an ex-

---

periment, (2) the stimulus precedes the supposed impacts, and (3) randomisation enables the distortionary effects of external variables to be neutralised.

✓ For a variety of reasons, experiments are only seldom applicable in evaluation studies. Thus, as a rule, non-experimental designs are used, whose greatest methodological weakness is that intervention effects are confounded by effects triggered by other variables. Through the lack of separation of programme impacts (outcomes) from the influences of extraneous confounding variables, the stringency of causal analysis is impaired. However, there are an array of non-experimental procedures which, although they may not attain the same degree of internal validityas experimental designs, instead exhibit greater external validity. In order to determine intervention effects with as much certainty as possible, sometimes elaborate non-experimental designs have been developed. The following applies here, though: "As in other matters, the better approaches to impact assessment generally require more skills and more time to complete, and they cost more" (Rossi, Freeman and Lipsey 1999: 237).

✓ The degree of certainty with which cause-effect statements can be formulated tends to rise as the methodological effort expended increases. For the sake of the quality of results, and thus their usefulness for decision-making processes, a certain minimum level should be reached in all cases. The formation of control groups, for instance, should only be foregone if no other course of action is possible, due either to the nature of the programme (e.g. in the case of "full-coverage" programmes) or to legal, ethical, or other compelling reasons.

✓ The employment of matched, or at least statistical controls, is a central requirement for being able to assess intervention impacts with at least some degree of certainty. Besides experiments, quasi-experiments offer far better prospects of achieving this than all other designs. Although panel and time-series designs do not involve control groups, they feature a series of measurement time-points, allowing changes over time to be identified.

✓ Less suitable for impact analyses are straightforward pretest-posttest designs, as well as judgemental approaches, under which impacts and their causes are assessed by neutral experts. The designs that merit the least faith are those based solely on the appraisals of programme administrators or on participant judgements.

4.4.2 Data collection methods

Just as all test designs that are well-established in empirical social research can also be applied for evaluation studies, *all data collection methods* can also be employed. This chapter can again only aim to provide an *overview* of the most frequently-used procedures suitable for obtaining data for answering the questions contained within the set of evaluation guidelines.

Document and file analysis

If certain services or programmes are planned and offered/implemented by organisations, a variety of *documents* are created (e.g. planning studies, concept papers, implementation plans, progress reports etc.), as well as *statistics* (e.g. about participants, brochures distributed, consultations carried out etc.). If a monitoring and evaluation system has been established, an array of quantitative and qualitative *data* are produced, which can be used for the analysis of programme development over time. No content-analytical approaches, in a strict sense, are applied here as a rule, under which, among other things, texts are subjected to quantifying analysis, but rather a targeted search is carried out for information that characterises the starting situation and development of a programme. The *evaluation guidelines* already developed can be used as a set of analysis guidelines to *structure* the information search.

The texts and other documents are used for obtaining information about reality. The texts or documents themselves are not the object of analytical interest (as may be the case, for example, within literary-scientific investigations), but rather serve as information carriers. The information documented represents an *indicator of underlying circumstances*, which Kromrey (2002: 311) distinguishes as follows:

- Events or situations described/depicted
- Intended statements/attitudes of the authors of documents
- Characteristics of the intended recipients/target groups of documents
- Political/social contexts of documented events/situations.

The issues of interest may either be manifestly documented in the texts (as 'statements about...'), or are able to be derived indirectly (latent content, 'between-the-lines' messages or information).

The *methodological problems* incurred in analysing texts and process-produced data are described extensively in the literature, and do not need to be repeated here.[140] Clearly, reports accumulated within an organisation do not represent an objective portrayal of reality, but rather their composition may have served manifold purposes. They may, for example, benefit the interests of the author, with certain circumstances (or people) being shown in a particularly favourable light, or they may be used to influence management decisions in a specific direction. Moreover, seemingly technical, factual justifications may only have been used to retroactively legitimise decisions that have already been made.

In addition, in written documents there is an overemphasis on the aspect of formal regulations, which, however, "only correspond to the reality of the activities regulated by them to a limited extent" (Hucke & Wollmann 1980: 226). Another serious problem is that the points of view of different groups of actors are registered to vastly varying degrees. In programme documents, the supporting organisation's view of the problem is

---

140   Cf. Friedrichs 1973: 314 ff.; Weiss 1974: 80 ff.; Webb, Campbell et al. 1975; Hucke & Wollmann 1980: 225 ff.; Caulley 1983: 19 ff.; Luckey et al. 1984: 300 ff.; Kromrey 1986: 168 ff.; Diekmann 1995: 481 ff.; Schnell, Hill, Esser 1999: 374 ff.; Kromrey 2002: 390 ff.

usually the dominant one. Insights obtained from file material should thus be interpreted and assessed with caution.

Surveys

In empirical social research, surveys, which René König (1972) once declared the "silver bullet" of social research, remain the most frequently used method of data collection. At the same time, it is also the procedure that is most developed. With regard to the type of communication employed, a distinction is made in principle between *oral surveys* (interviews), carried out *in person* (face-to-face) or *via telephone*, and *written surveys*.

Asking questions to obtain information seems very straightforward at first glance. Yet *language* as an instrument of information mediation is *by no means unproblematic*. In different social sub-cultures, 'different' languages are spoken. The same interview question, for example, is often understood in different ways, with differing interpretation occurring between the interviewer and interviewee and within different groups of respondents. If surveys are carried out in other countries, in order to obtain internationally comparable data, for example, these problems become magnified.

What is more – and this represents a serious limitation – the answers to questions asked do not always directly reveal the value of the feature of interest, but rather just act as indicators of its existence. Answers to questions of attitude, for example, are indicators of attitudes of interest which themselves are not directly identifiable. Yet even if it were possible to ascertain them directly, the reliability of this information can be extremely questionable. Not necessarily because the interviewee consciously hides his or her attitude or provides false statements – which can of course also occur – but rather because it is not the actual features that are surveyed (e.g. attitudes, income, education etc.), simply the knowledge or impressions of interviewees of the relevant issue at the point in time of the survey. This knowledge can, however, be erroneous, and impressions imprecise. Here it is to be expected that these become more inaccurate:

- The more complicated the issue asked about is for the interviewee
- The more limited his or her personal experience with the issue
- The longer ago the event asked about occurred (cf. Kromrey 2002: 348 ff.).

An *interview is not a conversation*, but rather a very special form of communication with a very 'artificial' atmosphere. Here it should be noted:

- That the persons engaged in interaction tend to be unfamiliar with each other, having not met beforehand
- That the social relationship is very asymmetric, with one person asking the questions and the other answering them
- That the situation differs from natural interactions in that it does not have any social consequences. The interviewer usually even alludes to this fact explicitly by assuring the interviewee that anonymity is protected.

Based on these *limitations*, it is not to be expected that surveys constitute a 'neutral' data collection procedure. On the contrary, the interview situation, interview conduct, and the way the measurement instrument, i.e. the questionnaire itself, is designed, all influence answers given.

Surveys can be differentiated, firstly, according to their degree of *structure* or standardisation. This can vary from 'completely structured' to 'unstructured/open'. And secondly, they can be differentiated based on whether questioning is of an *oral or written* nature.

In the case of a *completely structured* interview:
- All questions are asked
- In a predetermined order
- With specific answer categories given.

Open interviews have only minimal guidelines, which, in extreme cases, may consist solely of the definition of the survey topic. Everything else is then left to the conversation process. Hybrid designs are often used, with standardised and open questions (without answer options) combined. Such *partially standardised* interviews usually manage with just the outline of a questionnaire, with interviewers having the opportunity of contributing to the structuring of the survey situation themselves. This form of questioning, performed with the help of a set of guidelines, provides the possibility of asking about certain subjects in more detail, and ascertaining circumstances more intensively and in a more in-depth manner (and is therefore also labelled a guided, intensive or in-depth interview).

Strongly structured interviews are also referred to as 'quantitative' surveys, whilst less structured interview techniques (e.g. guided interviews, intensive interviews, narrative interviews) are classified as qualitative methods of questioning.

A systematic overview of the various forms of questioning can be found in Kromrey (2002: 377), and is illustrated here in figure 4.9.

In recent years, the personal (face-to-face) interview has experienced increasing competition from the telephone interview. As Internet coverage rises, online surveys are also becoming more important.

With regard to the *quality criteria* - objectivity, reliability, and validity - it can be assumed that highly-structured instruments fulfil the objectivity and reliability criteria to a greater extent than open ones, as they are less dependant on the person performing them.

Nevertheless, standardisation does come at a price. In the case of closed questions, obviously no information can be obtained outside of the scope of the answer categories provided. The application of standardised interviews only makes sense if substantial prior knowledge of the social situation being researched exists (cf. Diekmann 1995: 374).

Figure 4.9: Types of survey

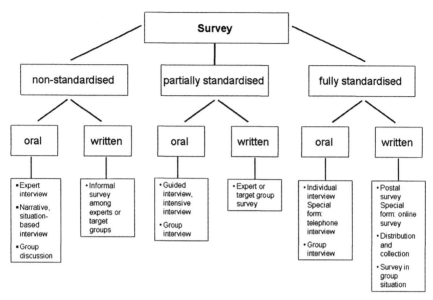

Source: based on Kromrey (2002: 377)

With interviews in general, the following *sources of error*, which can be divided up into three categories, can be identified:

(1) Interviewee characteristics
Distortionary effects can arise within interviews as a consequence of *social desirability*. This occurs if interviewees, seeking social acceptance, formulate their answers in such as way as to ensure that they correspond with the socially assumed 'mainstream'. If, for example, somebody is in favour of the death penalty, but does not consider this response 'politically correct' and therefore speaks out against the death penalty within an interview, contrary to his or her conviction, this would represent a (possibly putatively) socially desirable answer.

A *'response set'* is a systematic answer pattern of an interviewee that comes about independent of the content of questions. This would be the case if, for example, there were a tendency to agree (acquiescence), or a consistent trend towards positive or negative answers. This also includes the preference of some respondents for middle categories (in the case of uneven scales).

225

The phenomenon of *pseudo-opinions* is referred to if interviewees express views and judgements even if the issue under assessment is unfamiliar to them, or if it does not even exist.

(2) Question characteristics
It has been known for a long time – and yet is not always given sufficient consideration – that the *way questions are formulated* has considerable influence on responses provided. As has been shown by a series of split-ballot experiments, even the swapping of individual words can lead to significant shifts in answers.[141] Similar effects are also triggered by different *types of question*. For instance, under rating procedures (where the significance of an item is to be rated on a scale), higher values are obtained for the importance of the issue being assessed than under ranking procedures (where the interviewee has to arrange various topics in order of importance). The *nature and number of answer categories provided*, as well as the *positioning* of questions (halo effect or question order effect), can also influence response behaviour.

(3) Characteristics of the interviewer and the interview situation
The influence of the *external characteristics of interviewers* (gender, clothing, age) and of their *behaviour* on the responses of interviewees has also been the subject of multiple studies. The magnitude of influences depends on the specific questions asked. The *interview situation* can also have an effect, e.g. if a third party is present at a face-to-face interview. Even having knowledge of the commissioner of a study and his or her aims can bring about systematic bias in answers.

In compiling questionnaires and performing interviews, these aspects need to be given detailed consideration. Otherwise, the validity, reliability and objectivity of results are at risk. For the very reason that the survey appears so straightforward a tool at first glance, with questions simply written out one below the other and then speedily posed, it is *easy to underestimate* the *perils of this instrument*.

Surveys of an oral or written nature are also the data collection instruments most commonly used in evaluation research. Particularly appropriate for questioning 'important' groups of people about the programme and its development are *intensive interviews*. Among such groups are, notably (depending on the programme type), the following:

- Employees of the financing (sponsor) organisation (if this is not also the implementing organisation), who are responsible, at various hierarchical levels, for the implementation of the programme

---

141 A persuasive example is provided by the split-ballot experiment carried out by Schumann and Presser (1981) (as cited in Diekmann 1995: 393), in which the words 'not allow' and 'forbid', which are synonymous with each other, were used in an alternate manner, and led to completely different responses. The following questions were asked: do you believe that the USA should *forbid* public attacks on democracy? (Yes 54%; No 45%); do you believe that the USA should *not allow* public attacks on democracy? (Yes 75%; No 25%).

- Employees of the implementing organisation (executing agency) at various hierarchical levels and in various functional capacities
- Decision-makers of parent institutions (e.g. political departments, authorities)
- Members of the target group (towards whom the interventions are aimed and who are to benefit from them)
- Members of the non-target group (who are deliberately not affected by the interventions)
- People in the experimental and control groups
- Other stakeholders involved in the programme process or affected by it in some way or another.

The primary motivation for *questioning programme participants* is that "nobody [knows] the peculiarities and weak points of a programme better than those involved in its planning and implementation" (Brandstädter 1996: 224). Surveying those responsible for the programme above all serves to reveal something about the intended goals, the process of planning and implementation, management problems, conflicts of interest, acceptance problems etc.

When questioning employees of the executing agency, it should be ensured that as many departments and levels of the hierarchy as possible are surveyed, in order to take in a variety of different perspectives.

The *experimental and control groups* are *not equivalent* to the *target and non-target groups*. On the contrary, the experimental and control groups usually both belong to the target group, i.e. to the group among which the programme interventions are intended to produce an effect. In order to determine whether this impact occurs, the discrepancies in the selected target variables between the two groups are measured. As explained in chapter 4.4.1, the experimental and control groups should not differ from each other, so that the effect of the interventions can be measured as accurately as possible.

This can be illustrated with an *example*: a programme is aimed at comprehensive school pupils that have not found an apprenticeship position after leaving school (target group), but not at grammar school pupils (non-target group). The objective is to help the comprehensive school pupils take up a regular vocational training course through a year of occupational preparation. The graduates of the year of occupational preparation (experimental group) are thus compared with those that do not participate in it (control group), in order to determine whether the experimental group now has a greater chance of finding an apprenticeship. Beforehand, the comprehensive school pupils with no apprenticeship position were randomly allocated to either the experimental or control group.

If certain interviewees have already been involved with a programme since before it started, or from its inception, they can be questioned *retrospectively* about the starting situation, the beginning of support (tB), and the progress of the programme (t1-n). This provides an opportunity to supplement and 'verify' the findings obtained from file analysis. If the evaluation in question is of an ex-post nature, additional questions about the ending of support (tE) can also be posed.

Generally, it is possible to add to file analyses and the assessment of secondary statistical material with *retrospective interviews*, in order to explore the points of view of erstwhile decision-makers, employees, and other stakeholders. This not only allows supplementary information to be obtained, but it is often also the case that people who are no longer directly responsible for the programme or for decision-making provide franker, more open and critical answers than those currently responsible. File analysis should certainly precede interviews, as the knowledge obtained from it can be used to formulate targeted questions, in order, for example, to clear up ambiguities or fill in gaps in information.

To enhance the *reliability and validity* of data:
- The information obtained from file analysis should be examined in a purposeful manner with the help of interviews
- The same set of questions should be posed to different interview partners with comparable background experience, e.g. to persons formerly and currently responsible, to the managing and deputy director of an authority
- Similar questions should be put to people belonging to different departments, organisations, or hierarchical levels, in order to gather various perspectives on the same object of investigation; assuming, that is, that the question set is chosen in such a way that the respondents are able to answer the questions despite their differing background experience.

Subsequently, it is necessary to identify contradictions and commonalities between the interview statements and documents, as well as among interviewees. Here, statements need to be weighted according to their frequency of occurrence and the reliability of the information source.

For the *performance of interviews* with separate groups of people, specific sets of guidelines be drawn up in each case, which correspond to the supposed state of knowledge of respondents. The basic framework of the set of evaluation guidelines developed here can serve as an outline for this. However, the questions contained within these guidelines are not as a rule suitable as interview questions, meaning they would need to be reformulated beforehand.

Individual interviews have proved themselves – based on previous experience in numerous evaluation studies in the most diverse of contexts – to be methodologically superior to group interviews, as fewer confounding effects arise. The presence of third parties promotes 'socially desirable' answers, restricts critical statements, sometimes to a very great extent, and often leads to few people expressing the 'apparent' opinion of all. Contrary views are frequently not aired, and less eloquent people remain silent. Within individual interviews, even this kind of person can be induced to make statements, when under the protection of anonymity, which is of course not the case in group sessions, and critical, in-depth questions are also possible. The presence of superiors in group interviews can have a particularly disturbing effect, and is to be avoided in all cases.

The *anonymity* of statements should be assured and safeguarded unconditionally. If there is any doubt, audio and video recordings should be done without, by resorting instead to traditional written notes. All interviews are to be encrypted with a number code. If a sufficient amount of interviews have been carried out, so that specific statements cannot be traced to individual respondents, verbal statements can then also be quoted.

Standardised surveys have also proven their worth within evaluation studies. They are employed if larger groups are to be questioned, e.g. if very big implementing organisations are being dealt with, within which a lot of people need to be surveyed, or for questioning target and non-target groups as well as experimental and control groups. Here the primary objective is to ascertain the strengths and weaknesses of a programme, its usefulness for target groups, satisfaction with the services provided etc. Whilst in-depth questions in particular can be dealt with through qualitative interviews, standardised surveys facilitate above all the large-scale acquisition of representative answers.

Telephone interviews and, increasingly, online surveys, have proved the most effective methods of standardised questioning. Surprisingly, online surveys have even had a good deal of success in regions with low telephone density (e.g. in rural areas of southern and eastern countries) (cf. Heise und Stockmann 2004: 72 ff.).

Observation

Observation is an everyday activity. What distinguishes *scientific observation* from this is the reference to research hypotheses, as well as systematisation and control. Jahoda, Deutsch and Cook (1965: 77) consider scientific observation to be a valid emprical data collection technique if it:

- Serves a specific research purpose
- Is systematically planned
- Is systematically recorded
- Is related to more general judgements
- Is subjected to repeated checks and controls with regard to validity, reliability and accuracy.

The *objects of observation* are social processes and behavioural patterns. One problem is that the object of observation alters continually while being observed. In addition, the significance that an agent attaches to his or her actions can differ from that perceived and interpreted by the observer. Moreover, the process of observation is complicated by the fact that multiple activities are carried out simultaneously by various agents, and missed observations cannot be repeated. Even filming activity sequences – which is of course not always possible – is only able to redress such a situation to a limited extent, as only an extract of events can ever be recorded.

This means that considerable demands are placed on the observer, whose most important aid is a *categorisation scheme* for observation developed on the basis of relevant hypotheses. Here it is important to ensure that the categories are complete and mutually exclusive, and that there are not too many of them, so that the scheme is manageable.

Types of observation (cf. Schnell, Hill, Esser 1999: 359) can be differentiated based on whether:
- 'Objects' of observation are aware of the observation process or not (open/covert)
- The observer participates in the interactions or operates outside of the field (participative/non-participative)
- The observation is performed systematically based on a standardised framework, or simply in accordance with general instructions (structured/unstructured)
- The observation is carried out under field or laboratory conditions (natural/artificial observation situation)
- The observation performed is concerned with the behaviour of others or of oneself (external observation/self-observation).

Numerous *challenges* are involved with the method of observation. The observer plays a crucial role, having to perform activities of perception, selection, reduction, and interpretation. In doing so, a range of *errors* can arise (cf. Kromrey 2002: 338):
- Through selective attention, perception and recollection
- Through the tendency to combine even unrelated individual occurrences to form meaningful wholes, in accordance with one's own expectations, as well as to fill in gaps, and to structure the situation based on one's own interpretation.

Overall, observation is deemed a "largely problematic procedure...which, due to the difficulties entailed, e.g. in developing the categorisation scheme and performing the observation, is only relatively seldom" employed (Schnell, Hill, Esser 1999: 373; cf. also Diekmann 1995: 469 ff. and Kromrey 2002: 338).

This appraisal also applies within the *framework of evaluation research*. The technique of observation is most frequently used in studies that are strongly ethnological in their nature. It is used, for example, to document social actions and modes of behaviour (e.g. in organisations), as well as tuition or training situations. *'Site inspections'*, within which, for example, an organisation's technical equipment is examined with regard to its functional efficiency, state of repair and frequency of use, can also be classified as a form of observation.

Efficiency analysis
Procedures used for efficiency analysis do not represent further – economic – forms of data collection, but rather methods of appraisal, which nevertheless serve to supplement the set of tools applied in evaluations. They are employed in order to ascertain the cost-benefit ratio, an aspect often negelected in evaluations. In many cases it is not sufficient for the conclusive assessment of measures to know what intended and unintended impacts have occurred, and whether the programme or service goals have been attained. Rather, it is also of great interest to find out the relationship between these impacts and the costs incurred in achieving them. *Efficiency analyses are concerned with:*
- Measuring the costs associated with the impacts of a programme

- Tackling the question of whether the impacts justify these costs
- Choosing the most cost-effective (efficient) programme from alternative proposals.

Efficiency analyses[142] represent a specific type of evaluation, whose methodology comes from the field of economics. The most well-known techniques are cost-benefit analysis and cost-effectiveness analysis.[143] Both approaches are oriented towards determining the efficiency of a programme, but differ in how they measure impacts. Whilst *cost-benefit analysis* is concerned with ascertaining the utility of an object directly, in monetary terms, and comparing this with costs, which are likewise defined monetarily, in the case of *cost-effectiveness analysis*, only costs are specified in monetary terms, with impacts measured substantively. So, the central prerequisite of a cost-benefit analysis is that impacts recorded, as well as costs, can be specified in monetary units.

However, the services rendered by non-profit organisations, measured with the help of output indicators (e.g. the number of pupils educated, persons advised, sick persons cured etc.), and the resulting outcomes (e.g. improved knowledge, higher self-confidence, better quality of life), can frequently not be valued in monetary units. In such cases, the alternative is to define impacts in substantive results units (as in the examples just given), qualitatively and quantitatively, and to then contrast them with the monetary costs that have arisen.

Cost-benefit and cost-effectiveness analyses not only represent extremely complex, time-consuming procedures; they are also associated with numerous possibilities for manipulation, meaning they should only be applied by experts aware of the risks as well as the potential of these instruments. Evaluators can by all means leave the technical methods of efficiency analysis for accurately determining cost-benefit ratios - e.g. within a dam or bridge construction project - to auditors. However, they should nevertheless have as a minimum basic knowledge of the conceptual assumptions of these procedures, their

---

142 For introductory literature, cf. Gramblin 1990; Eddy 1992; Hanusch 1994; Mühlenkamp 1994; Nas 1996; Yates 1996; Greenberg 1998; Scholles 2001; Lassnigg & Steiner 2001; Domen 2001; Levin & McEwan 2001; Schönig 2002; Artner & Sinabell 2003; Rossi, Lipsey & Freeman 2004; Groh 2004. Interesting literature suggestions on the topic of efficiency measurement in general, as well as on specific subject areas (health, education, the environment etc.), can be found on the website of the European Commission: http://europa.eu.int/comm/regional_policy/sources/docgener/guides/cost/guide02_en.pdf; 127 ff.
The EU also has very informative handouts available for download:
http://europa.eu.int/comm/europeaid/qsm/ecofin/manual_tools_en.htm and
http://europa.eu.int/comm/europeaid/qsm/ecofin/documents/syllabus_base_en.pdf.
For supplementary information on cost accounting, cf. Jossé 2003; Hoitsch & Lingnau 2004.
143 Another established method is that of *utility analysis*, which, although it has a different makeup, only differs slightly from cost-effectiveness analysis, and is thus not dealt with here.

application, and their strengths and weaknesses, in order to be able to assess and incorporate the results of professional efficiency analyses, and to be able to carry out at least a rough estimate of efficiency themselves. As *efficiency* constitutes an important dimension for assessing *economic sustainability* in the *model of quality* developed in this book (cf. chapter 3.7, fig. 3.14), the practical application of the instruments will be illustrated using an evaluation-based example. Prior to this, the two most commonly used methods, cost-benefit and cost-effectiveness analysis, will be briefly discussed.

Cost-benefit analysis is based, on the one hand, on the normative concepts of welfare economics, and, on the other hand, on the insights provided by private industry capital budgeting (cf. Hanusch 1994: V). The aim of the analysis is to examine the economic efficiency of a measure in advance. Various alternatives are usually assessed, and the most economical (efficient) one selected. This procedure should ultimately – including in the field of public administration – lead to economically rational decisions. The central theme is the so-called 'economic minimum principle', which states that a given output should be achieved with minimal input. Efficiency analyses are intended to contribute towards identifying - through the comparison of programme alternatives - the solution that enables the attainment of programme goals with minimum resource input (personnel, costs etc.) under the relevant situational conditions.

Under this procedure of efficiency measurement, the benefits[144] of a programme, as well as all costs (directly attributable costs and opportunity costs[145]), are valued in monetary terms, and are thus suitable for comparison. This can be done, for example, by valuing both costs and benefits at market prices. Efficiency is then measured by simply subtracting the costs from the benefits, or by putting these two variables into a ratio (benefit/cost). This method differs from analyses of a purely business management nature (e.g. profitability calculations: income/expenditure ratio) in that macroeconomic costs and benefits are also incorporated in the assessment. Impacts that cannot be valued in monetary terms - so-called 'intangibles' - are also included, although they are merely described. A concise account of the individual steps followed in a cost-benefit analysis can be found in Scholles (2001).

The primary advantage of cost-benefit analyses is their uniform monetary assessment of various programme alternatives. This facilitates the selection of a programme based on straightforward comparisons and transparency. However, it remains questionable whether

---

144 'Benefits' refer to the (intended and unintended) net effects of a programme that are able to be measured in monetary terms. 'Costs' cover all direct and indirect inputs necessary for the implementation of an intervention (cf. Rossi, Freeman & Lipsey 1999: 364).

145 Opportunity costs are the costs of the alternative usage of a scarce factor. They represent the potential, yet foregone, benefit to be derived from a different usage of goods or funding. For example, an alternative use for empty office space may be to rent it out. In this case, the foregone benefit would be the rent, which has not been able to be obtained by leaving the office empty. The foregone rent could be calculated with the help of the local rent index, for example, and specified as the opportunity cost.

it is actually possible to place a monetary value on all the impacts of a project, and to give sufficient consideration to those impacts that cannot be valued in monetary terms, to the extent that they may be foreseeable.

Cost-effectiveness analysis is primarily used for projects within which, although inputs can be valued based on market prices, outputs cannot be measured in monetary terms (cf. Artner & Sinabell 2003). Under this analytical procedure, all direct and indirect impacts that arise as a result of a project are listed, and then contrasted with costs, which are ascertained in the same way as under cost-benefit analysis (cf. Hanusch 1994; Mühlenkamp 1994). The primary strength of a cost-effectiveness analysis is that impacts are recorded in substantive units rather than monetary values, meaning that this procedure is more flexible and can be employed in a greater array of situations. This also represents its biggest drawback, however, as only projects and programmes with similar aims and impact indicators can be compared in this way (cf. Rossi, Lipsey & Freeman 2004: 361 ff.). As complex projects not only have different impact dimensions, but also measure these based on different indicators, programme alternatives can barely be compared objectively with each other with regard to their efficiency, which is actually the main aim of cost-benefit and -effectiveness analyses. Decision-making is then only possible if subjective assessment criteria are drawn upon, which may be based, for example, on social norms or professional experience etc. Efficiency analyses also have to overcome other challenges in addition to this.

Investment costs and benefits do not arise at the same time, with impacts - depending on the nature of the programme - often only occurring with a long delay. This needs to be considered when calculating prices, as (potentially considerable) distortions are otherwise to be expected. This process of harmonisation over time is referred to as *discounting* (cf. Hanusch 1994: 97). Reasons given for the discounting of future project outcomes to the present include the time preferences of individuals and opportunity costs (cf. Mühlenkamp 1994: 166). Varying time preferences stem from the fact that "...future costs and benefits are usually valued lower than costs and benefits that arise in the present" (ibid.). This preference for the present is characterised by the 'uncertainty' and 'impatience' of individuals. In this case, opportunity costs refer to the costs incurred by individuals through waiting for the benefits of a project. They will only be prepared to bear these costs – according to the assumption – if expected future benefits exceed the costs of waiting. The discounting of future events to the present represents a huge challenge for the methods of efficiency measurement. Whilst the demand to assess projects at a single point in time makes sense in theory, in practice this leads to the question of what 'discount rate' to apply (cf. Mühlenkamp 1994: 177). Usually, an *interest rate* is used for this, set at a level similar to the long-term capital market rate or the rate offered by public bonds. However, such assumptions involve considerable risks when applied over long time periods. The choice of interest rate has significant implications for the calculation of the cost-benefit ratio, and "provides strong potential for manipulating cost-benefit analyses" (Scholles 2001: 14).

The application of efficiency analyses also involves further difficulties. At the outset, seminal *decisions* are made: is a measure to be viewed in isolation or as part of a system? In the case of an infrastructure project, for example the construction of a road, it should be decided whether the road is to be considered an isolated traffic route, or a component of the German or European transport network, taking railways into account. Moreover, it must be established what *goals* are to be included, and how they should be measured with monetary or other *indicators*. Scholles (2001: 11) thus advises: "These decisions are of a plainly political nature, and they should under no circumstances be left to an expert or even to the implementor of the project, as the latter will include everything that favours his or her measure, and, as far as possible, only consider those costs that cannot be dismissed".

The choice of the underlying *accounting perspective* can also lead to controversy. For example, (a) individual members of a target group, (b) the programme sponsors (financial backers), (c) implementing organisations, and (d) the local authorities in which the programme is embedded can all be used as the basis for the efficiency analysis. The resulting comparisons of costs and outcomes/impacts each produce different results, from which, in turn, different conclusions can be drawn (cf. the examples cited by Rossi, Lipsey & Freeman 2004: 351 & 353).

The *choice* of indirect (so-called secondary) *effects* to be included in the analysis also represents a problem; where should the line be drawn? Some impacts only occur as part of long chains of effect and with long delays, can only be identified or attributed to the intervention with great difficulty, or cannot be forecasted at all.

Intangible impacts, i.e. those that cannot be measured in monetary terms, cannot be incorporated in the calculation of the cost-benefit ratio. The cost-benefit analysis thus functions in a *structurally selective* way, as methodological rather than content-based considerations determine what circumstances are taken into consideration. Intangible impacts are indeed considered in cost-benefit analysis, by being described, but they have a weaker position than impacts that appear to have been calculated objectively in monetary terms. It is often the case that most social and ecological implications of measures belong to these intangible impacts, and they frequently fall behind supposed hard economic facts when appraised within efficiency analyses (cf. Scholles 2001: 12).

It remains the case that *cost-benefit and cost-effectiveness analyses* represent *important tools for determining efficiency*, and thus for the appraisal of measures, projects and programmes. The application of these procedures involves numerous problems, which can severely limit the informational value of these analyses. As a range of risky assumptions, specifications and selection decisions have to be made, which are based on experience or normative concepts, neither the procedures themselves nor the decisions made on the basis of their findings are impartial (cf. Artner & Sinabell 2003: 12). However, one advantage of these methods is that, if the individual procedural steps and assessment bases are accurately documented, all appraisals that have been carried out – as in the case of the impact analysis developed here – are open to scrutiny.

As elaborate cost-benefit and cost-effectiveness analyses are usually – as already mentioned – carried out by auditors rather than evaluators, the methods need not be presented here in any more depth. Moreover, the methods of efficiency measurement used for public authority projects cannot simply be automatically transferred to the whole of the non-profit sector. They take on a practical significance within the scope of the tasks of evaluation if a rough determination of the efficiency of measures, projects and programmes in the non-profit sector is to be carried out.

The use of basic principles of efficiency calculation enables evaluators to work out *assessment figures* within an appropriate time framework, and these provide information about the efficiency of resources deployed and allow an estimation of overall efficiency. Such operationalised figures, e.g. cost per participant, cost per case of advice or treatment, income growth per participant, facilitate, on the one hand, the observation of programme developments, and, on the other hand, comparisons with other, similarly positioned programmes (benchmarking).

How the various approaches may be *practically employed* to perform an estimation of efficiency within the scope of an impact-based evaluation will be illustrated using an example from the field of vocational training.[146] For this, a training programme in Jordan will be considered within the framework of an evaluation of efficiency aspects.

The aim of the programme is to enhance the efficiency of small and medium-sized enterprises (SMEs) and create new jobs, via further training in the area of "improvement management". The following data can be obtained from the project documents of the client and the training headquarters: the resources made available by a German non-profit development cooperation organisation for carrying out the training programme amounted to €300,000. Within the programme, 75 SME employees (participants) were to be trained. The implementation of the one-year training course was performed by a local training centre, which received €180,000 for this task. The remaining funding remained within the implementing organisation, and was used equally for travel costs and programme development.

The local training centre assigned the courses to five trainers, who carried out the training independently, each receiving a total payment of €15,000 (which also covered preparation of course content). The five trainers allocated each of the participants to one course of 14 days' duration, spread out over the year. In this period, the training centre building was structurally extended (building costs €100,000). However, these costs are not attributable to the "improvement management" training programme. This was an infrastructural measure for a training programme financed by a different donor. Thanks to this image gain and the improved equipment, in the same year the training centre was able to win three further training contracts for the field of "improvement management", worth a total of more than €300,000. Following the training, all 75 participants (P) were in a position to

---

146 This example is taken from the "Fortbildungsprogramm Evaluation in der Entwicklungszusammenarbeit" ("Evaluation in Development Cooperation Advanced Training Programme"), module 3, 2005 by Fritz Schöpf, www.feez.org (German language website).

reduce the production costs in their companies as planned. Per company (P), a savings potential of €40 a month was achieved. Twenty of the participating firms invested the resources saved in the diversification of their production, which led to the creation of a total of 20 new jobs. Employees (E) earn on average €500. Company earnings (profit) per employee amount to €50 a month. All newly employed workers have used a portion of their wages to purchase agricultural hand tools, which enable them to manage their sideline activities with 30% less time outlay. A further ten employees have put their new income towards buying consumer goods such as TV sets, radios, food processors etc. For this, in all cases it was necessary to take out a loan, of €2,000 on average, which had to be paid off in the first year after the training.

These circumstances can, based on the assessment criteria of cost-benefit and cost-effectiveness analysis, be illustrated as follows:

Figure 4.10: Measurement of all programme impacts[147]

Actor-oriented approach				
Actor	Costs/Benefits/Impacts			
Implementing organisation	Payment to training company	= €	180,000	C
	Travel costs	= €	60,000	C
	Programme development	= €	60,000	C
Training centre	New contracts	= €	300,000	UIPB
	Contract	= €	180,000	IB
	Image gain through int. trainers and building extension	= €		UIPI
Trainers	Sub-contract	= €	75,000	UIPB
Participants	Cost reduction (75 P * 12 months * €40)	= €	36,000	IB
	Operating result (20 E * 12 months * €50)	= €	12,000	IB
	Diversification of production in the case of 20 P			UIPI
Target group	20 new jobs			II
	Salary of (20 E * 12 months * €500)	= €	120,000	IB
	Hand tools: 30% more leisure time for 20 E			UIPI
	Consumer goods (10 E * €2,000)	= €	-20,000	UINB

Source: Fritz Schöpf, FEEZ course, module 3, 2005.

147 An alternative display format would be - borrowing from the field of accounting - an account (debit/credit). A balanced account (debit and credit equal) will of course never arise within such a display format. It simply serves to provide an overview. Which display format is most suitable depends on the problem or task of the evaluation.

Key:
C=   Costs
P=   Participants   E=   employees
II=   intended impact   IB=   intended benefit
UIPI=   unintended positive impact   UIPB=   unintended positive benefit
UINI=   unintended negative impact   UINB=   unintended negative benefit

On the basis of the information summarised in figure 4.10, *key data* for the internal and external assessment of the project can now be established.

For example, the following figures may be singled out:

-	Total cost per participant:	€300,000/75	=	€4,000
-	Direct training costs per participant:	€180,000/75	=	€2,400
-	Direct costs per training day:	€180,000/(5*14)	=	€2,571
-	Additional annual income per new employee:	€120,000/20	=	€6,000
-	Cost reduction per company/year	€36,000/75	=	€480

Viewed in isolation, these *key data* cannot be interpreted any further. They simply serve to illustrate how much the measure has cost per participant, and what the training costs per participant and day amount to. It has also been established, among other things, that 20 new jobs were created through the training programme (intended impact), and that, due to this, an additional annual income per new employee of €6,000 has been achieved, which strengthens spending capacity in the region and produces an improved quality of life for the families of these workers etc. A further figure is able to express the cost reduction per company/year. Whether the costs calculated are high or low relative to impacts produced, i.e. what the *efficiency* of this evaluated programme looks like, can only be determined through comparisons (benchmarking). To do this, however, similar programmes would be necessary. If these do not exist, it can ultimately only be decided on a subjective basis whether the resources invested are justifiable in relation to the benefits produced and impacts triggered. In order to rationalise such a judgement, overarching values or professional experience with similar programmes would then have to be drawn upon.

External programme comparison not only provides the possibility of relating the efficiency figures calculated to other, similar projects, ideally to the market-leading one, but also presents the chance of learning from others. Comparison facilitates the potential identification of the strengths and weaknesses of various programmes, with recommendations then able to be derived from these results as regards a more efficient attainment of project aims. Such a comparison may, for example, show that other programmes are offering services (e.g. new healing methods, consultation services) that prove to be more effective, or it may, for instance, be revealed that other programmes manage with less administrative expense etc. This type of comparison lends itself particularly to use by non-profit organisations if their programmes or services are quite homogenous, but with provision carried out decentrally. As the programmes/services are all similar to each other, the individual locations can be compared with each other. Taking the relevant country-specific and other situational conditions into account, the 'market-leading' site or 'market-leading' programme can be established on the basis of various efficiency data, and then serve as a 'benchmark'. In such a situation, it would also be possible to develop a combined monitoring-benchmarking-control system, in order to optimise efficiency, and thus quality, in all locations. When conducting external programme comparisons, it is important not only to compare programmes that are as alike as possible, but also to select those that are carried out in a similar situational environment. Even identical programmes within the same country can produce different figures, due, for example, to a different rent index, differing labour and living costs etc.

In addition to external programme comparisons (between similar programmes), *internal* comparisons are also possible, by observing the progress of a programme. The comparison of a single figure at different points in time provides information about the development of a programme's efficiency. Deviations, such as increasing total costs per participant, can be easily identified, constituting the starting point of the search for the causes. If direct training costs per participant remained constant during the same period, the cause of the change is likely to be found in rising administrative costs within the implementing organisation or the management of the school. In such a case, the increased cost ratio is by no means attributable to the training programme itself. Rather, new recruitments in the administrative department or a rise in office expenses may constitute possible explanations.

Efficiency assessment is thus able to provide management with important information for internal control. The routine collection of data relevant to efficiency measurement can be incorporated into a monitoring system. Even in the case of internal comparisons of key figures over time, situational conditions should not be ignored, as these, too, may represent the cause of changes in values. It is conceivable, for example, that the security situation in a region could dramatically worsen, necessitating additional guards or the installation of security systems in order to ensure safety in the training centre. Such an extraordinary burden would need to be appropriately considered when carrying out the assessment, and would not automatically be deemed to represent worsened programme efficiency.

The pragmatic approach presented here enables a straightforward, rough estimate of the efficiency of programmes to be made. Rough, because programme-specific conditions cannot be detected using the measurement methods put forward alone, and this is only possible in combination with other evaluation instruments. The methods of efficiency measurement dealt with here thus complement the primarily social-scientific methods used in this impact-based evaluation concept.

Multi-method approach

✓ In order to answer the investigative questions arranged within the set of evaluation guidelines according to subject area, various data collection methods must be employed. The combined use of different collection techniques, selection procedures, and test set-ups is referred to as 'triangulation'. The objective here is to compensate for the methodological weaknesses of one instrument with the strengths of others.

✓ In evaluations, it usually makes sense to combine qualitative and quantitative instruments: "If one wants to safeguard conclusions about relevant programme conditions and impacts through a framework of mutually supportive evidence, a multi-method approach generally provides a more comprehensive and meaningful picture than a single-method approach" (Brandstädter 1990b: 219).

✓ Through the use of file analyses, secondary statistical analyses of existing data, the carrying out of intensive interviews (some retrospectively), and standardised telephone or written (or online) surveys, as well as the supplementary use of observation procedures, a complex information picture is produced, encompassing the starting situation before/at the beginning of the programme, as well as the separate phases of implementation and, where applicable, the termination of support and the time thereafter, too.

✓ Through the use of numerous data collection methods, empirical findings are well backed up: as the data stem from different 'sources', and are collected with different tools, mutual 'cross-checking' is possible in order to review validity and reliability.

4.5 The social context of evaluation

4.5.1 The role of evaluators

Even though – as illustrated in the previous two chapters – all test designs and data collection methods well-known in the field of social research can be used for evaluation, it remains more than simply a particular form of this branch of research. What distinguishes it above all from this is the associated aspiration to *create value*. Evaluation endeavours to contribute towards configuring the planning and implementation of social interventions more effectively, whether they occur within the framework of individual measures of short-term projects, lasting programmes, or even permanent service provision, in order to ultimately improve the *quality of programmes and services*.

Evaluation research *differs* from basic research in numerous respects. Vedung (2004: 132) emphasises that "the basic difference between evaluation research and fundamental research is that the former is intended for use". While basic research may strive for insights in a relatively purposeless manner, evaluation research usually has a client, who is using it to pursue certain objectives, as well as an object of investigation (e.g. a programme or service) that is directly connected to population groups (target groups). These pursue different interests, objectives and goals, and have varying ideas as to who should benefit from a programme and in what way. Evaluation aims to support the development of programme initiatives and improve the planning of interventions in an ex-ante manner, as well as to configure the implementation of social measures more effectively and efficiently on an ongoing basis, in order to achieve a higher degree of effectiveness. It also aims to assess impacts produced on an ex-post basis, summatively and in a balanced way (cf. chapter 2.3.1, fig. 2.7). Because of this, it automatically gets caught up in a *field of conflict* of social and political interests. By performing functions of configuration, control, management and assessment within political impact fields, reporting its results back to the administrative and political process, it too becomes a *political tool*, operating "necessarily in a minefield of political, administrative and social interests" (Hellstern and Wollmann 1980: 61). Evaluation researchers thus need to consider the *social ecology of their working environment*. Various interest groups are directly or indirectly involved in evaluations, and can serve to hinder or support their implementation. These 'stakeholders' include, for example, political decision-makers, clients of evaluations, implementing organisations, executing agencies, programme participants, target and non-target groups, project employees, and competitors of a programme.

Evaluation research is thus characterised by *'duality'*. On the one hand, it belongs to the field of empirical social research, utilising its theories and methods, yet, on the other hand, it is part of the political process, which it also influences with its results, and is conversely subject to scientifically ignorant demands as a decision-making instrument for political management. In the course of the development of evaluation research, various methodological approaches have thus emerged, which tend to focus primarily either on scientific standards, the requirements of clients, or target group needs.

Now that the theoretical and methodological foundations of the evaluation concept developed here have been set out in the previous chapters, the focus will switch to shedding light on the *social context* in which this concept is to be employed. The *objective* is to explore the *role of the evaluator* in the evaluation process, his or her relationship to stakeholders, and potential areas of conflict that need to be observed, so that an evaluation not only progresses as smoothly as possible, but that a high level of benefit is also derived from its results, and recommendations for improving programme quality implemented.

For this purpose, a *participatory evaluation model* is developed, which, firstly, meets the demands of scientific quality, secondly, serves the information needs of stakeholders, and, thirdly, emphasises the (varying) interests of stakeholders as comprehensively as possible.

The evaluation concept developed here can be used for internal as well as external evaluations (cf. chapter 2.3.2), with a range of factors influencing the *role*, self-concept, and the approach and working method of an evaluator.

Internal evaluators have the advantage of being familiar with the programmes carried out, as well as with the associated aims, problems etc.; i.e. they have concrete situational knowledge, and can swiftly get going with the evaluation. Moreover, recommendations based on the results can be communicated via 'short' paths due to organisational proximity to decision-makers. On the other hand, because of their closeness to the people being dealt with, the organisational structures in which they are embedded, and especially because of their sound knowledge of the programme, there is a danger that internal evaluators lose their distance to the object of investigation and are not sufficiently open to alternative explanations, models and approaches. They may also be afraid of making critical comments (in order not to damage their career), and not consider the interests of stakeholders to an adequate extent.

The advantages and disadvantages associated with *external evaluators* are virtually a mirror image of this. They tend to act more independently, openly, and in a more distanced manner, yet experience difficulties in accessing information, winning acceptance, and penetrating complex organisational structures and processes etc. On the other hand, external evaluators can be expected to have a high level of theoretical and methodological competence, along with professional knowledge and extensive experience, enabling them to plan and implement evaluations that correspond to the relevant problem and also meet evaluation standards.

These statements are very typology-based, and will not always apply in concrete cases. However, the objective here is not to weigh up the benefits and drawbacks of internal and external evaluation, but rather to draw attention to the *difficulties* facing the evaluator in his or her *field of work*, which must be tackled when applying the evaluation concept developed here (and when performing evaluations in general). In doing so, internal and external evaluations place *different situational demands* on an evaluator, but in all cases *the same professional standards are valid*. That is to say, regardless of whether an evaluator operates 'internally' or 'externally', evaluation standards (including usefulness, feasibility, propriety and accuracy) apply.

The role of the evaluator of course also depends crucially on his or her *remit*, the aims of the evaluation, which phase of a programme the evaluation relates to, and what analytical perspective and cognitive interest are in the foreground etc. (cf. chapter 2.3.1, fig. 2.7). The evaluator must thus select an appropriate *evaluation paradigm* and *design*. As the evaluation concept in this book has been developed on the basis of the *empirical-scientific paradigm*, the evaluator's *understanding of his role* will also be assumed below to correspond to this. This is by no means intended to imply that this is the only correct, or the 'better', understanding. For every evaluation, the paradigm is to be chosen, and the design and data collection methods employed, that correspond to the relevant cognitive interest and the task at hand. Even though the diversity of the many approaches to evaluation may appear confusing, this is actually the source of its greatest heuristic value, with a broad range of alternatives available for different evaluation aims and tasks.

Regardless of which evaluation paradigm is selected, and whether an evaluation is carried out internally or externally, *communication* between the evaluator and stakeholders always plays a crucial role. The social interactions, or the fundamental relationship, between those involved in an evaluation and actors affected by it have an influence on the evaluation. Here, evaluators themselves, with their personal ideals and value perceptions vis-à-vis the various stakeholders, as well as their relationships with them, represent a potential 'source of interference': "Every evaluation is a reflection of the evaluator's personal beliefs, as well as a complex of interpersonal, financial, and organizational interrelationships between the evaluator and numerous other actors in the evaluation context" (Fitzpatrick et al. 2004: 416). Evaluators cannot suppress this fact, yet they must be aware of it and, through constant *self-reflection*, attempt to control their own behaviour.

Possible examples of how the personal attitudes and value positions of the evaluator can generate confounding effects are *ethnocentric perspectives*, or indeed the risk of *'going native'*. Ethnocentric distortions can arise (possibly unintentionally) if researchers are operating in foreign cultural contexts, yet apply theories, methods and tools that have been developed for the analysis of Western societies without reflection and without adapting them sufficiently to the relevant culture. Even in the formulation of the issue under investigation, as well as of supposed relationships, critical-rational research logic can come up against problems of understanding in foreign cultural contexts. 'Going native' refers to the tendency to adopt the perspective of individual actors or stakeholders. In this way, evaluators can lose their distance to the object of investigation and their independence from specific interests. This danger becomes greater, the longer an evaluator remains in the field, and the more intensive the exchange with stakeholders is.

The relationship with the client can be particularly problematic: "The more control the client has over the evaluators' job security, salary (or future consultant fees), and prerequisites, the less candor and objectivity the evaluator is likely to demonstrate in conducting the evaluation" (Fitzpatrick et al. 2004: 422).

Such influences, which affect the evaluator and can act to impair evaluation results, cannot be excluded, but the evaluator should be aware of them, so that he or she can take countermeasures. In practice, frequently occurring, more or less subtle *processes of influence* can stem from, among other things:

- The client defining desired and less desired outcomes as early as during the preparation of an evaluation
- Attempts to not register the interests of certain stakeholders or to attach a low value to them
- Evaluators being put under pressure to portray results differently
- Unwelcome findings being suppressed by stakeholders (including those other than clients)
- Results being selected or manipulated according to desired criteria
- Pressure being exerted to name informants who have been assured confidentiality
- Attempts to suppress questions relevant to the evaluation from the start
- Results not being made transparent and being concealed from superiors or the public.

This list could go on and on, and merely serves to provide a few examples of potential efforts to exert influence.

Evaluation *standards* should not only safeguard the usefulness, feasibility, and scientific nature of evaluations; they should also govern social interaction between evaluators and stakeholders in such a way that the two parties deal with each other with 'respect and fairness'. Below is a detailed list of the *propriety standards (P)* defined by the German Evaluation Society (cf. http://www.degeval.de):

P1 – Formal Agreement
Obligations of the formal parties to an evaluation (what is to be done, how, by whom, when) should be agreed to in writing, so that these parties are obligated to adhere to all conditions of the agreement or to renegotiate it.

P2 – Protection of Individual Rights
The evaluation should be designed and conducted in a way that protects the welfare, dignity, and rights of all stakeholders.

P3 – Complete and Fair Investigation
The evaluation should undertake a complete and fair examination and decription of strengths and weaknesses of the evaluand, so that strengths can be built upon and problem areas addressed.

P4 – Unbiased Conduct and Reporting
The evaluation should take into account the different views of the stakeholders concerning the evaluand and the evaluation findings. As with the entire evaluation process, the evaluation report should evidence the impartial position of the evaluation team. Value judgements should be made as unemotionally as possible.

P5 – Disclosure of Findings
To the extent possible, all stakeholders should have access to the evaluation findings.

Other guidelines also exist, besides these. The American Evaluation Association (AEA) (1994), for example, issued its *"Guiding Principles for Evaluators"*, which represent, to a certain extent, a code of conduct, encompassing five such guiding principles (Beywl and Widmer 2000: 282 f.), set out below.[148]

1. *Systematic enquiry*: evaluators conduct systematic, data-based inquiries.
2. *Competence*: evaluators provide competent performance to stakeholders.
3. *Integrity/honesty*: evaluators display honesty and integrity in their own behavior, and attempt to ensure the honesty and integrity of the entire evaluation process.
4. *Respect for people*: evaluators respect the security, dignity and self-worth of respondents, program participants, clients, and other evaluation stakeholders.
5. *Responsibilities for general and public welfare*: evaluators articulate and take into account the diversity of general and public interests and values that may be related to the evaluation.

---

148 These guiding principles have been taken directly from http://www.eval.org/Publications/GuidingPrinciples.asp.

Such sets of regulations[149] (standards) can contribute towards defusing conflicts that arise within evaluations, either preventatively or during the evaluation, but can of course not eliminate them entirely. What is more, the actual *interpretation* of these guidelines can only ever occur on a *situation-specific* basis. It is often the case that not all regulations can be adhered to simultaneously, meaning they have to be weighted and prioritised. However, they certainly represent an important *reference*, on the basis of which dialogue can be carried out and their observance insisted upon.

On top of clients, who provide the financial resources for an evaluation and define the so-called *'terms of reference'* - the requirement specifications - other stakeholders that influence an evaluation or are affected by it themselves can also be distinguished. Therefore, during the planning and implementation of an evaluation, it is not only the interests of the client that should be considered, but also the interests and needs of other actors. This is *not* primarily a *strategic measure* for eliminating 'confounding variables', so that nobody keeps information back, refuses to participate in an evaluation, or even boycotts it; the main objective here is to integrate various *points of view and perceptions*, so that results achieve broad acceptance. If this is not the case, it can hardly be expected that stakeholders will actively participate in the implementation of evaluation recommendations.

Part of the function of evaluations is to reveal deficiencies and undesirable developments, and to make these transparent, even if this involves casting doubt on the strategies and political positions of stakeholders, particularly of clients. Thus, even if all stakeholders are incorporated in an optimal fashion, it cannot be assumed that everyone will be enamoured with *evaluation results*:

> "This means that sponsors of evaluation and other stakeholders may turn on the evaluator and harshly criticise the evaluation if the results contradict the policies and

---

149 A further, comprehensive set of regulations are the "DAC Principles for Evaluation of Development Assistance" of the OECD (1998) (cf. http://www.oecd.org/dataoecd/63/50/2065863.pdf). These standards were compiled by the 'Expert Group on Aid Evaluation', founded in 1988, of the 'Development Assistance Committee' of the Organisation for Economic Cooperation and Development (OECD), and published for the first time in 1991. The DAC principles draw attention to eight central points: (1) Impartiality and Independence, (2) Credibility, (3) Usefulness, (4) Participation of Donors and Recipients, (5) Donor Cooperation, (6) Evaluation Programming, (7) Design and Implementation of Evaluations, and (8) Reporting, Dissemination and Feedback. All DAC member countries have pledged to adhere to these principles, which were subjected to a review process in 1998 (cf. OECD 1998).
Another set of regulations has been established by the United Nations Evaluation Group (UNEG). The 'Standards for Evaluation in the UN System' (2005) are divided up into four main categories: (1) Institutional Framework and Management of the Evaluation Function, (2) Competencies and Ethics, (3) Conducting Evaluations, (4) Evaluation Reports.
It is also interesting to conduct a comparison with the "Standards for Quality Assurance in Market and Social Research" (www.adm-ev.de).

perspectives they advocate. Thus, even those evaluators who do a superb job of working with stakeholders and incorporating their views and concerns in the evaluation plan should not expect to be acclaimed as heroes when the results are in. The multiplicity of stakeholder perspectives makes it likely that no matter how the results come out, someone will be unhappy." (Rossi, Lipsey & Freeman 2004: 43).

Because evaluations take place in a *political environment*, it may be that stakeholders react dismissively to results that contradict their own positions and expectations. Attempts may even be made to discredit the evaluation and those that have performed it. Evaluators should thus not be too surprised if their study, or even they themselves, get caught up in a cross-fire of *criticism*.

The following *typical patterns of criticism* can be identified from many years of evaluation practice:

(1) *Nothing new*
It sometimes occurs that the clients of the evaluation, evaluees, or other stakeholders claim that the results of the evaluation were already common knowledge before it was undertaken, and thus do not come as a surprise to anyone. It is indeed often true that stakeholders are aware of deficiencies and problems, or at least suspect their existence. The task of evaluation, however, goes beyond this, and is concerned with delivering empirically-founded evidence and robust findings. Regardless of this, in such a case it needs to be explained why, in spite of being aware of existing problems, those responsible did not act to rectify the 'well-known' shortcomings prior to the evaluation.

In evaluation research, as in the field of social science as a whole, it can also be observed that results which are counterintuitive, i.e. which do not correspond to general expectations, attract the most attention. Nevertheless, empirically-based insights that are in harmony with the mainstream of implicit or explicit suppositions and assumptions are no less significant.

(2) *Methodological deficiencies*
A particularly popular way of casting doubt on the results of an evaluation is to criticise the test design and methods employed. Here, it is always astounding how many (supposed) 'methodological experts' there are. Because many different approaches to an issue under investigation are indeed possible, only the selection of an appropriate test design and practicable methods can guard against unjustified criticism. An evaluator must therefore show convincingly that his or her methodological procedure is up to date with the latest developments in the field.

Problems can arise if the client does not even provide the necessary funding to finance a test design that is suitable for the task at hand. The very art of evaluation is often to obtain *as much robust information with as few resources as possible*. 'Second-best' approaches must frequently be accepted, as the evaluation cannot be carried out in any other way due to a lack of financial resources or time. However, there are clients who only provide a low level of funding for an evaluation and are tolerant enough accept a 'second-best' solution, but then criticise its methodological flaws at the end of the study. In order to prove that, during the preparation of an evaluation, the methodological difficulties and consequences for the quality of the evaluation associated with a 'second-best' solution were pointed out, it is advisable to document all procedural steps and to jointly agree upon protocols that have been prepared.

Ultimately, however, *responsibility for the quality* of an evaluation rests *with the evaluators*. Therefore, if they realise that the conditions necessary for an evaluation that is appropriate for the task at hand are not fulfilled, and that evaluation standards cannot be met, they should not take on the evaluation (cf. chapter 4.6).

The choice of interview partners should be made with great care. As representative (random) selections are often impossible, this should be done in a purposeful manner. It should be ensured that, as far as possible, all relevant perpectives and interests are represented. It is also advisable to agree on the selection with stakeholders (at least with the client), as otherwise there is a risk of the accusation being made that the 'wrong' people were questioned and 'incorrect' or distorted results thus arose; if the 'right' people had been interviewed, on the other hand, the assessment would have turned out to be completely different, i.e. more positive.

(3) *That which is not allowed to be, cannot be*

It sometimes occurs that findings are plainly denied. If this concerns facts and circumstances that can be proved indisputably with data, the issue can quickly be cleared up. If it concerns the expression of opinions (e.g. satisfaction with various aspects of a programme), then evidence needs to be provided in the form of a statistically-sufficient number of respondents. The data then 'tell their own story'. If it is a matter of the interpretations of the evaluator, a logical chain of argument should be stringently adhered to. The greater the extent to which statements that are not substantiated by existing data to a sufficient degree are avoided, the less an evaluation leaves itself open to attack. No evaluation should engage in pure speculation.

Particularly in the case of highly complex evaluands, factual errors can often not be completely eliminated, despite the greatest of care being taken. If these are queried by those responsible for or affected by a programme, who usually have far more extensive situational knowledge than the evaluators, they should of course be corrected after being subjected to close scrutiny. This is not the case, however, where substantiated assessments are concerned. Evaluators have not only the right, but also the professional duty, to stick to appraisals that are adequately backed up by facts, and to resist all possible attempts to influence them.

(4) *Painstaking search for errors*

When results summarised in the evaluation report are presented, it can sometimes be observed that criticism stemming from the client or evaluees consists merely of innumerable minor details. Due to superior concrete situational knowledge, it is almost always possible to reveal mistakes in presentation, even if they are only marginal. Even grammatical errors or the incorrect placement of commas in the final report can give rise to debate. In such cases it should be ensured that the central conclusions and insights of a study do not get overshadowed. There may by all means be method hidden behind such actions, i.e. the attempt to avoid having to deal, as far as possible, with uncomfortable information presented by the study.

(5) Implementation deficiencies
Not all evaluations are well arranged. If a situation arises in which the client does not grant the support agreed upon, e.g. by not providing the address data necessary for a survey, or if preassigned interview partners can never be found, or proceedings and decisions get delayed etc., these problems should be accurately documented by evaluators. This is the only way in which they can protect themselves against subsequent accusations, e.g. that the number of respondents is too low or the report was not finished within the specified time frame. Clearly, evaluators should make the client aware of such problems before then, and assist him or her – as far as they are able to – in solving them.

This list is not intended to give the impression that criticism of evaluation studies or evaluators is always unfounded, and that errors can only be due to the failures or lack of critical ability and willingness to learn of clients, evaluees, or other stakeholders. *Not at all. Of course, studies and evaluators frequently provide cause for justified criticism* if work has not been undertaken professionally. What is more, in the majority of cases, clients and evaluees are entitled to confront evaluation results in a constructive and open-minded way, especially if the development potential offered by evaluations is to be utilised. Moreover, experience shows that in organisations in which criticism is generally dealt with constructively, in which quality discussions are carried out openly, or in which an 'evaluation culture' exists, evaluation results and recommendations tend to be accepted to a greater extent and have a higher chance of being implemented (given that the evaluation is well-founded) than in organisations in which this is not the case.

Evaluators are as safe from unfounded criticism as they can be if:
- They have worked with scientific precision, so that the results can withstand methodological criticism
- Professional standards have been observed
- Stakeholders have been actively involved, ideally in the planning, and, if possible, also in the implementation of the evaluation
- The various interests of stakeholders have been sufficiently incorporated in data collection, analysis, and the interpretation of results.

However, the comprehensive *involvement of stakeholders* in all phases of the evaluation process also entails *risks*. It cannot always be assumed that an organisation or individual stakeholders are willing to learn. If an evaluation only meets with low acceptance, e.g. because it has been imposed upon the evaluees, the participatory approach favoured here can lead to severe conflicts, which can serve to hinder the planning and implementation of the evaluation to a considerable degree. If the most important stakeholders are involved as early as during the design phase of the evaluation, yet are not interested in constructive cooperation, it will be difficult to formulate mutual evaluation aims and assessment criteria, or to reach a consensus on the approach and the employment of selected methods. It is often the case that anxieties have to be overcome among evaluees, particularly if the closure of a facility or termination of a programme is feared. In such situations, evaluators need to develop a certain empathy for those affected, and display well-honed negotiating skills and persuasiveness. In showing understanding for stakeholders, however, it should not be forgotten that *evaluators bear responsibility for the professional implementation of an evaluation.* They must satisfy the requirements of clients, as well as the needs of affected parties (e.g. evaluees), and should adhere to scientific standards. This can sometimes constitute a difficult endeavour.

4.5.2 The participatory evaluation approach

For the implementation of the evaluation model developed here, a *participatory approach* is proposed, encompassing all stakeholders. If the various stakeholders are *actively involved* in *planning the evaluation,* thus being informed about the aims, test hypotheses, and the intended test design, as well as about data collection methods that are to be employed, there is a greater chance of winning their acceptance and support for the evaluation. This not only ensures that different perspectives are incorporated in the conception of the evaluation, but also that valuable knowledge of the various actors can be utilised, e.g. to obtain hints as to which actors should be questioned, to gauge the possibilities for forming control groups, to find out the availability of addresses and data etc. (cf. fig. 4.6).

If evaluation is organised as an *interactive process*, leading to intensive *dialogue* between the evaluators and people and institutions involved in the evaluation and in measures to be evaluated, this not only allows the various interests, values and needs of stakeholders to be ascertained, and their knowledge and experience to be used for developing the design; it can also serve to increase acceptance of the implementation and results of the evaluation, through the creation of a 'climate of trust'. What is more, this also increases the chances of evaluation findings being subsequently fed into development processes, with stakeholders viewing the evaluators not as external 'controllers', but rather as partners with complementary functions. Whilst the evaluators contribute *methodological knowledge*, stakeholders supply *professional, concrete, situational knowledge.*

As evaluators are often reliant on the voluntary, proactive cooperation of all stakeholders for performing a valid assessment of measures and occurrences, the validity of evaluation results can be improved with a participatory design. In an ideal scenario, this may mean that the evaluators and evaluees jointly agree on a proposal for the procedure of the evaluation, the actors to be incorporated etc. with the client.

Within the framework of this type of process of interaction, assessment criteria can also be developed collectively. This prevents the standards of the client from dominating, and the points of view of disadvantaged stakeholder groups, in particular, from getting a raw deal. Evaluators can either apply this set of criteria for their assessment, or alternatively develop their own criteria that are based on, for example, standards generally-accepted in certain sectors or for specific types of programme.

Within a procedure that has been agreed upon with stakeholders in this way, the evaluation instruments employed are also open to being continually adjusted, meaning that changing contextual conditions in the course of the evaluation process can be met with flexible reactions.

Whilst the first phase of an evaluation relies primarily on the methodological knowledge of evaluators, the *second phase* is concerned in particular with the collection of relevant information. During this phase, evaluees are most notably of significance as *information carriers,* representing the various perspectives that an evaluation is intended to collate in order to obtain as 'objective' a picture as possible of processes, structures and impacts. The involvement of stakeholders can be secured through the continuous dissemination of information about the progress of the evaluation, as well as through workshops.

Following the processing and analysis of data that have been collected with the help of as diverse an array of empirical social research methods as possible, the evaluation enters its *third phase*. Here, the data obtained by evaluators, which are ordered with the help of the analytical framework, and where applicable the recommendations that have already been derived from them as well, can be jointly discussed and appraised by stakeholders. The appraisal lines concluding each subject block of the set of evaluation guidelines can be used for this purpose (cf. chapter 4.3.2). The evaluator can only adopt the role of facilitator here, presenting the findings revealed within the scope of the evaluation and then releasing the results for assessment by the stakeholders. Evaluators can, however, along with their findings, also disclose the assessments they have made, presenting them for discussion.

Subsequently, feasible development strategies can be put together collectively, the realisation of which rests with the evaluees themselves, along with their organisations. The setting-up of a monitoring and evaluation system serves to keep an eye on implementation progress, and information obtained from this can then be used for management decisions.

With the approach developed here, *participation* in an evaluation is focused primarily on the *design and application phases*. The aims of an evaluation, the assessment criteria and, to a certain extent (as long as the scientific nature of the design is not damaged), the procedure, can be determined in a participatory manner, and constitute the guidelines for the evaluation. Information collection and analysis, on the other hand, is, with an empirical-scientific procedure, the job of evaluators. *Appraisal* of results can of course be carried out jointly with clients and the various stakeholders. The *application* of findings presented by an evaluation, and their translation into activities, is the sole responsibility of clients or other stakeholders. In contrast to quality management systems, evaluators, particularly if they are recruited externally, are not part of the implementation process. At most, they submit recommendations, for the realisation of which clients and stakeholders are responsible. The evaluator is no longer able to exert any influence when it comes to these processes.

Figure 4.11: Participatory approach

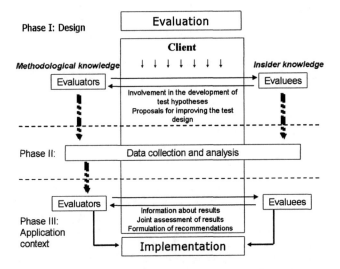

By way of qualification it must be emphasised that, within an evaluation project, it is scarcely possible to take all conceivable interests into account, or to incorporate all stakeholders in the process. *Non-organised interests* in particular, which are often prevalent among disadvantaged population groups, are in danger of not being adequately represented. There is also another problem with representation: who is authorised to represent the interests of specific groups, or at least entitled to articulate the majority opinion of those concerned? It will not always be possible to find such representatives. In such a case, the suggestion stemming from 'empowerment evaluation' and 'emancipatory evaluation', that evaluators should represent the interests of disadvantaged parties themselves, is of meagre assistance. This method would require that the evaluator actually knows the needs and demands of non-represented disadvantaged population groups (cf. Mertens 2004: 45 ff.; Lee 2004: 135 ff.).

The *participatory model* developed here is intended to contribute towards:

- The consideration of the interests and perspectives of the various stakeholders
- The utilisation of their knowledge and experience in the development of the evaluation design and selection of data collection methods
- Increasing acceptance of the evaluation and its results
- Safeguarding the usefulness of the evaluation, by ensuring that recommendations derived from the insights obtained are converted into actions: "In the end, the worth of evaluations must be judged by their utility" (Rossi, Lipsey and Freeman 2004: 411).

At the start of this chapter, it was once again pointed out that the purpose of evaluations is to create value. According to Beywl (2001: 160), the utility of an evaluation is proved by insights, information and conclusions being used, and affecting the actions of audiences in practice. The *utility standards* of the German Evaluation Society (2002) suggest that it must be ensured "that an evaluation is guided by both the clarified purposes of the evaluation and the information needs of its intended users". Here it is implicitly assumed that evaluation results are only made use of if these conditions are met. In order to ensure that this is the case, eight *utility standards (U)* are defined (cf. http://www.degeval.de):

U1 – Stakeholder Identification
Persons or groups involved in or affected by the evaluand should be identified, so that their interests can be clarified and taken into consideration when designing the evaluation.

U2 – Clarification of the Purposes of the Evaluation
The purposes of the evaluation should be stated clearly, so that the stakeholders can provide relevant comments on these purposes, and so that the evaluation team knows exactly what it is expected to do.

U3 – Evaluator Credibility and Competence
The persons conducting an evaluation should be trustworthy as well as methodologically and professionally competent, so that the evaluation findings achieve maximum credibility and acceptance.

U4 – Information Scope and Selection
The scope and selection of the collected information should make it possible to answer relevant questions about the evaluand and, at the same time, consider the information needs of the client and other stakeholders.

U5 – Transparency of Values
The perspectives and assumptions of the stakeholders that serve as a basis for the evaluation and the interpretation of the evaluation findings should be described in a way that clarifies their underlying values.

U6 – Report Comprehensiveness and Clarity
Evaluation reports should provide all relevant information and be easily comprehensible.

U7 – Evaluation Timeliness
The evaluation should be initiated and completed in a timely fashion, so that its findings can inform pending decision and improvement processes.

U8 – Evaluation Utilisation and Use
The evaluation should be planned, conducted, and reported in ways that encourage attentive follow-through by stakeholders and utilisation of the evaluation findings.

A distinction is made between three different *types of use*:

(1) Direct (instrumental) use
This refers to the immediate use of evaluation results by the management of the client entity and/or by other stakeholders. This is the case if, for instance, results are used in decision-making, if programmes are redesigned in accordance with evaluation recommendations, or if strategies and communication relations etc. are altered.

(2) Conceptual use
This arises if evaluation results influence the general thinking on problems. This occurs, for example, if it can be shown that the sustainability of programmes can only be measured by means of ex-post evaluations, and this realisation leads an organisation to employ ex-post evaluations as a supplementary procedure in future.

(3) Persuasive use
This is present if evaluation results serve to either underpin or undermine 'political' positions. This is the case if, for example, the results of evaluations are able to disprove deeply-rooted positions that are otherwise no longer challenged. In evaluating the sustainability of development projects, for instance, it becomes evident that the participation of target groups in the planning phase is not – as often claimed – a decisive variable for project success, but instead, other variables (such as goal acceptance, executing agency competence etc.) are far more significant.

A complaint heard frequently from evaluators is that evaluation findings and recommendations are not sufficiently heeded. Studies conducted in the '70s and '80s came to this conclusion again and again. Later investigations (cf. Fitzpatrick et al. 2004: 401; Stamm 2003: 183 ff.), however, show that this conclusion can only be confirmed to a limited extent, and that evaluation findings are even used instrumentally to a greater degree than is assumed. The initially strong focus of observations on the direct effects of evaluation results in particular proved to be too narrow to record their impacts. More comprehensive studies have shown that evaluations often tend to have indirect rather than direct implications for wider-reaching decision processes, by serving to promote processes of learning (conceptual use).

Studies concerned with the *use of evaluation results* have identified the following factors as being decisive for their practical implementation (cf. Fitzpatrick et al. 2004: 405; Rossi, Lipsey and Freeman 2004: 414):

- The relevance of the evaluation to decision-makers and/or other stakeholders
- The incorporation of stakeholders in the planning and reporting phases of the evaluation
- The reputation or credibility of the evaluator
- The quality of communication of results (currency, frequency, methodology)
- The development of supporting procedures to utilise the results, or the provision of recommendations for action.

The application of the participatory evaluation approach developed here, adherence to evaluation standards, as well as observance of the factors which support consideration of recommendations within decision-making processes and their practical implementation, should all contribute towards increasing the acceptance and level of utilisation of evaluation results, as the value of an evaluation ultimately depends on its usefulness.

Procedural instructions

✓ If evaluations are to contribute towards enhancing programme quality, in order to achieve as high a level of benefit as possible among target groups and other users, the application of a participatory approach, such as the one outlined here, is to be recommended.

✓ If the various stakeholders are involved in an evaluation from an early stage, their differing interests and perspectives can be better considered. This produces greater levels of acceptance of the evaluation among the stakeholders, and thus also a greater chance of evaluation findings being implemented over the long term. The primary benefit of this, however, is that it facilitates the development of an evaluation concept that avoids taking an overly narrow perspective under which realities are only depicted in part, and which therefore does not do justice to the complex contexts of real situations.

✓ The participatory approach proposed here can – in consultation with clients, and given their agreement – be used either very extensively or to a limited extent only. This depends on how prepared the relevant parties are to grant other stakeholders a say in the planning and implementation of the evaluation. Within an evaluation that aims to fulfil primarily control and/or legitimation functions, this will tend not to be the case to such an extent as when the focus is on cognitive interest and knowledge generation, with the objective of learning lessons for programme development and implementation (cf. chapter 2.3.1, fig. 2.9).

✓ If the most important stakeholders are integrated in the design phase of the evaluation, they can actively collaborate in describing the evaluand, developing test hypotheses, defining assessment criteria etc.

✓ Data collection and analysis are, for the reasons given (cf. chapter 4.4), the tasks of professional experts (evaluators) in the participatory approach presented here, in order to ensure the quality of results (validity, reliability, objectivity).

✓ Certain stakeholder groups (e.g. employees of an executing agency, target groups) can be given theoretical and methodological training within the scope of an evaluation process, so that they are able to actively cooperate in data collection and analysis, or possibly even assume these tasks themselves in the long run. This is especially important if a continual monitoring and evaluation system is to be created.

✓ In the third phase of the evaluation, the assessment of results, stakeholders should in all cases be reincorporated. Their comments and appraisals are of particular importance if very different points of view exist and are to be taken into consideration in the assessment process.

4.6 Evaluation planning and implementation

To conclude this book, the procedure of an evaluation will be outlined, at least roughly, with a description given of the individual steps to be taken. In addition, a number of practical tips will be given regarding the approach. Depending on the aims and functions of the evaluation, on situational conditions, and on client wishes, the procedure can be more or less participatory in its nature.

Evaluations can ideally be divided up into *three phases of activity* (cf. chapter 4.5.2, fig. 4.6):
(1) Design
(2) Data collection and analysis
(3) Application

However, it should be borne in mind that the planning and implementation of every evaluation is tied to its particular context, and that overlaps often arise between the separate phases, especially within formative evaluations. Nevertheless, the individual phases are directly dependent on each other, with one phase causally determining the next.

As discussed in chapter 2.3.1, for every evaluation, those in charge should clarify:
- What aims are being pursued with the evaluation
- To which phase of the programme it relates, what analytical perspective it is to adopt, what kind of cognitive interest it is to pursue

- What kind of test design and what methods are to be employed
- Who is to perform the evaluation, and who its audiences are.

These issues should be resolved during the *planning phase* of an evaluation. Every evaluation must be oriented towards goals that are either defined by the client or determined in a participatory manner with the various stakeholders, as well as towards a specified task. Planning can thus not take place on the basis of given, concrete, practical guidelines, but rather always represents a *creative act*, in which scientific demands, client requirements, the interests and needs of various stakeholder groups, and situational conditions need to be balanced. To ensure that the evaluation is realisable, it is necessary – according to the standards of the German Evaluation Society – that "an evaluation is planned (...) in a realistic, thoughtful, diplomatic and cost-effective manner" (cf. http://www.degeval.de).

In total, it is recommended that three *"feasibility standards" (F)* are adhered to:

F1 – Appropriate Procedures
Evaluation procedures, including information collection procedures, should be chosen so that the burden placed on the evaluand or the stakeholders is appropriate as regards the expected benefits of the evaluation.

F2 – Diplomatic Conduct
The evaluation should be planned and conducted so that it achieves maximal acceptance by the different stakeholders with regard to evaluation process and findings.

F3 – Evaluation Efficiency
The relation between cost and benefit of the evaluation should be appropriate.

In order to obtain as much acceptance as possible for the performance of the evaluation, and to avoid asking too much of those involved in an evaluation, so that the expense of carrying out an evaluation is ultimately justifiable in relation to its benefit, the starting questions of any evaluation - set out again above - should be dealt with within the planning phase as participatively as possible.

(1) Design and planning phase
It should first be clarified what *purpose* an evaluation is meant to fulfil. As explained in chapter 2.3.1, the following primary *goals* can be pursued with evaluations:
- Obtaining insights, in order to expand the knowledge base (evaluation for knowledge)
- Exerting control (evaluation for control)
- Legitimising programme results (evaluation for legitimisation)
- Learning for the further development of a programme (evaluation for action).

The task of the evaluator is first of all to get an overview of the evaluand. For this purpose, the guiding questions contained within the evaluation framework can be used, in particular those from subject block (1) 'programme and environment'. These contribute towards obtaining important programme data, as well as learning something about the goals and concept of the programme, and about the financial, human, technical and time resources deployed, the intended target group, the policy field, and the contextual conditions of the programme (cf. chapter 4.2). This should serve to reveal in what phase of its life-cycle the programme to be evaluated is (cf. chapter 2.3.1, fig. 2.10), and what analytical perspective should be adopted.

In order to determine in detail what *tasks* the evaluation is to fulfil (cf. chapter 2.3.1, fig. 2.11), a *'kick-off meeting'* should be held, which must in all cases involve the client. Within the participatory approach developed here, other stakeholders are also integrated in this process. The most important stakeholders can be identified using the 'programme and environment' analysis (subject block (1) of the evaluation framework).

Which of the stakeholders are actively incorporated depends not only on their significance for the development of the programme and the evaluation process, but also on very practical considerations, such as:

- Availability in terms of time
- Interest in participating in the evaluation and making a contribution to it
- The right to represent a stakeholder group
- The size of the planning committee
- The approval of the client to integrate certain stakeholders.

Once it has been resolved who is to participate in the clarification of goals and tasks, it should be determined what *function* this *'committee'* is to perform. It may convene just once as a 'clarification workshop', or be created as an *'advisory committee'* that is to be involved continually and consulted on important evaluation decisions.

The *function* of a *first meeting* is to:

- Reveal and discuss the various interests associated with the evaluation
- Determine the goals and purpose of the evaluation
- Develop questions for investigation
- Specify assessment criteria[150]
- Possibly also formulate methodological requirements
- Clarify the issue of resources
- Establish time frames.

Diffuse ideas about the aims of an evaluation are sometimes dominant among stakeholders, and these are not always compatible. Clear evaluation guidelines thus need to be compiled. This task becomes a particularly difficult undertaking if the stakeholder groups

---

150 If a second workshop is planned, this can also be done at a later point.

involved in the planning process cannot agree due to differing interests, or if sponsors and/or clients refuse to consider the interests of other stakeholders if they run counter to their own.

If no synthesis of the various objectives can be produced, the only alternative is to plan the evaluation exclusively from the perspective of one stakeholder group. This will usually be the perspective of the sponsor/client, which often associates an evaluation with aims that are specified from the start: e.g. the acquisition of information for the continued management of a programme (evaluation for action), or for the examination of programme progress thus far and of services rendered and impacts produced, or for the legitimate portrayal of achievements to the sponsor or a broad public.

The client sometimes not only stipulates what financial resources are available, the time framework, and the general aims and tasks of the evaluation, but also concrete questions, the nature and extent of stakeholder involvement, or even the methods to be employed etc. In such cases, the evaluation issues that are to be resolved cannot be negotiated in an open process between the sponsor/client, other stakeholders, and the evaluators, or at least to no more than a limited extent. All the same, an initial *joint evaluation workshop* should not be foregone, to ensure that all stakeholders are sensitised to the evaluation, to explain to them the aims and tasks, to canvass acceptance and active participation, and to exploit the remaining scope for cooperation.

The results of the kick-off meeting, which are negotiated either through dialogue with the client or within a participative workshop involving all relevant stakeholders, should in all cases be put down in writing, as they not only constitute the planning basis of the evaluation, but also protect evaluators against 'new' demands which may potentially arise later on.

Closely related to the objectives of an evaluation is the question of who the evaluation results should be *addressed* to. If the focus is primarily on the gaining of insights, scientists, for example, who are looking to reveal new relationships, or sponsors searching for new, successful strategies to realise their political beliefs, may be the main audiences. If the aspect of control or legitimation is at the forefront of considerations, the results may be oriented above all towards the sponsor and/or client, or towards a broader public. If the evaluation is aimed at improving programme activities, on the other hand, then the client, as well as the programme-implementing organisation, target groups, or other stakeholders may be the target audiences of results (cf. Rossi et al. 1999: 48, Rossi, Lipsey & Freeman 2004: 42; Fitzpatrick et al. 2004: 201).

Another issue that is closely related to the objectives and remit of an evaluation is the decision as to whether the evaluation should be carried out *internally or externally*. The respective advantages and disadvantages of these different approaches were dealt with in detail in chapter 2.3.2.

In order that the underlying aims of an evaluation can be achieved, the *questions* to be answered should each be written out explicitly in full. Here it is important to adapt the requirements of clients and/or other stakeholders in accordance with the feasible limits, given existing time and financial restrictions: "It is quite common for clients such as a steering committee, a school council or a middle-level manager to put forward a long list of issues which they would like addressed. The evaluator may need to work with the client to reduce this list" (Owen and Rogers 1999: 69). Questions that are central to the evaluation thus need to be separated from the less important ones. Against the background of the aims and tasks of the evaluation, as well as the information needs of the client and other stakeholders, the question of "who wants to know something and to what end?" can help to make the selection easier.

If important questions are wrongly left out, this can considerably diminish the value of an evaluation. On the other hand, a large number of 'unimportant' questions represents an undue burden on the usually limited time frame and scarce financial resources. In both cases, the credibility of evaluation results (and thus also that of the evaluator) can suffer. In the worst-case scenario, the evaluation then produces misleading results.

Closely related to the development of evaluation questions is the explicit definition of *assessment criteria*, on the basis of which the evaluand is ultimately to be judged. Such criteria are often oriented, as shown in chapter 2.3.1, towards the utility of an object, activity or development process for certain people or groups. The criteria can be specified by:

- The client (directive)
- The evaluator (knowledge-/experience-based)
- The target group and/or stakeholders (emancipatory), or
- Jointly by all of the above (participatory).

Vedung (2000: 224), after Dror (1968: 28), identifies the following *points of reference* for *assessments* performed within evaluations:

(1) *Historical comparison:* how does performance compare with that in the past?
(2) *Intra-national comparison:* how does performance compare with that of similar setups in the same regional or national area?
(3) *International comparison:* how does performance compare with that of similar setups in other countries?
(4) *Benchmarks:* how does the performance observed compare with best empirical practice?
(5) *Aims:* does the performance established reach formulated target values?
(6) *Target group expectations:* does the service rendered meet the expectations of target groups (audiences)?
(7) *Expectations of interested parties:* does performance meet the expectations of other stakeholders?
(8) *Professional standards:* do activities conform to widely-accepted occupational (professional, scientific) standards?
(9) *Minimum:* is performance high enough to satisfy minimum requirements?
(10) *Optimum:* is performance as high as possible in comparison to an ideal model?

Following the formulation and specification of evaluation questions, as well as the definition of assessment criteria, the next logical step is the *selection of a test design and appropriate methods of data collection and analysis,* in order to facilitate the empirical processing of the aims and tasks of the evaluation. Before this is undertaken, however, it is advisable to get an overview of available *resources,* as early as during the planning phase. Significant aspects for consideration here are:

▪ Available financial resources
▪ The personnel that are to carry out the evaluation
▪ The available time framework
▪ Existing information material (documents, monitoring data etc.) that can be used for the evaluation.

The evaluator must relate the available resources to the task at hand. Inexperienced clients in particular often have no clear ideas about what resources are required for dealing with certain questions. Sometimes clients and/or involved stakeholders are also not sure as to the achievement potential of an evaluation. The task of evaluators is thus to advise clients and/or stakeholders, and to inform them about alternative approaches and analytical models.

Usually, clients will only be prepared to provide the financial resources required for dealing with evaluation tasks if they have clear ideas about how they can sensibly deploy an evaluation to serve their purposes, and what benefit they can expect to derive from it. Here it is sometimes necessary to combat the preconception among programme managers, as well as among target groups, that the funding needed for an evaluation would be better invested in implementing the programme, or should be given directly to target groups. In such cases it is all the more important to elucidate the range of benefits offered by evaluations. If clients and/or stakeholders have already had bad experiences with evaluations, however, then they will be hard to disabuse. It is thus of crucial importance, on the one hand, to ensure that the planning and implementation of an evaluation conform to professional standards, and, on the other hand, to assess whether an evaluation can be carried out at all, given the prevailing situational conditions.

The *performance of an evaluation* would be *inappropriate if:*
▪ The evaluation is likely to generate merely trivial information, e.g. because an evaluation has only just taken place and no new results are to be expected
▪ It is to be anticipated that the results will not be utilised, e.g. because decision-makers reject the evaluation
▪ The financial resources provided and/or time frame allocated for implementation cannot be reconciled with the demands and expectations of clients, e.g. because comprehensive analyses are requested, but the funding and time required for this are not supplied
▪ No valid, useful results are to be expected, e.g. because situational conditions have changed in such a way (through natural disasters or wars, for instance) that it is no

longer possible to detect any programme impacts, or because a programme has not yet reached a certain phase of development that is actually intended for evaluation, due to time delays

- The evaluation approach requested by the client is unsuitable for the programme in question, or is incompatible with professional standards, e.g. if a request is made within the scope of an impact evaluation that the target group be left to collect its own data, or if other professional standards are violated
- The implementation is determined by political considerations alone (tactical evaluation), meaning that proper execution and subsequent suitable utilisation of results is not to be expected, e.g. if a decision on the continuation or termination of a programme has already been made, and is only intended to be given ex-post legitimacy through an evaluation.

In such cases it is better to refrain completely from performing an evaluation, as either the expectations of the client will not be able to be met or it will not be possible to adhere to professional standards.

Once the terms of reference for an evaluation have been clarified, and set out in a written document, the *drawing up of the evaluation concept and evaluation design* is begun. For this, the theoretical concept developed in this book, as well as the methodology based on it (in particular the set of evaluation guidelines), can be used. In addition, a range of designs suitable for evaluation, along with various methods of data collection, have been presented here.

The concern of the planning phase is now to develop an *evaluation or implementation plan* that is appropriate for the aims and tasks at hand, as well as for the investigative questions that are derived from these (not to be confused with the central questions within the subject blocks of the set of evaluation guidelines)[151]. This plan consists of:

- A description of the evaluand
- The formulation of the aims and tasks of the evaluation
- The specification of the target audiences of results
- The concrete specification of the individual evaluation questions and assessment criteria
- A test design that makes clear how the questions are to be dealt with empirically
- A selection of the methods with which the necessary data are to be collected
- A description of how the evaluation process is to be organised (internal and external evaluation elements, directive vs. participatory approach)
- A budget, personnel and time plan.

---

151 Investigative questions are those derived from the aims and tasks of an evaluation. The central questions in the evaluation framework, on the other hand, represent questions for assessing the state (at various points in time) of selected areas of evaluation (issues) (e.g. organisational competence, acceptance of programme goals, diffusion of programme impacts etc.).

The development of the *evaluation plan* demands of the evaluator social, mediation and negotiating skills in clarifying the remit, along with methodological knowledge for developing a design suitable for the evaluation aims and concrete analytical questions, and for selecting appropriate data collection methods. In addition, it also necessitates management competencies, in order to be able to produce a time plan for the evaluation process and to correctly estimate personnel and funding requirements.

Time schedules can easily be illustrated using histograms or critical path methods (cf. Wottawa and Thierau 2003: 114 ff.). It is more difficult, however, to realistically estimate how much time specific procedural steps will require. It is often the case that different activities are organised parallel to each other. Here, it should be ensured that these are intertwined and compatible with each other. For example, during the time in which a standardised written survey is circulating in the field, i.e. its return is being awaited, oral guideline-based interviews can be carried out. For postal, e-mail or online surveys, two or three 'follow-up waves' are to be scheduled, in which reminders of the survey are given. All in all, the challenge is, on the one hand, to develop a schedule that satisfies the usually restrictive demands of clients, i.e. that meets deadlines for the presentation of initial re-sults, and of the interim and final report, and, on the other hand, to incorporate sufficient time scope (buffers) for unexpected problems to be dealt with within the agreed time lim-its.

When carrying out *personnel planning*, it is important to establish which people are to perform which functions. This activity is primarily about task allocation between the evaluators, but should also consider when, and to what extent, personal input from the client (e.g. for meetings and workshops), from the project-executing agency, and from target groups and other stakeholders (e.g. for the compilation of material and data, the provision of addresses for surveys, logistical support in carrying out interviews, for an-swering questions etc.) will be required.

The production of the *evaluation budget* requires not only precise recording of the various types of cost, but also as accurate an estimate as possible of the level of costs that will accrue. The following cost types are to be considered (cf. Sanders 1983, as cited by Fitz-patrick et al. 2004: 282 ff.):

- Personnel costs for the evaluation team
- Costs for any consultants that may have to be employed (e.g. experts, specialists in certain subjects)
- Costs for the performance of quantitative surveys (e.g. telephone costs, IT specialists, method laboratory)
- Travel and accommodation costs
- Costs for communication media (postage, telephone, IT etc.)
- Printing costs (e.g. for reports, written surveys)
- Costs for necessary material purchases (technical equipment, literature, IT devices etc.)

- Costs for any subcontracts (e.g. for carrying out interviews, case studies, the procurement of material)
- Overheads (office expenses etc.).

If the evaluation contract is *tendered*, then the evaluation plan is usually requested in the form of an *offer*. This constitutes the basis of the awarding of the contract. As neither authorisation of the contract nor a participatively organised planning workshop has yet occurred at this stage, a number of details cannot be settled until after the contract has been awarded. In such a situation, there is a danger that the essential evaluation parameters have already been determined, and can no longer be fundamentally altered. Participatory planning is then only possible to a very limited extent. After presenting the evaluation plan, this should in all cases be agreed upon with the client, and better still, with the most important stakeholders. Once this has been done, the implementation of the evaluation can commence.

(2) Data collection and analysis
Although this phase of the evaluation takes the longest, of course, it is not necessary to discuss it any further at this point. Evaluation methodology and its application have been dealt with in detail in previous chapters. The concern now is with applying this knowledge for the implementation of the evaluation plan that has been generated. Any difficulties that arise (e.g. of a logistical nature, concerning the availability of interview partners, the preparedness to partake in the evaluation) should be discussed in good time with the client, and if necessary also with individual stakeholders, or the evaluation advisory committee if one has been set up, so that alternatives can be sought. Here too, the management and social competence of evaluators is of great importance.

In accordance with the evaluation model developed here, the first step is to gather the data required for answering the questions contained within the evaluation guidelines, on the basis of the evaluation design and using the various data collection methods, in order to be able to subsequently carry out appropriate assessments. The assessments should follow on logically from the data, and should be intersubjectively verifiable (cf. chapter 4.3). This can be approached either by the evaluators performing the assessments and entering outcomes in the designated appraisal lines of the set of guidelines, or by the stakeholders assessing the evaluation findings themselves, e.g. within a workshop.

(3) Presentation and application of results
Whether, and how, the results of an evaluation are utilised by the various stakeholders depends to a large extent on whether the evaluators succeed in conveying them convincingly within a process of communication. The most important media in this process are the *evaluation report* and the results *presentation*. The composition of the evaluation report should thus be given a great deal of attention. It should be preceded by an 'executive summary', containing the most important insights and recommendations. The main body

of the report may be based in terms of layout on the structure of the set of evaluation guidelines (cf. chapter 4.2, fig. 4.1), encompassing all significant findings, interpretations and assessments. The report can be made more interesting and easily readable through the inclusion of diagrams and tables, quotes that are either incorporated into the text or positioned separately in small 'boxes', and brief intermediate summaries. It usually concludes with concrete recommendations for action for the further development of the programme.

The results, along with the data on which they are based, should be presented clearly and unambiguously. The assessments that build on these should be intersubjectively verifiable, and the recommendations made should follow on 'logically' from the analysis and interpretation of results. In composing the report, a mode of expression is to be chosen that takes the audience into consideration, which does not always consist (solely) of the clients, but can also comprise other stakeholders. Evaluators must therefore, besides possessing the numerous competencies listed up to now, also be able to write 'appealingly' and comprehensibly.

However, a well-written evaluation report is no guarantee that the results will be utilised by clients and stakeholders: "In the past decade, evaluators have realized that it isn't enough to draft a good evaluation report. Indeed, evaluators have become increasingly aware that one can work hard to maximize the quality of their report and still find that the impact and influence it has on its stakeholders, programs, or policies is at best negligible and at worst, zero" (Fitzpatrick et al. 2004: 375). The communication of evaluation results should thus not be limited to just the written medium, but should also in all cases incorporate an *oral presentation*. Presentations allow the main results and recommendations to be displayed in condensed form, and important statements to be reemphasised. The chance should also be taken to discuss and comment on the results in detail. Here it should be ensured, however, that the discussion does not revolve merely around trivial matters (such as comma placement, spelling etc.), or around small factual 'errors' or misunderstandings. These can be observed in writing. Rather, the focus here should be on the substantive issues and results of the evaluation, as well as on the resulting recommendations (cf. chapter 4.5.1).

Such a *'concluding workshop'* is most effective if the evaluation report is distributed beforehand and all participants are aware of the results, so that the discussion can begin straight away. It is advisable to structure the discussion according to subject areas, and to draw up a time plan. It should be ensured that a climate of open communication prevails, and that all participants can express their comments and opinions freely. This is not always easy, for example if the client or sponsor has far-reaching sanctioning rights, i.e. is able to cut back or expand funding, or if certain stakeholder (groups) are economically dependent on the sponsor or client. In such cases, it can be useful to carry out separate workshops (with sponsors and clients on the one hand and other stakeholders on the other).

Figure 4.12: The evaluation process[152]

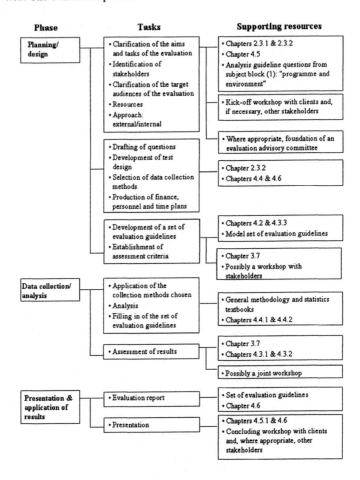

In general it can be observed that concluding workshops in which the most important stakeholders participate – as intended in the participatory model developed here (cf. chapter 4.5.2) – give rise to greater acceptance of evaluation results and recommendations,

---

152 Chapter information relates to the chapters in this book.

which thus have a (presumedly) higher chance of being implemented, than those which exclude stakeholders. A method that has proved itself especially well is the one under which the assessment of evaluation findings is carried out by the main stakeholders themselves rather than by the evaluators. This is approached as follows: the evaluators merely present evaluation findings successively, on a subject-by-subject basis in accordance with the set of guidelines, for instance within a workshop. Workshop participants can then enter into a discourse on, and appraise, the respective findings. The use of the 10-level scale contained within the guidelines has also proved unproblematic here. Experience has shown that affected parties are more likely to be prepared to recognise deficiencies and interpret them as problems if they have assessed the findings themselves. This is the central prerequisite of shortcomings being corrected and recommendations for the continued development of programmes implemented. Only if this is successfully achieved has an evaluation fulfilled its purpose.

The complete sequence of activities involved in an evaluation is depicted in summary form in fig. 4.7.

5 Summary, Review and Outlook

The aim of this book is to make a *contribution to quality development*, in particular that of non-profit organisations, by *means of evaluation*. As noted earlier on, the decades-old debate about quality management in business enterprises has, for a range of reasons, also been taken up in the non-profit sector. Non-profit organisations are increasingly trying to improve quality with the help of concepts and instruments developed for profit-oriented companies operating in competitive markets.

After examining particularly well-established concepts such as ISO and TQM, in particular EFQM, the question of to what extent these can be applied to non-profit organisations was posed. In order to answer this, the characteristics that non-profit organisations, by definition, exhibit, were identified. Here it became apparent that *ISO and TQM concepts* (such as EFQM) *can only be applied with difficulty in non-profit organisations*, as their situational and organisational conditions differ fundamentally from those of business enterprises.

Even the use of the *customer concept* is in many cases problematic, as in the non-profit sector the customer is lacking that which typically defines him or her, i.e. buyer authority to choose between alternative offers, the prices of which are determined through open competition. What is more, the customer concept cannot be defined in terms of a one-dimensional producer-customer relationship in the non-profit sector, but rather constitutes a multidimensional construct, which must also take non-customers into account. This is not always in a private enterprise sense, with non-customers representing a potential that is to be tapped if possible for the benefit of one's own products and services, but sometimes means completely the opposite, referring to a part of society that should preferably not become a 'customer' (e.g. an unemployed person, social welfare recipient, sick person, offender etc.). For the same reason, the *'customer'* of non-profit organisations can *not* – as is usual in free-market contexts – be drawn upon as the *highest authority for judging the quality* of products and services. Even if quality does not meet the needs and demands of 'customers' of non-profit organisations, this must by no means automatically lead to a negative assessment of quality, as the situation may appear very different from the point of view of non-customers. It is often the case that the services offered by non-profit organisations are not paid for (exclusively) by those that utilise them. Donors, for example, finance charitable institutions that are used by people in need, sick people, or citizens in search of advice. And all tax-paying citizens in Germany, for instance, fund the country's universities, even though they are only attended by a small, often affluent, section of society. The assessment criteria employed, and thus also the judgements of the quality of services rendered by non-profit organisations, can therefore vary enormously between the actual 'customers' (users) and all other citizens.

In contrast to private industry goods, in non-profit organisations it must be decided within a social process which activities are to be carried out at what prices for services that are to be financed by a community (e.g. education, security, social and pension insurance etc.). It is thus advisable, in the context of non-profit organisations, to refer to users, audiences or target groups rather than 'customers'.

In public administration, a sub-area of the non-profit sector, the management concepts of so-called New Public Management are favoured, which, in addition to customer, competition and quality orientation, also encompass a further management element, namely *output and outcome orientation*. These concepts attempt to adopt the free-market customer concept, putting it at the centre of their quality considerations, and endeavour to create competition-like conditions (either by opening up markets or through internal competition), and to employ business management tools (e.g. cost-performance analysis). However, these concepts reach their limits where this notion of customers and quality – as has just been briefly explained once again – can no longer be meaningfully employed, and where conditions of competition cannot be produced, or can only be simulated to a limited extent (e.g. in the case of social welfare and tax offices, chambers of commerce, and other compulsory associations etc.).

Furthermore, it should be kept in mind that, even in situations in which clear customer relationships can be identified, in which quality can be oriented towards the customer, and in which competition enables the customer to choose autonomously between products, in the non-profit sector the called-for businesslike behaviour nevertheless remains at times extremely limited. The scope for manoeuvre that would be required, for instance, in personnel policy or strategic decision-making, is often not allowed due to legal regulations. German universities are a prime example here: in future they are to be expected to stand their ground in a competitive environment, but will continue to be maintained by the state, to be subject to public budgetary and collective bargaining law, and to be dictated to by an array of detailed bureaucratic rules. The big development-political organisations too, such as the German Society for Technical Cooperation (GTZ) and the Kreditanstalt für Wiederafbau (KfW banking group), want to operate as business enterprises, but are restricted in many decisions due to their strategic remit. For instance, they have to carry out some programmes that are solely politically motivated and do not exhibit sufficient customer and quality orientation. What is more, they are active in an insular, protected market, which has (up to now at least) guaranteed them unrivalled state financing.

If not all socially necessary services are able to be provided by markets, for sociopolitical reasons as well as for reasons of market failure in certain social fields, the *existence of a non-profit sector cannot* be *foregone*. As mentioned earlier on, in Germany this sector encompasses more than seven million paid employees, on top of which are a large number of voluntary members and staff. Non-profit organisations not only constitute a *sector which is important in terms of employment and economic policy*, and which also exhibits *high growth dynamics*; they also have *great social and political potential* due to the wide scope of their activities.

However, it hardly appears possible, on the one hand, to justify the necessity of a non-profit sector by referring to socio-political requirements and market failure in certain social fields, whilst, on the other hand, simultaneously calling for the introduction of free-market principles, concepts, procedures, and instruments in order to make the non-profit sector as market-like as possible. Associated with this balancing act is the danger that elements that have been developed in the private, profit-oriented sector, and that indeed work well there, are transferred rashly to a sector that is characterised precisely by the fact that it exhibits fundamentally different legal, situational and organisational conditions. This *'differentness' of the non-profit sector* thus not only has *consequences* for the understanding of quality, and not only necessitates different tools (to those applied in the private sector) for measuring it, but also calls for different quality criteria, which cannot be one-sidedly oriented towards the fiction of a 'customer', which – as explained in detail – frequently does not even exist in the non-profit sector in the same way as it is understood in private industry.

The concepts of New Public Management, with their output and outcome orientation as a fourth strategic element, offer a possible alternative here. By moving away from the control of inputs to concentrate on output and outcome demands, the *achievement of intended goals and impacts becomes the most important quality feature. Quality* is measured by whether, and to what extent, services rendered by an organisation produce the intended effects among target groups (audiences, users) and in the policy fields in which interventions take place. According to this approach, the *quality development* of non-profit organisations should be *oriented towards the optimisation of outcomes*. In order to facilitate the management of non-profit organisations based on outputs and outcomes, and to thus ensure high levels of quality, appropriate appraisal concepts and analytical instruments are required, which should provide a valid, reliable information basis for rational management decisions.

The *concepts and tools of evaluation* are suitable for this purpose, as they facilitate not only the analysis of processes of planning and service provision, but also the empirical examination and assessment of services rendered, goals attained, and intended and unintended impacts produced. *Evaluation, in combination with management concepts* that are based on output- and outcome-oriented control, enables non-profit organisations to pursue *impact-based quality improvement* that is in line with their organisational and situational requirements.

The *aim of this book* has been to develop a theoretically and methodologically founded *evaluation concept* that can *form the basis of impact-based quality development*. This concept should thus not only consist of theoretical elements and their methodological/empirical implementation - in order to analyse processes of service provision and impacts triggered - but should also provide the possibility of deriving evaluation and quality criteria.

The *theoretical evaluation concept* is based on the assumption that non-profit organisations render services and/or carry out programmes, with the fundamental difference between the two types of activity being that programmes have a fixed time schedule whereas services are provided continuously and indefinitely.

As these activities are planned and administered in the form of services or programmes, they follow a specific sequence of phases, which is characterised by definable planning and implementation steps. To facilitate the understanding of this process flow, (1) the *concepts of life-cycle research* were utilised. Services and programmes are performed/carried out by organisations that have multifaceted relations with other organisations and social subsystems – i.e. with their environment. Therefore, for the analysis of relationships internal and external to the organisation, (2) *concepts of organisational theory* were employed. As services and, to an even greater extent, programmes frequently entail novel practices (innovations), (3) *concepts of innovation and diffusion research* facilitate the identification of conditions under which the introduction and diffusion of innovations enjoys the most success. And because many services and programmes have a long-term orientation, or are at least intended to trigger lasting changes, (4) a *multidimensional sustainability model* was developed.

These various theoretical approaches serve to *complement* one another: the life-cycle perspective highlights the processual nature of interventions, regardless of whether they occur in the form of continuous service provision or temporary programmes. The theoretical models of organisations, innovation and diffusion link organisational/structural and situational environmental conditions with the issue of the spread of innovations initiated by interventions. The sustainability model then finally deals with the permanence of impacts triggered by interventions, thus extending the life-cycle model beyond the termination of support (e.g. for a programme). So, the individual theoretical elements are closely related to one another, build on each other, and thereby form a *holistic theoretical concept*.

It is assumed that, irrespective of the policy field to which a service or programme belongs:

- Planning and implementation processes are always necessary in order to achieve intended goals and impacts
- Organisations are usually required for carrying them out
- It is usually necessary to introduce reforms (changes, innovations) and, if possible, also to diffuse them
- Impacts produced are usually not concerned with short-term effects, but rather with permanence and durability.

Thus, on the one hand, hypotheses about expected relationships can be derived, as well as, on the other hand, subject areas to be examined within an evaluation.

Based on these theoretical considerations, a *set of evaluation guidelines* was developed, which defines the central subject (assessment) areas for evaluation. In addition to a description of the object of investigation (programme and environment), it also contains questions on the programme process, on internal organisational structures and processes (of programme-implementing organisations), as well as on external areas of intervention - the audiences (target groups) and policy fields in which the programme interventions are intended to effect changes. The set of evaluation guidelines serves to structure and give direction to the search for information.

In order to *obtain information*, various data collection methods can be employed. For this, a *multi-method approach* was advocated, combining qualitative and quantitative procedures, in order to approach 'reality' from as many perspectives as possible. The *participatory approach* to evaluation also contributes to this, aiming to sensitise the various stakeholders to the evaluation and to win them over, in order to actively involve them in the process. Experience with this participatory evaluation approach has shown that, on the one hand, it enables the utilisation of the situational knowledge of stakeholders for the development of the evaluation design, and later on for the interpretation and assessment of results, and, on the other hand, it increases the chances of stakeholders being prepared to implement evaluation results and recommendations compared to a situation in which they are not involved. The participatory approach can thus enhance, sometimes significantly, the usefulness of an evaluation.

The *data collection and assessment process* is organised in such a way by the evaluation guidelines that a process of gradual information compression reduces the information gathered to a single value, which applies to a subject area-specific assessment dimension (e.g. goal acceptance or organisational competence). Comparisons with previous measurements facilitate the detection and assessment of changes over time. In order to establish impacts, as is well known, data must be available from at least two measurement time-points (before and after the intervention). As this indicates the so-called gross outcome, i.e. all recorded changes, the net effects, that is to say impacts that are solely attributable to the interventions (of the programme or service), are to be separated out. This core task of all evaluations – to record impacts and identify their causes – is made easier by the prior formulation of hypotheses, but still necessitates specific *test designs*, of which merely an overview has been given in this book.

The evaluation approach developed here provides an alternative to goal-free and goal-oriented evaluation with the *concept of a hypothesis-driven approach*. As has been shown, the idea that evaluations can be carried out without any knowledge of programme or service goals (goal-free approach) appears distinctly far-fetched, especially if funding is expected from clients for this. On the other hand, classic results evaluations, which merely examine the issue of goal attainment by comparing the target state (programme aims) with the actual state (degree of attainment), involve many risks, above all that of neglecting unintended impacts. As the evaluation concept in this book is designed to record as many intended and unintended impacts as possible, a hypothesis-based approach was developed instead. The hypotheses necessary for this can be derived from the theoretical considerations set out earlier on, and were incorporated in the construction of the *set of evaluation guidelines*. This can thus serve to structure the *hypothesis-driven search for information* about the process sequence, and about impacts within the executing agency and in external fields of activity (among audiences and in selected policy fields). Supplementary hypotheses should be developed for circumstances specific to the relevant policy field and programme/service, which can then be integrated into the model set of guidelines.

The guidelines encompass all *appraisal dimensions* of the evaluation, the ratings for which, within the framework of an objectifying approach, are established in such a way as to be transparent and intersubjectively verifiable. They represent the highest level of compression of information collected within the evaluation, and can be used to create a programme profile, which depicts an overview of programme development and facilitates systematic comparisons over time and with other programmes.

Based on the dimensions of service quality cited by Donabedian (1980), as well as the quality dimensions put forward by Garvin (1984), the evaluation criteria applied here can be adapted to form the following *quality dimensions*, which are appropriate for the organisational and situational conditions, and the tasks, of non-profit organisations:

(1) Planning and implementation quality,
which relates to the process of service provision.

(2) Internal impact-based quality,
which relates to the appraisal of intended and unintended impacts on the competence of the service-providing (programme-implementing) organisation, based on the criteria of goals/goal acceptance, personnel, organisational structure, financial resources, technical infrastructure, and organisational concept.

(3) External impact-based quality,
which relates to the appraisal of intended and unintended impacts with regard to the acceptance of service/programme goals among target groups, target group attainment, benefit (satisfaction), and diffusion within the policy fields of the intervention.

(4) Quality of sustainability
- *at the programme level,*
  of which a typology is formed, comprising the categories: project-/programme-oriented, output-oriented, system-oriented, and innovation-oriented.
- *at the macro level,*
  which relates to the appraisal of efficiency, social relevance, and environmental compatibility, and can thus also be referred to as economic, social and ecological sustainability.

These quality dimensions can be employed to assess the quality of services rendered by organisations and the associated impacts. They should thus be suited above all to those organisations whose quality management is carried out on the basis of output and outcome/impact control.

The evaluation concept presented in this book represents a *further development* of earlier concepts (cf. Stockmann 1996a). What is *new* is the linkage with models of quality, as well as the general extension to take in the tasks and requirements of non-profit organisations. The set of evaluation guidelines, which contains the assessment criteria central to evaluation, has been restructured on the basis of numerous evaluation experiences, and in accordance with the broadened scope of its tasks, and supplemented with an additional four quality dimensions for the appraisal of the outputs and impacts of (non-profit) organisations. Furthermore, application-oriented presentation is intended to make using the evaluation concept easier.

Further development with regard to application for *network evaluations* still remains to be done. The network approach is becoming increasingly significant, especially in international politics. The background to this is the observation that, in the course of globalisation, the capacity for governance of the nation state is declining. Attempts are being made to counter this by incorporating civil actors in political decision-making processes and their implementation, e.g. via networks. From an evaluation point of view, in addition to the continuing problem of the sustainable embedding of project structures within executing agencies, the question also arises of how the cooperation of multiple independent organisations can be lastingly ensured and optimised to create sustainable effectiveness. Consequently, from a theoretical perspective, the organisational/ sociological principles of the evaluation concept developed here need to be supplemented with insights from network research (cf. CEval annual report 2004: 5).

The advancement of theories and methods of evaluation research often occurs in conjunction with studies and evaluation assignments, for which theoretical concepts have to be updated or creative designs developed. This was also the case here: the evaluation concept presented is based on concepts developed in numerous studies, and thus on experiences gained in the 'field'. A number of *studies* that were of great *importance* for the development of the evaluation concept will therefore be presented below. The primary reason for doing this is to document the broad scope of tasks and application, which, through the further theoretical and methodological development of the model, now also facilitates its extension - in particular to take in non-profit organisations of all kinds, as well as for undertaking impact-based quality development in general.

The original version was developed for the *ex-post evaluation of the effectiveness and sustainability of vocational training programmes and projects in development cooperation* (cf. Stockmann 1996a). For this, programmes and projects that had been carried out by the German Society for Technical Cooperation were examined for the first time within the framework of an ex-post study. This triggered a debate about the sense and purpose of ex-post analyses that continues to this day.[153] This evaluation, designed as a scientific

---

153 Cf. Elshorst 1993a & b; Stockmann 1989, 1993a & b; 1994; 1995b; 1996; 1998; 1999b; 2001; 2002a & b; Caspari & Stockmann 2001; Caspari, Kevenhörster & Stockmann 2003.

study, primarily served the acquisition of insights. However, as it was also intended to contribute towards remedying the lack of meaningful studies on the effectiveness of development cooperation, it was also of a legitimising nature. A further objective was to discover the factors that constitute or impede a sustainably successful development policy, so that these could be considered in the case of future support programmes. That is to say, the insights obtained served primarily a learning-/development-oriented purpose (cf. fig. 2.8, chapter 2.3.1).

In a follow-up evaluation study on the effectiveness of vocational training cooperation that took place at the end of the 1990s, for the first time in Germany a direct *comparison of state and non-state programmes* was carried out (cf. Stockmann et al. 2000). The aim was to examine the effectiveness of vocational training projects in PR China with regard to the different support concepts, strategies, procedures, and conditions of action of a state-run implementing organisation (GTZ) and a non-profit organisation (the Hanns Seidel Foundation, HSF). One question of interest here was whether a non-profit organisation actually does provide its services more efficiently and effectively than a state-run organisation. As this was merely a case study, the results obtained can by no means be generalised. Still, to provide a very brief summary, the tendency was for the programmes of both organisations to be similarly effective and sustainable, yet the services of the non-profit organisation had been provided with significantly lower personnel, financial and time costs. The results of the evaluation and resulting recommendations led to changes, some of a far-reaching nature, in the support strategies (particularly in the case of the GTZ) and methods of working (particularly in the case of the HSF) of both implementing organisations.

There is a need for further research here. As mentioned earlier on, the discussion on the performance capacity of non-profit organisations ranges from glorification to destructive criticism, without sufficient evidence being provided of this. A comparative examination of business enterprises, state and non-state non-profit organisations active in a particular policy field (e.g. health, education or development cooperation) may shed light on their different performance capacities, as well as on the quality of the services they provide and the impacts they trigger.

Whilst it is frequently the case that concepts and models developed and tested in the industrialised world are exported to Third World countries, the original model of the evaluation concept further developed here took the opposite path. Initially developed for the ex-post evaluation of development cooperation projects and programmes in Latin America and Asia, at the end of the 1990s the concept was used for the *evaluation of environmental programmes* in Germany. The programme of the German Environment Foundation[154] under evaluation was a very extensive, complex support construct with

---

154 The German Environment Foundation ('Deutsche Bundesstiftung Umwelt', DBU), based in Osnabrück, began its work in 1991. With the privatisation revenues of Salzgitter AG as its endowment capital, which amounted to around 2.5 billion German marks, the DBU is one of the largest foundations in Europe. The earnings from the foundation's assets are used to

various goals and goal levels, numerous executing agencies, and multiple target groups. The purpose of this evaluation, which was likewise summative in its nature and carried out on an ex-post basis, was to provide legitimation, as well as being learning-oriented. On the one hand, the sustainability of the programme was to be evaluated, whilst on the other hand recommendations for future support strategies were to be derived from the analysis of causes and relationships.

At the beginning of the current decade, the evaluation concept was used with the same objectives for the *evaluation of environmental communication projects in the field of skilled crafts* (cf. Meyer et al. 2005). This field of activity constitutes a focus for the support of the German Environment Foundation, with almost 55 million German marks invested in it since the DBU's foundation in 1991. The evaluation was intended to deliver an analysis and appraisal of the support programme as a whole, as well as performing an examination of the success and sustainability of individual projects, in order to derive specific improvement strategies. Here too, the multi-layered support structure - with over 30 executing agencies – as well as the heterogeneity of target groups and the variety of programme goals made a complex evaluation concept necessary. Application of the participatory approach contributed substantially to overcoming the initial scepticism of some of the executing agencies under evaluation, whilst the multi-method approach (including document analysis, 1600 standardised telephone interviews with craft/trade businesses, and over 100 intensive interviews, primarily with persons responsible for the programme) facilitated data collection and analysis that was as broadly based and in-depth as possible. Using the set of evaluation guidelines, the multi-faceted information was able to be structured, and subjected to hypothesis-driven analysis.

As early as the 1990s, the evaluation concept and methodological tools were employed in numerous scientific works and studies.[155] The most extensive investigation thus far on the basis of this model was carried out by the German Federal Ministry for Economic Cooperation and Development from 1998 to 2000, in order to, for the first time (!), evaluate the sustainability of its projects and programmes (cf. BMZ 2000)[156]. This meant the evaluation model was applied in the *policy fields of basic health care, agriculture, water provision, sewage and waste disposal, and basic education*, with more than 50 evaluators selected by the BMZ requiring training in the application of the methodological tools, in order to carry out 32 separate evaluations in 19 different countries. The evaluation was

---

promote schemes for protecting the environment, with particular consideration given to mid-sized businesses.

155 Including of the Bundesrechnungshof (1992), the Deutsche Stiftung für Internationale Entwicklung (Capacity Building International) (1993), Enfants du Monde (1994), the Institut für Raumplanung und Regionalentwicklung Wien (Institute for Spatial Planning, Vienna) (1994) etc. Cf. also Stockmann 1996a: footnote 2, p. 399.

156 For the case history of the study, cf. e.g. Caspari 2004: 121 ff.; Caspari, Kevenhörster & Stockmann 2003; Stockmann & Kevenhörster 2001; Stockmann & Caspari 2001; Stockmann, Caspari & Kevenhörster 2000.

primarily of a legitimising nature, with the aim of confronting the growing criticism of development cooperation with substantiated evaluation findings. In this context, practical assistance was generated for the first time with regard to adapting the set of evaluation guidelines and applying the most important instruments and assessment procedures.

Whilst the evaluation concept had thus far been applied for summative, ex-post evaluations in various policy fields in Germany and numerous Third World countries, its use for formative evaluations, as well as for the creation of impact-based monitoring and evaluation systems, constituted another milestone for the further theoretical, and above all methodological, development of the concept.

Formative evaluations, which are above all concerned with supplying ongoing projects or programmes with information for constructive management decisions in a process-oriented manner, have been carried out in different policy fields, primarily in collaboration with, among others, various government departments, foundations, the German Federal Institute for Vocational Education and Training[157], as well as with the German Academic Exchange Service[158] (for more detail, cf. annual reports of the Center for Evaluation 2002–2008).[159]

The application of the evaluation concept for the *creation of monitoring and evaluation systems* necessitated not only further development in terms of content, the extension of the participatory approach, and the use of different data collection methods, but also extensive training measures for those that were to operate these systems. The scope here ranges from the development and implementation of a monitoring system for further training institutions in Germany, via the creation of programme/system monitoring and evaluation systems for the introduction of dual vocational training in Egypt, the Philippines, Vietnam, and a number of provinces of PR China, right the way to environmental monitoring and evaluation systems in Mexico City and Costa Rica.

These evaluations not only mark important steps in the evolution of the evaluation concept into its current form, but at the same time also illustrate the *scope of its application* up to now:

(1) Whilst the concept was initially used predominantly for ex-post evaluations, it is now also employed increasingly for formative purposes, as well as for the creation of impact-based monitoring and evaluation systems.

---

157 Bundesinstitut für Berufsbildung (BIBB).
158 Deutscher Akademischer Austauschdienst (DAAD).
159 The following is a selection of formative studies that have been carried out: Brandt 2004, Jacoby et al. 2004; Krapp & Meiers 2004; Stockmann, Krapp & Baltes 2004; Baltes, Krapp & Stockmann 2004; Baltes 2003a & b; Brandt & Meyer 2003; Heise & Stockmann 2003; Krapp 2003; Krapp & Gräber 2002; Schäffer & Meyer 2002; Jacoby & Hauschnik 2002. For additional studies, cf. CEval annual reports 2002-2008..

(2) The 'original version' was developed primarily for carrying out scientific studies. Subsequently it served, in addition to the acquisition of insights, above all programme development and legitimation purposes.

(3) The fields of policy and practice of evaluation have so far spanned such diverse areas as:
- Vocational training
- Basic education
- Higher education
- Education and training
- The environment
- Water provision, sewage and waste disposal
- Agriculture
- Health

(4) The predecessor versions of this evaluation concept have thus far been employed in over 50 countries.

Experiences gathered up to now lead one to conclude that the evaluation concept developed here can in principle be employed in all fields of policy and activity, and for all phases of service provision, from planning (ex-ante), via implementation (ongoing), right up to beyond the termination of support (ex-post). The basic model is configured sufficiently flexibly to be adapted to any evaluand. What is more, the concept can not only be used for performing evaluations, but also for the creation of monitoring systems. Previous experience with the use of the various predecessor versions, along with the judgements of clients[160], reveals a *high level of practical feasibility* of the concept for a diverse range of tasks and in a wide array of policy fields.

The further development of the concept presented in this book predestines it for use in organisations that pursue *output and outcome-based quality management*. It is thus primarily suited to management and quality development in non-profit organisations, and those organisations that, due to a high level of social responsibility, are concerned not only with the intended, but also the unintended, consequences of their corporate actions, and that align their corporate strategy with sustainable development. The development of quality dimensions oriented towards the organisational and situational conditions of non-

---

160 The clients of evaluations carried out on the basis of this concept of the Center for Evaluation are *highly satisfied* with the process flow, as well as with the value created for them by the evaluation results for future activities. Since the introduction of an internally-developed monitoring system at CEval, following the completion of an evaluation the satisfaction of clients is surveyed using a range of criteria. Modelled on German school grades, values from (1) 'very satisfied' to (6) 'very dissatisfied' can be awarded. The participatory approach, with an average of 1.14, is rated especially highly. The benefit of the evaluation to the commissioning organisation is rated at 1.5, the usefulness of recommendations for future action at 1.57 (for more detail, cf. CEval annual report 2004: 23 f.).

profit organisations, as well as towards their quality requirements, provides an alternative to ISO and EFQM-based standards/criteria.

Characteristics of the evaluation concept

To conclude, the *characteristics* of the *evaluation concept* developed here can be summarised as follows:

✓ It is a concept of evaluation based on four theoretical approaches (the life-cycle perspective, organisational, innovation and diffusion theory, and sustainability), at the core of which is a *set of evaluation guidelines* containing the central assessment criteria and quality dimensions. In contrast to numerous other approaches, primarily stemming from the field of quality management, the *criteria* applied here have been derived theoretically. This is also true of the *four quality dimensions*, which can be formed by bundling together the evaluation criteria, and which facilitate the appraisal of (1) the quality of service provision, (2) the quality of impacts produced within the executing agency, (3) among audiences (target groups), and in the fields of intervention (policy fields), as well as (4) the quality of sustainability at the programme and macro levels.

✓ The evaluation concept is primarily oriented towards the establishment and assessment of *impacts*, as well as the detection of their causes. To this end, the evaluation neither procedes in a goal-free manner, nor is it based directly on the aims of a programme or service. Rather, it follows a *hypothesis-driven approach*, which is governed by the set of evaluation guidelines.

✓ The *performance* of the evaluation is organised *participatively*, in order, on the one hand, to utilise the situational knowledge of stakeholders for the development of the evaluation design and the interpretation and assessment of results, and, on the other hand, to enhance the usefulness of the evaluation by motivating these parties to actively support it.

✓ *Data collection* is carried out on the basis of a *multi-method approach*. The methodological weaknesses of one procedure should be compensated for by the strengths of another. Furthermore, the use of numerous different methods should serve to ascertain as many perspectives on the evaluand as possible, in order to maximise the validity, reliability and objectivity of description and assessment.

✓ *Data analysis* is performed on the basis of the set of evaluation guidelines, within a process of gradual information compression. The information gathered with the various collection methods is condensed through a step-by-step procedure *('funnel method')* to form subject area-specific indicators, which can then, in turn, be applied for the assessment of quality.

✓ The evaluation concept exhibits a *management orientation*, in that primarily data relevant for output- and outcome-based control are collected and assessed. To this end, it endeavours to combine classic evaluation methodology with quality management approaches. Here it becomes clear, however, that existing quality management models developed for profit-oriented firms that are subject to market competition hardly deal sufficiently with the particular organisational and situational conditions of non-profit organisations. Even New Public Management approaches, used especially in public administration, are largely based on the market model. What is pioneering, though, is the strategy of aligning management with the provision of outputs and the resulting outcomes. Evaluation can, in principle, supply management-relevant data for management models of any kind. However, the potential of evaluation can best be realised in *conjunction with an output- and outcome-oriented management model.*

✓ The *evaluation concept* developed here is thus oriented towards making a contribution to *impact optimisation*, and therefore to *impact-based quality improvement*, in particular in non-profit organisations.

✓ The *evaluation methodology* presented in detail in this book, along with the instructions for performing analysis, are intended to contribute towards the concept and its tools being used as frequently as possible, in order to achieve the most important aim of any evaluation, which is to create *value.*

279

6 References

Abraham, Martin/Büschges, Günter (2004): Einführung in die Organisationssoziologie. Wiesbaden: VS-Verlag.

Adelmann, Gerd (2000): Erfolg durch Qualität: Leitfaden zur Einführung von Qualitätsmanagement in die Umweltberatung. Bremen: Asendorf.

Ahn, Heinz (2003): Effektivitäts- und Effizienzsicherung: Controlling-Konzept und Balanced-Scorecard. Frankfurt a.M.: Lang.

Albach, Horst (1994): Culture and Technical Innovation. A Cross-Cultural Analysis and Policy Recommendations. Berlin/New York: de Gruyter.

Alber, Jens (1989): Der Sozialstaat in der Bundesrepublik Deutschland 1950-1983. Frankfurt a.M./New York: Campus.

Aldrich, Howard E. (1979): Organizations and Environments. Englewood Cliffs, NJ: Prentice Hall.

Alkin, Marvin C. (Hg.) (2004): Evaluation roots: Tracing Theorists' Views and Influences. Thousand Oaks: Californien.

Allmendinger, Jutta (1995): Die sozialpolitische Bilanzierung von Lebensverläufen. In: Berger, Peter A./Sopp, Peter (Hg.): Sozialstruktur und Lebensverlauf, S.179-201. Opladen: Leske + Budrich.

Altmann, Franz-Lothar/Hösch, Edgar (1994): Reformen und Reformer in Osteuropa. Regensburg: Pustet.

Anheier, Helmut K. (1997): Der Dritte Sektor in Zahlen: ein sozioökonomischses Porträt. In: Anheier, Helmut K./Priller, Eckhard/Seibel, Wolfgang/Zimmer, Annette (Hg.): Der Dritte Sektor in Deutschland. Organisationen im gesellschaftlichen Wandel zwischen Markt und Staat. Berlin: edition sigma, S. 29-74.

Anheier, Helmut K./Priller, Eckhard/Zimmer, Annette (2000): Zur zivilgesellschaftlichen Dimension des Dritten Sektors. In: Klingemann, Hans-Dieter/Neidhardt, Friedhelm (Hg.): Die Zukunft der Demokratie. Herausforderungen im Zeitalter der Globalisierung. Berlin: edition sigma.

Anheier, Helmut K./Seibel, Wolfgang/Priller, Eckhard/Zimmer, Annette (2002): Der Nonprofit-Sektor in Deutschland. In: Badelt, Christoph (Hg.): Handbuch der Nonprofit-Organisation: Strukturen und Management. Stuttgart: Schäffer-Poeschel, S. 19-44.

Anthony, Robert N. (1988): The Management Control Function. In: Management. Boston.

Aregger, Kurt (1976): Innovation in sozialen Systemen. Erste Einführung in die Innovationstheorie der Organisation. Bern/Stuttgart: Haupt.

Argyris/Schön (1999): Die lernende Organisation. Stuttgart: Klett-Cotta.

Arnold, Rolf (1997): Qualitätssicherung in der Erwachsenenbildung. Opladen: Leske + Budrich.

Arnold, Ulli (2003): Qualitätsmanagement in Sozialwirtschaftlichen Organisationen. In: Arnold, Ulli/Maelicke, Bernd (Hg): Lehrbuch der Sozialwirtschaft. Baden-Baden: Nomos Verlagsgesellschaft (2., überarb. Auflage).

Arnold, Ulli/Maelicke, Bernd (Hg) (2003): Lehrbuch der Sozialwirtschaft. Baden-Baden: Nomos Verlagsgesellschaft (2., überarb. Auflage).

Artner, Astrid/Sinabell, Franz (2003): Grundlegendes zur Cost-effectiveness-Analyse. Positionspapier zu Teilmodul 3 / Leitbildentwicklung für ausgewählte Flusslandschaften (Möll/Kärnten) im Rahmen des Forschungsprojekts Flusslandschaftstypen Österreichs – Leitbilder für eine nachhaltige Entwicklung von Flusslandschaften. Wien.

Astley, W. Graham (1985): The two ecologies: Population and Community Perspectives on Organizational Evolution. In: Administrative Science Quarterly 30, S. 224-241

Badelt, Christoph (Hg.) (2002): Handbuch der Nonprofit-Organisation: Strukturen und Management. Stuttgart: Schäfer-Poeschel (3., überarb. u. erw. Auflage).

Badelt, Christoph (2002): Zwischen Marktversagen und Staatsversagen? Nonprofit-Organisationen aus sozioökonomischer Sicht. In: Badelt, Christoph (Hg.): Handbuch der Nonprofit-Organisation: Strukturen und Management. Stuttgart: Schäffer-Poeschel, S. 107-128.

Badelt, Christoph (2002): Ausblick: Entwicklungsperspektiven des Nonprofit-Sektors. In: Badelt, Christoph (Hg.): Handbuch der Nonprofit Organisation: Strukturen und Management. Stuttgart: Schäffer-Poeschel.

Bähr, Uwe (2002): Controlling in der öffentlichen Verwaltung. Sternenfels: Verlag Wissen und Praxis.

Baier, Peter (2002): Praxishandbuch Controlling: Planung & Reporting, bewährte Controllinginstrumente, Balanced Scoredard, Value Management, Sensitivitäts-analysen, Fallbeispiele (Nachdruck). Wien: Ueberreuter.

Baltes, Katrin (2003a): Evaluation des Leonard-Euler-Stipendienprogramms im Auftrag des DAAD. Saarbrücken.

Baltes, Katrin (2003b): Evaluation deutsch-japanischer Hochschulpartnerschaften im Auftrag des DAAD. Saarbrücken.

Baltes, Katrin (2004): Fallstudie Großbritannien im Rahmen der Programmbereichsevaluation „Stipendien für Ausländer" im Auftrag des DAAD. Saarbrücken.

Baltes, Katrin/Krapp, Stefanie/Stockmann, Reinhard (2004): Begleitende Evaluation des Kommunikations- und Informationssystems Berufliche Bildung (KIBB). Erster Zwischenbericht. Saarbrücken.

Baltes, Marget M/Baltes, Paul B. (Hg.) (1986): The Psychology of Control and Aging. Hillsdale, N.J.: Lawrence Erlbaum Associates.

Bamberger, Michael (1989): The Monitoring and Evaluation of Public Sector Programs in Asia: Why are Development Programs Monitored but not Evaluated? In: Evaluation Review 13 (3), S. 223-242.

Bank, Volker/Lames, Martin (2000): Über Evaluation. Kiel: bajOsch-Hein, Verlag für Berufs- und Wirtschaftspädagogik.

Barnard, Chester Irving (1938): The Functions of the Executive. Cambrigde, Mass.: Harvard University Press.

Barnett, Homer G. (1953): Innovation: The Basis of Cultural Change. New York u.a.: McGraw-Hill.

Barnett, John H. (1988): Non-Profits and the Life-Cycle. In: Evaluation and Programm Planning 11, S. 13-20.

Bauer, Rudolph (1997): Zivilgesellschaftliche Gestaltung in der Bundesrepublik. Möglichkeiten oder Grenzen? Skeptische Anmerkungen aus der Sicht der Nonprofit-Forschung. In: Schmals, Klaus M./Heinelt, H. (Hg.): Zivile Gesellschaften. Opladen: Leske + Budrich, S. 133-153.

Bauer, Rudolph (2001): Personenbezogene soziale Dienstleistungen. Wiesbaden: Westdeutscher Verlag.

Baum, Heinz-Georg (2004): Strategisches Controlling. Stuttgart: Schäffer-Poeschel (3., überarb. u. erw. Auflage).

Bea, Franz Xaver/Göbel, Elisabeth (2002): Organisation: Theorie und Gestaltung. Stuttgart: Lucius und Lucius.

Bechmann, Gotthard/Grunwald, Armin (1998): „Was ist das Neue am Neuen, oder: wie innovativ ist Innovation?" In: TA-Datenbank-Nachrichten 7 (1), S. 4-11.

Beck, Ulrich (1997): Was ist Globalisierung? Irrtümer des Globalismus – Antworten auf Globalisierung. Frankfurt a.M.: Suhrkamp.

Beckmann, Christof (Hg.) (2004): Qualität in der sozialen Arbeit: zwischen Nutzerinteresse und Kostenkontrolle. Wiesbaden: Verlag für Sozialwissenschaft.

Behrendt, Heiko (2005): Evaluation der Logik und der Wirkungsweise von Projekten. In: Berufsbildung. Bd. 91/92. Jg. 59, S. 38-40.

Behrens, Johann/Voges, Wolfgang (Hg.) (1996): Kritische Übergänge. Statuspassagen und sozialpolitische Institutionalisierung. Frankfurt a.M.: Campus.

Beikirch-Korporal, Elisabeth/Korporal, Johannes (2002): Debatte um die integrierte Pflegeausbildung: Rahmenbedingungen der Reform von Pflegeausbildungen in Deutschland. In: Igl, Gerhard/Schiemann, Doris/Gerste, Bettina/Klose Joachim (Hg.): Qualität in der Pflege: Betreuung und Versorgung von pflegebedürftigen alten Menschen in der stationären und ambulanten Altenhilfe. Stuttgart: Schattauer.

Benz, Arthur (1995): Politiknetzwerke in der horizontalen Politikverflechtung. In: Jansen, Dorothea/Schubert, Klaus (Hg.): Netzwerke und Politikproduktion. Konzepte, Methoden, Perspektiven. Marburg: Schüren, S. 185-204.

Berger, Peter A./Sopp, Peter (Hg.) (1995): Sozialstruktur und Lebenslauf. Opladen: Leske+Budrich.

Berger, Ulrike/Bernhard-Mehlich, Isolde (1993): Die Verhaltenswissenschaftliche Entscheidungstheorie. In: Kieser, Alfred (Hg.): Organisationstheorien. Stuttgart u.a.: Kohlhammer, S. 141ff.

Bethke, Franz Sieber (2003): Controlling, Evaluation und Reporting von Weiterbildung und Personalentwicklung. Bremen: Institut zur Entwicklung moderner Unterrichtsmedien.

Beyer, Horst-Tilo (1992): Neue Technik bleibt erfolglos ohne die soziale Innovation. In: Der Arbeitgeber 44 (5), S. 163-168.

Beyme, Klaus von (1996): Das politische System der BRD. München: Piper.

Beywl, Wolfgang; Schobert, Berthold (2000): Evaluation – Controlling – Qualitätsmanagement in der betrieblichen Weiterbildung. Kommentierte Auswahlbibliographie. (3. aktualisierte und übererbeitete Auflage). Bielefeld: Bertelsmann.

Beywl, Wolfgang; Speer, Sandra (2004): Data- and Literature-Based Reflections on Western European Evaluation Standards and Practices. In Russon, C.; Russon, G. (Hg.): International Perspectives on Evaluation Standards. New Directions for Evaluation, 104 (S. 43-54). San Francisco: Jossey-Bass.

Beywl, Wolfgang; Taut, Sandy (2000): Standards: Aktuelle Strategie zur Qualitätsentwicklung in der Evalaution. In: Deutsches Institut für Wirtschaftsforschung Berlin (Hg.): Evaluierung im Spannungsfeld zwischen Wissenschaft und Politik. Vierteljahresheft zur Wirtschaftsforschung. Heft 4/2000 (S.358-370). Berlin: Duncker & Humblot.

Beywl, Wolfgang; Widmer, Thomas (2000): Handbuch der Evaluationsstandards. Die Standards des „Joint Committee for Educational Evaluation". Opladen: Leske + Budrich.

Binnendijk, Annette L. (1989): Donor Agency Experience with the Monitoring and Evaluation of Development Projects. In: Evaluation Review 13 (3), S. 206-222.

Binstock, Robert H./George, Linda K. (Hg.) (1990): Handbook of Aging and the Social Sciences. New York: Academic Press.

Blau, Peter M. (1970): A Formal Theory of Differentiation in Organizations. In: American Journal of Sociological Review 35, S. 201-218.

Blau, Peter M./Scott, Richard W. (1963): Formal Organizations: A Comparative Approach. London: Routledge and Kegan.

Blossfeld, Hans-Peter (1989): Kohortendifferenzierung und Karriereprozess – Eine Längsschnittstudie über die Veränderung von Bildungs- und Berufschancen im Lebenslauf. Frankfurt a.M.: Campus-Verlag.

Blossfeld, Hans-Peter (1990): Berufsverläufe und Arbeitsmarktprozesse. Ergebnisse sozialstruktureller Längsschnittuntersuchungen. In: Mayer, Karl Ulrich (Hg.): Lebensverläufe und Sozialer Wandel. (Sonderheft der Kölner Zeitschrift für Soziologie und Sozialpsychologie). Opladen: Westdeutscher Verlag.

Blossfeld, Hans-Peter (1990): Unterschiedliche Systeme der Berufsbildung und Anpassung an Strukturveränderungen im internationalen Vergleich. In: Bundesinstitut für Berufsbildung (Hg.): Die Rolle der beruflichen Bildung und Berufsbildungsforschung im internationalen Vergleich. Eine Tagungsdokumentation. Berlin/Bonn.

Blossfeld, Hans-Peter (1990c): Changing educational careers in the Federal Republic of Germany. In: Sociolgy of Education 63, S. 165-177.

Blossfeld, Hans-Peter/Drobnik, Sonja (2001): Careers couples in contemporary society. From male breadwinner to dual-earner families. Oxford: Oxford University Press.

Blossfeld, Hans-Peter/Drobnic, Sonja/Schneider, Thorsten (2001): Pflegebedürftige Personen im Haushalt und das Erwerbsverhalten verheirateter Frauen. In: Zeitschrift für Soziologie 30 (5), S. 362-383.

Blossfeld, Hans-Peter/Huinink, Johannes (2001): Lebensverlaufsforschung als sozialwissenschaftliche Forschungsperspektive. Themen, Konzepte, Methoden und Probleme. In: BIOS 14 (2), Opladen: Leske + Budrich, S. 5-31.

Blossfeld, Hans-Peter/Shavit Y. (1993): Persisting Barriers: Changes in Educational Opportunities in Thirteen Countries. In: Shavit, Y./Blossfeld, Hans-Peter (Hg.): Persistent Inequality: Changing Educational Stratification in Thirteen Countries. Boulder, Col.: Manuskript.

Blossfeld, Hans-Peter/Stockmann, Reinhard (Hg.) (1998/99): Globalization and Changes in Vocational Training Systems in Developing and Advanced Industrialized Societies. International Journal of Sociology. Special Issue.

Bode, Ingo (2000): Die Bewegung des Dritten Sektors und ihre Grenzen. In: Forschungsjournal Neue Soziale Bewegungen 13 (1), S. 48-52.

Boeßenecker, Karl-Heinz (1998): Spitzenverbände der freien Wohlfahrtspflege in der BRD. Eine Einführung in die Organisationsstruktur und Handlungsfelder. Münster: votum (2. Auflage).

Boeßenecker, Karl-Heinz u.a. (Hg.) (2003): Qualitätskonzepte in der sozialen Arbeit. Weinheim: Beltz.

Bollmann, Petra (1990): Technischer Fortschritt und wirtschaftlicher Wandel. Eine Gegenüberstellung neoklassischer und evolutorischer Innovationsforschung. Heidelberg: Physica.

Bornemeier, Olaf (2002): Benchmarking in der Gesundheitsversorgung: Möglichkeiten und Grenzen. Berlin: Autorenverlag: Scheriau.

Bosetzky, Horst/Heinrich, Peter (1994): Mensch und Organisation. Aspekte bürokratischer Sozialisation. Köln: Dt. Gemeindeverlag.

Boudon, Raymond (2002): „Sociology that Really Matters". In: European Sociological Review 18 (3), S. 371-378.

Boysen, Thies/Strecker, Marius (2002): Der Wert der sozialen Arbeit: Qualitätsmanagement in Non-Profit-Organisationen. München: Herbert Utz Verlag.

Brandt, Tasso/Meyer, Wolfgang (2003): Zwischenevaluierung des Regionalmanagements und der regionalen Partnerschaft „Vis à Vis" (Zwischenbericht). Saarbrücken.

Brandt, Tasso (2004): Zwischenbericht des Regionalmanagements und der regionales Partnerschaft „Vis a Vis e.V. " Saarbrücken.

Brandtstädter, Jochen (1990a): Entwicklung im Lebenslauf. Ansätze und Probleme der Lebensspannen-Entwicklungspsychologie. In: Mayer, Karl Ulrich (Hg.): Lebensverläufe und Sozialer Wandel. (Sonderheft der Kölner Zeitschrift für Soziologie und Sozialpsychologie). Opladen: Westdeutscher Verlag.

Brandtstädter, Jochen (1990b): Evaluationsforschung: Probleme der wissenschaftlichen Bewertung von Interventions- und Reformprojekten. In: Zeitschrift für Pädagogische Psychologie 4 (4), S. 215-228.

Brauer, Jörg-Peter (2002): DIN EN ISO 9000-2000ff. umsetzen: Gestaltungshilfen zum Aufbau Ihres Qualitätmanagementsystems. München: Hanser.

Braun, Norman/Engelhardt, Henriette (1998): Diffusionsprozesse und Ereignisdatenanalyse. In: Kölner Zeitschrift für Soziologie und Sozialpsychologie 50 (2), S. 263-282.

Brinckmann, Hans (1994): Strategien für eine effektivere und effizientere Verwaltung. In: Naschold, F./Pröhl, M. (Hg.): Produktivität öffentlicher Leistungen. Gütersloh: Bertelsmann Stiftung.

Brinkerhoff, Derick W./Goldsmith, Arthur A. (1992): Promoting the Sustainability of Development Institutions: A Framework for Strategy. In: World Development 20 (3), S. 369-383.

Brückner, Erika/Mayer, K. U. (1998): Collecting life history data: Experiences from the German Life History Study. In: Giele, Z. J./Elder, G. H.: Methods of life course research: Qualitative and quantitative approaches. S. 152-181.

Brüderl, Joseph (1991): Mobilitätsprozesse in Betrieben. Frankfurt a.M.: Campus.

Bruhn, Manfred (1998): Wirtschaftlichkeit des Qualitätsmanagements. Berlin.

Bruhn, Manfre/Geogri, Dominik (1999): Kosten und Nutzen des Qualitätsmanagements. Grundlagen – Methoden – Fallbeispiele. München: Carl Hanser.

Budäus, Dietrich/Dobler, Christian (1977): Theoretische Konzepte und Kriterien zur Beurteilung der Effektivität von Organisationen. In: Management International Review 17, S. 61ff.

BUND & Misereor (Hg.) (1996): Zukunftsfähiges Deutschland. Ein Beitrag zu einer global nachhaltigen Entwicklung. Berlin: Birkhäuser.

Bundesministerium für Wirtschaftliche Zusammenarbeit und Entwicklung (Hg.) (2000): Langfristige Wirkung deutscher Entwicklungszusammenarbeit und ihre Erfolgsbedingungen. Bonn: BMZ.

Bungard, Walter (1992): Qualitätszirkel in der Arbeitswelt – Ziele, Erfahrungen, Probleme. Göttingen: Verlag für Angewandte Psychologie.

Bungard, Walter (1991): Qualitätszirkel: ein soziotechnisches Instrument auf dem Prüfstand. Ludwigshafen: Ehrenhof-Verlag.

Bungard, Walter/Wiendiek, H. (Hg.) (1986): Qualitätszirkel als Instrument zeitgemäßer Betriebsführung. Landsberg a.L.

Buschor, Ernst (2001): Evaluation und New Public Management. Speyer: DeGEVal Jahrestagung.

Buschor, Ernst. (1993): Zwanzig Jahre Haushaltsreform – Eine verwaltungswissenschaftliche Bilanz. In: Brede/Buschor (Hg.): Das neue öffentliche Rechnungswesen. Betriebswirtschaftliche Beiträge zur Haushaltsreform in Deutschland, Österreich und der Schweiz. Schriften zur öffentlichen Verwaltung und öffentlichen Wirtschaft 133. Baden-Baden: Nomos.

Buschor, Ernst (2002): Evaluation und New Public Management. In: Zeitschrift für Evaluation 1 (1), S. 61-74.

Buss, Eugen (1995): Lehrbuch der Wirtschaftssoziologie. Berlin: De Gruyter.

Busse, Thomas (2003): Qualitätsmanagement in der Pflege: ein Leitfaden zur Einführung. Frankfurt a.M.: Fachhochschulverlag.

Bussmann, Werner u.a. (Hg.) (1997): Einführung in die Politikevaluation. Basel: Helbing und Lichtenhahn.

Cameron, Kim S. (1978): Measuring Organizational Effectiveness in Institutions of Higher Education. In: ASQ 23, S. 604ff.

Cameron, Kim S./Whetten, David R. (Hg.) (1983): Organizational Effectiveness: A Comparison of Multiple Models. Orlando: Academic Press.

Camp, Robert C. (1994): Benchmarking. München: Hanser

Camp, Robert C. (1995): Business process benchmarking. Milwaukee: ASQC Quality Press.

Campbell, John P. (1977): On the Nature of Organizational Effectiveness. In: Goodman, Paul S./Pennings, Johannes S. (Hg.): New Perspectives on Organizational Effectiveness. San Francisco: Jossey-Bass.

Campbell, Donald T. (1969): Reform as Experiments. In: American Psychologist 24 (4), S. 409-429.

Campbell, Donald T./Stanley, J.C. (1963): Experimental and Quasi-Experimental Designs in Research on Teaching. In: Gage, N.L. (Hg.) Handbook of Research on Teaching. Chicago: Rand McNally.

Cappis, Marc C. (1998): Von ISO 9001 über EQA Assessment zu TQM. In: Boutellier, Roman/Masing, Walter (Hg.): Qualitätsmanagement an der Schwelle zum 21. Jahrhundert. München u.a.: Hanser, S. 33-52.

Carrington, Peter/Scott, John/Wassermann Stanley/Granovetter, Mark (Hg.) (2005): Models and Methods in Social Network Analysis. Cambridge: Cambridge University Press.

Carroll, Glenn R. (1984): Organizational Ecology. In: Annual Review of Sociology 10, S. 71-93.

Carroll, Glenn. R. (Hg.) (1988): Ecological Models of Organizations. Cambridge, MA: Ballinger.

Carroll, Glenn R./Haveman, Heather/Swaminathan, Anand (1990): Karrieren in Organisationen. Eine ökologische Perspektive. In: Mayer, Karl Ulrich (Hg.): Lebensverläufe und Sozialer Wandel (Sonderheft der Kölner Zeitschrift für Soziologie und Sozialpsychologie). Opladen: Westdeutscher Verlag.

Caspari, Alexandra (2004): Evaluation der Nachhaltigkeit von Entwicklungszusammenarbeit. Zur Notwendigkeit angemessener Konzepte und Methoden. Wiesbaden: VS Verlag

Caspari, Alexandra/Kevenhörster, Paul/Stockmann, Reinhard (2000): Langfristige Wirkungen der staatlichen EZ. Ergebnisse einer Querschnittsevaluierung zur Nachhaltigkeit. In: Entwicklung und Zusammenarbeit 41, S. 10.

Caspari, Alexandra/Kevenhörster, Paul/Stockmann, Reinhard (2003): Das Schweigen des Parlaments: Die vergessene Frage der Nachhaltigkeit deutscher Entwicklungszusammenarbeit. In: Aus Politik und Zeitgeschichte 13/14.

Caulley, Darrel N.(1983): Document Analysis in Program Evaluation. In: Evaluation and Program Planning 6, S. 19-29.

CEDEFOP (Hg.) (1997): Qualitätsfragen und -entwicklungen in der beruflichen Bildung und Ausbildung in Europa. Thessaloniki: CEDEFOP.

CEDEFOP (Hg.) (1998): Indikatoren aus verschiedenen Perspektiven. Thessaloniki.

Centrum für Evaluation (Hg.) (2002): Jahresbericht 2002. Saarbrücken: CEval.

Centrum für Evaluation (Hg.) (2003): Jahresbericht 2003. Saarbrücken: CEval.

Centrum für Evaluation (Hg.) (2004): Jahresbericht 2004. Saarbrücken: CEval.

Chambers, Nicky/Simmons, Craig/Wackernagel, Mathis (2000): Sharing Nature's Interest: ecological footprints as an indicator of sustainability. London: Earthscan.

Chelimsky, Eleanor (1995): New dimensions in evaluation. In: World Bank Operations Evaluations Department (OED): Evaluation and Development: proceedings of the 1994 World Bank Conference. Washington D.C., S. 3-11.

Chelimsky, Eleanor/Shadish, William R. (Hg.) (1997): Evaluation for the 21st century. A Handbook. Thousand Oaks/London/New Delhi: Sage (Nachdruck).

Chelimsky, Eleanor (1997): Thoughts for a new evaluation society. Keynote speech at the UK Evaluation Society Conference 1996. In Evaluations 3, S. 97-108.

Chelimsky, Eleanor/Shadish, William R. (Hg.) (1999): Evaluation for the 21st century. A Handbook. Thousand Oaks/London/New Delhi: Sage.

Chen, Huey/Rossi, Peter H. (1980): The Multi-Goal, Theory-driven Approach to Evaluation: A Model Linking Basic and Applied Social Science. In: Social Forces 59, S. 106-122.

Child, John (1972): Organizational Structure, Environment and Performance: The Role of Strategic Choice. In: Sociology, S. 369-93.

Christensen, Tom (2002): New Public Management: the transformation of ideas and practise. Aldershot: Ashgate.

Clutterbuck, David u.a. (1993): Inspired Customer Service: Strategies for Service Quality. London: Kogan Page.

Collin, A./Brown, J.S./Newmann, S.E. (1989): Cognitive apprenticeship: Teaching the crafts of reading, writing, and mathematics. In: Resnick, L.B. (Hg.): Knowing, learning, and instruction. Essays in honor of Robert Glaser. Hillsdale: Erlbaum, S. 453-494.

Commission on Global Governance (1995): Our Global Neighborhood: The Report of the Commission on Global Governance. Oxford: Oxford University Press.

Connolly, T./Conlon, E.J./Deutsch, S.J (1980): Organizational Effectiveness. In: Academy of Management Review 5, S. 211ff.

Cook, T.D./Matt, G.E. (1990): Theorien der Programmevaluation. In: Koch, Uwe/ Wittman, Werner W. (Hg.): Evaluationsforschung: Bewertungsgrundlage von Sozial- und Gesundheitsprogrammen. Berlin u.a.: Springer, S. 15-38.

Cramer, Friedrich (1997): Überfluss und „neue Askese". In: Schenk, Herrad (Hg.): Vom einfachen Leben. Glücksuche zwischen Überfluss und Askese. München: Beck, S. 278-280.

Cronbach, Lee J. (1982): Designing Evaluations of Educational and Social Programs. San Francisco u.a.: Jossey-Bass.

Cronbach, Lee J. u. a. (1981): Toward Reform of Program Evaluation. San Franciso u.a.: Jossey-Bass.

Cross, Rob/Parker, Andreas/Cross, Robert L. (2004): The Hidden Power of Social Networks. Understanding How Work Really Gets Done in Organisations. Boston: Harvard Business School.

Czenskowsky, Torsten (2002): Grundzüge des Controlling: Lehrbuch der Controlling-Konzepte und Instrumente. Gernsbach: Deutscher Betriebswirte Verlag.

DANIDA (Hg.) (1999): Environmental assistance to developing countries: annual report. Copenhagen: DANIDA.

Daumenlang, Konrad/Palm, Wolfgang (1997): Qualitätsmanagement in Non-Profit-Organisationen. Landau: Fachbereich 8, Psychologie, Universität Koblenz-Landau.

Davies, Ian C. (1999): Evaluation and Performance Management in Government. In: Evaluation 5 (2), S. 150-159.

Davis, Kingsley (1949): Human Society. New York: Macmillan.

Deitmer, Ludger (2004): Zum Forschungszusammenhang: Innovation und Region. In: Deitmer, Ludger: Management regionaler Innovationsnetzwerke: Evaluation als Ansatz zur Effizienzsteigerung regionaler Innovationsprozesse. Baden-Baden: Nomos.

Deming, William Edwards (1952): Elementary Principles of the statistical control of quality. Tokyo: Nippon Kegaku Gijutsu Remmei.

Deming, William Edwards (1982): Quality, productivity, and competitive position. Cambridge: Massachusetts Inst. of Technology.

Dent, Mike (Hg.) (2004): Questioning the new public management. Aldershot: Ashgate.

Deppe, Joachim (1992): Quality Circle und Lernstatt. Ein integrativer Ansatz. Wiesbaden: Gabler (3., erw. Auflage).

Derlien, Hans-Ulrich (1976): Die Erfolgskontrolle staatlicher Planung. Eine empirische Untersuchung über Organisation, Methode und Politik der Programmevaluation. Baden-Baden: Nomos.

Derlien, Hans-Ulrich (Hg.) (1991): Programmforschung in der öffentlichen Verwaltung. Werkstattbericht der Gesellschaft für Programmforschung. München.

Deutsch, Karl W. (1985): On Theory and Research in Innovation. In: Merritt, Richard L./Anna J. Merritt (Hg.): Innovation in the Public Sector. Beverly Hills u.a.: Sage, S. 17-35.

Deutsche Gesellschaft für Evaluation (2002): Standards für Evaluation. Köln: DeGEval.

Deutsche Gesellschaft für Qualität e.V. (Hg.) (2001): Qualitätsmanagement in der Weiterbildung. Berlin: Beuth.

Deutscher, Irvin; Ostrander, Susan A. (1985): Sociology and Evaluation Research: Some Past and Future Links. In: History of Sociology 6, S. 11-32.

Deutscher Bundestag (Hg.) (1989): Drucksache 11/5105 vom 28.8.1989. Bonn: Deutscher Bundestag.

Deutscher Bundestag (Hg.) (1989): Drucksache 13/10857: Systematische Erfolgskontrolle von Projekten und Programmen der bilateralen Entwicklungszusammenarbeit. Bonn: Deutscher Bundestag.

Deutsches Institut für Normung (Hg.) (2002): Der Weg von DIN EN ISO 9000ff. zu Total Quality Management (TQM).

Deutsches Institut für Normung (Hg.) (2004): ISO 9000ff. – Die neuen Qualitätsmaßstäbe 2004 (Tagungsband der DIN-Tagung). Berlin: Deutsches Institut für Normung.

Deutsches Institut für Normung (Hg.) (2004): Qualitätsmanagement DIN EN ISO 9000ff. Berlin: Beuth.

Deyhle, Albrecht (1995): Controller Praxis: Führung durch Ziele, Planung und Kontrolle. Gauting/München: Management-Service-Verlag.

Deyle, Albrecht (2000): Controller Praxis: Führung durch Ziele, Planung und Controlling. Offenburg u.a.: Verlag für ControllingWissen.

Deyle, Albrecht (2002): Controlling Controller: Trends in der Controller Praxis. In: Betriebswirtschaft und Mediengesellschaft im Wandel, S. 429-451.

Deyle, Albrecht (2003): Controller-Handbuch: Enzyklopädisches Lexikon für die Controller-Praxis. Offenburg u.a.: Verlag für ControllingWissen (5., neu geschriebene Auflage).

Diani, Marion/McAdam, Dough (2004): Social Movements and Networks. Relational Approaches to Collective Action. Oxford: Oxford University Press.

Diekmann, Andreas (1995): Empirische Sozialforschung. Grundlagen, Methoden, Anwendungen. Reinbek b. Hamburg: Rowohlt.

Diekmann, Andreas (2004): Empirische Sozialforschung. Grundlagen, Methoden, Anwendungen. Reinbek b. Hamburg: Rowohlt.

Diekmann, Andreas/Weick, Stefan (Hg.) (1993): Der Familienzyklus als sozialer Prozeß: bevölkerungssoziologische Untersuchungen mit den Methoden der Ereignisanalyse. Berlin: Duncker & Humblot.

Diensberg, Christoph (2001): Balanced Scorecard – kritische Anregungen für die Bildungs- und Personalarbeit, für Evaluation und die Weiterentwicklung des Ansatzes. In: Diensberg, Christoph/Krekel, Elisabeth M./Schobert, Berthold (Hg.): Balanced

Scorecard und House of Quality: Impulse für die Evaluation in Weiterbildung und Personalentwicklung. Schriftenreihe des Bundesinstituts für Berufsbildung 53. Bonn: BIBB, S. 21-38.

Diewald, Martin/Huinink, Johannes/Heckhausen, Jutta (1996): Lebensverläufe und Persönlichkeitsentwicklung im gesellschaftlichen Umbruch. Kohortenschicksale und Kontrollverhalten in Ostdeutschland nach der Wende. In: Kölner Zeitschrift für Soziologie und Sozialpsychologie 48, S. 219-248.

Diewald, Martin/Mayer, Karl Ulrich (Hg.) (1996): Zwischenbilanz der Wiedervereinigung: Strukturwandel und Mobilität im Transformationsprozess. Opladen: Leske + Budrich.

Donabedian, Avesis (1980): The definition of quality and approaches to its assessment. Ann Arbor, Mich.: Health Administration Press.

Doppler, Klaus/Lauterburg, Christoph (2000): Change Management. Den Unternehmenswandel gestalten. Frankfurt a.M.: Campus.

Drescher, Peter (2003): Moderation von Arbeitsgruppen und Qualitätszirkeln: ein Handbuch. Göttingen: Vandenhoeck und Ruprecht.

Dror, Yehezkel (1968): Public policymaking re-examined. Scranton, Pennsylvania: Chandler.

Druwe, Ulrich (1987): Politik. In: Görlitz, Axel/Prätorius, Rainer: Handbuch Politikwissenschaft. Grundlagen-Forschungsstand-Perspektiven. Hamburg: Rohwolt, S. 393-397.

Dunn, William N. (2004). Public policy analysis: an introduction. Prentice-Hall: Pearson.

Dye, Thomas R. (1978): Policy-Analysis: What Governments Do, Why They Do It, and What Difference it Makes. Alabama: University of Alabama.

Eder, Ferdinand (Hg.) (2002): Qualitätsentwicklung und Qualitätssicherung im österreichischen Schulwesen. Innsbruck: Studien-Verlag.

Eddy, David M. (1992): Cost-Effectiveness-Analysis: Is it Up to the Task? In: Journal of the American Medical Association 267, S. 3342-3348.

EFQM (2003a): Die Grundkonzepte der Excellence. Frankfurt a.M.: EFQM.

EFQM (2003b): Excellence einführen. Frankfurt a.M.: EFQM.

EFQM (2003c): Das EFQM-Modell für Excellence: Version für den Öffentlichen Dienst und soziale Einrichtungen. Frankfurt a.M.: EFQM.

Egger, Martin/Schübel, Ulrich F./Zink, Klaus J. (2002): Total Quality Management (TQM) in Werkstätten für behinderte Menschen (WfbM): Abschlussbericht; Entwicklung und Erprobung eines Verfahrens zur kontinuierlichen Verbesserung von umfassender Qualität in WfbM [CD-Rom Ausgabe]. Kaiserslautern: Universität, Institut für Technologie und Arbeit.

Ehlers, Ulf-Daniel/Schenkel, Peter (2004): Bildungscontrolling im E-Learning. Berlin: Springer.

Elder, Glen H./Caspi, Avsholm (1990): Persönliche Entwicklung und sozialer Wandel. Die Entstehung der Lebensverlaufsforschung. In: Mayer, Karl Ulrich (Hg.): Lebensverläufe und Sozialer Wandel (Sonderheft der Kölner Zeitschrift für Soziologie und Sozialpsychologie). Opladen: Westdeutscher Verlag.

Ellwein, Thomas (1977): Das Regierungssystem der BRD. Opladen: Westdeutscher Verlag.

Elsweiler, Bernd (2002): Erweitertes Monitoring- und Benchmarkingsystem zur strategischen Unternehmenslenkung. Aachen: Shaker.

Endruweit, Günter (2004): Organisationssoziologie. Stuttgart: Lucius & Lucius (2., überarb. u. erw. Auflage).

Engelhardt, Hans D. (2001): Total Quality Management: Konzept, Verfahren, Diskussion. Schwerpunkt Management. Augsburg: Ziel.

Ermert, Karl (Hg.) (2004): Evaluation in der Kulturförderung: Über Grundlagen kulturpolitischer Entscheidungen.

Eschenbach, Rolf (1996) (Hg.): Controlling. Stuttgart: Schäffer-Poeschel Verlag.

Eschenbach, Rolf (1996): Zukunft des Controlling. In: Eschenbach, Rolf (Hg.): Controlling. Stuttgart: Schäffer-Poeschel Verlag, S. 715-727.

Eschenbach, Rolf (1998): Führungsinstrumente für die Nonprofit-Organisation: bewährte Verfahren im Einsatz. Stuttgart: Schaeffer-Poeschel.

Eschenbach, Rolf (1999): Einführung in das Controlling. Konzeption und Institution; ein Arbeitsbuch zur Einführung für den Gebrauch an Fachhochschulen. Wien: Service-Fachverlag (2. Auflage).

Eschenbach, Rolf (2000): Rechnungswesen und Controlling in NPOs. In: Badelt, Christoph (Hg.): Handbuch der Nonprofit-Organisation. Stuttgart: Schäffer-Poeschel.

Eschenbach, Rolf/Horak, Christian (Hg.) (2003): Führung der Nonprofit-Organisation: bewährte Instrumente im praktischen Einsatz. Stuttgart: Schäffer-Poeschel.

Eschenbach, Rolf/Niedermayr, Rita (1996): Controlling in der Literatur. In: Eschenbach, Rolf (Hg.): Controlling. Stuttgart: Schäffer-Poeschel Verlag, S. 49-65.

Eschenbach, Rolf/Niedermayr, Rita (1996): Die Konzeption des Controlling. In: Eschenbach, Rolf (Hg.): Controlling. Stuttgart: Schäffer-Poeschel Verlag, S. 65-95.

Escher, Norbert (1997): Qualität und Qualitätsmanagement im Gesundheitswesen. In: Maelicke, Bernd (Hg.): Qualität und Kosten sozialer Dienstleistungen. Baden-Baden: Nomos.

Etzioni, Amitai (1973): The Third Sector and Domestic Missions. Public Administration Review 33, S. 314-323.

Etzioni, Amitai (1971): Two Approaches to Organizational Analysis: a Critique and a Suggestion. In: Ghorpade. S. 33 ff.

Etzioni, Amitai. (1961): A Comparative Analysis of Complex Organizations. New York: The Free Press.

European Foundation for Quality Management (Hg.) (1998): Die Leistung steigern mit dem EFQM-Modell für Business Excellence. Brüssel.

Eversheim, Walter/Jaschinski, Christoph/Reddemann, Andreas (Hg.), (1997): Qualitätsmanagement für Nonprofit-Dienstleister. Ein Leitfaden für Kammern, Verbände und andere Wirtschaftsorganisationen. Berlin: Springer.

Eversheim, Walter (Hg.) (1997): Qualitätsmanagement für Dienstleister: Grundlagen, Selbstanalyse, Umsetzungshilfen. Berlin: Springer.

Eversheim, Walter (Hg.) (2000): Qualitätsmanagement für Dienstleister: Grundlagen, Selbstanalyse, Umsetzungshilfen. Berlin: Springer.

Ewers, H.-J./Brenck, A. (1992): Innovationsorientierte Regionalpolitik: Zwischenfazit eines Forschungsprogramms. In: Birg, H./Schalk, H.-H. (Hg.): Regionale und sektorale Strukturpolitik. Münster: Institut für Siedlungs- und Wohnungswesen.

Ewert, Wolfgang (2004): Handbuch Projektmanagement und öffentliche Dienste: Grundlagen, Praxisbeispiele und Handlungsanleitungen für die Verwaltungsreform durch Projektarbeit. Bremen u.a.: Sachbuchverlag Kellner.

Fahrni, Fritz/Völker, Rainer/Bodmer, Christian (2002): Erfolgreiches Benchmarking in Forschung und Entwicklung, Beschaffung und Logistik. München: Hanser.

Faßhauer, Uwe/Basel, Sven (2005): Qualitätsoptimierung oder Bewertungsritual. In: Berufsbildung. Bd. 91/92, Jg. 59, S. 30-35.

Feick, Jürgen/Jann, Werner (1988): Nations matter – Vom Eklektizismus zur Integration in der vergleichenden Policy-Forschung? In: Schmidt, Manfred G. (Hg.): Staatstätigkeit. International und historisch vergleichende Analysen (PVS-Sonderheft 19). Opladen: Westdeutscher Verlag.

Feuchthofen, Jörg E./Severing, Eckart (Hg.) (1995): Qualitätsmanagement und Qualitätssicherung in der Weiterbildung. Neuwied u.a.: Luchterhand.

Fitzpatrick, Jody L./Sanders, James R./Worthen, Blaine R. (2004): Program Evaluation. Alternative Approaches and Practical Guidelines. Boston u.a.: Pearson.

Fratschner, F. A. (1999): Balanced Scorecard – Ein Wegweiser zur strategiekonformen Ableitung von Zielvereinbarungen über finanzwirtschaftliche Ziele hinaus. In: Controller Magazin 1999 (1), S. 13-17.

Freeman, John H. (1982): Organizational Life Cycles and Natural Selection Processes. In: Staw, Barry/Cummings, Larry (Hg.): Research in Organizational Behavior. Greenwich, CT: JAI-Press.

Freeman, John/Hannan, Michael (1975): Growth and Decline Processes in Organizations. In: ASR 40, S. 215-228.

Frehr, Hans-Ulrich (1994): Total-quality-Management: unternehmensweite Qualitätsverbesserung; ein Praxis-Leitfaden für Führungskräfte. München: Hanser.

Frese, Erich (1992): Organisationstheorie: Historische Entwicklung – Ansätze – Perspektiven. Wiesbaden: Gabler.

Fricke, Reiner (2000): Qualitätsbeurteilung durch Kriterienkataloge: Auf der Suche nach validen Vorhersagemodellen. In: Schenkel, Peter/Tergan, Sigmar-Olaf/Lottmann, Alfred: Qualitätsbeurteilung multimedialer Lern- und Informationssysteme. Nürnberg: Verlag Bildung und Wissen, S.75-88.

Friedag, Herwig R. (1998): Die Balanced Scorecard – Alter Wein in neuen Schläuchen? In: Controller Magazin 1998 (4), S. 291-294.

Friedag, Herwig R./Schmidt, Walter (2004): Balanced Scorecard. Planegg: Haufe (2., aktual. Ausgabe).

Friedl, Birgit (2003): Controlling. Stuttgart: Lucius & Lucius [u.a.].

Friedrichs, Jürgen (1973): Methoden empirischer Sozialforschung. Hamburg: Rowohlt.

Friedrichs, Jürgen/Kamp, Klaus (1978): Methodologische Probleme des Konzepts „Lebenszyklus". In: Kohli, Martin (Hg.): Soziologie des Lebenslaufs. Darmstadt u.a.: Luchterhand.

Fuchs-Heinritz, Werner (1990): Biographische Studien zur Jugendphase. In: Mayer, Karl Ulrich (Hg.): Lebensverläufe und Sozialer Wandel. (Sonderheft der Kölner Zeitschrift für Soziologie und Sozialpsychologie). Opladen: Westdeutscher Verlag.

Fuhr (1998): Qualitätsmanagement im Bildungssektor. In: Hochschulrektorenkonferenz: Qualitätsmanagement in der Lehre. Bonn: Hochschulrektorenkonferenz, S. 47-67.

Gabler, Theo (Hg.) (1994): Wirtschaftslexikon. Wiesbaden: Gabler.

Galbraith, Jay (1973): Designing Complex Organizations. Reading, Mass.: Addison-Wesley.

Garms, Silke (2000): Qualitätsmanagement in sozialen Projekten: Chancen und Risiken von Qualitätsentwicklung. Berlin: RosenholzVerlag.

Garvin, David A. (1984): What does ‚Product Quality' really mean? In: Sloan Management Review. S. 25-43.

Gaschler, Christine (2002): Qualitätsmanagement in sozialen Dienstleistungsunternehmen unter dem Fokus der Mitarbeiterzufriedenheit. Frankfurt a.M.: Hochschulschrift.

Gebert, Alfred J./Kneubühler, Hans-Ulrich (2001): Qualitätsbeurteilung und Evaluation der Qualitätssicherung in Pflegeheimen: Plädoyer für ein gemeinsames Lernen. Bern: Huber.

German Federal Statistical Office (Hg.) (2004): Datenreport 2004. Bonn: Statistisches Bundesamt. http://www.destatis.de/datenreport/d_datend.htm.

Gerlich, Petra (1999): Controlling von Bildung, Evaluation oder Bildungs-Controlling? Überblick, Anwendung und Implikationen einer Aufwand-Nutzen-Betrachtung von Bildung unter besonderer Berücksichtigung wirtschafts- und sozialpsychologischer Aspekte am Beispiel akademischer Nachwuchskräfte in Banken. München: Hampp.

Geschka, H. (1974): Innovationsideen: Ihre Herkunft und die Technik ihrer gezielten Hervorbringung. In: Meissner, H.G./Kroll, H.A. (Hg.): Management technologischer Innovationen. Pullach: Verlag Dokumentation.

George, Clive/Kirkpatrick, Colin (2003): A Practical Guide to Strategic Impact Assessment for Enterprise Development. University of Manchester: Institute for Development Policy and Management.

Giebenhain, Dagmar (2005): Evaluation in Entwicklungsvorhaben. In: Berufsbildung. Bd. 91/92, Jg. 59, S. 55-56.

Gillwald, Katrin (2000): Konzepte sozialer Innovation. Veröffentlichungsreihe der Querschnittsgruppe Arbeit und Ökologie beim Präsidenten des Wissenschaftszentrum Berlin für Sozialforschung. Nr. P00-519. Berlin: Wissenschaftszentrum Berling für Sozialforschung GmbH (WZB).

Gissel-Palkovich, Ingrid (2002): Total Quality Management in der Jugendhilfe? Von der Qualitätssicherung zur umfassenden Qualitätsentwicklung in der Sozialen Arbeit. In: Pädagogik: Forschung und Wissenschaft. Bd. 2. Münster: Lit.

Glagow, Manfred (Hg.) (1990): Deutsche und internationale Entwicklungspolitik. Zur Rolle staatlicher, supranationaler und nicht-regierungsabhängiger Organisationen im Entwicklungsprozeß der Dritten Welt. Opladen: Westdeutscher Verlag.

Glagow, Manfred (1992): Die Nicht-Regierungsorganisation in der internationalen Entwicklungszusammenarbeit. In: Nohlen, Dieter/Nuscheler, Franz (Hg.): Handbuch der Dritten Welt. Bonn: Dietz (3., überarb. Auflage), S. 304-326.

Glatzer, Wolfgang/Zapf, Wolfgang (Hg.) (1984): Lebensqualität in der Bundesrepublik. Objektive Lebensbedingungen und subjektives Wohlbefinden. Frankfurt a.M.: Campus.

Glowalla, U./Schoop, E. (1992): Entwicklung und Evaluation computerunterstützter Lehrsysteme. In: Glowalla, U./Schoop, E. (Hg.): Hypertext und Multimedia: Neue Wege in der computerunterstützten Aus- und Weiterbildung. Berlin/Heidelberg: Springer, S. 21-38.

Glowalla, U. (1992): Evaluation computerunterstützten Lernens. In: Glowalla, U./Schoop, E. (Hg.): Hypertext und Multimedia: Neue Wege in der computerunterstützten Aus- und Weiterbildung. Berlin/Heidelberg: Springer, S. 39-40.

Gohl, Eberhard (2000): Prüfen und lernen: praxisorientierte Handreichung zur Wirkungsbeobachtung und Evaluation. Bonn: VENRO.

Grabatin, Günther (1981): Effizienz von Organisationen. Berlin u.a.: de Gruyter.

Gramlich, Edward M. (1990): A Guide to Benefit-Cost Analysis. Ebglewood Cliffs, NJ: Prentice Hall.

Greenberg, David H./Appenzeller, Ute (1998): Cost Analysis Step by Step: A How-to Guide for Planners and Providers of Welfare-to-Work and Other Employment and Training Programs. New York: Manpower Demonstration Research Corporation.

Greiling, Michael (2001): Die Balanced Scorecard. In Diensberg, Christop/Krekel, Elisabeth M./Schobert, Berthold (Hg.): Balanced Scorecard und House of Quality: Impulse für die Evaluation in Weiterbildung und Personalentwicklung. Schriftenreihe des Bundesinstituts für Berufsbildung 53. Bonn: BIBB, S. 9-20.

Greiling, Michael (1998): Das Innovationssystem – Eine Analyse zur Innovationsfähigkeit von Unternehmungen. Frankfurt a.M.: Lang.

Greinert, Wolf-Dietric/Heitmann, Werner/Stockmann, Reinhard (Hg.) (1996): Ansätze betriebsbezogener Ausbildungsmodelle. Beispiele aus dem islamisch-arabischen Kulturkreis. Berlin: Overall-Verlag.

Greinert, Wolf-Dietrich/Heitmann, Werner/Stockmann, Reinhard/West, Brunhilde (Hg.) (1997): Vierzig Jahre Berufsbildungszusammenarbeit mit Ländern der Dritten Welt. Die Föderung der beruflichen Bildung in den Entwicklungsländern am Wendepunkt? Baden-Baden: Nomos.

Greulich, Andreas (2002): Balanced Scorecard im Krankenhaus: von der Planung bis zur Umsetzung. Heidelberg: Economica-Verlag.

Grieble, Oliver (2004): Modellgestütztes Dienstleistungsbenchmarking. Lohmar/Köln: Eul.

Grochla, Erwin (Hg.) (1978): Einführung in die Organisationstheorie. Stuttgart: Poeschel.

Groh, Peter E. (2004): Kosten-Nutzen-Analyse als Instrument des Qualitätsmanagements. Kissing: WEKA-Media.

Grupp, Michael (1979): Science and Ignorance. In: Nowotny, H./Rose, H. (Hg.): Counter-Movements in the Sciences. Dordrecht: Reidel.

Grupp, Hariolf/Schmoch, Ulrich (1995): Beschreibung und Erklärung innovationsgerechter Vorgänge. In: Technik und Gesellschaft. Jahrbuch 8: Theoriebausteine der Techniksoziologie. Frankfurt a.M.: Campus, S. 227-243.

GTZ (2004): Qualitätsbericht GTZ China EFQM-Zyklus 2003/2004. Eschborn: GTZ.

GTZ (2003): Orientierung auf Wirkung ist das gemeinsame Thema von vier aktuellen Reformen. Eschborn: GTZ.

GTZ (2002): Die Anwendung des „EFQM-Modells for Excellence" in der GTZ. Informationspapier. Eschborn:GTZ.

GTZ (1999): Wegweiser für die Projektfortschrittskontrolle (PFK). Eschborn: GTZ.

GTZ (HG.) (1999): Bericht zur 5. Querschnittsanalyse. Wirkungsbeobachtung von den in den Jahren 1993 bis 1997 laufenden und abgeschlossenen TZ-Vorhaben. Teil 1 und 2. Eschborn: GTZ.

Guba, Egon G./Stufflebeam, Daniel L. (1968): Evaluation: The Process of Stimulating, Aiding and Abetting Insightful Action. Bloomington, Ind.: Measurement and Evaluation Center in Reading Education, Indiana University.

Gucanin, Ane (2003): Total Quality Management mit dem EFQM-Modell: Verbesserungspotentiale erkennen und für den Unternehmenserfolg nutzen. Berlin: uni-edition.

Guhl, Martin (1998): Total Quality Management im Dienstleistungsbereich. Bad Urbach: Verl. Inst. für Arbeitsorganisation.

Habersam, Michael (1997): Controlling als Evaluation – Potentiale eines Perspektivenwechsels. München und Mering: Rainer Hampp.

Hage, Gerald/Aiken, Michael (1969): Routine Technology, Social Structure, and Organization Goals. In: ASQ. Vol 14, S. 366-376.

Hagestad, Gunhild (1990): Social Perspectives on the Life Course. In: Binstock, R./George, L. (Hg.): Handbook of Aging and the Social Sciences. New York: Academic Press.

Haindl, Maria (2003): ‚Total Quality Management' in Schulen: Ein Modell für die Evaluation von Schulqualität? Innsbruck: Studienverlag.

Halfar, Bernd (1987): Nicht-intendierte Handlungsfolgen. Stuttgart: Enke.

Hall, R.H. (1980): Closed-System, Open-System, and Contingency-Choice Perspectives. In: Etzioni, A./Lehman, E.W. (Hg.): A Sociological Reader on Complex Organizations. New York: Holt, Rinehart & Winston.

Hamschmidt, Jost (2001): Die Wirksamkeit von UMS nach ISO 14001 in Schweizer Unternehmen. Ergebnisse einer empirischen Untersuchung. Wien: Universität St. Gallen.

Hannan, Michael T./Freeman, John (1977): The Population Ecology of Organisations. In: American Journal of Sociology 82, S. 929-964.

Hannan, Michael T./Freeman, John (1988a): Density Dependence in the Growth of Organizational Populations. In: Carroll, G.R. (Hg.): Ecological Models of Organizations. Cambridge, MA: Ballinger.

Hannan, Michael T./Freeman, John (1988b): The Ecology of Organizational Mortality: American Labor Unions 1836-1985. In: American Journal of Sociology 94, S. 25-52.

Hannan, Michael T./Freeman, John (1989): Organizational Ecology. Cambridge, MA: Harvard University Press.

Hansen, Wolfgang/Kamiske, Gerd F. (Hg.) (2003): Qualitätsmanagement im Dienstleistungsbereich: Assessment – Sicherung – Entwicklung. Düsseldorf: Symposion.

Hanusch, Horst (1994): Kosten-Nutzen-Analyse. München: Vahlen (2., überarb. Auflage).

Härtel, Michael/Stockmann, Reinhard/Gaus, Hansjörg (Hg.) (2000): Berufliche Umweltbildung und Umweltberatung. Grundlagen, Konzepte und Wirkungsmessung. Bielefeld: Bertelsmann-Verlag.

Hartwich, Hans Hermann (Hg.) (1985): Policy-Forschung in der Bundesrepublik Deutschland. Ihr Selbstverständnis und ihr Verhältnis zu den Grundfragen der Politikwissenschaft. Opladen: Westdeutscher Verlag.

Haubrich, Karin; Lüders, Christian (2004a): Evaluation – hohe Erwartungen und ungeklärte Fragen. Sozialwissenschaftlicher Fachinformationsdienst: Jugendforschung 2004. Bd. 1, S. 9-15.

Haubrich, Karin; Lüders, Christian (2004b): Evaluation – mehr als ein Modewort? Recht der Jugend und des Bildungswesens, 3/2004, S. 316-337.

Hauff, Volker (Hg.) (1987): Unsere gemeinsame Zukunft. Der Brundtland-Bericht der Weltkommission für Umwelt und Entwicklung. Greven: Eggenkamp-Verlag.

Hauschildt, Jürgen (1980): Zielsysteme. In: Handwörterbuch der Organisation. Stuttgart: Poeschel, S. 2419ff.

Hauschildt, Jürgen/Hamel, Winfried (1978): Empirische Forschung zur Zielbildung in Organisationen – auf dem Weg in eine methodische Sackgasse. In: Hamburger Jahrbuch für Wirtschafts- und Gesellschaftspolitik 23, S. 237-250.

Heckhausen, Jutta (1990): Erwerb und Funktion normativer Vorstellungen über den Lebenslauf. Ein entwicklungspsychologischer Beitrag zur sozio-psychischen Konstruktion von Biographien. In: Mayer, Karl Ulrich (Hg.): Lebensverläufe und Sozialer Wandel. (Sonderheft der Kölner Zeitschrift für Soziologie und Sozialpsychologie). Opladen: Westdeutscher Verlag.

Heiner, Maja (Hg.) (1996): Qualitätsentwicklung durch Evaluation. Freiburg i.B.: Lambertus.

Heinrich, Tina/Meyer, Wolfgang (2005): Entwicklung eines Monitoring-Systems für die politische Weiterbildung – Ansatz und Erfahrungen am Beispiel des Bildungszentrums Kirkel. In: Zeitschrift für Evaluation 3 (2), S. 271-291.

Heinrich, Werner M. (1996): Einführung in das Qualitätsmanagement. Eichstätt: Brönner & Daentler.

Heinz, Walter R. (1995): Arbeit, Beruf und Lebenslauf: eine Einführung in die berufliche Sozialisation. Weinheim/München: Juventa-Verlag.

Heise, Maren/Stockmann, Reinhard (2003): Evaluationsstudie zum DAAD-Förderprogramm „Nachbetreuung ehemaliger Studierender aus Entwicklungsländern". Teilbericht: Methodische Konzeption und Alumni Survey. Saarbrücken.

Heise, Maren/Stockmann, Reinhard (2004): Nachbetreuung ehemaliger Studierender aus Entwicklungsländern. Teilbericht: Methodische Konzeption und Ergebnisse des Alumni Surveys. In: DAAD (Hg.): Programmstudie. Nachbetreuung ehemaliger Studierender aus Entwicklungsländern. Bonn: DAAD.

Heller, Robert (1993): The quality makers: TQM. Zürich/Schweiz: Orell Füssli

Hellstern, Gerd-Michael/Wollmann, Hellmut (1980a): Evaluierung in der öffentlichen Verwaltung – Zweck und Anwendungsfelder. In: Verwaltung und Fortbildung. S. 61 ff.

Hellstern, Gerd-Michael/Wollmann, Helmut (Hg.) (1984): Handbuch zur Evaluierungsforschung. Bd. 1. Opladen: Westdeutscher Verlag.

Henderson, Hazel (1988): The Politics of the Solar Age. Alternatives to Economics. Indianapolis: Knowledge Systems.

Hennemann, Carola (1997): Organisationales Lernen und die lernende Organisation: Entwicklung eines praxisbezogenen Gestaltungsvorschlags aus ressourcenorientierter Sicht. München u.a.: Hampp.

Hens, L./Nath, Bhaskar (2003): The Johannesburg Conference. In: Environment, Development and Sustainability 5, S. 7-39.

Héritier, Andrienne (Hg.) (1993): Policy-Analyse. Kritik und Neuorientierung (PVS-Sonderheft 24). Opladen: Westdeutscher Verlag.

Herlth, Alois/Strohmeier, Klaus Peter (1989): Lebenslauf und Familienentwicklung: Mikroanalysen des Wandels familialer Lebensformen. Opladen: Leske + Budrich.

Heß, Martin (1997): TQM-Kaizen-Praxisbuch: Qualitätszirkel und verwandte Gruppen im Total-quality-Management. Köln: Verl. TÜV Rheinland.

Hesse, Joachim J./Ellwein, Thomas (2004): Das Regierungssystem der BRD. Berlin: de Gruyter Recht und Politik (9., vollst. neu bearb. Auflage).

Heuß, Ernst (1965): Allgemeine Markttheorie. Tübingen: St. Galler wirtschaftswissenschaftliche Forschungen.

Hickson, David J. u.a. (1971): A Strategic Contingencies' Theory of Interorganizational Powers. In: Administrative Science Quaterly 16, S. 216-229.

Hill, Wilhelm u.a. (1974): Konzeption einer modernen Organisationslehre. In: Zeitschrift für Organisation.

Hill, Hermann (Hg.) (1997): Die kommunikative Organisation. Change Management und Vernetzung in öffentlichen Verwaltungen. Köln u.a.: Carl Heymanns.

Hiller, Petra (2005): Organisationswissen: Eine wissenssoziologische Neubeschreibung der Organisation. Wiesbaden: VS-Verlag.

Hillmert, Steffen (2001): Ausbildungssysteme und Arbeitsmarkt: Lebensverläufe in Großbritannien und Deutschland im Kohortenvergleich. Opladen: Westdeutscher Verlag.

Hochschulrektorenkonferenz (Hg.) (1998): Qualitätsmanagement in der Lehre. TQL 98. Beiträge zur Hochschulpolitik 1998 (5). Bonn.

Hoeth, Ulrike/Schwarz, Wolfgang (2002): Qualitätstechniken für die Dienstleistung: die D7. München: Hanser.

Hoffmann, Werner H./Niedermayr, Rita/Risak, Johann (1996): Führungsergänzung durch Controlling. In: Eschenbach, Rolf (Hg.): Controlling. Stuttgart: Schäffer-Poeschel Verlag, S. 3-49.

Hoitsch, Hans-Jörg/Lingnau, Volker (2004): Kosten- und Erlösrechnung: Eine controllingorientierte Einführung. Berlin: Springer.

Holenstein, Hildegard (1999): Fähig werden zur Selbstevaluation: Erfahrungsberichte und Orientierungshilfen. Chur/Zürich: Rüegger.

Holla, Bernd (2002): Qualitätsentwicklung in der Weiterbildung durch praxisorientierte Evaluation. Frankfurt a.M. u.a.: Lang.

Holtappels, Heinz Günter (2003): Schulqualität durch Schulentwicklung und Evaluation. München: Luchterhand.

Horak, Christian (1997): Management von NPOs. In: Badelt, Christoph (Hg.): Handbuch der Nonprofit Organisation. Stuttgart: Schäffer-Poeschel , S. 123-134.

Horak, Christian (1998): Zukünftiger Entwicklungsbedarf an Instrumenten in NPOs. In: Eschenbach, Rolf (Hg.): Führungsinstrumente für die Nonprofit Organisatin

Horak, Christian (1999): Controlling in Nonprofit-Organisationen: Erfolgsfaktoren und Instrumente. Wiesbaden: DUV (2. Auflage, Nachdruck).

Horak, Christian/Matul, C./Scheuch, F. (2002): Ziele und Strategien von NPOs. In: Badelt, Christoph (Hg.): Handbuch der Nonprofit Organisation. Stuttgart: Schäfer-Poeschel, S. 197-224.

Horbach, Andreas (2000): Strategien zur Umsetzung von Total Quality Management bei Non-Profit-Dienstleistern. Hochschulschrift. Chemnitz: Technische Universität.

Horváth, Peter (2002): CotrollingMünchen: Vahlen (8., vollst. überarb. Auflage).

Horváth, Peter (1996): Controlling. München: Vahlen (6. Auflage).

Horváth, Peter/Gaiser, B. (2000): Implementierungsverfahren mit der Balanced Scorecard im deutschen Sprachraum – Anstöße zur konzeptionellen Weiterentwicklung. In: Betriebswirtschaftliche Forschung und Praxis 2000 (1), S. 17-35.

Horváth, Peter/Kaufmann, L. (1998): Balanced Scorecard – Ein Werkzeug zur Umsetzung von Strategien. In: Harvard Business Manager 1998 (5), S. 39-48.

Horváth & Partners (2004): Balanced Scorecard umsetzen. Stuttgart: Schäffer-Poeschel (3., vollst. überarb. Auflage).

HRK (2005): Qualität messen – Qualität managen: Leistungsparameter in der Hochschulentwiclung. Projekt Qualitätssicherung. Beiträge zur Hochschulpolitik 2005 (6). Bonn: Hochschulrektorenkonferenz.

HRK (2004a): Metaevaluation. Evaluation von Studium und Lehre auf dem Prüfstand: Zwischenbilanz und Konsequenzen für die Zukunft. Projekt Qualitätssicherung. Beiträge zur Hochschulpolitik 2004 (5). Bonn: Hochschulrektorenkonferenz.

HRK (2004b): Evaluation – ein Bestandteil des Qualitätsmanagements an Hochschulen. Projekt Qualitätssicherung. Beiträge zur Hochschulpolitik 2004 (9). Bonn: Hochschulrektorenkonferenz.

Hucke, Jochen/Wollmann, Hellmut (1980): Methodenprobleme der Implementationsforschung. In: Mayntz, Renate (Hg.): Implementation politischer Programme. Königstein: Athenäum.

Huinink, Johannes (1995): Kollektiv und Eigensinn: Lebensläufe in der DDR und danach. Berlin: Akademie-Verlag.

Huninink, Johannes (1995): Warum noch Familie? Zur Attraktivität von Partnerschaft und Elternschaft in unserer Gesellschaft. Frankfurt a.M.: Campus-Verlag.

Huinink, Johannes/Wagner, Michael (1989): Regionale Lebensbedingungen, Migration und Familienbildung. In: Kölner Zeitschrift für Soziologie und Sozialpsychologie 41, S. 669-689.

Hullen, Gert (1998): Lebensverläufe in West- und Ostdeutschland. Opladen: Leske + Budrich.

Hummel, Thomas (1999): Erfolgreiches Bildungscontrolling: Praxis und Perspektiven. Heidelberg: Sauer.

Hummel, Thomas/Malorny, Christian (1997): Total Quality Management: Tipps für die Einführung. München u.a.: Hanser (2. Auflage).

Hummel, Thomas/Malorny, Christian (2002): Total Quality Management: Tipps für die Einführung. München u.a.: Hanser (3. Auflage).

Igl, Gerhard/Schiemannn, Doris/Gerste, Bettina; Klose/Joachem (Hg.) (2002): Qualität in der Pflege: Betreuung und Versorgung von pflegebedürftigen alten Menschen in der stationären und ambulanten Altenhilfe. Stuttgart: Schattauer.

International Organization for Standards: Norm DIN EN ISO 8402.

Ishikawa, Kaoru (1980): Guide to Quality Control. Tokyo: Asian Productivity Organisation

Jackson, Norman (Hg.) (2000): Benchmarking for higher education. Buckingham: Society for Research into Higher Education.

Jacoby Klaus-Peter (2002): Möglichkeiten und Grenzen von Evaluation in der Verwaltungspolitik. In: Zeitschrift für Evaluation 1 (1), S. 115-126.

Jacoby, Klaus-Peter/Hauschnik, Peter (2002): Wirkkungsmonitoring. Beispielhafte Einführung eines Monitoring- und Evaluierungssystems (M&E) in Projekten der deutschen technischen Zusammenarbeit in Mexiko. In: WBF im Dialog (6. Ausgabe).

Jacoby, Klaus-Peter/Meyer, Wolfgang/Schneider, Vera/Stockmann, Reinhard (2004): Abschlussbericht: Evaluation von Projekten der Umweltkommunikation im Handwerk, im Auftrag der DBU. Saarbrücken.

Jaedicke, Wolfgang/Thrun, Thomas/Wollmann, Hellmut (2000): Modernisierung der Kommunalverwaltung: Evaluierungsstudie zur Verwaltungsmodernisierung im Bereich Planen, Bauen und Umwelt. IFS Institut für Stadtforschung und Strukturpolitik. Stuttgart: Kohlhammer.

Jahoda, Maria/Deutsch, Morton/Cook, Stuart W. (1965): Beobachtungsverfahren. In König, René (Hg.): Beobachtung und Experiment in der Sozialforschung. Köln: Kiepenheuer & Witsch (3. Auflage), S. 77-96.

Jahns, Christopher (2003): Strategisches Benchmarking: Arbeitsbuch. Sternenfels: Verlag Wissenschaft und Praxis Dr. Brauner.

Jansen, Dorothea (2002a): Netzwerkansätze in der Organisationsforschung. In Allmendinger, Jutta/Hinz, Thomas (Hg.) Organisationssoziologie (Sonderheft 42/2002 der Kölner Zeitschrift für Soziologie und Sozialpsychologie). Wiesbaden: Westdeutscher Verlag, S. 88-118.

Jansen, Dorothea (2002b): Einführung in die Netzwerkanalyse. Grundlagen, Methoden, Anwendungen. Wiesbaden: VS-Verlag.

Jansen, Dorothea (2000): Netzwerke und soziales Kapital. Methoden zur Analyse struktureller Einbettung. In: Weyer, Johannes (Hg.): Soziale Netzwerke. Konzepte und Methoden der sozialwissenschaftlichen Netzwerkforschung. München/Wien: Oldenbourg, S. 35-62.

Jann, Werner (1994): Politikfeldanalyse. In: Nohler, Dieter/Kuz, Jürgen/Schulze, Rainer-Olaf (Hg.): Lexikon der Politik. Bd. 2: Politikwissenschaftliche Methoden. München: Beck, S. 308-314.

Jossé, Germann (2003): Basiswissen Kostenrechnung: Kostenarten, Kostenstellen, Kostenträger, Kostenmanagement. München: Deutscher Taschenbuchverlag.

Jossé, Germann (2005): Balanced Scorecard: Ziele und Strategien messbar umsetzen. München: Deutscher Taschenbuchverlag.

Jung, Hans (2003): Controlling. München: Oldenbourg.

Juran, Joseph M. (1988): Juran's quality control handbook. New York: McGraw-Hill.

Juran, Joseph M. (1951): Quality Control Handbook. New York: MacGraw-Hill.

Juran, Joseph M. (1991): Handbuch der Qualitätsplanung. Landsberg/Lech : Verl. Moderne Industrie.

Juran, Joseph M. (1999): Juran's quality handbook. New York: McGraw-Hill.

Juran, Joseph M. (1988): Juran on planning for quality. New York: Free Press.

Juran, Joseph M./Gryna, Frank M. (1993): Quality planning an analysis: from product development through use. New York: McGraw-Hill.

Käfler, Hans (2005): Qualitätsmanagement mit EFQM. In: Berufsbildung. Bd. 91/92, Jg. 59, S. 14-15.

Kamiske, Gerd F. (2003): Qualitätsmanagement: eine multimediale Einführung; mit CD-ROM „Lernprogramm Qualitätsmanagement". München u.a.: Fachbuchverlag Leipzig im Carl-Hanser-Verlag.

Kamiske, Gerd F. (Hg.) (2000): Der Weg zur Spitze: business excellence durch Totalquality-Management; der LeitfadenMünchen u.a.: Hanser (2., vollst. überarb. u. erw. Auflage).

Kaplan, R. S./Norton, D.P. (1997): Balanced Scorecard – Strategien erfolgreich umsetzen. Stuttgart: Schäffer-Poeschel.

Kasarda, John D./Bidwell, Charles E. (1984): A Human Ecological Theory of Organizational Structuring. In: Micklin, M./Choldin, H.M. (Hg.): Sociological Human Ecology. New York: Academic Press.

Kastenholz, H.G./Erdmann, K.-H./Wolff, M. (Hg.) (1996): Nachhaltige Entwicklung. Zukunftschancen für Mensch und Umwelt. Berlin/Heidelberg/New York: Springer.

Katz, Elihu/Levin, Martin L./Hamilton, Herbert (1963): Traditions of research on the diffusion of innovations. In: American Sociological Review 28, S. 237-252.

Kegelmann, Monika (1995): CERTQUA: Zertifizierung von Qualitätsmanagementsystemen nach DIN/EN/ISO 9000ff. in der beruflichen Bildung. In: Feuchthofen, Jörg E./Severing, Eckart (Hg.), 1995: Qualitätsmanagement und Qualitätssicherung in der Weiterbildung. Neuwied u.a.: Luchterhand. S. 155-178.

Kempfert, Guy; Rolff, Hans-Günter (2005): Qualität und Evaluation: ein Leitfaden für pädagogisches Qualitätsmanagement. Weinheim: Beltz.

Kieser, Alfred (1985): Entstehung und Wandel von Organisationen. Ein evolutionstheoretisches Konzept. Mannheim: Univeröffentlichtes Arbeitspapier.

Kieser, Alfred (1988): Darwin und die Folgen für die Organisationstheorie. In: Die Betriebswirtschaft 48, S. 603-620.

Kieser, Alfred (1989): Entstehung und Wandel von Organisationen. Ein evolutionstheoretisches Konzept. In: Bauer, L./Matis, H. (Hg.): Evolution – Organisation – Management. Berlin: Duncker & Humblot.

Kieser, Alfred (1993f): Der situative Ansatz. In: Kieser, Alfred (Hg.): Organisationstheorien. Stuttgart u.a.: Kohlhammer.

Kieser, Alfred (2002) (Hg.): Organisationstheorien. Stuttgart: Kohlhammer (5. Auflage).

Kieser, Alfred/Kubicek, Herbert (1992): Organisation. Berlin u.a.: de Gruyter.

Kieser, Alfred/Walgenbach, Peter (2003): Organisation. Stuttgart: Schäffer-Poeschel (4., überarb. u. erw. Auflage).

Kimberley, John R./Miles, Robert H. (1980): The Organizational Life Cycle: Issues in the Creation, Transformation, and Decline of "Organizations". San Francisco: Jossey-Bass.

Kirkpatrick, Colin/George, Clive (2003): Sustainability Impact Assessment of Proposed WTO Negotiations: Sector Studies for Market Access, Environmental Services and Competition: Final Report. University of Manchester: Institute for Development Policy and Management.

Kissling-Näf, Ingrid/Knoepfel, Peter/Marek, Daniel (1997): Lernen in öffentlichen Politiken. Basel: Helbing & Lichtenhahn.

Klages, Helmut (1998): Verwaltungsmodernisierung. „Harte" und „weiche" Aspekte II. Speyer: Forschungsinstitut für öffentliche Verwaltung bei der Deutschen Hochschule für Verwaltungswissenschaften (2. Auflage).

Klausegger, Claudia/Scharitzer, Dieter (1998a): Adjunktivität bei Dienstleistungen: die Bedeutung personenbezogener adjunktiver Güter in Bezug auf die Qualitätswahrnehmung prozeßorientierter Dienstleistungen. In: Perspektiven des Dienstleistungsmarketing. Wiesbaden: Deutscher Universitätsverlag, S. 11-22.

Klausegger, Claudia/Scharitzer, Dieter (1998b): Instrumente für das Qualitätsmanagement in NPOs. In: Eschenbach, Rolf (Hg.): Führungsinstrumente für die Nonprofit-Organisation. Stuttgart: Schäffer-Poeschel.

Knoepfel, Peter u.a. (1997): Lernen in öffentlichen Politiken. Basel/Frankfurt a.M.: Helbing und Lichtenhahn.

Koch, Christian (2003): Balanced Scorecard (BSC). In Boeßenecker, Karl-Heinz u.a. (Hg.): Qualitätskonzepte in der Sozialen Arbeit. Weinheim: Beltz, S. 15-22.

Koch, Rainer (2004a): New Public Management als Referenzmodell für Verwaltungsmodernisierungen. In: Strohmer, Michael F. (Hg.): Management im Staat. Frankfurt a.M.: Lang.

Koch, Rainer (2004b): Umbau öffentlicher Dienste: internationale Trends in der Anpassung öffentlicher Dienste an ein New Public Management. Wiesbaden: Deutscher Universitäts-Verlag.

Kohler-Koch, Beate (1991): Inselillusion und Interdependenz: Nationales Regieren unter den Bedingungen von „international governance". In: Blanke, Bernhard/Wollmann, Hellmut (Hg.): Die alte Bundesrepublik. Opladen: Westdeutscher Verlag, S. 45-67.

Kohli, Martin (1978b): Erwartungen an eine Soziologie des Lebenslaufs. In: Kohli, Martin (Hg.): Soziologie des Lebenslaufs. Darmstadt u.a.: Luchterhand.

Kohli, Martin (Hg.) (1978a): Soziologie des Lebenslaufs. Darmstadt u.a.: Luchterhand.

Kohli, Martin (1985): Die Institutionalisierung des Lebenslaufs: Historische Befunde und theoretische Argumente. In: Kölner Zeitschrift für Soziologie und Sozialpsychologie 37, S. 1-29.

Kohli, Martin/Künemund, Harald (Hg.) (2000): Die zweite Lebenshälfte: gesellschaftliche Lage und Partizipation im Spiegel des Alters-Surveys. Opladen: Leske + Budrich.

Konietzka, Dirk (1999): Ausbildung und Beruf. Die Geburstjahrgänge 1919-1961 auf dem Weg von der Schule in das Erwachsenenleben. Opladen: Westdeutscher Verlag.

König, René (Hg.) (1972): Handbuch der empirischen Sozialforschung. Stuttgart: Enke.

Kortman, Walter (1995): Diffusion, Marktentwicklung und Wettbewerb: Eine Untersuchung über die Bestimmungsgründe zu Beginn des Ausbreitungsprozesses technologischer Produkte. Frankfurt a.M.: Europäische Hochschulschriften.

Koschatzky, K./Zenker, A. (1999): Innovationen in Ostdeutschland – Merkmale, Defizite, Potenziale. Ausarbeitung für das Bundesministerium für Bildung und Forschung im

Rahmen der Vorarbeiten zum Förderprogramm „InnoRegio". Arbeitspapier Regionalforschung 17. Karlsruhe: Frauenhoferinstitut für Systemtechnik und Innovationsforschung.

Kraemer-Fieger, Sabine (Hg.) (1996): Qualitätsmanagement in Non-Profit-Organisationen: Beispiele, Normen, Anforderungen, Funktionen, Formblätter. Wiesbaden: Gabler.

Krämer, Walter (1994): So überzeugt man mit Statistik. Frankfurt: Campus.

Krapp, Stefanie (2003): Synoptic Analysis of Dual Training System (DTS): Monitoring and Evaluation Results. Desk Study for the TESDA-GTZ-Project in the Philippines. Saarbrücken.

Krapp, Stefanie (2005): Auftragsklärung und prozessbegleitende Abstimmung bei Evaluationen. In: Berufsbildung. Bd. 91/92, Jg. 59, S. 57-59.

Krapp, Stefanie/Gräber, Christian (2002): TESDA/GTZ-Project "Expansion of Dual Education and Training in the Philippines". Results of the 2nd Survey Phase. Saarbrücken.

Krapp, Stefanie/Meiers, Ralph/Stockmann, Reinhard (2004): eBUt – eLearning in der Bewegungs- und Trainingswissenschaft. Evaluationsbericht. Saarbrücken.

Kreutzberg, Joachim (2000): Qualitätsmanagement auf dem Prüfstand. Universität Zürich: Dissertation.

Krönes, Gerhard (2001): Die balanced scorecard als Managementinstrument für Nonprofit-Organisationen. Weingarten: Fachhochschule Ravensburg-Weingarten.

Kromey, Helmut (2002): Empirische Sozialforschung: Modelle und Methoden der standardisierten Datenerhebung und Datenauswertung. Opladen: Leske + Budrich.

Kromphardt, Jürgen/Teschner, Manfred (1986): Neuere Entwicklung der Innovationstheorie. In: Vierteljahreshefte zur Wirtschaftsforschung. S. 235-248.

Kromrey, Helmut (1986): Empirische Sozialforschung. Modelle und Methoden der Datenerhebung und Datenverarbeitung. Opladen: Leske + Budrich.

Kromrey, Helmut (2001): Evaluation – Ein vielschichtiges Konzept. Begriff und Methodik von Evaluierung und Evaluationsforschung. Empfehlungen für die Praxis. In: Sozialwissenschaften und Berufspraxis 24 (2), S. 105-31.

Kromrey, Helmut/Meyer, Wolfgang/Stockmann, Reinhard (2002): Beiträge zur Evaluationsforschung auf dem 31. Kongress der Deutschen Gesellschaft für Soziologie in Leipzig vom 7.-11.10.2002. In: Zeitschrift für Evaluation 1 (2), S. 317-326

Kubicek, Herbert (1981): Unternehmensziele, Zielkonflikte und Zielbildungsprozesse. Kontroversen und offene Fragen in einem Kernbereich betriebswirtschaftlicher Theoriebildung. In: WiSt 10, S. 458-466.

Kückmann-Metschies, Hedwig (2001): Total-Quality-Management: Ein Weg zur Qualitätssicherung an Fachhochschulen für Sozialpädagogik? In: Dortmunder Beiträge zur Pädagogik 28. Bochum: Projekt-Verlag.

Kuhlmann, Christian (1997): Diffusion von Informationstechnik. Wiesbaden: Gabler.

Kuhlmann, Sabine/Bogumil, Jörg/Wollmann, Hellmut (Hg.) (2004): Leistungsmessung und -vergleich in Politik und Verwaltung: Konzepte und Praxis. In: Stadtforschung aktuell 96. Wiesbaden: Verlag für Sozialwissenschaften.

Kuhlmann, Stefan/Holland, Doris (1995): Evaluation von Technologiepolitik in Deutschland. Konzepte, Anwendung, Perspektiven. Heidelberg: Physika.

Küpper, Hans-Ulrich (Hg.) (1990): Unternehmensführung und Controlling. Wiesbaden: Gabler.

Küpper, Hans-Ulrich/Weber, Jürgen/Zünd, André (1990): Zum Verständnis und Selbstverständnis des Controlling: Thesen zur Konsensbildung. In: Zeitschrift für Betriebswirtschaft.

Kürzl, Albert (1989): Qualität und Qualitätsmanagement. Aus der Praxis für die Praxis. Berlin: Walter de Gruyter.

Lachenmann, Gudrun (1987): Soziale Implikationen und Auswirkungen der Basisgesundheitspolitik. In: Schwefel, D. (Hg.): Soziale Wirkungen von Projekten in der Dritten Welt. Baden-Baden: Nomos.

Landsberg, Georg von/Weiß, Reinhold (Hg.) (1995): Bildungs-Controlling. Stuttgart: Schäffer-Poeschel.

Landwehr, Norbert (2005): Qualität durch Evaluation und Entwicklung. In: Berufsbildung. Bd. 91/92, Jg. 59, S. 20-22.

Lang, Christian (2000): Qualitätssicherung und Qualitätsmanagement in der Weiterbildung – systemisches Denken als Alternative? Lüneburg: Hochschulschrift.

Lange, Elmar (1983): Zur Entwicklung und Methodik der Evaluationsforschung in der Bundesrepublik Deutschland. In: Zeitschrift für Soziologie 12 (3), S. 253-270.

Langguth, Heike (1994): Strategisches Controlling. Ludwigsburg: Verl. Wiss. und Praxis.

Langnickel, Hans (2003): Das EFQM-Modell für Excellence – Der Europäische Qualitätspreis. In: Boeßenecker, Karl-Heinz: Qualitätskonzepte in der sozialen Arbeit. Weinheim: Beltz.

Langthaler, Silvia (2002): Mehrdimensionale Erfolgssteuerung in der Kommunalverwaltung: konzeptionelle und praktische Überlegungen zum Einsatz der Balanced Scorecard im kommunalen Management. Linz: Trauner.

Lawrence, Paul R./Lorsch, Jay W. (1967): Differentiation and Integration in Complex Organizations. In: ASQ 12, S. 1-47.

Lawrence, Paul R./Lorsch, Jay W. (1969): Organization and Environment. Homewood, Ill.: Irwin.

Lauterbach, Wolfgang (1994): Berufsverläufe von Frauen. Erwerbstätigkeit, Unterbrechung und Wiedereintritt. Frankfurt a.M.: Campus-Verlag.

Lee, B. (2004). Theories of Evaluation. In: R. Stockmann (Hg.), Evaluationsforschung. Grundlagen und ausgewählte Forschungsfelder. Opladen: Leske + Budrich (2. Aufl.), S. 135-173.

Leicht, René/Stockmann, Reinhard (1997): Qualifikation in kleinen Betrieben Thailands. Ein Modell für die partizipative Erhhebung und Auswertung von Daten. Berlin: Overall-Verlag.

Leidig, Guido/Sommerfeld, Rita (2003): Balanced-Scorecard-Handbuch. Wuppertal: TAW-Verlag.

Lewan, Lillemor/Simmons, Craig (2001): The Use of Ecological Footprint and Biocapacity Analyses as Sustainability Indicators for Subnational Geographical Areas: A Recommended Way Forward. Abschlussbericht des European Common Indicators Project EUROCITIES vom 27. August 2001. Online verfügbar unter http://www.bestfoodforward.com/downloads.

Levin, Henry M./McEvan, Patrick J. (2001): Cost-Effectiveness-Analysis: Methods and Applications. Thousand Oaks: Sage.

Lewin, H.Y./Minton, J.W. (1986): Determing Organizational Effectiveness. In: Management Science 32, S. 514ff.

Liebald, Christiane (2003): Das Qualitätsmodell für dezentrale Weiterbildungsinstitutionen und ihre Landesorganisationen. Mainz: Evangelische Landesarbeitsgemeinschaft für Erwachsenenbildung.

Lienhard, Andreas (2005): 10 Jahre New Public Management in der Schweiz: Bilanz, Irrtümer, Erfolgsfaktoren. Bern: Haupt.

Light, Paul C. (2004): Sustaining Nonprofit Performance: The Case for Capacity Building and the Evidence to Support it. Washington: Brookings Institution Press.

Linz, Manfred (2004), Weder Mangel noch Übermaß. Über Suffizienz und Suffizienzforschung, Wuppertal: Wuppertal Institut (Wuppertal Papers 145, im Internet unter: http://www.wupperinst.org/Publikationen/WP/WP145.pdf).

Luckey, James W. u.a. (1984): Archival Data in Program Evaluation and Policy Analysis. In: Evaluation Studies 9, S. 300-307.

Ludwig, Martina/Koglin, Ebba (2003): eBuT-Projektevaluation. In: dsv-Informationen, Vierteljahresschrift der Deutschen Vereinigung für Sportwissenschaft, 18. Jg. Hamburg: Deutsche Vereinigung für Sportwissenschaft.

Maelicke, Bernd (Hg.) (1997): Qualität und Kosten sozialer Dienstleistungen. Baden-Baden: Nomos.

Mai, Diethard (1993): Nachhaltigkeit und Ressourcennutzung. In: Stockmann, Reinhard/Gaebe, Wolf (Hg.): Hilft die Entwicklungshilfe langfristig? Bestandsaufnahme zur Nachhaltigkeit von Entwicklungsprojekten. Opladen: Westdeutscher Verlag.

Malorny, Christian (1996): Vergleichen Sie sich mit den Besten – Benchmarks TQM-geführter Unternehmen. In: Kaminske, Gerd F. (Hg.): Rentabel durch Total-Quality-Management. München u.a.: Hanser, S. 225-257.

Malorny, Christian (1999): TQM umsetzten. Weltklasse neu definieren; Leistungsoffensive einleiten; Business Excellence erreichen. Stuttgart: Schäffer-Poeschel.

Malorny, Christian; Hummel, Thomas (1998): Total Quality Management. Tips für die Einführung. München: Hanser.

Mandl, H./Gruber, H./Renkl, A. (1997): Situiertes Lernen in multimedialen Lernumgebungen. In: Issing, L. J./Klimsa, P. (Hg.): Information und Lernen mit Multimedia, Weinheim: Psychologie Verlags Union (2., überarb. Auflage), S. 167-178.

March, James G./Olsen, Johann P. (1976): Ambiguity and Choice in Organizations. Bergen: Universitetsforlaget.

March, James G./Simon, Herbert A. (1958): Organizations. New York: John Wiley.

Martin, Lawrence L. (1993): Total Quality Management in Human Service Organizations. Newburry Park: Sage.

Marwede, Manfred (2005): Qualitätsmanagement mit DIN ISO 9001. In: Berufsbildung. Bd. 91/92, Jg. 59, S.16-19.

Masing, Walter (1998): Die Entwicklung des Qualitätsmanagements in Europa: heutiger Stand, zukünftige Herausforderungen. In: Boutellier, Roman/Masing, Walter (Hg.): Qualitätsmanagement an der Schwelle zum 21. Jahrhundert. München u.a.: Hanser, S. 19-32.

Mastronardi, Philippe (2004): New Public Management in Staat und Recht: ein Diskurs. Bern u.a.: Haupt.

Matul, Christian/Scharitzer, Dieter (2002): Qualität der Leistungen in NPOs. In: Badelt, Christoph (Hg.): Handbuch der Nonprofit-Organisation: Strukturen und Management. Stuttgart: Schäffer-Poeschel, S. 605-632.

Mayer, Elmar/Weber, Jürgen (Hg.) (1990): Handbuch Controlling. Stuttgart: Poeschel.

Mayer, Karl-Ulrich (1987): Lebenslaufforschung. In: Voges, Wolfgang (Hg.): Methoden der Biographie- und Lebenslaufforschung. Opladen: Westdeutscher Verlag.

Mayer, Karl Ulrich (1990b): Lebensverläufe und sozialer Wandel. Anmerkungen zu einem Forschungsprogramm. In: Mayer, Karl Ulrich (Hg.): Lebensverläufe und Sozialer Wandel. (Sonderheft der Kölner Zeitschrift für Soziologie und Sozialpsychologie) Opladen: Westdeutscher Verlag.

Mayer, Karl Ulrich (1996): Lebensverläufe und gesellschaftlicher Wandel: Eine Theoriekritik und eine Analyse zum Zusammenhang von Bildungs- und Geburtenentwicklung. In: Behrens, Johann/Voges, Wolfgang (Hg.): Kritische Übergänge: Statuspassagen und sozialpolitische Institutionalisierungen. Frankfurt a.M.: Campus, S. 43-72.

Mayer, Karl Ulrich (1997): Notes on a comparative political economy of life courses. In: Comparative Social Research 16, S. 203-226.

Mayer, Karl Ulrich (2001): Lebensverlauf. In: Schäfers, B./Zapf, W. (Hg.): Handwörterbuch zur Gesellschaft Deutschlands. Opladen: Leske + Budrich (2. Auflage), S. 446-460.

Mayer, Karl Ulrich/Huinink, Johannes (1990): Alters-Perioden- und Kohorteneffekte in der Analyse von Lebensverläufen oder: Lexis a de. In: Mayer, Karl Ulrich (Hg.): Lebensverläufe und sozialer Wandel. Sonderheft 31 der Kölner Zeitschrift für Soziologie und Sozialpsychologie. Opladen: Westdeutscher Verlag, S. 442-459.

Mayer, Karl Ulrich/Müller, Walter (1989): Lebensverläufe im Wohlfahrtsstaat. In Weymann, Ansgar (Hg.): Handlungsspielräume. Stuttgart: Enke, S. 41-60.

Mayländer, Franziska (2000): Qualitätsmanagement in der stationären Altenhilfe. Konstanz: Hartung-Gorre.

Mayntz, Renate (1977): Die Implementation politischer Programme: Theoretische Überlegungen zu einem neuen Forschungsgebiet. In: Die Verwaltung. S. 51ff.

Mayntz, Renate (1980c): Die Entwicklung des analytischen Paradigmas der Implementationsforschung. In: Mayntz, Renate (Hg.): Implementation politischer Programme. Königstein: Athenäum.

Mayntz, Renate (1985): Über den begrenzten Nutzen methodologischer Regeln in der Sozialforschung. In: Bonß, Wolfgang/Hartmann, Heinz (Hg.): Zur Relativität und Geltung soziologischer Forschung (Soziale Welt Sonderband 3). Göttingen: Schwartz.

Mayntz, Renate/Roghmann, Klaus/Ziegler, Rolf (1977): Handbuch der empirischen Sozialforschung, Bd. 9: Organisation, Militär. Stuttgart: Enke.

Mayntz, Renate/Ziegler, Rolf (1976): Soziologie der Organisation. In: König, René (Hg.): Handbuch der empirischen Sozialforschung, Bd. 9. Stuttgart: Enke.

McKelvey, Bill/Aldrich, Howard E. (1983): Populations, Natural Selection, and Applied Organizational Science. In: ASQ 28, S. 101-128.

McLaughlin, Kate (Hg.) (2002): New Public Management: current trends and future prospects. London: Routledge.

Mead, Margaret (1955): Cultural Patterns and Technical Change. New York: New American Library.

Meadows, Donella H./Meadows, Dennis L./Randers Jorgen/Behrens William W. (1972): The Limits of Growth: A Report for the Club of Rome's Project on the Predicament of Mankind. New York: University Press.

Meffert, Heribert/Bruhn Manfred (2000): Dienstleistungsmarketing: Grundlagen, Konzepte, Methoden. Wiesbaden: Gabler.

Meffert, Heribert/Bruhn Manfred (2003): Dienstleistungsmarketing: Grundlagen, Konzepte, Methoden. Wiesbaden: Gabler (2. Auflage).

Meister, Dorothee M. (Hg.) (2004): Evaluation von E-Learning: Zielrichtungen, methodologische Aspekte, Zukunftsperspektiven. Münster: Waxmann.

Mertens, Donna M. (1998): Research methods in education and psychology: Integrating diversity with quantitative and qualitative approaches. Thousand Oaks, CA: Sage.

Mertens, Donna M. (2004): Institutionalizing Evaluation in the United States of America. In: Stockmann, Reinhard (Hg.): Evaluationsforschung. Opladen: Leske + Budrich, S. 45-60.

Mertins, Kai (Hg.) (2004): Spezialreport Benchmarking: Leitfaden für den Vergleich mit den Besten. Düsseldorf: Symposion.

Mertins, Kai/Süssenguth, Wolfram/Jochem, Roland (1994): Modellierungsmethoden für rechnerintegrierte Produktionsprozesse: Unternehmensmodellierung, Softwareentwurf, Schnittstellendefinition, Simulation. München u.a.: Hanser.

Meulemann, Heiner (1990): Schullaufbahnen, Ausbildungskarrieren und die Folgen im Lebensverlauf. Der Beitrag der Lebenslaufforschung zur Bildungssoziologie. In: Mayer, Karl Ulrich (Hg.): Lebensverläufe und Sozialer Wandel. (Sonderheft der

Kölner Zeitschrift für Soziologie und Sozialpsychologie). Opladen: Westdeutscher Verlag.

Meyer, John W.; Rowan, Brian (1977): Institutionalized Organisations: Formal Structures as Myth and Ceremony. In: American Journal of Sociology. Vol 83. S. 340-363.

Meyer, Katharina (Hg.) (2002): Nonprofit-Management auf dem Prüfstand: Konzepte – Strategien – Lösungen. Frankfurt a.M. u.a.: Lang.

Meyer, Wolfgang (2000): Wegweiser zur „nachhaltigen" Gesellschaft? Die Evaluationspraxis im Umweltbereich. Vortrag in der Ad-hoc-Gruppe" Gute Gesellschaft gestalten: Der Beitrag von Evaluationen" am Soziologie-Kongress 26.09.2000 in Köln. Vortragsmanuskript. Saarbrücken: Universität des Saarlandes.

Meyer, Wolfgang (2002): Was ist Evaluation. CEval-Arbeitspapier No. 5. http://www.ceval.de/

Meyer Wolfgang (2002a): Regulating Environmental Action of Non-Governmental Actors. The impact of communication support programs in Germany. In: Biermann, F./Brohm, R./Dingwerth, K. (Hg.): Global Environmental Change and the Nation State: Proceedings of the 2001 Berlin Conference of the Human Dimensions of Global Environmental Change. Potsdam: Potsdam Institute for Climate Impact Research (forthcoming).

Meyer, Wolfgang (2002b): Sociology Theory and Evaluation Research. An Application and its Usability for Evaluation Sustainable Development. Paper presented on EASY-Eco-Conference, Vienna 23.-25.05.02 (als download unter der Internetadresse http://www.ceval.de zu finden).

Meyer, Wolfgang (2005): Wie zukunftsfähig ist die deutsche Zivilgesellschaft? Zur Umsetzung des Leitbildes nachhaltiger Entwicklung in deutschen Interessenorganisationen. Habilitationsschrift. Saarbrücken: Universität des Saarlandes.

Meyer, Wolfgang/Jacoby, Klaus-Peter/Stockmann, Reinhard (2003): Umweltkommunikation in Verbänden: Von der Aufklärungsarbeit zur institutionellen Steuerung nachhaltiger Entwicklung. In: Linne, Gudrun/Schwarz, Michael (Hg.): Ein Handbuch für nachhaltige Entwicklung. Opladen: Leske + Budrich.

Meyer, Wolfgang/Stockmann, Reinhard (2005): Evaluation. In: Michelsen, Gerd/ Godemann, Jasmin (Hg.): Handbuch Nachhaltigkeitskommunikation. München: Oekom.

Meyer-Krahmer, Frieder (1997): „Innovation und Nachhaltigkeit." In: Ökologisches Wirtschaften – IÖW/VÖW Informationsdienst 11 (1), S. 20-22.

Meyer-Krahmer, Frieder (Hg.) (1998): Innovation and Sustainable Development. Lessons for Innovation Policies. Heidelberg: Physica.

Michels, Karin (2004): Qualitätsmanagement für Pflegeschulen: Grundlagen – Implementierung – Verfahrensanweisungen. Stuttgart: Kohlhammer.

Möller, Michael (Hg.) (2003): Effektivität und Qualität sozialer Dienstleistungen: ein Diskussionsbeitrag. Kassel: kassel university press.

Mohr, Hans-Walter (1977): Bestimmungsgründe für die Verbreitung von neuen Technologien. Berlin: Duncker & Humblot.

Morganski, Bernd (2003): Balanced-Scorecard: Funktionsweise und Implementierung. Kissing: WEKA.

Mühlenkamp, Holger (1994): Kosten-Nutzen-Analyse. München/Wien: Oldenbourg.

Mülbert, Thomas (2002): New Public Management: ein Vergleich der Diskussionen zwischen Deutschland und Großbritannien. Universität Konstanz: Diplomarbeit.

Müller, Markus/Zenz, Andreas (1996): Qulitätsmanagement und Qualitätscontrolling. In: VDI 4, S. 40-43.

Müller, Armin (2002): Controlling-Konzepte. Stuttgart: Kohlhammer.

Müller, Verena/Schienstock, Gerd (1978): Der Innovationsprozess in westeuropäischen Industrieländern. Bd. 1: Sozialwissenschaftliche Innovationstheorien. München: Ducker & Humblot.

Müller, Walter (1980): The Analysis of Life Histories: Illustrations of the Use of Life History Plots. In: Clubb, Jerome M./Scheuch, Erwin K. (Hg.): Historical Life Research. The Use of Historical and Process-Produced Data. Stuttgart: Klett.

Müller-Jentsch, Walther (2003): Organisationssoziologie. Eine Einführung. Frankfurt a.M.: Campus.

Nas, Tevfik F. (1996): Cost-Benefit Analysis: Theory and Application. Thousand Oaks: Sage.

Naschold, Frieder (1995): Ergebnissteuerung, Wettbewerb, Qualitätspolitik. Entwicklungspfade des öffentlichen Sektors in Europa. Berlin: Sigma.

Naschold, Frieder (1997): Umstrukturierung der Gemeindeverwaltung: eine international vergleichende Zwischenbilanz. In: Naschold/Oppen/Wegener (1997): Innovative Kommunen. Internationale Trends und deutsche Erfahrungen. Stuttgart: Kohlhammer, S. 15-48.

Naschold, Frieder u.a. (1998): Kommunale Spitzeninnovationen. Konzepte, Umsetzung, Wirkungen in internationaler Perspektive. Berlin: edition sigma.

Naschold, Frieder/Bogumil, Jörg (2000): Modernisierung des Staates. New Public Management in deutscher und internationaler Perspektive. Opladen: Leske + Budrich.

Naschold, Frieder/Oppen, Maria/Wegener, Alexander (1997): Innovative Kommunen. Internationale Trends und deutsche Erfahrungen. Stuttgart: Kohlhammer.

Nauck, Bernhard/Schönpflug, Ute (1997): Familien in verschiedenen Kulturen. Stuttgart: Enke.

Nauendorf, Wolfgang (2004): Total Quality Management als Vertrauensmanagement. Mering: Hampp.

Neubert, Susanne (1998): Die soziale Wirkungsanalyse. Ein Beitrag zur Methodendiskussion in der Entwicklungszusammenarbeit. Berlin: Deutsches Institut für Entwicklungspoltik.

Neumann, Andreas 2000: ISO 9000 in der Praxis. Eine Kosten-Nutzen-Analyse zertifizierter Qualitätsmanagementsysteme am Beispiel kleinerer und mittelständischer Betriebe. Aachen: Shaker-Verlag.

Neun, Hansjörg (1985): Projektübergabe bei der Technischen Zusammenarbeit mit Entwicklungsländern.: Maro-Verlag.

Niedermayr, Rita (1996): Die Realität des Controlling. In: Eschenbach, Rolf (Hg.): Controlling. Stuttgart: Schäffer-Poeschel Verlag, S. 127-177.

Niven, Paul R. (2003): Balanced Scorecard – Schritt für Schritt: Einführung, Anpassung und Aktualisierung. Weinheim: Wiley-VCH.

Niven, Paul R. (2003): Balanced Scorecard step-by-step for government and nonprofit agencies. Hoboken: Wiley.

Nolte, Rüdiger (2005): Changemanagement in der öffentlichen Verwaltung: "Management des Wandels" – Veränderungsprozesse im Kontext der Reformbewegung des New Public Management und des neuen Steuerungsmodells. In: Verwaltungsarchiv, Zeitschrift für Verwaltungslehre, Verwaltungsrecht und Verwaltungspolitik 96, S. 243-266.

Norton, D. P.; Kappler, F. (2000): Balanced Scorecard Best Practices. Trends and Research Implications. In: Controlling 2000 (1), S. 15-21.

Nöthen, Joachim (2004): New Public Management: Aufgaben, Erfahrungen und Grenzen der Verwaltungsmodernisierung in Deutschland. In: Moldaschl, Manfred (Hg.): Reorganisation im Non-Profit-Sektor. München: Hampp.

Nowotny, Helga (1989): The Sustainability of Innovation. A preliminary reserach agenda on innovation and obsolescence. In: WZB-Schriftenreihe Nr. P89-001. Berlin: Wissenschaftszentrum Berlin für Sozialforschung.

Nowotny, Helga (1996): Über die Multiplizität des Neuen. In: Technik und Gesellschaft. Jahrbuch 9: Innovation – Prozesse, Produkte, Politik. Frankfurt a.M.: Campus, S. 33-54.

Nüllen, Helmut (2004): Lehrbuch Qualitätsmanagement in der Arztpraxis: Entwicklung und Einführung eines QMS. Köln: Deutscher Ärzte-Verlag (2., überarbeitete Auflage).

Oakland John (2003): TQM. Oxford: Butterworth Heinemann.

OECD (Hg.) (1986): Methods and Procedures in Aid Evaluation: A Compendium of Donor Practice and Experience. Paris: OECD.

OECD (Hg.) (1989): Sustainability in Development Programmes: A Compendium of Evaluation Experience. Paris: OECD/DAC.

OECD (Hg.) (1998): Review of the DAC Principles for Evaluation of Development Assistance. Paris: OECD/DAC.

Oess, Attila (1994): Total Quality Management (TQM): Eine ganzheitliche Unternehmensphilosophie. In: Stauss, Bernd (Hg.): Qualitätsmanagement und Zertifizierung: Von DIN ISO 9000 zum Total Quality Management. Wiesbaden: Gabler, S. 199-222.

Ogburn, William F. (1923): Social Change. With Respect to Culture and Original Nature. London: Allen & Unwin.

Ogburn, William F. (1957): "Cultural Lag as Theory". In: Sociology and Social Research 41 (3), S. 167-174.

Ogburn, William F./Nimkoff, Meyer F. (1950): A handbook of sociology. London: Routledge & Kegan Paul.

Olbertz, Jan-Hendrik/Otto, Hans-Uwe (2001): Qualität von Bildung: vier Perspektiven. Wittenberg: Institut für Hochschulforschung.

Oppen, Maria (1996): Qualitätsmanagement: Grundverständnisse, Umsetzungsstrategien und ein Erfolgsbericht: die Krankenkassen Berlin: Ed. Sigma.

Ossadnik, Wolfgang (2003): Controlling. München: Oldenbourg (3., überarb. u. erw. Auflage).

Ösze, Daniel (2000): Managementinformationen im New Public Management am Beispiel der Steuerverwaltung des Kantons Bern. Dissertation. Bern u.a.: Haupt.

Owen, John M./Rogers, Patricia J. (1999): Program Evaluation. Forms and Approaches. London u.a.: Sage.

Pappi, Franz Urban/König, Thomas/Knoke, David (1990): Entscheidungsprozesse in der Arbeits- und Sozialpolitik. Der Zugang der Interessengruppen zum Regierungssystem über Politikfeldnetze: Ein deutsch-amerikanischer Vergleich. Frankfurt a.M./New York: Campus

Patton, Michael Q. (1997): Utilization – Focused Evaluation: The New Century Text. Thousand Oaks/London/New Delhi: Sage (3. Auflage).

Pede, Dr. Lars (2000): Wirkungsorientierte Prüfung der öffentlichen Verwaltung. Bern: Haupt.

Perger, Eugen (2002): Total Quality Management im Bankwesen: Umsetzung des TQM in Universalbanken aufgrund des EFQM-Modells. Bern u.a.: Haupt.

Perrow, Charles (1965): Hospitals: Technoloy, Structure and Goals. In: March, J.G. (Hg.): Handbook of Organizations. Chicago: Rand McNally.

Perrow, Charles (1967): A Framework for the Comparative Analysis of Organizations. In: American Sociological Review 32, S. 194-208.

Peterander, Franz; Speck, Otto (Hg.) (1999): Qualitätsmanagement in sozialen Einrichtungen. München: Reinhard.

Pfeffer, Jeffrey/Salancik, Gerald R. (1978): The External Control of Organizations: A Resource Dependence Perspective. New York: Harper & Row.

Pfeifer, Thilo (2001): Qualitätsmanagement: Strategien, Methoden, Techniken. München: Hanser.

Pfeiffer, Dietmar (1976): Organisationssoziologie. Eine Einführung. Stuttgart: Kohlhammer.

Pfister, Gerhard/Renn, Ortwin (1997): Zukunftsfähiges Deutschland. Studie des Wuppertaler-Institutes im Vergleich zum Nachhaltigkeitskonzept der Akademie für Technikfolgeabschätzung. Arbeitsbericht 75/Juni. Stuttgart: Akademie für Technikfolgeabschätzung.

Pierer, Heinrich v./Oetinger, Bolko v. (1997): Wie kommt das Neue in die Welt. München: Hanser.

Pinter, Erwig (1999): ISO und EFQM sind keine Gegensätze. In: Krankenhaus Umschau, Sonderheft EFQM – das Qualitätsmodell der European Foundation for Quality Management. Kulmbach: Baumann, S. 26.

Piontek, Jochem (2003): Controlling. München: Oldenbourg (2., erw. Auflage).

Pira, Andreas (1999): Total-quality-Management im Spitalbereich auf der Basis des EFQM-Modells. Zürich: Hochschulschrift.

Pitschas, Rainer (2004): Looking behind New Public Management: "new" values of public administration and the dimensions of personnel management in the beginning of the 21st century. Speyer: Forschungsinstitut für Öffentliche Verwaltung bei der Deutschen Hochschule für Verwaltungswissenschaft.

Poister, Theodore H. (2003): Measuring performance in public and nonprofit organizations. San Francisco: Jossey-Bass.

Pollitt, Christopher (1998): Evaluation in Europe: Boom or Bubble? In: Evaluation 4 (2), S. 214-224.

Pollitt, Christopher (2000): Public management reform: a comparative analysis. New York: Oxford Univ. Press.

Posavac, Emil J./Carey, Raymond G. (1997): Program evaluation: methods and case studies. NJ: Prentice-Hall.

Preisendörferr, Peter/Burgess, Yvonne (1988): Organizational dynamics and career patterns: Effects of organizational expansion and contraction on promotion changes in a large West German company. European Sociological Review 4, S. 32-45.

Preißner, Andreas (2003): Balanced Scorecard anwenden. Kennzahlengestützte Unternehmenssteuerung. München: Hanser.

Price, James L. (1986): Organizational Effectiveness. Homewood, Ill.: Richard D. Irvin.

Priller, Eckhard/Zimmer, Annette (Hg.) (2001): Der Dritte Sektor international: mehr Markt – weniger Staat? Berlin: Edition Sigma.

Pugh, D.S./Hickson, D.J./Hinings, C.R. (1969): An Empirical Taxonomy of Structures of Work Organizations. In: Administrative Science Quarterly 14, S. 115-126

Puschmann, Norbert O. (2000): Benchmarking: Organisation, Prinzipien und Methoden. Unna: Externbrink-Puschmann.

PwC Deutsche Revision (2001): Die Balanced Scorecard im Praxistest: Wie zufrieden sind die Anwender? Frankfurt a.M. (im pdf-Format auch herunterzuladen unter: http://www.pwc.de).

Radtke, Philipp/Wilmes, Dirk (1997): European Quality Award – die Kriterien des EQA umsetzen. München u.a.: Hanser.

Radtke, Philipp; Wilmes, Dirk (2002): European Quality Award – die Kriterien des EQA umsetzen. 3. Auflage. München u.a.: Hanser.

Raidl, Monika (2001): Qualitätsmanagement in Theorie und Praxis – eine Verbindung von Instrumenten der empirischen Sozialforschung und der Einsatz und Nutzen für die Praxis. Eine empirische Studie in einer süddeutschen Privatklinik. München u.a.: Hampp.

Rat von Sachverständigen für Umweltfragen (1994): Umweltgutachten 1994. Für eine dauerhaft-umweltgerechte Entwicklung. Stuttgart: Metzler-Poeschel.

Rehbinder, Manfred (2002): New Public Management: Rückblick, Kritik und Ausblick. In: Eberle, Carl-Eugen (Hg.): Der Wandel des Staates vor den Herausforderungen der Gegenwart. München: Beck.

Reichard, Christoph (2002): Institutionenökonomische Ansätze und New Public Management. In: König, Klaus (Hg.): Deutsche Verwaltung an der Wende zum 21. Jahrhundert. Baden-Baden: Nomos.

Reichard, Christoph (2004): New Public Management als Reformdoktrin für Entwicklungsverwaltungen. In: Benz, Arthur (Hg.): Institutionenwandel in Regierung und Verwaltung. Berlin: Duncker & Humblot.

Reinhold, Gerd (Hg.) (1992): Soziologie-Lexikon. München: Oldenbourg (2., überarb. Auflage).

Reinmann-Rothmeier, G./Mandl, H. (1998): Wissensvermittlung. Ansätze zur Förderung des Wissenserwerbs. In: Klix, F./Spada, H. (Hg.): Enzyklopädie der Psychologie: Wissen, Bd. 6. Göttingen u.a.: Hogrefe, S. 457-500.

Riedel, Dieter (2000): Die Diffusion von Innovationen unter besonderer Berücksichtigung von ERS-SAR-Fernerkundungsdaten. Oberpfaffenhofen: Deutsches Fernerkundungsdatenzentrum.

Rischer, Klaus/Titze, Christa (1998): Qualitätszirkel – Problemlösung durch Gruppen im Betrieb. Renningen-Malmsheim: expert Verlag (4., erw. Auflage).

Rittberger, Volker (Hg.) (2002): Global Governance and the United Nations System. New York: United Nations University Press.

Ritz, Adrian (2003): Evaluation von New Public Management: Grundlagen und Empirische Ergebnisse der Bewertung von Verwaltungsreformen in der schweizerischen Bundesverwaltung. Bern: Haupt.

Röber, Manfred/Schröter, Eckhard/Wollmann Hellmut (Hg.) (2002): Moderne Verwaltung für moderne Metropolen: Berlin und London im Vergleich. In: Stadtforschung aktuell 82. Wiesbaden: Verlag für Sozialwissenschaften.

Rogers, Everett M (1995): Diffusion of innovations. 4th edition. New York.

Rogers, Everett M./Shoemaker, F. F. (1971): Communication of innovations: A cross-cultural approach. New York: Free Press.

Rogers, Everett M./Jouong-Im Kim (1985): "Diffusion of Innovations in Public Organizations." In: Merritt, Richard L./Merritt, Anna J. (Hg.): Innovations in the Public Sector. Beverly Hills u.a.: Sage, S. 85-107.

Rohe, Christoph (1999) (Hg.): Werkzeuge für Innovations-Management. So schaffen Sie eine lebendige und erfolgreiche Wachstumskultur. Frankfurt a.M.: Frankfurter Allgemeine Zeitung für Deutschland.

Rölle, Daniel/Blättel-Mink, Birgit (1998): Netzwerke in der Organisationssoziologie – neuer Schlauch für alten Wein? In: Österreichische Zeitschrift für Soziologie 23 (3), S. 66-87.

Rondinelli, Dennis A. (1983): Secondary cities in developing countries: policies for diffusing urbanization Beverly Hills: Sage.

Rossi, Peter H. (1978): Issues in the Evaluation of Human Services Delivery. In: Evaluation Quarterly. S. 573-599.

Rossi, Peter H./Lyall, Katharine (1976): Reforming Public Welfare: A Critique of the Negative Tax Experiment. New York: Russel Sage Foundation.

Rossi, Peter H./Berk, Richard A./Lenihan, Kenneth, J. (1980): Money, Work and Crime. New York: Academic Press.

Rossi, Peter H./Lipsey, Mark W./Freeman, Howard E. (1999): Evaluation. A Systematic Approach. Thousand Oaks u.a.: Sage (6. Auflage).

Rossi, Peter H./Freeman, Howard E./Hofmann, Gerhard (1988): Programm Evaluation: Einführung in die Methoden angewandter Sozialforschung. Stuttgart: Enke.

Rossi, Peter H./Lipsey, Mark W./Freeman, Howard E. (2004): Evaluation: a systematic approach. Thousand Oaks, Calif.: Sage.

Rossmann, Bruno (2003): Die Reform in der öffentlichen Verwaltung in den Jahren 2000 bis 2002: Versuch einer Evaluierung. Wien: Kammer für Arbeiter und Angestellte für Wien.

Rothlauf, Jürgen (2004): Total Quality Management in Theorie und Praxis: zum ganzheitlichen Unternehmensverständnis. München: Oldenbourg (2., neubearbeitete und erweiterte Auflage).

Royse, David u.a. (2001): Program Evaluation. An Introduction. Australia: Brooks/Cole.

Rühl (1998): ISO 9000 – Erfahrungsbericht aus einem technischen Entwicklungszentrum. In: Hochschulrektorenkonferenz: Qualitätsmanagement in der Lehre. Bonn: Hochschulrektorenkonferenz, S. 21-47.

Runge, Joachim H. (1994): Schlank durch Total Quality Management – Strategien für den Standort Deutschland. Frankfurt a.M.: Campus.

Rüschemeyer, Dietrich (1971): Partielle Modernisierung. In: Zapf, Wolfgang (Hg.): Theorien des sozialen Wandels. Köln: Kiepenheuer und Witsch.

Saatweber, Jürgen (1994): Inhalt und Zielsetzung von Qualitätsmanagementsystemen gemäß den Normen DIN ISO 9000 bis 9004. In: Stauss, Bernd (Hg): Qualitätsmanagement und Zertifizierung: Von DIN ISO 9000 zum Total Quality Management. Wiesbaden: Gabler, S. 63-91.

Sackmann, Reinhold; Wingens, Matthias (Hg.) (2001): Strukturen des Lebenslaufs: Übergang – Sequenz – Verlauf. Weinheim: Juventa-Verlag.

Salen, S. H. (1984): Preface zu Heden. In: King, C.G./King, A. (Hg.) Social Innovations for Development. Oxford: Pergamon, S. v-vii.

Saner, Raymond (2002): "Quality management is training generic or sector-specific? In: ISO Management Systems. Online verfügbar unter http://www.iso.org/iso/en/iso9000-14000/addresources/articles/pdf/survey_4-02.pdf., S. 53-61.

Saner, Raymond (2002): „Quality Assurance for Public Administration: A Consensus Building Vehicle. In: Public Organization Review: A Global Journal. Netherlands: Kluwer, S. 407-414.

Sauer, Dieter/Lang, Christa (1999) (Hg.): Paradoxien der Innovation. Perspektiven sozialwissenschaftlicher Innovationsforschung. München: Campus.

Schäfer, Erik/Meyer, Wolfgang (2002): Evaluation ausgewählter TWINNING-Projekte im Auftrag des Bundesumweltministeriums. Saarbrücken: Universität des Saarlandes.

Schauer, Reinbert/Blümle, Ernst-Bernd/Witt, Dieter/Anheier, Helmut K. (2000): Non-profit-Organisationen im Wandel: Herausforderungen, gesellschaftliche Verantwortung, Perspektiven. Eine Dokumentation. Linz: Trauner Druck.

Schedler, Kuno/Proeller, Isabella (2000): New Public Management. Bern: Haupt (1. Auflage).

Schedler, Kuno/Proeller, Isabella (2003): New Public Management. Bern: Haupt (2., überarbeitete Auflage).

Scheiber, Konrad (1999): ISO 9000 – die große Revision. Wien: Österreichische Vereinigung für Qualitätssicherung (2. Auflage).

Schenkel, Peter/Tergan, Sigmar-Olaf/Lottmann, Alfred (2000) (Hg.): Qualitätsbeurteilung multimedialer Lern- und Informationssysteme: Evaluationsmethoden auf dem Prüfstand. Nürnberg: Verlag Bildung und Wissen.

Scherer, Andrea G./Alt, Jens M. (Hg.) (2002): Balanced Scorecard in Verwaltung und Non-Profit-Organisationen. Stuttgart: Schäffer-Poeschel.

Schiersmann, Christiane (2001): Organisationsbezogenes Qualitätsmanagement: EFQM-orientierte Analyse und Qualitätsentwicklungs-Projekte am Beispiel der Familienbildung. Opladen: Leske + Budrich.

Schildknecht, Rolf (1992): Total Quality Management: Konzeption und State of the Art. Frankfurt a.M. u.a.: Campus.

Schlemmer, Frank (2002): Management by Balanced Scorecard: Grundlagen, Techniken, Implementierung (mit Seminarkonzept und Foliensatz zur Einführung in Unternehmen). Düsseldorf: VDM-Verlag Müller.

Schmid, Josef (1998): Verbände. Interessenvermittlung und Interessenorganisation: Lehr- und Arbeitsbuch. München/Wien: Oldenbourg.

Schmidheiny, Stephan (1992): Kurswechsel: Globale unternehmerische Perspektiven für Entwicklung und Umwelt. München: Artemis & Winkler.

Schmidt, Manfred G. (Hg.) (1988): Staatstätigkeit. International und historisch vergleichende Analysen (PVS-Sonderheft 19). Opladen: Westdeutscher Verlag.

Schneider, Werner (1994): Erfolgsfaktor Qualität: Einführung und Leitfaden. Berlin: Cornelsen.

Schnell, Rainer/Hill, Paul B./Esser, Elke (1999): Methoden der empirischen Sozialforschung. München: Oldenbourg.

Schnell, Rainer/Hill, Paul B./Esser, Elke (2005): Methoden der empirischen Sozialforschung. München: Oldenbourg (7., vollständig überarbeitete und erweiterte Auflage).

Scholles, Frank (2001): Die Kosten-Nutzen-Analyse. Manuskript. Verfügbar unter: http://www.laum.uni-hannover.de/ilr/lehre/Ptm/Ptm_BewKna.htm.

Schön, Franz (2001): Die Balanced Scorecard in der Jugendarbeit. Berlin: Bundesministerium für Familie, Senioren, Frauen und Jugend.

Schott, Franz (2000): Evaluation aus ganzheitlicher, theoriegeleiteter Sicht. In: Schenkel, Peter/Tergan, Sigmar-Olaf/Lottmann, Alfred: Qualitätsbeurteilung multimedialer Lern- und Informationssysteme, S. 106-124. Nürnberg: Verlag Bildung und Wissen.

Schreyögg, Georg (1999): Organisation: Grundlagen moderner Organisationsgestaltung. Wiesbaden: Gabler.

Schröder, Patricia (Hg.) (1998): Qualitätsentwicklung im Gesundheitswesen: Konzepte, Programme und Methoden des Total Quality Management. Bern: Huber.

Schröter, Eckhard/Wollmann, Hellmut (1998): New Public Management. In: Bandemer, Stephan v. u.a. (Hg.): Handbuch zur Verwaltungsreform. Opladen: Leske + Budrich, S. 59-69.

Schüberl, Ulrich F./Egger, Martin (2001): Organisationsentwicklung durch Total Quality Management in Werkstätten für Behinderte. In: Schubert, Hans-Joachim/Zink, Klaus: Qualitätsmanagement im Gesundheits- und Sozialwesen. Neuwied: Luchterhand.

Schubert, Hans-Joachim (2001): Von Leistungs- und Prüfvereinbarungen zur Umsetzung umfassender Qualitätsmanagementkonzepte. In: Schubert, Hans-Joachim/Zink, Klaus: Qualitätsmanagement im Gesundheits- und Sozialwesen. Neuwied: Luchterhand.

Schubert, Hans-Joachim/Zink Klaus (2001): Qualitätsmanagement im Gesundheits- und Sozialwesen. Neuwied u.a.: Luchterhand (2., erw. und überarb. Auflage).

Schubert, Hans-Joachim/Zink, Klaus (1997): Qualitätsmanagement im Gesundheits- und Sozialwesen. Neuwied. u.a.: Luchterhand.

Schubert, Hans-Joachim/Zink, Klaus (1997): Qualitätsmanagement in sozialen Dienstleistungsunternehmen. Neuwied: Luchterhand.

Schubert, Hans-Joachim/Zink, Klaus (2001): Eine Einführung in das Werk: Zur Qualität sozialer Dienstleistungen. In: Schubert, Hans-Joachim/Zink, Klaus: Qualitätsmanagement im Gesundheits- und Sozialwesen. Neuwied: Luchterhand.

Schubert, Klaus (1991): Politikfeldanalyse. Opladen: Westdeutscher Verlag.

Schubert, Klaus/Bandelow, Nils C. (2003): Lehrbuch der Politikfeldanalyse. München: Oldenbourg.

Schuhen, Axel (2002): Nonprofit Governance in der freien Wohlfahrtspflege (Schriften zur öffentlichen Verwaltung und öffentlichen Wirtschaft 181). Baden-Baden: Nomos.

Schulz, Susanne M. (2003): Qualitätsmanagement in Nonprofit-Organisationen: Analyse der Übertragbarkeit betriebswirtschaftlicher Konzepte des Qualitätsmanagements auf sozialwirtschaftliche Organisationen. Veröffentlichte Hochschulschrift der Universität Lüneburg.

Schumpeter, Joseph A. (1911): Theorie der wirtschaftlichen Entwicklung. Eine Untersuchung über Unternehmergewinn, Kapital, Kredit, Zins und den Konjunkturzyklus. München: Duncker & Humblot.

Schumpeter, Joseph A. (1939): Business Cycles: a theoretical, historical and statistical analysis of the capitalist process. New York: McGraw-Hill Book Co.

Schumpeter, Joseph A. (1947): „The Creative Response in Economic History." In: The Journal of Economic History 7 (2), S. 149-159.

Schumpeter, Joseph A. (1961): Konjunkturzyklen. Eine theoretische, historische und statistische Analyse des kapitalistischen Prozesses. 2 Bde. Göttingen: Vandenboeck & Ruprecht, insb. Bd. 1, Kap. III und IV.

Schumpeter, Joseph A. (1964): Theorie der wirtschaftlichen Entwicklung. Eine Untersuchung über Unternehmergewinn, Kapital, Kredit, Zins und den Konjunkturzyklus. Berlin: Dunck & Humblot.

Schwan, Renate/Kohlhaas, Günther (2002): Qualitätsmanagement in Beratungsstellen: Selbstbewertung nach dem EFQM-Modell am Beispiel Studienberatung. Weinheim: Deutscher Studien-Verlag.

Schwefel, Detlef (Hg.) (1987a): Soziale Wirkungen von Projekten in der Dritten Welt. Baden-Baden: Nomos.

Schwefel, Detlef (1987b): Evaluation sozialer Auswirkungen und Nebenwirkungen von Projekten. In: Schwefel, Detlef (Hg.): Soziale Wirkungen von Projekten in der Dritten Welt. Baden-Baden: Nomos.

Schwefel, Detlef (1987c): Soziale Auswirkungen von Infrastrukturen und Industrien. In: Schwefel, Detlef (Hg.): Soziale Wirkungen von Projekten in der Dritten Welt. Baden-Baden: Nomos.

Schweizerische Normen-Vereinigung SNV (Hg.) (2002): Qualitätsmanagement in der öffentlichen Verwaltung. Berlin: Beuth.

Schweri, Jürg u.a. (2003): Kosten und Nutzen der Lehrlingausbildung aus der Sicht Schweizer Betriebe. Beiträge zur Bildungsökonomie, Bd. 2. Zürich: Rüegger.

Scott, W. Richard (1977): Effectiveness of Organizational Effectiveness Studies. In: Goodman, Paul S./Pennings, Johannes S. (Hg): New Perspectives on Organizational Effectiveness. San Francisco: Jossey-Bass.

Scott, W. Richard u.a. (1978): Organizational Effectiveness and the Quality of Surgical Care in Hospitals. In: Meyer, Marshall W. (Hg.): Environments and Organizations. San Francisco: Jossey-Bass.

Scott, Richard W. (2003): Organizations: Rational, Natural, and Open Systems. New Jersey: Prentice Hall (5. Auflage).

Scriven, Michael (1967): The Methodology of Evaluation. In: Stake, R.E. (Hg.): AERA Monograph Series on Curriculum Evaluation Vol. 1. Chicago: Rand McNally.

Scriven, Michael (1972): Die Methodologie der Evaluation. In: Wulf, Christoph (Hg.): Evaluation. Beschreibung und Bewertung von Unterricht, Curricula und Schulversuchen. München: Piper.

Scriven, Michael (1972): Pros and Cons About Goal-Free Evaluation. In: Evaluation Comment, S. 1-4.

Scriven, Michael (1980): The Logic of Evaluation. California: Edgepress.

Scriven, Michael (1983): Evaluation Ideologies. In: Madaus, G.F./Scriven, M./ Stufflebeam, D.L. (Hg.): Evaluation Models: Viewpoints on Educational and Human Services Evaluation. Boston: Kluwe-Nijhoff.

Scriven, Michael (1991): Evaluation Thesaurus. Newbury Park u.a.: Sage (1. Auflage).

Scriven, Michael (2002): Evaluation Thesaurus. Newbury Park u.a.: Sage (4. Auflage).

Sebaldt, Martin/Straßner, Alexander (2004): Verbände in der Bundesrepublik Deutschland: eine Einführung. Wiesbaden: Verlag für Sozialwissenschaft.

Seghezzi, Hans Dieter (1994): Qualitätsmanagement: Ansatz eines St. Galler Konzepts. Integriertes Qualitätsmanagement. Jg. 10, IFB Schriften. St.Gallen: Schäffer-Poeschel Verlag und Verlag Neue Zürcher Zeitung.

Seghezzi, Hans Dieter (2003): Integriertes Qualitätsmanagement: Das Sankt Gallener Konzept. München: Hanser Fachbuchverlag (2., vollst. überarb. u. erw. Auflage).

Seghezzi, Hans Dieter/Hansen, Jürgen R. (1993): Qualitätsstrategien: Anforderungen an das Management der Zukunft. München u.a.: Hanser.

Seibel, Hans Dieter (1992): Datenarchivierung, vergleichende Analyse, Praxisbezug. Ziel und Nutzen des ESE-Projekts. In: Reichert, Ch./Scheuch, Erwin K./Seibel, Hans Dieter (Hg.): Empirische Sozialforschung über Entwicklungsländer. Methodenprobleme und Praxisbezug. Saarbrücken: Breitenbach.

Seibel, Wolfgang (1992): Funktionaler Dilettantismus. Erfolgreich scheiternde Organisationen im „Dritten Sektor" zwischen Markt und Staat. Baden-Baden: Nomos.

Selbmann, Hans-Konrad (1999): EFQM – Ein Finales Qualitäts-Modell? Qualitätsmanagement aus Sicht der Gesundheitspolitik. In: Krankenhaus Umschau, Sonderheft EFQM – das Qualitätsmodell der European Foundation for Quality Management, Kulmbach: Baumann, S. 4-8.

Shadish, Wiliam R. (1990): Amerikanische Erfahrungen mit der Evaluation von Sozial- und Gesundheitsprogrammen. In: Koch, Uwe/Wittman, Werner W. (Hg.): Evaluationsforschung: Bewertungsgrundlage von Sozial- und Gesundheitsprogrammen. Berlin u.a.: Springer, S. 159-182.

Shadish, Wiliam R./Cook, Thomas D./Leviton, Laura C. (1991): Foundations of Program Evaluation: Theory and Practice. London: Sage.

Shand, David/Arnberg, Morton (1996): „Background Paper". Responsive Government: Service Quality Initiatives. Paris: OECD, pp.15-38

Shavelson, Richard J./McDonnell, Lorraine/Oakes, Jeannie (1991): What are educational indicators and indicator systems? Washington, D.C.: ERIC Clearinghouse on Tests, Measurement, and Evaluation.

Sherrill, Sam (1984): Identifying and Measuring Unintended Outcomes. In: Evaluation and Program Planning 7, S. 27-34.

Sieber Bethke, Frank (2003): Controlling, Evaluation und Reporting von Weiterbildung und Personalentwicklung. Bremen: Medieninstitut.

Siebert, Gunnar (Hg.) (2002): Performance Management: Leistungssteigerung mittels Benchmarking, Balanced Scorecard und Business-Excellence-Modell. Stuttgart: Deutscher Sparkassen-Verlag.

Siebert, Gunnar (2002): Benchmarking: Leitfaden für die Praxis. München: Hanser.

Simon, Herbert A. (1981): Entscheidungsverhalten in Organisationen. Landsberg: Verlag Moderne Industrie.

Simsa, Ruth (2000): Gesellschaftliche Funktionen und Einflussformen von Nonprofit-Organisationen. Wien: Lang.

Simsa, Ruth (Hg.) (2001): Management der Nonprofit-Organisation: gesellschaftliche Herausforderungen und organisationale Antworten. Stuttgart: Schäffer-Poeschel.

Simsa Ruth (2001): Hoffnungen auf Zivilgesellschaft und die gesellschaftliche Funktion von NPOs im Spannungsfeld von Schadensbegrenzung und aktiver Mitgestaltung. In: Simsa, Ruth (Hg.): Management der Nonprofit-Organisation: gesellschaftliche Herausforderungen und organisationale Antworten. Stuttgart: Schäffer-Poeschel.

Simsa, Ruth (2002): NPOs und die Gesellschaft: Eine vielschichtige und komplexe Beziehung – Soziologische Perspektiven. In: Badelt, Chrisoph (Hg.): Handbuch der Nonprofit Organisation: Strukturen und Management. Stuttgart: Schäffer-Poeschel, S. 129-152.

Simson, Uwe/Schönherr, Siegfried (1985): Innovationsfixierung, Kultur und Entwicklungszusammenarbeit. In: Internationales Afrikaforum 21 (1), S. 75-81.

Sommer, Joachim (2001): Qualitätszirkel: Ziele, Aufgaben und Handlungsfelder. Frankfurt a.m.: Deutscher Sportbund, Bundesvorstand Breitensport.

Sontheimer, Kurt (1977): Grundzüge des politischen Systems der Bundesrepublik Deutschland. München: Piper.

Sontheimer, Kurt (2003): Grundzüge des politischen Systems Deutschlands. Bonn: Bundeszentrale für politische Bildung(aktualisierte Neuausgabe).

Sontheimer, Kurt/Bleek, Wilhelm (2000): Grundzüge des politischen Systems der Bundesrepublik Deutschland. München: Piper.

Sorensen, Aage B./Weinert, Franz E./Sherrod, Lonnie R (1986) (Hg.): Human Development and the Life Course. Multidisciplinary Perspectives. Hillsdale, N.J.: Lawrence Erlbaum Associates.

Spalink, Heier (1999) (Hg.): Werkzeuge für das Change-Management. Prozesse erfolgreich optimieren und implementieren. Frankfurt a.M.: Frankfurter Allgemeine Zeitung.

Speck, Otto (1999): Die Ökonomisierung sozialer Qualität. Zur Qualitätsdiskussion in Behindertenhilfe und Sozialer Arbeit. München: Reinhardt.

Spiel, Christiane (2001): Evaluation universitärer Lehre: zwischen Qualitätsmanagement und Selbstzweck. Münster u.a.: Waxmann.

Spraul, Artur (2004): Controlling. Stuttgart: Schäffer-Poeschel.

Spray, S.L. (Hg.) (1976): Organizational Effectiveness. Kent: State University.

Staehle, W.H./Grabatin, G. (1979): Effizienz von Organisationen. In: Die Betriebswirtschaft, S. 88-102.

Stahl, Thomas/Severing, Eckhart (2002): Qualitätssicherung in der beruflichen Bildung – Europäische Konzepte und Erfahrungen. In: Arnold, Rolf (Hg): Qualitätssicherung in der Entwicklungszusammenarbeit. Baden-Baden: Nomos Verlagsgesellschaft

Stamm, Margit (2003): Evaluation im Spiegel ihrer Nutzung: Grand idée oder grande illusion des 21. Jahrhunderts?. In: Zeitschrift für Evaluation 2 (2), S.183-200.

Stark, Gerhard (2000): Qualitätssicherung in der beruflichen Weiterbildung durch Anwendungsorientierung und Partizipation: Ergebnisse aus einem Modellversuch. Bielefeld: Bertelsmann.

Statistical Yearbook (2004). Wiesbaden: Statistisches Bundesamt.

Staudt, Erich/Hefkesbrink, Joachim/Treichel, Heinz-Reiner (1988): Forschungs-management durch Evaluation: Das Beispiel Arbeitsschwerpunkt Druckindustrie. Frankfurt a.M.: Campus.

Stausberg, Michael (2003): Qualitätsmanagement-Methoden: Auswahl, Einführung, Durchführung. Augsburg: WEKA, Fachverlag für technische Führungskräfte.

Stauss, Bernd (1995): Qualitätsmanagement und Zertifizierung: von DIN ISO 9000 zum Total Quality Management. Wiesbaden: Gabler.

Steers, Richard M. (1975): Problems in the Measurement of Organizational Effectiveness. In: Administrative Science Quarterly 20, S. 546-558.

Steers, Richard M. (1977): Organizational effectiveness: a behavioral view. Santa Monica: Goodyear Publ. Comp.

Steffens, Franz (1980): Technologie und Organisation. In: Grochla, Erwin (Hg.): Hand-wörterbuch der Organisation. Stuttgart: Poeschel.

Steinacher, Alexander (2002): Balanced Scorecard: das innovative Controlling-Instrument. Düsseldorf: VDM-Verlag.

Steinmann, Horst/Gerum, Elmar (1978): Reform der Unternehmensverfassung. Metho-dische und ökonomische Grundüberlegungen. Köln u.a.: Heymann.

Stockmann, Reinhard (1987): Gesellschaftliche Modernisierung und Betriebsstruktur. Die Entwicklung von Arbeitsstätten in Deutschland 1875-1980. Frankfurt a.M.: Campus.

Stockmann, Reinhard (1998b): Nachhaltigkeit als Prüfstein erfolgreicher Entwicklungs-politik. In: Entwicklung und Zusammenarbeit 6.

Stockmann, Reinhard (1992a): Die Nachhaltigkeit von Entwicklungsprojekten. Eine Me-thode zur Evaluierung am Beispiel von Berufsbildungsprojekten. Opladen: West-deutscher Verlag.

Stockmann, Reinhard (1992b): Ein Analyse- und Erhebungsinstrumentarium zur Erfas-sung der Nachhaltigkeit von Entwicklungsprojekten. In: Reichert, Christoph/ Scheuch, Erwin K./Seibel, Hans D. (Hg.): Empirische Sozialforschung über Ent-wicklungsländer – Methodenprobleme und Praxisbezug. Saarbrücken u.a.: Breiten-bach.

Stockmann, Reinhard (1993a): Die Nachhaltigkeit von Entwicklungsprojekten. Eine Me-thode zur Evaluierung am Beispiel von Berufsbildungsprojekten. Opladen: West-deutscher Verlag (2. Auflage).

Stockmann, Reinhard (1993b): Langfristige Wirkungen – bisher wenig untersucht. In: Entwicklung und Zusammenarbeit 2.

Stockmann, Reinhard (1993c): Sind Ex-post-Analysen wirklich nutzlos? Replik auf den Beitrag von Hans-Jörg Elshorst. In: Entwicklung und Zusammenarbeit 2.

Stockmann, Reinhard (1993d): Die Bewertung der Entwicklungszusammenarbeit. In: Stockmann, Reinhard; Gaebe, Wolf (Hg.): Hilft die Entwicklungshilfe langfristig? Bestandsaufnahme zur Nachhaltigkeit von Entwicklungsprojekten. Opladen: West-deutscher Verlag.

Stockmann, Reinhard (1993e): Die Nachhaltigkeit von Berufsbildungsprojekten. In: Stockmann, Reinhard/Gaebe, Wolf (Hg.): Hilft die Entwicklungshilfe langfristig?

Bestandsaufnahme zur Nachhaltigkeit von Entwicklungsprojekten. Opladen: West-deutscher Verlag.

Stockmann, Reinhard (1993f): Nachhaltigkeit. Bilanz eines Themas. In: Stockmann, Reinhard/Gaebe, Wolf (Hg.): Hilft die Entwicklungshilfe langfristig? Bestands-aufnahme zur Nachhaltigkeit von Entwicklungsprojekten. Opladen: Westdeutscher Verlag.

Stockmann, Reinhard (1995a): Ein methodisches Konzept zur Evaluierung der Wirksam-keit von Entwicklungsprojekten. In: Heitmann, Werner/Greinert, Wolf-Dietrich (Hg.): Analyseinstrumente in der Berufsbildungszusammenarbeit. Berlin: Overall-Verlag.

Stockmann, Reinhard (1995b): Die Krise der Entwicklungszusammenarbeit. Viel Kritik – aber wenig empirisches Wissen über Nachhaltigkeit. In: Trappe, Paul (Hg.): Krisen-kontinent Afrika – Ansätze zum Krisenmanagement. Social Strategies, Bd. 27. Basel: Karger Libri.

Stockmann, Reinhard (1996a): Die Wirksamkeit der Entwicklungshilfe. Eine Evaluation der Nachhaltigkeit von Programmen und Projekten der Berufsbildung. Opladen: Westdeutscher Verlag.

Stockmann, Reinhard (1996b): Defizite in der Wirkungsbeobachtung. Ein unabhängiges Evaluationsinstitut könnte Abhilfe schaffen. In: Entwicklung und Zusammenarbeit 8.

Stockmann, Reinhard (1997a): The Evaluation of Sustainability of Development Projects. Baden-Baden: Nomos.

Stockmann, Reinhard (1997b): Ein Modell zur partizipativen Partnerqualifizierung für die Erhebung und Auswertung von Daten. In: Leicht, René/Stockmann, Reinhard (Hg.): Qualifikation in kleinen Betrieben Thailands. Berlin: Overall-Verlag.

Stockmann, Reinhard (1997c): The Sustainability of Development Projects: An Impact Assessment of German Vocational-Training Projects in Latin America. In: World Development 25 (11).

Stockmann, Reinhard (1998a): La efficacia de la ayuda al desarollo. Baden-Baden: No-mos.

Stockmann, Reinhard (1998b): Viel Kritik – aber wenig profundes Wissen: Der Mangel an Erkenntnissen über die Wirksamkeit der Entwicklungszusammenarbeit und wie er behoben werden könnte. In: Brüne, Stefan (Hg.): Erfolgskontrolle in der entwick-lungspolitischen Zusammenarbeit. Hamburg: Schriften des Übersee-Instituts.

Stockmann, Reinhard (1998c): Globalization and Changes in Vocational Training Sys-tems in Developing and Advanced Industialized Countries – The German Dual Sys-tem in Comparative Perspecitve. In: Blossfeld, Hans-Peter; Stockmann, Reinhard (Hg.): Globalization and Changes in Vocational Training Systems in Developing and Advanced Industialized Societies (I). International Journal of Sociology. Bd. 28, Nr.2, S. 3-28.

Stockmann, Reinhard (1999a): The Implementation of Dual Vocational Training Struc-tures in Developing Countries – An Evaluation of „Dual Projects" Assisted by the GTZ. In: Blossfeld, Hans-Peter/Stockmann, Reinhard (Hg.): Globalization and

Changes in Vocational Training Systems in Developing and Advanced Industialized Societies (III). International Journal of Sociology. Bd. 29, Nr.2, S.29-65

Stockmann, Reinhard (1999b): Wirkungsevaluation in der Entwicklungszusammenarbeit: Notwendige Grenzüberschreitungen. In: Grenzenlose Gesellschaft? 29. Kongress der Deutschen Gesellschaft für Soziologie. Bd. II/2 Ad-hoc-Gruppen. Pfaffenweiler: Centaurus Verlagsgesellschaft.

Stockmann, Reinhard (1999c): Grenzenlose Evaluation? In: Grenzenlose Gesellschaft? 29. Kongress der Deutschen Gesellschaft für Soziologie. Bd. II/2 Ad-hoc-Gruppen. Pfaffenweiler: Centaurus Verlagsgesellschaft.

Stockmann, Reinhard (Hg.), (2000a). Evaluationsforschung. Grundlagen und ausgewählte Forschungsfelder. Opladen: Leske + Budrich.

Stockmann, Reinhard (2000b): Evaluation in Deutschland. In: Stockmann, Reinhard (Hg.): Evaluationsforschung. Grundlagen und ausgewählte Forschungsfelder. Opladen: Leske + Budrich.

Stockmann, Reinhard (2000c): Evaluation staatlicher Entwicklungspolitik. In: Stockmann, Reinhard (Hg.): Evaluationsforschung. Grundlagen und ausgewählte Forschungsfelder. Opladen: Leske + Budrich.

Stockmann, Reinhard (2000d): Methoden der Wirkungs- und Nachhaltigkeitsanalyse: Zur Konzeption und praktischen Umsetzung. In: Müller-Kohlenberg, Hildegard/Münstermann, K. (Hg.): Qualität von Humandienstleistungen. Opladen: Leske + Budrich.

Stockmann, Reinhard (2000e): Wirkungsevaluation in der Entwicklungspolitik. In: Vierteljahreshefte zur Wirtschaftsforschung 69 (3).

Stockmann, Reinhard (2000f): Evaluation der Nachhaltigkeit von Umweltberatungsprogrammen: Theoretische und methodische Grundlagen. In: Härtel, Michael/ Stockmann, Reinhard/Gaus, Hansjörg (Hg.): Berufliche Umweltbildung und Umweltberatung. Bielefeld: Bertelsmann.

Stockmann, Reinhard (2001): Evaluation der Nachhaltigkeit von Umweltberatung. In: Stockmann, Reinhard u.a. (Hg.): Umweltberatung und Nachhaltigkeit. Berlin u.a.: Erich Schmidt Verlag.

Stockmann, Reinhard (2002a): Nachhaltigkeit der Entwicklungszusammenarbeit. Ein mehrdimensionales Nachhaltigkeitskonzept und seine Anwendung. In: Jäggi, Victoria/Mäder, U./Windisch, K. (Hg.): Entwicklung, Recht, Sozialer Wandel. Festschrift für Paul Trappe. Bern u.a.: Peter Lang.

Stockmann, Reinhard (2002b): Herausforderungen und Grenzen, Ansätze und Perspektiven der Evaluation in der Entwicklungszusammenarbeit. In: Zeitschrift für Evaluation 1 (1).

Stockmann, Reinhard (2002c): Qualitätsmanagement und Evaluation – Konkurrierenden oder sich ergänzende Konzepte? In: Zeitschrift für Evaluation 1 (2).

Stockmann, Reinhard (2003a): Eine Konzeption zur Evaluation der Nachhaltigkeit politischer Programme. In: Allmendinger, Jutta (Hg.): Entstaatlichung und Soziale Sicherheit. 31. Kongress der Deutschen Gesellschaft für Soziologie. Bd. Ad-hoc-

Gruppen. Opladen: Leske + Budrich (auf CD-ROM; Beitrag zur Sitzung der gleichnamigen Gruppe).

Stockmann, Reinhard (2003b): Die Standards für Evaluation zeigen, worauf es bei 'guten' Evaluationen ankommt. In: Berufsbildung und Wissenschaft 32 (6).

Stockmann, Reinhard (Hg) (2004a). Evaluationsforschung. Grundlagen und ausgewählte Forschungsfelder. Opladen: Leske + Budrich (2., überarb. Auflage).

Stockmann, Reinhard (2004b): Institutionelle Qualitätssicherung statt Programmevaluation? In: Hochschulrektorenkonferenz (Hg.): Qualitätssicherung an Hochschulen – neue Herausforderungen nach der Berlin-Konferenz. Bielefeld: Bertelsmann.

Stockmann, Reinhard (2004c): Evaluationsforschung – Ansatz und Methoden. In: EvaNet (http://www.llevanet.his.de).

Stockmann, Reinhard (2004d): Was ist eine gute Evaluation? Einführung zu Funktionen und Methoden von Evaluationsverfahren. In: Ermert, Karl (Hg.): Evaluation in der Kulturförderung. Wolfenbüttel: Bundesakademie für kulturelle Bildung.

Stockmann, Reinhard (2005a): Zur Umgestaltung des Evaluationssystems der Entwicklungszusammenarbeit. In: Schriften des Vereins für Socialpolitik (Hg.): Zur Bewertung der Entwicklungszusammenarbeit. Berlin: Duncker & Humblot.

Stockmann, Reinhard (2005b): Qualitätsmanagement und Evaluation bei eLearning Programmen. In: Igel, Christoph/Daugs, Reinhard (Hg.): Handbuch eLearning. Schorndorf: Hofmann.

Stockmann, Reinhard (2007): Handbuch zur Evaluation. Eine praktische Handlungsanleitung. Münster: Waxmann Verlag.

Stockmann, Reinhard u.a. (2000): Wirksamkeit deutscher Berufsbildungsarbeit. Opladen: Leske + Budrich.

Stockmann, Reinhard u.a. (2001): Nachhaltige Umweltberatung. Opladen: Leske + Budrich.

Stockmann, Reinhard/Blossfeld, Hans-Peter (Hg.) (1999): Globalization and Changes in Vocational Training Systems in Developing and Advanced Industrialized Societies. International Journal of Sociology. Special Issue.

Stockmann, Reinhard/Caspari, Alexandra (2001): Nachhaltigkeit deutscher EZ-Projekte. Eine operationale Nachhaltigkeitsdefinition und ihre Anwendung. In: epd-Entwicklungspolitik 14.

Stockmann, Reinhard/Caspari, Alexandra/Kevenhörster, Paul (2000): Langfristige Wirkungen der staatlichen Entwicklungszusammenarbeit. Ergebnisse einer Querschnittsevaluierung zur Nachhaltigkeit. In: Entwicklung und Zusammenarbeit 10.

Stockmann, Reinhard/Gaebe, Wolf (1993): Hilft die Entwicklungshilfe langfristig? Bestandsaufnahme zur Nachhaltigkeit von Entwicklungsprojekten. Opladen: Westdeutscher Verlag.

Stockmann, Reihnard/Heise, Maren (2004): Nachbetreuung ehemaliger Studierender aus Entwicklungslndern. Teilbericht: Methodische Konzeption und Ergebnisse des Alumni Survey. In: DAAD (Hg.): Programmstudie. Nachbetreuung ehemaliger Studierender aus Entwicklungsländern. Bonn: DAAD.

Stockmann, Reinhard/Kevenhörster, Paul (2001): Wissenschaftlicher Rigorismus oder praxisorientierter Pragmatismus? Zum Verhältnis zwischen Entwicklungspolitik und Wissenschaft. In: Entwicklung und Zusammenarbeit 42 (4).

Stockmann, Reinhard/Kohlmann, Uwe (1998): Transferierbarkeit des Dualen Systems. Eine Evaluation dualer Ausbildungsprojekte in Entwicklunsländern. Berlin: Overall Verlag.

Stockmann, Reinhard/Krapp, Stefanie/Baltes Katrin (2004): DAAD-Ergebnisübersicht: Evaluation des DAAD-Programmbereichs Stipendien für Ausländer. Saarbrücken: Centrum für Evaluation..

Stockmann, Reinhard/Kreuter, Frauke (1996): Anwendungsprobleme empirischer Erhebungsmethoden in Entwicklungsländern. In: Greinert, Wolf-Dietrich/Heitmann, Werner/Stockmann, Reinhard (Hg.): Ansätze betriebsbezogener Auswertungsmodelle. Beispiele aus dem islamisch-arabischen Kulturkreis. Berlin: Overall-Verlag.

Stockmann, Reinhard/Leicht, René (1997): Implementationsbedingungen eines kooperativen Ausbildungssystems in Ägypten. Berlin: Overall Verlag.

Stockmann, Reinhard/Meyer, Wolfgang/Krapp, Stefanie/Köhne, Gerhard (2000): Wirksamkeit deutscher Berufsbildungszusammenarbeit. Ein Vergleich staatlicher und nicht-staatlicher Programme in der Volksrepublik China. Wiesbaden: Westdeutscher Verlag.

Stockmann, Reinhard/Meyer, W./Kohlmann, U./Gaus, H-J./Urbahn, J. (2001): Nachhaltige Umweltberatung. Eine Evaluation von Umweltberatungsprojekten. Opladen: Leske + Budrich.

Stoll, Bettina (2003): Balanced scorecard für soziale Organisationen: mehr Qualität durch strategisches Management, Handbuch für die Praxis sozialer Arbeit. Regensburg u.a.: Walhalla-Fachverlag.

Straumann, Ursula (2000): Professionelle Beratung. Bausteine zur Qualitätsentwicklung und Qualitätssicherung. Heidelberg: Roland Asanger Verlag.

Stufflebeam, Daniel L. (2001): Evaluation Models. San Francisco: Jossey-Bass.

Stufflebeam, Daniel L./Madaus, George F./Kellaghan, Thomas (2000): Evaluation Models: Viewpoints on Educational and Human Services Evaluation.

Tenberg, Ralf (2005): Change-Management. In: Berufsbildung. Bd. 91/92, Jg. 59, S. 3-6.

Tergan, Sigmar-Olaf (2000): Grundlagen der Evaluation: Ein Überblick. In: Schenkel, Peter/Tergan, Sigmar-Olaf/Lottmann, Alfred (Hg.): Qualitätsbeurteilung multimedialer Lern- und Informationssysteme. Nürnberg: Verlag Bildung und Wissen, S. 22-51.

Tergan, Sigmar-Olaf (2000): Bildungssoftware im Urteil von Experten: 10 + 1 Leitfragen zur Evaluation. In Schenkel, Peter/Tergan, Sigmar-Olaf/Lottmann, Alfred (Hg.): Qualitätsbeurteilung multimedialer Lern- und Informationssysteme. Nürnberg: Verlag Bildung und Wissen, S. 137-163.

Tergan, Sigmar-Olaf (2000): Vergleichende Bewertung von Methoden zur Beurteilung der Qualität von Lern- und Informationssystemen: Fazit eines Methodenvergleichs. In Schenkel, Peter/Tergan, Sigmar-Olaf/Lottmann, Alfred (Hg.): Qualitätsbeurteilung multimedialer Lern- und Informationssysteme. Nürnberg: Verlag Bildung und Wissen, S. 329-347.

Tews, Kerstin (2004): Diffusion als Motor globalen Politikwandels) Potentiale und Grenzen. FU-Report 01-2004. Berlin: Freie Universität.

Thompson, Randal Joy (1990): Evaluators as Change Agents. The Case of a Foreign Assistance Project in Morroco. In: Evaluation and Program Planning 13, S. 379-388.

Thompson, James D. (1967): Organizations in Action. New York: McGraw-Hill.

Thompson, James D./Bates, Frederick L. (1957/58): Technology, Organization, and Administration. In: ASQ 2, S. 325-343.

Tonnesen, Christian T. (2002): Die balanced scorecard als Konzept für das ganzheitliche Personalcontrolling: Analyse und Gestaltungsmöglichkeiten. Wiesbaden: Deutscher Universitäts-Verlag.

Töpfer, Armin/Mehrdorn, Hartmut (1994): Total Quality Management: Anforderungen und Umsetzung im Unternehmen. Neuwied u.a.: Luchterhand (3. Auflage).

Töpfer, Armin/Mehrdorn, Hartmut (2002): Total Quality Management: Anforderungen und Umsetzung im Unternehmen. Neuwied u.a.: Luchterhand (Neuauflage).

Tremmel, Jörg (2003): Nachhaltigkeit als politische und analytische Kategorie. Der deutsche Diskurs um nachhaltige Entwicklung im Spiegel der Interessen der Akteure. München: ökonom-Verlag.

Türk, Klaus (1978): Soziologie der Organisation. Eine Einführung. Stuttgart: Enke.

Türk, Klaus (Hg.), (2000): Hauptwerke der Organisationstheorie. Wiesbaden: Westdeutscher Verlag.

Tushmann, Michael; Anderson, Philip (1997): Managing Strategic Innovation and Change. New York: University Press.

Tweraser, Stefan (1998): Besonderheiten der Implementierung von Instrumenten in NPOs. In: Eschenbach, Rolf (Hg.): Führungsinstrumente für die Nonprofit Organisationen. Stuttgart: Schäffer-Poeschel.

Udy, Stanley H. Jr. (1959): 'Bureaucracy' and 'Rationality' in Weber's Organization Theory. In: American Sociological Review 24, S. 791-795.

Uebel, Matthias F./Helmke, Stefan (2003): FAQ Balanced Scorecard und Controlling. Troisdorf: Bildungsverlag EINS.

Uehlinger, Kurt/Allmen, Werner von (2001): TQM Praxis: Total Quality Management nach dem europäischen Modell für Excellence). Kilchberg: SmartBooks Wirtschaft (2., aktual. u. erw. Auflage).

UNDP (1988a): Technical Co-Operation: Its Evolution and Evaluation (Diskussionspapier). UNDP.

UNDP (2000a): Development Effectiveness. Review of Evaluative Evidence. New Work: UNDP.

United Nations Evaluation Group (2005): Standards for Evaluation in the UN System. New York: UNEG.

USAID (1999): Agency Performance Report 1998. Washington D.C.: USAID/CDIE.

Van den Berg, J.M./Verbruggen, H. (1999): Spatial sustainability, trade and indicators: an evaluation of the ecological footprint. In: Ecological Economics 29 (1), S. 61-72.

Van den Bulte, Christophe/Lilien, Gary L. (1999): Integrating Models of Innovation Adoption: Social Network Tresholds, Utility Maximation, and Hazad Models, Report 27-1999. Pennsylvania State University: Institute for Studying Business Markets (ISBM).

Van Kooten, G.C./Bulte, E. (2000): The Economics of Nature: Managing Biological Assets. Oxford: Blackwell.

Vedung, Evert (1999): Evaluation im öffentlichen Sektor. Wien u.a.: Böhlau.

Vedung, Evert (2000): Evaluation Research and Fundamental Research. In: Stockmann, Reinhard (Hg.): Evaluationsforschung. Opladen: Leske + Budrich, S. 103-127.

Vedung, Evert (2004): Evaluation Research and Fundamental Research. In: Stockmann, Reinhard (Hg.): Evaluationsforschung. Opladen: Leske + Budrich (2. Auflage), S. 111-134.

Vilain, Michael (2003): DIN EN ISO 9000 ff.: 2000. In: Boeßenecker, Karl-Heinz: Qualitätskonzepte in der sozialen Arbeit. Weinheim: Beltz.

Voges, Wolfgang (1983b): Alter und Lebenslauf. Ein systematisierender Überblick über Grundpositionen und Perspektiven. In: Voges, Wolfgang (Hg.): Soziologie der Lebensalter. Alter und Lebenslauf. München: Sozialforschungsinstitut.

Voges, Wolfgang (Hg.) (1983a): Soziologie der Lebensalter. Alter und Lebenslauf. München: Sozialforschungsinstitut.

Voges, Wolfgang (Hg.) (1987): Methoden der Biographie- und Lebenslaufforschung. Opladen: Westdeutscher Verlag.

Vöhringer, Bernd (2004): Computerunterstützte Führung in Kommunalverwaltung und -politik: Steuerung mit New Public Management und Informationstechnologie. Wiesbaden: Deutscher Universitätsverlag.

Vomberg, Edeltraud; Wallrafen-Dreisow, Helmut (2002): Qualitätsmanagement mit dem EFQM-Modell für Excellence als partizipativer Ansatz – auch in der Pflege? In: Igl u.a.: Qualität in der Pflege. Stuttgart: Schattauer.

Voss, Rödiger/Stoschek, Julia (2005): Studie: Unterschiede zwischen ISO 9001: 2000 und EFQM-Modell. Text im www verfügbar unter http://euro.hanser.de/qm/overview_basic.asp?task=4&basic_id=23223475230&bt=0 0100.00020&xid=1850@Sa9e261IcF1J2K7QSRP0MK4

Wächter, Hartmut; Vedder, Günther (Hg.) (2001): Qualitätsmanagement in Organisationen: DIN ISO 9000 und TQM auf dem Prüfstand. Wiesbaden: Betriebswirtschaftlicher Verlag Gabler.

Wackernagel, Mathis et al. (2002): Strategic sustainable development – selection, design and synergies of applied tools. In: Journal of Cleaner Production, 10 (3), S. 197-214.

Wackernagel, Mathis/Rees, William E. (1997): Unser ökologischer Fußabdruck. Basel: Birkhäuser.

Wagner, Michael (1997): Scheidung in Ost- und Westdeutschland. Zum Verhältnis der Ehestabilität und Sozialstruktur seit den 30er-Jahren. Frankfurt a.M.: Campus-Verlag.

Walter-Busch, Emil (1996): Organisationstheorien von Weber bis Weick. Amsterdam: G+B Verlag Fakultas.

Webb, E.J./Campbell, D.T u.a. (1975): Nicht-reaktive Messverfahren. Weinheim: Beltz.

Weber, Jürgen (1991): Controlling in öffentlichen Organisationen (Non-Profit-Organizations). In: Risak, Johann/Deyhle, Albrecht (Hg.): Controlling – State of the Art und Entwicklungstendenzen. Wiesbaden: Gabler.

Weber, Jürgen (1995): Grundbegriffe des Controlling. Stuttgart: Schäffer-Poeschel.

Weber, Jürgen/Schäffer, Utz (2000): Balanced Scorecard und Controlling. Implementierung – Nutzen für Manager und Controller – Erfahrungen in deutschen Unternehmen. Wiesbaden: Gabler (2., aktual. Auflage).

Weber, Jürgen (2002): Einführung in das Controlling. Stuttgart: Schäffer-Poeschel (9., kompl. überarb. Auflage).

Weber, Max (1976): Wirtschaft und Gesellschaft. Grundriss der verstehenden Soziologie. Tübingen: Mohr.

Weick, Karl E. (1977): Re-Punctuating the Problems. In: Goodman, Paul S./Pennings, Johannes S. (Hg.): New Perspectives on Organizational Effectiveness. San Francisco: Jossey-Bass.

Weinert, Franz E. (Hg.) (2001): Leistungsmessung in Schulen. Weinheim: Beltz.

Weiss, R.S.; Rein, M. (1969): The Evaluation of Broad-Aim Programs: A Cautionary Case and a Morale. In: Annals of the American Academy of Political and Social Science, S. 133-142.

Weiss, Carol H. (1974): Evaluierungsforschung. Opladen: Westdeutscher Verlag.

Weiß, Peter (2000): Praktische Qualitätsarbeit in Krankenhäusern: ISO 9001:2000; Total Quality Management (TQM). Wien: Springer Verlag.

Welge, Martin K./Fessmann, Klaus-D. (1980): Effizienz, organisatorische. In: Grochla, Erwin (Hg.): Handwörterbuch der Organisation. Stuttgart: Poeschel.

Werkmann, Alexander/Braun, Andreas (2001): Die Theorie des Total-Quality-Managements als ganzheitliches Instrument progressiver Unternehmensführung und deren Übertragung auf eine Zahnarztpraxis. Nürtingen: Hochschulschrift.

Wex, Thomas (2004): Der Nonprofit-Sektor der Organisationsgesellschaft. Wiesbaden: Deutscher Universitäts-Verlag.

White, Louise G. (1986): An Approach to Evaluating the Impact of AID Projects. Washington: US.AID.

Wholey, Joseph S. (1979): Evaluation: Promise and Performance. Washington, D.C.: Urban Institute.

Widmer, Thomas (2001): Qualitätssicherung in der Evaluation – Instrumente und Verfahren. In: LeGES – Gesetzgebung und Evaluation 12. Bern, S. 9-41.

Widmer, Thomas (2002): Staatsreformen und Evaluation: Konzeptionelle Grundlagen und Praxis bei Schweizer Kantonen. In: Zeitschrift für Evaluation 1 (1), S. 101-114.

Widmer, Thomas/Schenkel, Walter/Hirschi, Christian (2000): Akzeptanz einer nachhaltigen Verkehrspolitik im politischen Prozess: Deutschland, Niederlande und Schweiz im Vergleich Bern: BBL, EDMZ.

Wilmes, Dirk/Radtke, Philipp (1998): Das Modell für Business Excellence durch TQM. In: Kamiske, Gerd F. (Hg.): Der Weg zur Spitze. München u.a.: Hanser, S. 13-25.

Windhoff-Héritier, Adrienne (1983): Policyanalyse. Eine Einführung. Frankfurt a.M.: Campus.

Witte, Andreas (1993): Integrierte Qualitätssteigerung im Total Quality Management. Diss. Münster u.a.: Lit Verlag.

Wittmann, Werner (1985): Evaluationsforschung. Aufgaben, Probleme und Anwendungen. Berlin u.a.: Springer.

Wittwer, Günther (2003): Keine Angst vor Controlling! Einführung in ein einfaches Steuerungsinstrument für die erfolgreiche Unternehmensführung. Kissing: Weka Media.

Woehrle, Armin (2003): Grundlagen des Managements in der Sozialwirtschaft. Baden-Baden: Nomos.

Wollmann, Hellmut (1994): Evaluierungsansätze und -institutionen in Kommunalpolitik und -verwaltung. Stationen der Planungs- und Steuerungsdiskussion. In: Schulze-Böing, Matthias/Johrendt, Norbert (Hg.): Wirkungen kommunaler Beschäftigungsprogramme. Methoden, Instrumente und Ergebnisse der Evaluation kommunaler Arbeitsmarktpolitik. Basel/Boston/Berlin: Birkhäuser.

Wollmann, Hellmut (1998): Kommunale Verwaltungsmodernisierung in Ostdeutschland. Zwischen Worten und Taten. Diskussionspapier. Humboldt-Universität zu Berlin.

Wollmann, Hellmut (1998): Modernisierung der kommunalen Politik- und Verwaltungswelt - Zwischen Demokratie und Managementschub. In: Grunow, Dieter/Wollmann, Hellmut (Hg.): Lokale Verwaltungsreform in Aktion: Fortschritte und Fallstricke. Basel u.a.: Birkhäuser, S. 400-439.

Wollmann, Hellmut (1999): Politik- und Verwaltungsmodernisierung in den Kommunen: Zwischen Managementlehre und Demokratiegebot. Die Verwaltung, Schwerpunktheft 3.

Wollmann, Hellmut (2000): Staat und Verwaltung in den 90er Jahren: Kontinuität oder Veränderungswelle? In: Czada, Roland; Wollmann, Hellmut (Hg.): Von der Bonner zur Berliner Republik. 10 Jahre Deutsche Einheit, Leviathan-Sonderheft 19/1999. Opladen: Westdeutscher Verlag.

Wollmann, Hellmut (2002): Verwaltungspolitik und Evaluierung. Ansätze, Phasen und Beispiele im Ausland und in Deutschland. In: Zeitschrift für Evaluation 1 (1), S. 75-100.

Wollmann, Hellmut (Hg.) (2003): Evaluation in Public Sector: Reform Concepts and Practice in International Perspective. Cheltenham: Edward Elgar Publishing Limited.

Woodward, Joan (1965): Industrial Organization. Theory and Practice. New York: Oxford University Press.

Wottawa, Heinrich/Thierau, Heike (1998): Lehrbuch Evaluation. Bern: Huber (2. Auflage).

Wottawa, Heinrich/Thierau, Heike (2003): Lehrbuch Evaluation. Bern: Huber (3., überarb. Auflage).

Wüst, Marcella (2001): Der Balanced-Scorecard-Ansatz: Darstellung der grundlegenden Konzeption und ihrer Erweiterung um Risikoaspekte (Diplomarbeit). Aschaffenburg: Fachhochschule.

Wunder, Helmut (1995): ISO 9000 – Entwicklung des Qualitätsmanagements und Vorteile ganzheitlichen Qualitätsmanagements. In: Feuchthofen, Jörg E./Severing, Eckart (Hg.): Qualitätsmanagement und Qualitätssicherung in der Weiterbildung. Neuwied u.a.: Luchterhand.

Wunder, Thomas (2004): Transnationale Strategien: anwendungsorientierte Realisierung mit Balanced Scorecard. Wiesbaden: Deutscher Universitäts-Verlag.

Wunderer, Rolf (1998): Beurteilung des Modells der Europäischen Gesellschaft für Qualitätsmanagement (EFQM) und dessen Weiterentwicklung zu einem umfassenden Business Excellence-Modell. In: Boutellier, Roman/Masing, Walter (Hg.): Qualitätsmanagement an der Schwelle zum 21. Jahrhundert. München u.a.: Hanser, S. 53-68.

Wunderer, Rolf/Gerig, Valentin/Hauser, Rainer (1997): Qualitätsmanagement durch und im Personalmanagement – Konzeptionelle Grundlagen und Folgerungen für die Personalwirtschaft. In: Wunderer, Rolf/Gerig, Valentin/Hauser, Rainer (Hg.): Qualitätsorientiertes Personalmanagement: Das europäische Qualitätsmodell als unternehmerische Herausforderung. München u.a.: Hanser, S. 1-104.

Yates, Brian T. (1996): Analyzing Costs, Procedures, Processes and Outcomes in Human Services. Thousand Oaks: Sage.

Yuchtman, Ephraim/Seashore, Stanley E. (1976): A System Resource Approach to Organizational Effectiveness. In: American Sociological Review 32, S. 891-903.

Zammuto, R. F. (1984): A Comparison of Multiple Constituencey Models of Organizational Effectiveness. In: Academy of Management Review 9, S. 606ff.

Zapf, Wolfgang (Hg.) (1977): Probleme der Modernisierungspolitik. Meisenheim: Anton Hain.

Zapf, Wolfgang (1989): Über soziale Innovationen. In: Soziale Welt 40 (1/2), S. 170-183.

Zapf, Wolfgang (Hg.) (1997): Wohlfahrtsentwicklung im vereinten Deutschland: Sozialstruktur, sozialer Wandel und Lebensqualität. Berlin: Ed. Sigma.

Zbaracki, Mark J. (1998): The rhetoric and reality of Total Quality Management. In: Administrative Science Quarterly, 43. S. 602-636.

Zech, Rainer (1996): Mittelmäßigkeit als Machtressource. Über die Lernunfähigkeit politischer Organisationen. In: Zeitschrift für Politische Psychologie 4, S. 255-271.

Zimmer, Annette/Priller, Eckhart (1997): Die Zukunft des Dritten Sektors in Deutschland. In: Anheier, Helmut u.a. (Hg.): Der Dritte Sektor in Deutschland. Organisationen zwischen Staat und Markt im gesellschaftlichen Wandel. Berlin: Ed. Sigma, S. 249-283.

Zink, Klaus (2001): Neuere Entwicklungen im Qualitätsmanagement – Relevanz in Werkstätten für Behinderte. In: Schubert, Hans-Joachim/Zink, Klaus: Qualitätsmanagement im Gesundheits- und Sozialwesen. Neuwied: Luchterhand.

Zink, Klaus J. (1995): TQM als integriertes Managementkonzept: Das europäische Qualitätsmodell und seine Umsetzung. München u.a.: Hanser.

Zink, Klaus J. (Hg.) (1995): Erfolgreiche Konzepte zur Gruppenarbeit – aus Erfahrung lernen. Neuwied: Luchterhand.

Zink, Klaus J. (1994): Total Quality als europäische Herausforderung. In: Zink, Klaus J. (Hg.): Business excellence durch TQM: Erfahrungen europäischer Unternehmen. München u.a.: Hanser. S. 1-29.

Zink, Klaus J. (1992): Qualitätszirkel und Lernstatt. In: Frese, E. (Hg.): Handwörterbuch der Organisation. Stuttgart: Poeschel Verlag (3., völlig neu gestaltete Ausgabe), S. 2129-2140.

Zollondz, Hans-Dieter (2002): Grundlagen Qualitätsmanagement: Einführung in Geschichte, Begriffe, Systeme und Konzepte. München, u.a.: Oldenbourg.

7 Appendix

7.1 Index of tables and figures

7.2 Set of evaluation guidelines for development cooperation

Guidelines for evaluating programmes and projects in the field of development cooperation

	Overview
1.	**Programme and environment**
	Programme description
1.0	Programme data
1.1	Programme concept
1.2	Innovation concept
1.3	Resources (Inputs)
	Environmental/contextual conditions
1.4	Country characterisation
1.5	Field of practice/policy (social subsystems)
1.6	Target groups (audiences, users)
2.	**Programme process**
2.1	Preparation/planning
	Implementation
2.2	Programme management
2.3	Preparation for termination of support
2.4	Aftercare support
3.	**Internal impact fields (executing agency)**
3.1	Goal acceptance
3.2	Personnel
3.3	Organisational structure
3.4	Financial resources
3.5	Technology: technical infrastructure
3.6	Technology: organisational agenda/concept
3.7	Internal programme impacts (balance)
4.	**External impact fields (audiences, fields of policy/practice)**
4.1	Goal acceptance among target groups
4.2	Target group attainment (diffusion effects within the target group)
4.3	Benefit to target groups
4.4	Target group-spanning impacts (diffusion effects outside of the target group)
4.5	Impacts in the field of policy/practice (in social subsystems)
4.6	Policy field-spanning impacts
4.7	External programme impacts (balance)
5.	**Programme quality**
5.1	Planning and implementation quality
5.2	Internal impact-based quality
5.3	External impact-based quality
5.4	Sustainability at the programme level
	Sustainability at the macro level
5.5	Efficiency
5.6	Social relevance
5.7	Environmental compatibility

1

335

1. Programme and environment

Programme description

1.0 Programme data

1. Programme title:
2. Partner country:
3. Type of programme (e.g. structural support):
4. Sector/system of intervention (e.g. education system):
5. Executing agency structure (description of designated organisations):
   - Formal (parent) project executing agency (political institution):
   - Direct project executing agency (implementing partner):

1.1 Programme concept

1. Description of targeted goals and intended impacts:
2. What intervention measures are employed to realise the programme goals?
3. At what analytical levels (individuals, organisations, systems) and along what dimensions (behaviour, structures, processes) are impacts to be produced?
4. What is the programme theory? What relationships are assumed to exist between interventions and impacts?
5. What cause-effect hypotheses can be formulated on the basis of the three theoretical approaches applied here (the life-cycle model, and organisational and innovation/diffusion theory)? What impacts are to be expected based on these? Have the most important cause-effect relationships been considered in the programme theory?
6. Does the programme concept take the current status of international discussion/research into account?

Logic of programme concept	1	2	3	4	5	6	7	8	9	10
	very low									very high

1.2 Innovation concept

1. Description of the innovations introduced. What kind of innovations are they (product/service, procedural, organisational/structural, personnel innovations)?

2. Is the innovation oriented more towards the traditional sector or the modern sector?

3. How are the specific characteristics of the innovation to be assessed (from the point of view of potential users)?

   - Relative benefit in comparison to previous problem solutions
   - Compatibility with existing solutions
   - Degree of complexity (extent to which the application of the innovation turns out to be relatively difficult to understand and hard to manage)
   - Testability, observability, degree of maturity?

4. How are the chances of diffusion to be appraised given the specific characteristics of the innovation, the competence of the executing agency (see section 3 of the set of guidelines), and external conditions (e.g. values, norms, traditions, laws, spatial structures, ecological environment etc.) (see sections 1.4 and 1.5 of the set of guidelines)?

5. Is the executing agency qualified to introduce and spread the innovation (see section 3.6 of the set of guidelines)?

6. How favourably are external conditions (laws, values, norms etc.) to be assessed with regard to the introduction and diffusion of the innovation (see section 1.5 of the set of guidelines)?

Conformity of the innovation with the situation of the partner country

1	2	3	4	5	6	7	8	9	10
very low									very high

1.3 Resources (Inputs)

1. Financial resources
   - German contribution:
   - Partner contributions:
   - Third-party contributions:

2. Human resources
   - Number and length of stay of German (foreign) long-term experts:
   - Deployment of short-term experts:
   - Partner country personnel:
   - Value of human resources provided:

3. Technical resources
   - Description of equipment supplied within the framework of the support:
   - Description of the technological know-how transferred:

© Reinhard Stockmann 2005

3

337

- Description of expert reports produced (advisory reports, studies etc.):
- Value of technical resources provided:

4. Time resources
    - Start/end of German support:
    - Start/end of partner's support:
    - Duration of support programme:

Availability of resources	1	2	3	4	5	6	7	8	9	10
	very low									very high

Environmental/contextual conditions

1.4 Country characterisation

Description of contextual conditions relevant (!) to programme implementation, e.g.:

- The political/social system of the partner country (e.g. government system and political development, party system, the roll of associations, trade unions, social groups, administration, the legal system, social security systems such as health insurance, old-age/pension insurance, unemployment insurance):
- The economic system (e.g. economic constitution, economic development, foreign trade development, the labour market, employment trends by sector, the credit system, level of debt):
- Social structure (e.g. social differentiation, social inequality, social stratification, social mobility):
- The cultural system (e.g. ethnic and linguistic homogeneity, predominant religions, the role of family):
- The population structure (e.g. age distribution, population development):
- Settlement patterns (urban-rural contrast, regional economic centres, conurbations, spatial concentration/urbanisation, spatial mobility):
- Other relevant social subsystems (contextual conditions):

    (Sources: e.g. World Development Reports of the World Bank, country reports of national statistical offices, country notes of the foreign office, national statistical data and descriptions etc.).

Country-related contextual conditions for programme implementation	1	2	3	4	5	6	7	8	9	10
	very low									very high

4

338

1.5 Field of practice/policy (social subsystems)

1. Description of the main features of the policy field relevant (!) to programme implementation:

    -   In particular the actors (e.g. the state, non-governmental organisations, private industry) in terms of their areas of responsibility, functions, significance, interest and power structures, competition, and cooperation

    -   The underlying normative, legal, traditional etc. conditions in the policy field

    -   Other conditions of the policy field not listed here that are relevant to programme implementation.

2. Description of the sector policy, programmes and concepts of the partner country (where applicable taking international guidelines into account). How does the programme/project fit in with this sector policy?

3. Description of complementary (including past) projects and programmes supported by foreign donors:

4. Description of other bilateral and multilateral projects/programmes within the policy field. Description of the demarcation from, or overlap with, equivalent support measures of other donors or initiatives of the developing country itself:

Contextual conditions in the policy field relevant to programme implementation

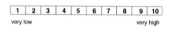

1	2	3	4	5	6	7	8	9	10
very low									very high

1.6 Target groups (audiences/users)

1. Target group definition

    -   At what target groups is the innovation aimed?

    -   How were the target groups identified, defined and delimited?

    -   What groups are not incorporated or excluded (i.e. made non-target groups)?

    -   What were the reasons for favouring the selected target groups over other groups?

2. Target group description:

    -   E.g. based on socio-economic structure, age, gender, employment/income structure, social stratification, family status, education, literacy etc. (depending on relevance):

    -   Based on their values, norms, attitudes and traditions:

    -   What different potential common interests and conflicts exist in the target groups (e.g. between women and men, old and young, the poor and the rich etc.), and what allowances have been made for these?

    -   What allowances have been made for the poor and particularly needy in the target groups, and how have they been incorporated in the project/programme? To what extent are their specific interests accommodated?

3. Relevance of the programme/project to target groups:

5

339

- What benefit should the target groups derive from the project/programme?
- In what way do the target groups benefit from the services (access opportunities)?
- What do the target groups expect of the programme and the innovations introduced? Are these expectations met?
- What services can the target groups render on their own account, and which of these are actually rendered? What resources do they have available to them?
- How would the lives of the target groups be different if the programme did not exist?

Relevance of the programme to target groups	1	2	3	4	5	6	7	8	9	10
	very low									very high

2. Programme process

2.1 Planning/programme preparation

Assessment of preparation prior to the start of the programme:

1. Is there a proposal on the part of partners? Who created it (initiative)? What is the quality of the partner proposal (is it informative and meaningful; is a concept discernable; is it based on development-political guidelines and oriented towards sustainability)?

2. What planning steps were carried out (pre-feasibility study, feasibility study, project appraisal)? Who carried them out?

3. Were all of the following performed during the preparation phase:
   - Problem analysis/situation analysis?
   - Goal analysis?
   - Target group analysis/stakeholder analysis?
   - Analysis of the executing agency and the structure of partners?
   - Need analysis?
   - Micro-/macroeconomic analysis?

4. Were all relevant aspects taken into account here with regard to programme implementation (in terms of sustainability in particular)?

5. Were development-political alternatives given consideration? If so, which ones? How were they assessed?

6. Were all important people, social groups and institutions identified that make decisions within the framework of the implementation, or play an active part in, or are affected by, the project? Who was actively involved in the planning process?

Quality of programme planning/preparation	1	2	3	4	5	6	7	8	9	10
	very low								very high	

Implementation

2.2 Programme management

1. Is there adaptation of programme planning to meet the requirements of the executing agency/contextual conditions during the respective implementation phases? If so, why? How is the adjustment to be rated?

2. Is a well-functioning monitoring and evaluation system in existence (regular, open, comprehensive, problem-based)?

3. What is the quality of reporting and (internally and externally performed) evaluations?

4. Is a well-functioning quality management system in place that makes rational decisions on the basis of monitoring and evaluation data, controls their implementation, and contributes to overall quality development?

5. How is the foreign contribution managed by the foreign implementing organisation (on site and through the headquarters) (in a problem-based manner, effectively, participatively)?

6. How is the programme managed on the side of the partner?

7. How is the collaboration between the ministry of development cooperation, the implementing organisation and partner institutions to be assessed?

8. Are all important people, social groups and institutions incorporated in the implementation?

Quality of programme management	1	2	3	4	5	6	7	8	9	10
	very low								very high	

2.3 Preparation for termination of support

1. What preparations are made for the termination of support for the programme?

2. Is a realistic target system developed for the post-support phase? Is this done in conjunction with the partner?

3. Is the provision of advice and funding reduced gradually?

4. Are the functions of consultants (in the case of personnel projects) gradually assumed by the partners?

5. What sub-areas are entrusted to the sole responsibility of partners, and when?

6. Are partners involved in the decision to terminate support?

© Reinhard Stockmann 2005   7

Quality of preparation for the termination of support	1 2 3 4 5 6 7 8 9 10
	very low ⟶ very high

2.4 Aftercare support

1. Is aftercare support for the programme provided? If so, what measures are implemented to this end, with what aims, and what degree of success?

2. Is systematic follow-up monitoring of the programme carried out? By whom? Is an ex-post evaluation performed?

3. What insights does this provide? For what purpose are these used?

4. Are the results fed into the knowledge management system of the implementing organisation and made available to others?

Quality of aftercare support	1 2 3 4 5 6 7 8 9 10
	very low ⟶ very high

3. Internal impact fields (executing agency)

3.1 Goal acceptance

3.1.1 Goal acceptance within the parent executing agency (political institution)

1. Level of knowledge among managers about the programme (its goals, activities, intended impacts etc.):

2. Appraisal of the programme by managers:

3. Relative importance of programme goals in the overall context of organisational aims:

4. Support for the programme (e.g. through the provision of sufficient resources, active espousal of aims, participation in workshops etc.):

5. Are the activities agreed upon performed?

Goal acceptance within the political executing agency	1 2 3 4 5 6 7 8 9 10
	very low ⟶ very high

3.1.2 Goal acceptance within the direct executing agency (implementing partner)

1. Level of knowledge among managers about the programme (its goals, activities, intended impacts etc.):

2. Appraisal of the programme by managers:

3. Relative importance of programme goals in the overall context of organisational aims:

4. Support for the programme (e.g. through the provision of sufficient resources, active espousal of aims, participation in workshops etc.):

5. Are the activities agreed upon performed?

6. Preparedness of other departments to work together with the programme-implementing departments, to exchange information, and to support their work:

7. Development of their own proposals and innovative ideas (with regard to the programme):

Goal acceptance within the implementing organisation	1	2	3	4	5	6	7	8	9	10
	very low									very high

3.2 Personnel

1. Number and qualification profile of (external) experts/consultants employed on site (target/actual).

   (Qualification particularly in terms of: technical qualification, strategic/conceptual competence, consultancy and management skills, communication skills, team skills, intercultural competence, linguistic competence, evaluation and quality assurance:)

2. Employee turnover, length of vacancies among external long-term experts:

3. Number and qualification profile of domestic personnel/CPs/consultants (target/actual).

   (Qualification particularly in terms of: technical qualification, strategic/conceptual competence, consultancy and management skills, communication skills, team skills, intercultural competence, linguistic competence, evaluation and quality assurance:)

4. Recruitment and employee turnover problems, as well as the duration of vacancies among implementing personnel (considering the general condition of the job market and the attractiveness of the implementing organisation as an employer):

5. Training (on site/in donor country) of the personnel of the implementing organisation (e.g. managers, administrative employees, technical staff etc.). What kind? What is the degree of institutionalisation?

Level of qualification of implementing personnel

(incl. external personnel component)*

1	2	3	4	5	6	7	8	9	10

very low   very high

*can, if necessary, be displayed separately

3.3 Organisational structure

1. How is the organisational structure of the executing agency configured (organigrams, job charts, task descriptions)? Where in the structure is the programme located? From where is it managed?

2. How efficient are the individual organisational subsystems (e.g. administration, procurement, service and maintenance etc.)? Is the degree of division of labour/specialisation efficient for the long-term task completion of the implementing organisation?

3. How is work organised and coordinated? Is this appropriate for the nature of the task?

4. How is the decision-making structure within the executing agency arranged: on a centralised or decentralised basis (decision paths, duration)?

5. Are responsibilities clearly assigned (job charts, task descriptions)?

6. How does information flow and cooperation function within the project team and the project implementing agency, as well as between these and the parent (political) project executing agency and the target group (formally and informally)?

7. Is the programme 'correctly' integrated in the structure of the executing agency (i.e. in a way conducive to goal attainment); from where is it managed; are sufficient management competencies present?

8. How high is the decision autonomy of the executing agency? Does it have sufficient competencies for fulfilling its tasks? What important decision-makers is it dependent upon? What decision processes need to be gone through (duration)?

9. With whom does the executing agency have intensive communication (e.g. political departments, chambers of commerce, associations, other donors etc.)? In what networks is it incorporated?

10. How does the quality management system of the executing agency function, and to what extent is the M&E of the programme incorporated?

Potential of the executing agency's organisational structure

1	2	3	4	5	6	7	8	9	10

very low   very high

3.4 Financial resources

1. How high is the budget of the executing agency, and how is it developing (income/expenditure)?

2. Are there any mid- or long-term financing plans in place?

3. How does the executing agency cover its costs? Who is involved in the financing (significance of self-financing mechanisms)?

4. Are the financial resources of the executing agency sufficient to cover all costs (including for wages and salaries, service and maintenance, new and replacement investment)? Are measures discontinued for reasons of costs? Are salary payments made regularly, or do financial bottlenecks arise frequently during the fiscal year?

Financial capacity of the executing agency

1	2	3	4	5	6	7	8	9	10
very low									very high

3.5 Technology: technical infrastructure

1. Description of the technical equipment of the executing agency:

2. Does the equipment (incl. that supplied within the framework of the support – see 1.3) meet the requirements of the programme and innovation concept (see 1.1 and 1.2) (considering goals/target groups – see 1.6)?

3. How does the level of technical equipment compare with the domestic standard, as well as with internationally (biogeographically and socio-economically) comparable regions?

4. How is the condition of the technical equipment to be assessed?

5. How high is the rate of utilisation of equipment?

6. Are the technologies introduced aligned with ecological conditions (strains on, and risks for, the environment)?

Technical standard and condition of the executing agency's equipment

1	2	3	4	5	6	7	8	9	10
very low									very high

3.6 Technology: organisational agenda/concept

1. What is the concept of the executing agency (the organisational agenda)?

2. Who are the organisational aims oriented towards; who is the target group of the executing agency's service offering?

345

3. How are the organisational aims (the organisational agenda) implemented?

4. To what extent is the executing agency in a position to adapt its organisational concept to changing conditions?

5. What competencies does the executing agency have in terms of developing and implementing innovations itself?

6. Are the innovations introduced within the framework of support developed further by the executing agency (see section 1.2 of the set of guidelines)?

Innovation potential of the executing agency	1	2	3	4	5	6	7	8	9	10
	very low									very high

3.7 Internal programme impacts

1. Which of the changes listed under points 3.1 to 3.6 (= gross outcome) are attributable to the programme interventions (= programme or net effects)? Which of these are to be rated positively, and which negatively?

2. Which of the programme impacts were intended (= programme goals), and which were not?

3. Which of the targeted (planned/intended) goals have been achieved (= effectiveness or goal attainment according to a target/actual comparison)?

Internal impact balance	1	2	3	4	5	6	7	8	9	10
	very low									very high

4. External impact fields (audiences, fields of policy/practice)

4.1 Goal acceptance among target groups

1. How are the programme, its goals and measures, and the intended impacts assessed by the (where applicable various) target groups?

2. To what extent do the target groups participate in the design and implementation of the programme, through financial and human contributions (e.g. through involvement and cooperation in meetings, workshops etc.)?

3. To what extent do the target groups develop there own proposals and innovative ideas with regard to the (further) development of the programme?

Goal acceptance among target groups	

4.2 Target group attainment

1. Are the selected target groups reached (differentiated according to socio-economic structure, age, gender, employment/income structure, social stratification, family status etc.)?
2. Are parts of the target groups not reached, or do they not utilise the services? What are the reasons for this?
3. What proportion of the target groups is reached?
4. What proportion of the target groups adopts the innovations introduced?
5. How, and to what extent, are the target groups provided with information? What measures are implemented to reach target groups?

Degree of diffusion within target groups	

4.3 Benefit to target groups

1. What value does the programme create for its target groups?
2. What drawbacks for the target groups arise from the programme?
3. To what extent do the target groups utilise the programme's services (differentiated according to socio-economic structure, age, gender, employment/income structure, social stratification, family status etc.)?
4. Are the expectations and requirements of the target groups met?
5. How satisfied are the target groups with the service offering?
6. To what extent have the target groups' living conditions, as well as other spheres of life relevant to the programme (e.g. participation and solidarity behaviour, organisational ability, self-help skills etc.), changed?
7. Has the programme contributed towards reducing poverty among the target groups?

Benefit to target groups	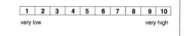

13

347

4.4 Target group-spanning impacts

1. Which other groups does the programme benefit in addition to the target groups? In what way?
2. To what extent are other social groups disadvantaged? Which ones, and why?
3. What other groups have adopted the innovations stemming from the programme? Why?
4. How did the non-target groups learn of these?
5. Are the innovations developed further by non-target groups?
6. Are further groups of users (beyond the target groups) accessed; through what measures?

Target group-spanning diffusion effects

1	2	3	4	5	6	7	8	9	10

very low   very high

4.5 Impacts in the policy field (social subsystem)

1. What diffusion effects can be identified within the policy field (classified as either: product innovation, procedural innovation, organisational/structural innovation, personnel innovation)?
2. Diffusion of the innovations beyond the executing agency, to other organisations: have the innovations been adopted and developed further by other organisations? Which ones?
3. Have system-shaping effects been successfully produced (e.g. through the changing of legal regulations and laws, the creation of new institutions, the production of system alterations, the founding of new organisations?
4. What further effects can be identified in the policy field?

Diffusion effects within the policy field

1	2	3	4	5	6	7	8	9	10

very low   very high

4.6 Policy field-spanning impacts

1. What diffusion effects have arisen in relevant policy fields that are linked to the policy field in which the programme was implemented?
2. What effects have arisen in other social subsystems relevant to the programme, e.g. in:
   - The system of values and norms

14

- The social system (e.g. a change in living habits, the roll of women, social inequality, migration etc.)
- The macroeconomic system (e.g. import substitution, exports, the balance of trade)
- The political system (e.g. an increase in political participation, promotion of democracy)
- The ecological system (land, water, climate, noise, air)?

Diffusion effects in neighbouring policy fields*	1	2	3	4	5	6	7	8	9	10
	very low									very high

* In the case of several policy fields, these are to be specified and listed separately.

4.7 External programme impacts

1. Which of the changes listed under points 4.1 to 4.6 (= gross outcome) are attributable to the programme interventions (= programme or net effects)? Which of these are to be rated positively, and which negatively?

2. Which of the programme impacts were intended (= programme goals), and which were not?

3. Which of the targeted (planned/intended) goals have been achieved (= effectiveness or goal attainment according to a target/actual comparison)?

External impact balance	1	2	3	4	5	6	7	8	9	10
	very low									very high

5. Programme quality

5.1 Planning and implementation quality

For this appraisal, the following points of the set of evaluation guidelines should be given particular attention:

2.1   Preparation/planning

2.2   Programme management

2.3   Preparation for the termination of support

2.4   Aftercare support

1.   How is the quality of programme planning and implementation to be appraised

overall?

2. What consequences does programme quality have for the internal and external, intended and unintended impacts produced?

Planning and implementation quality

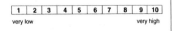

1	2	3	4	5	6	7	8	9	10

very low   very high

5.2 Internal impact-based quality

For this appraisal, the following points of the set of evaluation guidelines should be given particular attention:

1.1   *Programme concept*

1.2   *Innovation concept*

1.3   *Resources*

3.1.1   *Goal acceptance within the parent executing agency (political institution)*

3.1.2   *Goal acceptance within the direct executing agency (implementing partner)*

3.2   *Personnel*

3.3   *Organisational structure*

3.4   *Financial resources*

3.5   *Technology: technical infrastructure*

3.6   *Technology: organisational agenda/concept*

3.7   *Internal programme impacts*

1. How is the organisational competence of the executing agency to be appraised overall?

2. What intended and unintended impacts have the programme interventions had on the competence of the executing agency; has it been successfully improved?

3. What intended and unintended consequences does the competence of the executing agency have for external impact fields?

Internal impact-based quality

1	2	3	4	5	6	7	8	9	10

very low   very high

16

5.3 External impact-based quality

For this appraisal, the following points of the set of evaluation guidelines should be given particular attention:

1.4   *Country characterisation*

1.5   *Field of practice/policy*

1.6   *Target groups (audiences, users)*

4.1   *Goal acceptance among target groups*

4.2   *Target group attainment (diffusion effects within the target group)*

4.3   *Benefit to target groups*

4.4   *Target group-spanning impacts (diffusion effects outside of the target group)*

4.5   *Impacts in the policy field*

4.6   *Policy field-spanning impacts*

4.7   *External programme impacts*

1.   All in all, what consequences do intended and unintended impacts have in terms of:
   - Target group attainment?
   - Diffusion effects among target groups?
   - Benefit to target groups?
   - Target group-spanning diffusion effects?
   - Diffusion effects within the policy field in which the programme interventions take place?
   - Diffusion effects in neighbouring policy fields and social subsystems?

2.   To what extent are they attributable to programme interventions? To which ones?

External impact-based quality	1	2	3	4	5	6	7	8	9	10
	very low									very high

5.4 Sustainability at the programme level

The sustainability of a programme can only be appraised once support has ended. For the assessment, subject areas (3) and (4) of the set of evaluation guidelines should be given particular attention.

For the creation of a sustainability profile, the following questions are to be answered:

1.   Does the target group/executing agency continue the innovations/improvements out of self-interest and for their own benefit?

2.   Have other groups/organisations adopted the innovations out of self-interest and for

---

their own benefit on a lasting basis?

3. Do the innovations lead, via processes of diffusion, to an increase in the performance of the system as a whole (e.g. the health/education/economic system)?

4. Does the target group/executing agency have innovation potential that allows it to react flexibly and appropriately to changed environmental conditions?

5. To what extent have the quality of the planning and implementation process, along with the competence of the executing agency, contributed to sustainability?

Sustainability profile

Dimension	I	II	III	IV
achieved				

Sustainability at the macro level

5.5 Efficiency

For this appraisal, the following points of the set of evaluation guidelines should be given particular attention:

1.3 Resources (inputs)

3.7 Internal programme impacts

4.2 Target group attainment (diffusion effects within the target group)

4.3 Benefit to target groups

4.4 Target group-spanning impacts (diffusion effects outside of the target group)

4.5 Impacts in the policy field

4.6 Policy field-spanning impacts

4.7 External programme impacts

1. What is the relationship between input and output?

2. What is the relationship between input and outcome?

3. What is the relationship between input and internal and external impacts?

Efficiency

1	2	3	4	5	6	7	8	9	10

very low   very high

© Reinhard Stockmann 2005   18

5.6 Socio-political relevance

For this appraisal, the following points of the set of evaluation guidelines should be given particular attention:

1.0   Programme data

1.1   Programme concept

1.2   Innovation concept

1.4   Country characterisation

1.5   Field of practice/policy

1.6   Target groups

3.7   Internal programme impacts

4.1   Goal acceptance among target groups

4.2   Target group attainment (diffusion effects within the target group)

4.3   Benefit to target groups

4.4   Target group-spanning impacts (diffusion effects outside of the target group)

4.5   Impacts in the policy field

4.6   Policy field-spanning impacts

4.7   External programme impacts

1.   To what extent are the programme and its intended and unintended impacts relevant to:

- The socio-political aims of the government of the partner country?

- The aims and concepts of political programme-executing agencies?

- The aims and concepts of the implementing organisation?

- The expectations, needs and demands of target groups?

2.   To what extent are the programme and its intended and unintended impacts of development-political and overall social significance (e.g. for social justice, equality of opportunity, poverty reduction etc.)?

Social relevance

1	2	3	4	5	6	7	8	9	10

very low   very high

5.7 Environmental compatibility

For this appraisal, the following points of the set of evaluation guidelines should be given particular attention:

1.1   Programme concept

1.   To what extent is the programme characterised by the conservation of resources in the production of goods and services?

2.   To what extent are solutions applied that avoid environmental damage and are ecologically innovative?

3.   To what extent have negative ecological effects arisen?

Environmental compatibility	1	2	3	4	5	6	7	8	9	10
	very low									very high

7.3 M & E Indicators for the Mubark-Kohl-Program, Cairo

UNIVERSITÄT DES SAARLANDES

Lehrstuhl für Soziologie FR. 6.3
Prof. Dr. Reinhard Stockmann

Zi. E19, Geb. 35	Tel. 0681 / 302-3372 + 3320
Im Stadtwald	Fax 0681 / 302-3899
Postfach 151150	Email: r.stockmann@rz.uni-sb.de
D- 66041 Saarbrücken	

M & E – System

for projects of the

MKI-Initiative

Final Version

27.08.1999

- Some of the indicators can be used in several respects, not only when it is explicitly mentioned
- Figures will always rely on "per year", otherwise it is mentioned

1.	**Goal Acceptance**	*Source*
1.1	**Implementing Agency (RUDS or others)**	
1.1.1	Egyptian Project budget for training material per trainee	*Documents*
1.1.2	Budget of RUDS or other implementing agency per trainee	*RUDS Files*
1.1.3	Percentage attendance of leaders at workshops and meetings	*min.o.meet.*
1.1.4	Ratio of the actually available RUDS staff to the needed staff (according to the plan)	*RUDS Director*
1.1.5	Ratio of the actually available school staff to the needed staff (according to the plan)	*School Director*
1.1.6	Number of companies visited by RUDS staff (or other implementing agency)	*RUDS Files*
1.2	**Teaching personnel**	*Teacher Survey*
1.2.1	Number of teachers involved in the Dual System	*School Files*
1.2.2	Ratio of teachers in the project to all teachers in the TSS	*RUDS Files*
1.2.3	Number of teachers attending upgrading courses for the Dual System (also to 2.1)	*RUDS Files*
1.3	**Training Personnel (in the companies)**	*Company Survey*
1.3.1	Number of in-company-trainers involved in the Dual System	*RUDS Files*
1.3.2	Ratio of all in-company-trainers to the total number of trainees	*RUDS Files*
1.3.3	Number of in-company-trainers attending upgrading courses for the Dual System	*RUDS Files*

Anhang 2 _ S.355-3622

© Prof. Dr. Reinhard Stockmann; Universität des Saarlandes

356

1.4	**Target Group: Companies**	*Company Survey*
1.4.1	Number of companies participating in the dual system in the project area	*RUDS Files*
1.4.2	Number of companies that would like to join the Dual System	*RUDS Files*
1.4.3	Number of training places offered by the companies	*RUDS Files*
1.4.4	Number of trainees in the companies	*RUDS Files*
1.4.5	Ratio of trainees in the companies to total number of workers	*RUDS Files*
1.4.6	Number of graduates employed by companies	*RUDS Files*
1.4.7	Percentage of companies paying RUDS fees	*RUDS Files*
1.4.8	Percentage of companies paying training fees	*RUDS Files*
1.4.9	Percentage of companies paying pocket money	*RUDS Files*
1.4.10	Ratio of all participating companies accepting visits	*RUDS Files*
1.4.11	Salary of graduates vs. non graduates of the Dual System	*Company Survey/ Graduate Survey*

1.5	**Target group: Trainees**	*School Files*
1.5.1	Number of applicants	
1.5.2	Number of graduates	
1.5.3	Drop out rate	

2. Qualification of personnel

2.1	**Qualification of teaching personnel (in schools)**	*School Files/ RUDS Files*
2.1.1	Graduation level	
2.1.2	Ratio of number of courses visited to the total number of teachers (always main area of the course)	
	- theoretical	
	- practical	
	- pedagogical	
	- language	
	- computer	
	- school management	
2.1.3	Working experience in years	*Teacher Survey*
	- Total	
	- In the current job	
	- In the Company (maintenance/production line/training/others)	
	- In job beside the school	
2.1.4	Following the curriculum	
2.1.5	Use of training aids	

Anhang 2 _ S.355-3623

© Prof. Dr. Reinhard Stockmann; Universität des Saarlandes

2.2	**Qualification of training personnel in companies**	*Trainer Survey*
2.2.1	Graduation level	
2.2.2	Number of courses visited (always main area of the course)	

- theoretical
- practical
- pedagogical
- language
- computer
- management

| 2.2.3 | Working experience in years |

- Total (maintenance/production line/training/other)
- In the current job
- In job beside the company

| 2.2.4 | Following the curriculum |

2.3	**Quality of teaching and training**	*Trainees/Trainers/ Teachers/Companies/ Graduates Surveys*
2.3.1	Satisfaction with:	

- training in the companies
- teaching in schools
- technical equipment in school
- technical equipment in company
- qualification of teacher in school
- qualification of trainer in company
- cooperation between school and company

3. Effectiveness of organizational structures

3.1	**Fulfillment of training schedule**	
3.1.1	Ratio of taught lessons to planned lessons	*School Files*
3.1.2	Same as 2.1.4	
3.1.3	Same as 2.2.4	

3.2	**Personnel**	*School Files*
3.2.1	Fluctuation of personell in schools	
3.2.2	Ratio of available number of teachers to planned number of teachers	
3.2.3	Ratio of available number of administrators to planned number of administrators	

Anhang 2 _ S.355-3624

© Prof. Dr. Reinhard Stockmann; Universität des Saarlandes

3.3	**Cleaning, Maintenance and Attendance**	*School Files*
3.3.1	Existence of a cleaning plan	
3.3.2	Frequency of cleaning according to the plan	
3.3.3	Existence of a maintenance plan	
3.3.4	Frequency of maintenance according to the plan	
3.3.5	Existence of staff responsible for maintenance	
3.3.6	Days of absence of students (ratio)	
3.3.7	Days of absence of teachers (ratio)	

3.4	**Communication**	*RUDS Files*
3.4.1	Frequency of meetings in the implementing agency	
3.4.2	Attendance to these meetings in the implementing agency	
3.4.3	Frequency of meetings between projects	
3.4.4	Attendance to these meetings between projects	
3.4.5	Quality of cooperation:	*Company Survey*
	- between projects	
	- between schools and companies	
	- between RUDS and companies	
	- between schools and RUDS	

4. **Financial Effectiveness of implementing agency** *RUDS/*
Ministry of Education

4.1	Amount of annual budget for training (if it is the RUDS, then the total budget)	
4.2	Cost per trainee	
	- In the regular TSS (not participating in the Dual System)	
	- In the Dual System	
	- In the RUDS	
4.3	Ratio of costs of Dual System trainee (incl. RUDS costs) to costs per regular TSS-trainee	
4.4	Amount of money earned by own activities per year (fees, production, services etc.)	*School director*

Anhang 2 _ S.355-3625

5.   Quality of technical facilities

5.1	**Implementing Agency (schools)**	*Teachers Survey*
5.1.1	Complimentary equipment to enterprises according to curriculum contents	
5.1.2	Condition of equipment (efficiency of operation)	
5.1.3	Availability of substitutes for equipment	
5.1.4	Availability of training aids	
5.1.5	Quality of training aids	
5.1.6	Use of training aids	
5.1.7	Degree of utilization of classrooms	
5.1.8	Degree of utilization of workshops	
5.1.9	Degree of utilization of labs	
5.1.10	Days without electrical power	*School Files*

5.2	**Companies**	*Trainers / Trainees Survey*
5.2.1	Existence of equipment according to curriculum contents	
5.2.2	Trainees trained with this equipment (also to 2.3)	

6.   Quality of Training Model

6.1	**Conformity to education level**	*School Files/Ministry*
6.1.1	Grades of applicants (after basic school)	
6.1.2	Grades of applicants (after basic school) of regular TSS and Dual TSS in the governerates	
6.1.3	Number of new applicants	
6.1.4	Percentage of students passing aptitude test	
6.1.5	Grades in the aptitude tests (average)	
6.1.6	Percentage of students passing course tests (during training) - practical tests - theoretical tests	
6.1.7	Grades in these tests (average)	
6.1.8	Percentage of students passing final tests - practical tests - theoretical tests	
6.1.9	Grades in these final tests	
6.1.10	Percentage of repeaters	
6.1.11	Percentage of leaving students without graduating (drop-out rate)	
6.1.12	Percentage of women (from total of all trainees)	
6.1.13	Graduates of MKI in the TOP 10	

Anhang 2 _ S.355-3626

6.2	**Conformity to employment system**	*Company/Graduates Survey*
6.2.1	Curricula oriented toward the qualifications required by companies	*Company Survey*
6.2.2	Time period between graduation and finding work (also to 8 and 2.3)	*Company/Graduates Survey*
6.2.3	Percentage of those successfully graduating finding a position of work appropriate to their training	*Company/Graduates Survey*
6.2.4	Percentage of graduates employed in adequate jobs after five years passing the diploma	*Graduate Survey*
6.2.5	Job situation for Dual System graduates on the labor market (also to 8)	*Company/Graduates Survey*
6.2.6	Percentage of Dual System graduates working in international companies or joint ventures (also to 8)	*Company/Graduates Survey*
6.2.7	Size of companies offering jobs for graduates (size classes)	*Company/Graduates Survey*
6.2.8	Size of companies offering training places for trainees (size classes)	*Company/Graduates Survey*
6.2.9	Prospects of promotion for Dual System graduates in comparison to others	*Company Survey*
6.2.10	Salaries of graduates to comparable average	*Company/Graduates Survey*
6.2.11	Assessment of the qualification of graduates of the Dual System in comparison to graduates not being trained in the Dual System	*Company Survey*
6.2.12	Percentage of tasks, the Dual System graduates have to do although not being trained or educated for (in comparison to other graduates)	*Company/Graduates Survey*

7.	**Diffusion effects in vocational training system**	*RUDS Files*
7.1	**Training Model**	
7.1.1	Number of schools participating in the Dual System (also to 8)	
7.1.2	Number of trainees in the Dual System	
7.1.3	Number of graduates in the dual system	
7.1.4	Number of new vocations in the Dual System (also to 8)	
7.1.5	Number of new trades in the Dual System (also to 8)	
7.1.6	Ratio of dual graduates to the total number of graduates in TSS	
7.1.7	Number of Dual System contracts between RUDS and companies per year (also to 8)	
7.1.8	Number of institutions running the system (RUDS, NGO's...) (also to 8)	
7.1.9	Number of governerates participating in Dual System (also to 8)	*PPIU*
7.2	**Methods**	
7.2.1	Number of teachers and instructors from other schools trained by MKI	*RUDS Files*
7.2.2	Availability of teaching aids needed for the Dual System in new schools	*School Director*

Anhang 2 _ S.355-3627

| 7.3 | **Qualification** | *RUDS Files/PPIU* |
| 7.3.1 | Number of courses per year according to the Dual System organized | |

for teachers and in-company-trainers:
- Courses with / in technical subjects
- Introductory courses in the Dual System
- Courses with / in pedagogical subjects
- School management
- others

7.3.2   Number of participants to these courses
- Teachers
- In-company-trainers

8.	**Diffusion effects in the employment system**	*Company Survey/ RUDS Files*
8.1	Number of companies participating in Dual System	*RUDS Files*
8.2	Reasons for participating in the Dual System	*Company Survey*
8.3	Number of supplied training places by the companies (also to 7.1)	*RUDS Files/Company Survey*
8.4	Percentage of Dual System graduates working in their Vocation	*Graduates Survey/ Company Survey*
8.5	Percentage of Dual System graduates working in other companies not participating in the Dual System	*Graduates Survey/ Company Survey*
8.6	Number of graduates establishing own companies	*Graduates Survey*
8.7	Number of graduates becoming trainers	*Graduates Survey/ Company Survey*
8.8	Number of companies that refused to hire the trainees after graduation	*Graduates Survey/ Company Survey*
8.9	Reasons for refusing to hire the trainees after graduation	*Company Survey*
8.10	Number of companies quitting dual system	*RUDS Files*
8.11	Reasons for quitting the Dual System	*Company Survey*

> Annotation: The different surveys (Company Survey, Graduate Survey, Teacher Survey, Trainer Survey, Trainee Survey) will include a lot of additional questions which can be transformed to indicators and added to this list in the following steps

Anhang 2 _ S.355-362B

© Prof. Dr. Reinhard Stockmann; Universität des Saarlandes

Isabell Welpe / Britta Thege / Shirley Henderson (eds.)

The Gender Perspective

Innovations in Economy, Organisation and Health within the Southern African Development Community (SADC)

Frankfurt am Main, Berlin, Bern, Bruxelles, New York, Oxford, Wien, 2004.
439 pp., num. tab. and graf.
ISBN 978-3-631-52599-9 · pb. € 71.70*

The constitutional and legislative framework within the Southern African Development Community provides a positive institutional environment to ensure mainstreaming gender concerns. However, the translation and implementation of the gender perspective is at times lacking. Both agenda setting as an instrument of change management and reorganisation procedures are not used enough in the fields of economy, organisation and health. These three areas are crucial partly due to their interconnectivity and also because of their vital importance to the successful sustainable development of SADC nations. This volume results from the findings of a conference hosted by the Institute of Women and Gender Studies, Kiel, and the Institute for Women's and Gender Studies, Pretoria.

Contents: Gender · Gender Mainstreaming · SADC · Economy · Organisation · Health

Frankfurt am Main · Berlin · Bern · Bruxelles · New York · Oxford · Wien
Distribution: Verlag Peter Lang AG
Moosstr. 1, CH-2542 Pieterlen
Telefax 00 41 (0) 32 / 376 17 27

*The €-price includes German tax rate
Prices are subject to change without notice
Homepage http://www.peterlang.de